Globalization and the State: Volume II

Also by Carlos M. Peláez and Carlos A. Peláez:

THE GLOBAL RECESSION RISK
Dollar Devaluation and the World Economy

INTERNATIONAL FINANCIAL ARCHITECTURE
G7, IMF, BIS, Debtors and Creditors

GOVERNMENT INTERVENTION IN GLOBALIZATION

Globalization and the State: Volume II

Trade Agreements, Inequality, the Environment, Financial Globalization, International Law and Vulnerabilities

Carlos M. Peláez

and

Carlos A. Peláez

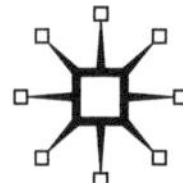

First published 2008 by
PALGRAVE MACMILLAN

Palgrave Macmillan in the UK is an imprint of Macmillan Publishers Limited, registered in England, company number 785998, of Houndmills, Basingstoke, Hampshire RG21 6XS.

Palgrave Macmillan in the US is a division of St Martin's Press LLC, 175 Fifth Avenue, New York, NY 10010.

Palgrave Macmillan is the global academic imprint of the above companies and has companies and representatives throughout the world.

Palgrave® and Macmillan® are registered trademarks in the United States, the United Kingdom, Europe and other countries.

ISBN-13: 978–0–230–20531–4 hardback
ISBN-10: 0–230–20531–3 hardback

This book is printed on paper suitable for recycling and made from fully managed and sustained forest sources. Logging, pulping and manufacturing processes are expected to conform to the environmental regulations of the country of origin.

A catalogue record for this book is available from the British Library.

A catalog record for this book is available from the Library of Congress.

10 9 8 7 6 5 4 3 2 1
17 16 15 14 13 12 11 10 09 08

Printed and bound in Great Britain by
CPI Antony Rowe, Chippenham and Eastbourne

Contents

List of Tables	ix

List of Chart	x

List of Abbreviations	xi

Acknowledgments	xvi

Introduction	1

1 Trade Agreements	3
Introduction	3
The economic analysis of trade agreements	4
The European Union	8
NAFTA	10
APEC	15
ASEAN	17
MERCOSUR	24
OPEC	28
Summary	34

2 Poverty, Inequality, the Environment and Social Issues	35
Introduction	35
Global poverty and inequality	35
Regional, international and global public goods	46
The environment	48
Climate change	52
Political regime	63
Summary	72

3 Financial Globalization	73
Introduction	73
Finance, efficiency and growth	73
Financial repression and restraint	81
Financial globalization	86
Capital account liberalization	90
Financial crises	102
Financial reversals and the modified private
  interest view	108
Summary	112

4   International Economic Law   **114**
Introduction   114
Soft law, standards and codes   114
Basel II capital requirements   126
Implementing Basel II in Europe and the United States   143
Self-regulatory organizations, the SEC and the FSA   148
Sarbanes-Oxley   155
US competitiveness in capital markets   168
Summary   179

5   Vulnerabilities of the Global Economy   **180**
Introduction   180
US external deficits and the global recession risk   182
The challenge to the international financial system   194
Regulation, trade and devaluation wars   205
Summary   209

Conclusion: The Credit/Dollar Crisis   **211**

Notes   214

References   215

Index   233

List of Tables

1.1	World exports and imports of merchandise US$ Billion, 2005	4
1.2	GDP, GDP per capita, exports and imports of the EU countries	9
1.3	GDP, GDP per capita, exports and imports in NAFTA 2005	10
1.4	GDP, GDP per capita, exports and imports in APEC 2005	15
1.5	GDP, GDP per capita, exports and imports in ASEAN 2005	18
1.6	Trade of ASEAN and China US$B, 2005	21
1.7	GDP, GDP per capita, exports and imports in MERCOSUR 2005	24
1.8	Projections of US oil price and consumption	29
1.9	GDP, GDP per capita, exports and imports in OPEC 2005	30
2.1	GDP growth in Russia and China 1991–2000 in %	42
2.2	Discount factors of future values	60
2.3	DICE model simulations by Nordhaus (2006)	61
3.1	Functions of financial intermediation	75
3.2	Interest rate liberalization and prudential bank behavior	83
3.3	Benefits of financial sector foreign direct investment	89
3.4	United States international transactions, 2005 US$ Billions	91
3.5	Thailand, Korea and Indonesia, indicators during the Asian crisis	103
3.A	Countries in financial crisis	103
3.6	The modified private interest view of Rajan and Zingales	110
4.1	Institutions of strengthening financial standards and codes	116
4.2	Process based on internal ratings (IRB)	133
4.3	Risk components of Basel II	134
4.4	IRB risk weights for unexpected loss	137
4.5	Minimum requirements for IRB entry and use	138
4.6	Treatment of securitization exposures	140
4.7	Definitions in Basel II	142
4.8	Selected stock and futures exchanges	149
4.9	Corporate scandals according to Coffee	156
4.10	Structure of SOX	157
4.11	The loss of competitiveness of US capital markets	170
4.12	Proposals for enhancing US competitiveness in financial markets	177
5.1	US, current account, NIIP, fiscal balance, debt and nominal GDP $ Billions	183
5.2	Global imbalances $B and %	184
5.3	Summary of results by Croke *et al.* (2005)	185
5.4	US, exports, imports and trade balance $ Million	189
5.5	IMF regional policies of shared responsibility	193
5.6	US GDP growth 1930–45%	206

List of Chart

5.1 Fed funds rate 1990–2008   200

List of Abbreviations

ABCP	Asset-backed commercial paper
ABS	Asset-backed security
ADB	Asian Development Bank
ADR	American Depository Receipt
AIG	Accord Implementation Group
AIM	Alternative Investment Market
AMA	Advanced Management Approach
AMEX	American Stock Exchange
ANPR	Advanced notice of proposed rulemaking
APEC	Asia-Pacific Economic Cooperation
APO	ASEAN plus One
APT	ASEAN plus Three
AR4	Fourth assessment report
ARM	Adjustable rate mortgage
ASEAN	Association of Southeast Asian Nations
AUM	Assets under management
BCBS	Basel Committee on Banking Supervision
BCP	Basel Core Principles of Banking Supervision
BEA	Bureau of Economic Analysis
BIS	Bank for International Settlements
BOE	Bank of England
BOJ	Bank of Japan
CA	Current account
CAD	Current account deficit
CAN	Andean Community of Nations
CCF	Credit conversion factors
CCMR	Committee on Capital Markets Regulation
CDO	Collateralized debt obligation
CEBS	Committee of European Banking Supervisors
CEU	Central and Eastern Europe
CFTC	Commodities Futures Trading Commission
CGFS	Committee on the Global Financial System
CIR	Covered interest arbitrage
CLO	Chief legal officer
CPI	Consumer price index
CPSS	Committee on Payment and Settlement Systems
CRD	Capital Requirements Directive
CRM	Credit risk mitigation
CSN	South-American Community of Nations
CU	Customs union

D&O	Directors and officers
DDR	Doha Development Round
DI	Debt intolerance
DICE	Dynamic integrated model of climate and the economy
EAEG	East Asian Economic Grouping
EAI	Enterprise for ASEAN Initiative
EC	European Commission
ECA	Export credit agency
ECAI	External credit assessment institution
ECB	European Central Bank
EEC	European Economic Community
EIA	Energy Information Administration
EKC	Environmental Kuznets curve
EL	Expected loss
EME	Emerging market economies
EMU	European Monetary Union
EPA	US Environmental Protection Agency
ERM	Enterprise risk management
EU	European Union
EWS	Early warning systems
FCPA	Foreign Corrupt Practices Act of 1976
FDI	Foreign direct investment
FDIC	Federal Deposit Insurance Corporation
FRBNY	Federal Reserve Bank of New York
FRBO	Federal Reserve Board
FRS	Federal Reserve System
FSA	Financial Services Authority
FSAP	Financial Sector Assessment Program
FSF	Financial Stability Forum
FSFDI	Financial sector FDI
FSI	Financial sector indicators
FSMA	Financial Services and Market Act of 2000
FTA	Free trade area
FTAA	Free Trade Area of the Americas
FTAAP	Free Trade Agreement of Asia and the Pacific
GAADP	Generally Agreed Auditing Principles
GAAP	Generally Agreed Accounting Principles
GAO	US General Accounting Office
GATT	General Agreement on Tariffs and Trade
GBP	UK pound
GHG	Greenhouse gas
GPG	Global public good
G7	Group of Seven
G10	Group of Ten
HF	Hedge fund

IAP	Individual Action Plan
IEA	International Energy Agency
IEFP	International economic and financial policy
IFA	International financial architecture
IFI	International financial institutions
IFRS	International Financial Reporting Standards
IMF	International Monetary Fund
IMFC	International Monetary and Financial Committee
IOSCO	International Organization of Securities Commissions
IPCC	Intergovernmental Panel on Climate Change
IPL	International poverty line
IPO	Initial public offering
IPR	International property rights
IRB	Internal-Ratings Based
ISI	Import substitution industrialization
ITO	International Trade Organization
IV	Instrumental variable
JPY	Japanese yen
KP	Kyoto Protocol
LBO	Leveraged buyout
LE	London exchanges
LGD	Loss given default
LSE	London Stock Exchange
LTCM	Long Term Capital Management
mbod	Million barrels of oil per day
MBS	Mortgage backed securities
MDB	Multilateral development banks
MERCOSUR	Common Market of the South
MFN	Most-favored nation
MKC	McKinsey & Co.
MMC	Ministerial Monitoring Committee
MNC	Multinational corporation
MPC	Monetary Policy Committee
MTM	Mark-to-market
NAFTA	North American Free Trade Agreement
NIC	Newly industrialized countries
NIIP	Net international investment position
NPR	Notice of proposed rulemaking
NYC	New York City
NYE	New York Exchanges
NYS	New York State
OCC	Office of the Comptroller of the Currency
OECD	Organization for Economic Co-operation and Development
OLS	Ordinary least squares
OMB	Office of Management and Budget

OPEC	Organization of Petroleum Exporting Countries
OTC	Over the counter
OTS	Office of Thrift Supervision
pbo	Per barrel of oil
PCA	Prompt corrective action
PCAOB	Public Company Accounting Oversight Board
PE	Private equity
PECC	Pacific Economic Cooperation Council
ppb	Parts per billion
ppm	Parts per million
PPP	Purchasing power parity
PSE	Public sector enterprises
PTA	Preferential trade agreement
PWGFM	President's Working Group on Financial Markets
PWT	Penn World Tables
QIS	Quantitative impact study
QLCC	Qualified legal compliance committee
ROSC	Report on Standards and Codes
RPG	Regional public good
RPIX	Retail price index excluding mortgage payments
RSRA	Reverse sale and repurchase agreement
RTA	Regional trade agreement
SCP	Structured credit product
SDRT	Social discount rate
SEC	Securities and Exchange Commission
SIV	Structured investment vehicle
SOE	State-owned enterprise
SOX	Sarbanes – Oxley Act of 2002
SPE	Special purpose entity
SRA	Sale and repurchase agreement
SRO	Self-regulatory organizations
SS	Sudden stop
TAR	Third Assessment Report
TFIPCC	Task Force on National Greenhouse Gas Inventories
TFP	Total factor productivity
TPG	Transnational public good
UIP	Uncovered interest parity
UN	United Nations
UNEP	UN Environment Programme
USCC	US Chamber of Commerce
USD	US dollar
VaR	Value at risk
VC	Venture capitalist

WB	World Bank
WFE	World Federation of Stock Exchanges
WGI	Working Group I (IPCC)
WGII	Working Group II (IPCC)
WGIII	Working Group III (IPCC)
WHO	World Health Organization
WMO	World Meteorological Organization
WTO	World Trade Organization

Acknowledgments

This is the sixth book around this subject that we have published over a decade. It is the expanded, advanced form of *Government Intervention in Globalization*. We are very grateful to Taiba Batool, Economics Editor of Palgrave Macmillan, for the encouragement of the project and for important improvements. Two perceptive reviewers of Palgrave Macmillan also contributed extremely valuable suggestions. We are most grateful to Alec Dubber at Palgrave Macmillan for steering the manuscript to publication. Geetha Naren at Integra Software Services revised the manuscript with highly useful suggestions and competent typesetting for final publication.

We began work on this project already during the publication of *The Global Recession Risk* by Palgrave under the highly valuable guidance of Amanda Hamilton. Hard times undermine international cooperation, accentuating the damage of economic and employment losses. Currently, we are working on another volume on the regulatory wars of finance that are already beginning.

We are grateful to many friends who helped us in this effort. A partial list includes Professor Antonio Delfim Netto, Ambassador Richard T. McCormack, Senator Heráclito Fortes, Professor Paulo Yokota and Eduardo Mendez. Magnolia Maciel Peláez, DDS, reviewed the manuscript providing many suggestions deriving from her long experience in health regulation.

Our intention is providing a comprehensive source for the reader to acquire tools with which to analyze and develop own views on what may be the most important current event, government intervention in national affairs.

In writing this book we remembered dear friends and colleagues who helped and motivated in the interest on scholarly work and international affairs, Clay and Rondo Cameron and Otilia and Nicholas Georgescu-Roegen. We are solely responsible for the shortcomings and errors in this work.

Carlos M. Peláez and Carlos A. Peláez
Atlantic City and New York City

Introduction

The dream of economists after World War II was a system of multilateral trade through the International Trade Organization (ITO) to reverse the protectionism of the Great Depression. There is major criticism by economists of the existing system of preferential trade agreements (PTA). Chapter 1 provides the economic analysis of PTAs. It also analyzes the major agreements, such as the European Union (EU), North American Free Trade Agreement (NAFTA), Asia-Pacific Economic Cooperation (APEC), Association of Southeast Asian Nations (ASEAN) and the Common Market of the South (MERCOSUR). The Free Trade Area of the Americas (FTAA) is stalled. There is also discussion of the analytical critique of bilateral agreements of the United States and the EU. The fact is that most of the trade of the world is processed through PTAs. The Organization of Petroleum Exporting Countries (OPEC) is an agreement that intends to restrict production and trade in oil to maintain a high price. The rising price of oil and its role in international trade imbalances is generating proposals for taxation of oil products.

The critique of globalization is analyzed in Chapter 2. The major technical debate on the measurement and evolution of global poverty and inequality is analyzed in a separate section. The theory of public goods is extended to the analysis of regional, international and global public goods (GPG). The environment and climate change are important issues in globalization and are analyzed in individual sections. The relation of globalization to the choice of political regime is creating an active academic debate.

The widest dissent on the benefits of globalization is centered on financial globalization. Many proponents of free trade argue that financial flows should be controlled. Our experience is that capital controls do not function if there is the opportunity to engage in international trade. China and Brazil provide important illustrations. There are multiple mechanisms to transfer capital from the internal economy to other countries and for the reverse process. In the case of an overvalued exchange rate, economic agents transfer capital abroad in the expectation of gaining from future devaluation by means of overvaluing import invoices, undervaluing export invoices, anticipating dividend remittances and engaging in price transfers through multinational corporations (MNCs). In the case of an undervalued exchange rate, importers undervalue invoices, exporters overvalue invoices and companies delay dividend remittances and engage in price transfers as forms of repatriating capital to gain from revaluation. The growth and sophistication of financial instruments allows shorting country risk through derivative transactions and the closing of trade finance lines. Free trade finances capital flows openly or in hidden transactions, rendering capital controls ineffective.

Chapter 3 provides the theoretical and empirical analysis of financial globalization. The benefits of efficiency and growth of financial liberalization in general are considered in the first section, followed by the analysis of financial repression and restraint. There is analysis of the vast literature trying to relate financial liberalization and economic growth. Various economists argue that financial globalization must be preceded by regulatory measures and institutions because of the prevalence of adverse selection and moral hazard resulting from imperfect information. Many economists blame the international financial institutions (IFI) for the capital account liberalization that allegedly caused the financial crises of emerging markets. Financial reversals are analyzed by means of the modified private interest view introduced in Chapter 5 of Volume I.

Chapter 4 focuses on international economic law. Significant part of the effort of the international financial architecture (IFA) (Peláez and Peláez 2005, 239–300) is centered on international standards and codes. There is a first section introducing the analysis of soft law, standards and codes. The most accomplished soft law is the Basel II framework of capital requirements that are adopted by banks accounting for most international banking assets. The implementation of Basel II in Europe and the United States is analyzed in separate sections. The balance of this chapter focuses on the analysis of regulatory measures that have allegedly caused the loss of competitiveness of finance by the United States. The analysis and major proposals to reverse this loss are considered in detail.

The vulnerabilities of the global economy are analyzed in Chapter 5. The major threat is in the US current account deficit (CAD) that absorbs over two-thirds of the external surpluses of the world. There is risk of a global recession in case of a fire sale of US debt ignited by the US real estate downturn (Peláez and Peláez 2007). Interest rates could rise in an abrupt exit by investors out of US securities, crashing stock markets, devaluing the dollar and raising inflation. The international credit contraction is also threatening economic activity and the international financial system. International economic cooperation is likely to decline. The politics of polarization and conflict continue in confrontations in the Middle East and Asia. The fear of protectionism and trade wars is present in view of the experience during the Great Depression. The US Congress is challenging the exchange rate policy of China and confrontation is possible if the US economy deteriorates.

There is a conclusion at the end of the volume, summarizing the issues and prospects of international economic and financial policy (IEFP). The notes and references are collected at the end together with an index.

1
Trade Agreements

Introduction

The members of the World Trade Organization (WTO), as it was the case of the contracting parties to the General Agreement on Tariffs and Trade (GATT), must notify the regional trade agreements (RTA) in which they participate. Nearly all of the WTO (2007) members have engaged in an RTA and some members are party to 20 or more. GATT received 124 notifications of RTAs by its contracting parties in 1948–94 and the WTO has received 130 additional notifications since its creation in 1995. Not all these RTAs are in force currently but many have been redefined in a different RTA. Currently, there are 170 RTAs in force and the WTO estimates that an additional 70 are operational but not yet notified. The WTO estimates that by 2005 about 300 RTAs were operational.

The subject of this chapter is PTAs. The first section below covers the definitions and economic analysis of these trade agreements. The proliferation of the agreements creates frustrating preferential trade maps of such complexity that Bhagwati (1995, 2003) characterizes them as resembling a "spaghetti bowl."

The EU is one of the oldest and largest agreements, initially incorporating a few countries in Western Europe but subsequently extending through Eastern Europe. The largest producers of bilateral agreements are the United States and the EU. NAFTA is almost equal in output to the EU but not as high in trade because of the lower percentage of trade relative to GDP in the United States. APEC is a special forum of consultation and voluntary movement toward free trade of the countries in the Pacific area. ASEAN is a free trade area (FTA) of South East Asian nations, which have intentions of increasing integration. MERCOSUR is an agreement of four countries in the South American southern cone but now includes Venezuela as a formal member and other South American countries as associate members. The FTAA is an attempt to create an FTA of 34 countries in the Western Hemisphere that is currently stalled. OPEC is the well-known cartel of oil producers. The summary to this chapter provides some conclusions.

The economic analysis of trade agreements

The effort of multilateral trade negotiation continues through first the GATT and subsequently the WTO. However, the world is composed of multiple RTAs. Table 1.1 shows the WTO data for world exports and imports of merchandise with the corresponding data for the major RTAs. It is difficult to include APEC because it is mainly a forum of consultation with voluntary movement toward reduction of barriers to trade and investment. Nearly all the world's trade is processed through RTAs. It is possible to improve the welfare of the countries engaged in a customs union (CU) and a PTA without reducing the welfare of the world. This does not mean that it is technically feasible or common. Many economists distrust the possible excuse of PTAs to disguise protectionism, especially behind complex rules of origin. PTAs have become a reality for world trade.

The PTA consists of a group of countries that impose the same tariff rates on the trade of goods produced in member countries and a common higher tariff on trade produced in non-member countries (Panagariya 2000, 288). The FTA is a PTA in which the tariffs of goods produced in member countries are entirely eliminated. In the CU there are no tariffs on goods produced in member countries, as in an FTA, but there is a common tariff on any good produced in a non-member country. The difference between an FTA and a CU is that the CU imposes the same tariff on non-members while the FTA member can have different tariffs on goods and services produced in non-members (Krueger 1999, 112). This difference can result in what Krueger (1999, 112) calls trade deflecting, which consists of imports shifting to enter the FTA through the lowest tariff member. As a result, there are additional negotiations on rules of origin to prevent imports of all goods through the lowest tariff country; these rules define the conditions under which a good is considered to have its origin in the member of the area. These negotiations are the target of lobbies of producers. For example, there are 200 pages of rules of origin

Table 1.1   World exports and imports of merchandise US$ Billion, 2005

	Exports		Imports	
	Value	%	Value	%
NAFTA	1,478	14.5	2,285	21.7
United States	904	8.9	1,732	16.5
European Union 25	4,001	39.4	4,135	39.3
MERCOSUR	163	1.6	114	1.1
ASEAN	653	6.4	594	5.7
Asia	2,779	27.4	2,599	24.7
Japan	595	5.9	515	4.9
China	762	7.5	660	6.3
World	10,159	100	10,511	100

Source: World Trade Organization, http://www.wto.org/english/res_e/statis_e/its2006_e/its06_byregion_e.pdf.

in the final NAFTA agreement (Krueger 1999, 112). Protectionism occurs when the rules favor higher cost producers of intermediate products, such as auto parts, to gain access to a member country in detriment of lower cost producers.

NAFTA and the EU were created by appeal to an exception of preferences in GATT. Article XXIV section 2 of GATT (1986) defines a customs territory as a geographical unit that maintains separate tariffs and other regulations relative to the commerce of a significant part of that territory with other territories. Article XXIV subsection 8(a) defines a CU as the replacement of two or more custom territories with a single customs territory. The CU eliminates the duties and other regulations of commerce for a significant part of the trade between the members of the CU by subsection 8(a)(i) and applies the same duties and other regulations of commerce by each member of the union to trade with territories outside the union by subsection 8(a)(ii). Article XXIV subsection 8(b) defines an FTA as two or more custom territories that eliminate the duties and other regulations of commerce for trade between the member territories. Article XXIV section 4 recognizes that the development of voluntary agreements of integration between parties of GATT is desirable for the increase of free trade. The intention of the CU and the FTA is to facilitate trade among members. There is no intention in CUs and FTAs to increase trade barriers against other members of GATT.

Article XXIV subsection 5 provides three conditions for CUs and FTAs. The first condition is that the duties and other regulations imposed against non-members of CUs should not be higher or more restrictive than those prevailing before the formation of the union or the adoption of the interim agreement. There is a similar provision with respect to FTAs not to raise duties or impose more restrictive regulations of commerce than those existing before the formation of the FTA or the interim agreement. The third condition is that any interim agreement for both CUs and FTAs should include a schedule for the formation of the CU or FTA. That is, at some point in the future there would be a 100 percent reduction of tariffs among the members. The result of these conditions was to move PTAs closer to the idea of a CU to avoid the older approach of sector-by-sector bilateral negotiations of tariffs (Krueger 1999, 106).

Article I of GATT (1986) provides for "general MFN [most-favored nation]." Article I section (1) requires that "any advantage, favor, privilege or immunity" given by a member of GATT to trade with "any other country" shall be extended to all other members of GATT. This is the central provision of GATT (Panagariya 2000, 288), implying that its members shall not discriminate other members with their tariff policies. The creation of PTAs or the less encompassing varieties such as CUs and FTAs conflicts with Article I of GATT that provides that preferences in trade be extended to all GATT contracting members.

The departing contribution for analysis of CUs is the classic work by Viner (1950). Consider a simple example by Panagariya (2000, 290–1) in which there are two potential members of the CU, X and Y, and the rest of the world, Z. Assume that X imports pins. The cost of producing pins in X, C_X, is higher than in Y, C_Y, and in turn higher than in Z, C_Z, that is, $C_X > C_Y > C_Z$. There is a tariff of t per pin imposed by X on imports of pins such that: $C_X > C_Y + t > C_Z + t$, that is, the cost is higher in X than the imports with tariff from Y and both are higher than the imports with tariff from Z. Country Z, or the rest of the world, is the lowest cost producer. In this case, X is importing from the lowest cost producer, Z, at the price (equal to cost) of $C_Z + t$.

Suppose that country X maintains the tariff $t > C_Y - C_Z$ on Z and eliminates it for Y. Thus, X imports from Y because $C_X > C_Z + t > C_Y$. This agreement is trade diverting in Viner's analysis because imports shift from the lowest cost producer, Z, to a higher cost producer, Y. Assuming with Meade (1955), as analyzed by Panagariya (2000, 290–1), that there is perfect competition, zero elasticity of demand (vertical demand curve) and constant marginal costs equal to average cost (horizontal supply curve), the trade-diverting CU causes a loss of welfare as measured by the decrease of consumer surplus. Suppose that X had a tariff at such a level, t', that it was too costly to import from either Y or Z: $C_Z + t' > C_Y + t' > C_X$. If X eliminated the tariff against Y but maintained it against Z, instead of producing pins at home, X would buy them from a lower cost source, Y. In the analysis of Viner (1950), this union would be trade creating. With the assumptions of perfect competition, horizontal supply and vertical demand, it is immediately evident that the union is beneficial to X, increasing consumer surplus (Panagariya 2000, 291). Viner argued that in the real world it would be quite difficult to determine if a trade agreement would be beneficial because of the diverse types of trade creating and trade diverting effects. Unfortunately, the solution to the issue of the welfare of the member countries and the world as a whole is even more complex than this initial analysis by Viner.

Panagariya (2000) provides a comprehensive survey of substantial literature on the welfare effects of PTAs. It is possible for countries to form a CU or an FTA such as to make the union or area better off without reducing world welfare (Bhagwati and Panagariya 1996, 83, Kemp 1964, Kemp and Wan 1976, Ohyama 1972, Panagariya 2000, 307, Vanek 1965). The basic theorem for CUs is intuitively as follows. Consider again countries X and Y. Assume that the vector of trade of X and Y with the rest of the world is rigid. Using the external trade vector as a constraint, it is possible to maximize the joint welfare of X and Y by means of the standard equality of marginal rates of product transformation and marginal rates of substitution for each pair of goods for all agents in the union. This is achieved by the elimination of all trade barriers among union members and choosing the common external tariff vector in such a way that the external trade vector outside the union remains the same as before the union. There is Pareto improvement for the union without reduction of the welfare of the world. There is an extension of this argument to FTAs (Panagariya 2000, 295–7). The theoretical feasibility of gains for the members of PTAs without a loss for the rest of the world does not imply that this is a likely outcome or that it is feasible to attain it with policy instruments.

Krueger (1999, 116) argues that "efforts to translate these arguments into firm rules about when PTAs are more or less likely to lead to welfare improvement have been only partially successful." The welfare effects are likely to differ according to trade structure with the rest of the world, level of tariffs before the PTA and economic structures. There are not very meaningful arguments on when PTAs will likely improve the welfare of members. It becomes difficult to assess a situation when a PTA increases welfare for its members while being neutral in welfare outside the area.

There has been debate of whether PTAs could be building blocks for multilateral trade or actually stumbling blocks. Krueger (1999, 117–9) surveys the literature finding the following arguments in favor of the building block proposition:

- *Trade creating PTAs.* The majority of PTAs are trade creating and thus will lead to further multilateral liberalization. Krueger (1999, 117) warns that lobbies may grow in strength within the PTAs to protect their gains.
- *Locking liberalization gains.* Developing countries try to lock in their gains from liberalization by engaging in PTAs with developed countries to increase the flow of investment.
- *Lowering tariffs.* Producers will lobby to lower multilateral tariffs to the level of the low input tariff partner.
- *Bargaining threat.* The threat of potential creation of a PTA may speed up multilateral bargaining.
- *Liberalizing beyond.* Members of a PTA can liberalize among themselves more than what could be obtained with more negotiating parties within multilateral negotiations. This was a motivation for the United States in creating FTAs.

There are equally strong arguments for the proposition that PTAs discourage multilateral trade liberalization (Krueger 1999, 119):

- *Increasing barriers against non-members.* The countries within the PTA tend to increase barriers against non-members. Bhagwati (1995) argues that trade diversion occurs even when tariffs are low.
- *Increasing protectionism.* There may be acceptance of protectionism to avoid the truly optimal outcome of multilateralism.
- *Exhausting negotiation resources.* Trade ministries have limited resources that become exhausted in negotiating PTAs instead of multilateral liberalization.

The proliferation of bilateral trade agreements is considered by Bhagwati (2003) to be a systemic problem. World and regional maps have become full of connecting lines and curves resembling what Bhagwati (1995, 2003) calls the "spaghetti bowl" problem "with preferences like noodles, crisscrossing all over the place." Bhagwati (2003) ponders that "the great economists who warned us against preferences during the 1930s when competitive tariff-raising was creating fragmented markets worldwide would have been horrified to see that, in the name of free trade, we are now re-enacting such fragmented markets on a parallel scale, and feeling virtuous about it." The proliferation of bilateral agreements, according to Bhagwati (2003), weakens the resolve to continue multilateral trade negotiations. He argues that bilateral agreements between the United States and developing countries require that they use US products, such as fabrics in textiles. The negotiations on textiles and agriculture have suffered because of the unwillingness of countries to engage in MFN negotiations that would erode the preferences of PTAs. Conditions on capital controls, labor and environmental standards are included in the bilateral agreements, thus building an unfavorable template for multilateral trade negotiations. Trade negotiations are used to promote agendas that do not have a relation to the economic criteria of efficiency and welfare and that should be pursued in different forums.

In 1930, the average European tariff was 30.4 percent and that in the United States 37 percent. By 2000, the average European tariff declined to 4.2 percent and that for the United States to 4 percent (Baldwin (2006, 4) using data in Findlay and O'Rourke (2007)). Japanese average tariffs declined from 18 percent in the early 1960s to 3 percent in 2000. Brazil lowered its average tariff from 99 percent in the early 1960s to 17 percent in 2000 (Baldwin (2006, 5) using data in Findlay and O'Rourke (2007)). The interest of Baldwin (2006) is in developing a political economy explanation of how the spaghetti bowls of PTAs can become building blocks toward free trade. Offshoring is the driving force that motivates regionalism toward multilateral liberalization of trade.

The European Union

The EU is the most complex agreement because it is leading to full economic and political integration of the members. There are more complex institutions in the EU than in other RTAs. It also is the largest RTA in terms of total trade. The entire agenda of the EU is centered on an increase in productivity by renewed R&D investment and reorganization of its production and use of knowledge. The renewed Lisbon strategy is a set of policies at the national and community level designed to recover the leadership of Europe in innovation and its competitiveness in the individual countries and in world markets (Peláez and Peláez 2007).

The effort to integrate the economies and societies of Europe began in 1952 with the establishment of the European Coal and Steel Community. The European Economic Community (EEC) was created by the Treaties of Rome in March 1957 (EEC 1957). The initial six members were Belgium, Germany, France, Luxembourg and the Netherlands. Subsequently, other members joined the community: Denmark, Ireland and the United Kingdom in 1973, Greece in 1981, Spain and Portugal in 1986 and East Germany in 1990 with the reunification of Germany. There were two objectives in the creation of the EEC. The common market would "transform the conditions of trade and manufacture on the territory of the community" (EEC 1957). The second objective was the development of a political Europe, constituting a step toward the unification of the continent. The elimination of the barriers dividing Europe would provide better living and working conditions to the members, with balanced trade and fair competition. The common trade policy would lead to the elimination of all barriers to trade.

The purpose of the EEC was to establish a CU or common market. The treaty abolished quotas and customs duties among the member states and imposed an external frontier for products that replaced the tariffs of the members. A common trade policy complemented the CU and would be managed at the community

Table 1.2 GDP, GDP per capita, exports and imports of the EU countries

	GDP per capita		GDP	Exports	Exports	Imports
	PPP US$ 2003	PPP EU25 = 100 2006	US$B 2005	% GDP	US$B 2005	US$ 2005
Austria	29,506	123	306	53.2	163	146
Belgium	28,132	118	371	70.0	260	253
Denmark	29,874	122	259	48.6	126	114
Finland	27,428	113	193	38.9	75	68
France	27,760	107	2,126	26.0	555	575
Germany	26,302	110	2,795	40.1	1,121	982
Greece	19,411	85	225	20.9	47	63
Ireland	32,975	139	202	80.2	162	136
Italy	26,119	99	1,762	26.3	464	465
Luxembourg	51,088	257	36	158.3	57	49
Netherlands	29,105	126	624	71.1	444	393
Portugal	18,320	70	183	28.4	52	68
Spain	23,825	98	1,125	25.4	286	344
Sweden	28,119	116	358	48.6	174	146
United Kingdom	29,032	117	2,199	26.1	574	660
Total EU			12,764		4,560	4,462
United States	37,765	150	12,456	10.5	1,303	2,020

Sources: PPP US, EUROSTAT, http://www.unece.org/stats/trends2005/Sources/127_GDP%20per%20capita, %20PPP%20USD.pdf.
EU25 PPP, UN European Commission for Europe, http://epp.eurostat.ec.europa.eu/portal/page?_pageid= 1996,39140985&_dad=portal&_schema=PORTAL& screen=detailref&language=en&product=Yearlies_ new_economy&root=Yearlies_new_economy/B/B1/B11/eb011.
GDP, Exports and Imports, United Nations, http://unstats.un.org/unsd/snaama/countryList.asp.

level instead of the state level. The common market would be established over a transition period of 12 years composed of three stages of 4 years each.

The treaty of 1992 (European Union 2006) provided new powers and duties to the institutions of the community, creating the EU. It also provided cooperation in different ways. In 1995, Austria, Finland and Sweden joined the EU. The disintegration of the USSR brought ten more members to the EU, raising the total to 25 members. The territorial extension of the EU is about two-fifths of the United States but its population is 57 percent larger, standing at around 457 million. Table 1.2 provides the dimensions of the EU. It is the largest RTA in force in terms of total trade.

There are a number of important institutions in the EU (Europa 2007):

- *The European Parliament.* The people of Europe elect a parliament every 5 years. The parliament elected in June 2004 has 732 members from all 25 countries of the EU. The main responsibility of parliament is to pass European laws.

- *Council of the EU.* It shares with the parliament the responsibility of passing laws and taking decisions on policy. It is also primarily responsible for foreign and security policy. There are up to four summit meetings at the council of the presidents and/or prime ministers of member states to decide on overall EU policy.
- *The European Commission (EC).* It is independent of national governments, representing and defending the interests of Europe. It conducts most of the administrative duties, implementing policies, spending funds and drafting proposals for new European laws. The EC has powers of oversight of compliance with treaties and laws, taking violators to court. It also negotiates international agreements between the EU and other nations. The EC is composed of 25 members, one per EU state. It has a staff of 24,000 and is located in Brussels.
- *The Court of Justice.* It is located in Luxembourg and has one member per EU state. It ensures that the EU law is applied in all members in the same way and that the states and institutions comply with the EU law.
- *The Court of Auditors.* It audits the expenditures of the EU. It is located in Luxembourg and has authority to audit any entity that uses EU funds.
- *The European Economic and Social Committee.* It consists of 317 members that represent multiple interests.
- *The Committee of the Regions.* It is a consultative body with 317 members from local and regional government.

NAFTA

The FTA among Canada, Mexico and the United States, NAFTA, has a combined GDP of $14,335 billion. NAFTA was signed by the United States, Mexico and Canada on December 17, 1992, taking effect on January 1, 1994. There is no RTA in the world with this immense output, shown in Table 1.3. Even total trade is significantly high. There have been few FTAs that created such political debate in the member countries. NAFTA became an important electoral issue in at least Mexico and the United States. The rules of origin in the agreement required about 200 pages, raising intriguing issues of political economy.

Table 1.3   GDP, GDP per capita, exports and imports in NAFTA 2005

	GDP	GDP per capita	Exports	Imports
	US$B	US$	US$B	US$B
Canada	1,131	35,073	519	467
Mexico	768	7,180	250	264
United States	12,456	41,768	1,303	2,019
Total	14,335		2,072	2,750

Source: United Nations, http://unstats.un.org/unsd/snaama/countryList.asp.

The USTR (2006) provides data, not necessarily reflecting causality, of the performance of trade and investment flows and economic indicators in the first decade of NAFTA:

- Trade among members increased by 173 percent in 1993–2005, from $297 billion to $810 billion; the daily trilateral trade of members is $2.2 billion.
- The merchandise exports of the United States to NAFTA members increased by 133 percent in 1993–2005, much higher than growth of 77 percent with the rest of the world.
- Canada and Mexico accounted for 36 percent of US foreign markets and for 36 percent of US export growth to the world.
- Canada and Mexico were responsible for 55 percent of the increase in US agricultural exports since the creation of NAFTA in 1993.
- Mexican agriculture benefited from NAFTA in 1993–2005, with agricultural exports to and from the United States increasing by $5.6 billion.
- Real GDP growth in 1993–2005 was 48 percent for the United States, 40 percent for Mexico and 49 percent for Canada.
- US employment increased by 22.6 million jobs, or 20.1 percent, from 112.2 million jobs in December 1993 to 134.8 million jobs in February 2006. The average unemployment rate declined from 7.1 percent in 1982–93 to 5.1 percent in 1994–2005.
- The average real compensation of manufacturing workers in the United States increased at the average yearly rate of 2.3 percent in 1993–2005 in contrast with a yearly growth rate of only 0.4 percent between 1987 (when data became available) and 1993.
- The rate of productivity growth in the US business sector increased at 2.6 percent per year in 1993–2005, totaling 36.2 percent. In contrast, in 1981–93, the yearly rate of growth of productivity was 1.8 percent for a cumulative 24.3 percent.
- US non-residential fixed investment increased by 104 percent in 1993–2005 in contrast with an increase of 37 percent in 1981–93.

Evidently, there is no attempt to claim that NAFTA contributed to these economic conditions. However, it is difficult to argue that NAFTA could have been detrimental to economic performance because of its huge share in US trade of about one-third. Adverse effects from such a large share of trade could have affected aggregate economic performance. However, there is still the elusive counterfactual in economics of whether the United States and its partners could have grown more rapidly and efficiently without NAFTA.

The exports to Mexico from the United States were $50.8 billion in 1994 jumping to $110.8 billion in 2004 while imports from Mexico increased from $49.5 billion in 1994 to $155.8 billion in 2004 according to the data by Nica *et al.* (2006). The trade balance with Mexico changed from a surplus of $1.3 billion in 1994 to a deficit of $45.1 billion in 2004. Econometric research by Nica *et al.* (2006) shows that exports of the United States to Mexico were not affected by NAFTA while the agreement caused a significant increase in imports from Mexico. There was a short-term trade deficit between the United States and Mexico that is likely to increase temporarily with further integration of the two countries.

There have been warnings of the role of lobbies in negotiating rules of origin in PTAs with NAFTA being an important case (Krueger 1999, 122). These rules of origin cause costs to producers in PTA member countries in the form of higher prices of inputs and costs of administrative compliance (Cadot *et al.* 2005). Research is focusing on the constraints of rules of origin on the performance of PTAs.

There was a symposium at the World Bank (WB) to analyze the first ten years of NAFTA (Lederman and Servén 2005). An objective of the symposium was to draw general conclusions on PTAs involving developed and developing countries. There were contributions of the effects of NAFTA on Mexico in terms of economic geography, trade, wages, migration and foreign direct investment (FDI). Various problems remained after NAFTA such as continuing trade barriers among members, income differences among regions in Mexico, relation of labor markets to migration, trade and FDI. The flows of FDI did not appear to be related to the trade agreement. Trade creation and diversion effects appear negligible.

The trade preferences of the PTA create rents to exporters in the member countries (Cadot *et al.* 2005). Conventional trade flows are not useful in determining the distribution of these rents, which is crucial in assessing the welfare effects of preferences combined with rules of origin. The effect of preferences on prices is the required information. Cadot *et al.* (2005) estimate the pass-through effects of tariff preferences on consumer prices, which is the increase in foreign producer prices caused by tariff preferences in the PTA. Cadot *et al.* (2005) use the estimates of pass-through of tariffs preferences in the US markets to export prices for Mexican producers to simulate the welfare effects for Mexican exporters of preferential access in textiles and apparel under US rules of origin. The rules of origin halve the tariff preference margin of 8 percent of apparel producers in Mexico. The costs of intermediate inputs to producers in Mexico did not decline after the elimination of the tariff on imports from the United States. Producers in Mexico pay 12–13 percent more for intermediate goods imported from the United States than the price of exports by US producers to non-preferential destinations, with 4 percentage points explained by technical requirements, a form of rules of origin in textiles and apparel.

The literature on FDI distinguishes the effects of PTAs on FDI depending on whether industries are vertically or horizontally integrated. In vertical integration, offshoring occurs for many basic activities that rely on low-cost labor while management and technology are centralized in the headquarters in the more advanced country (Cuevas *et al.* 2005, 475). A vertical integration strategy assumes trade without major restrictions because the offshore production must serve the home market. In the strategy of horizontal FDI, there are similar basic manufacturing plants in various countries, each one serving the local market. There are differences in factor endowments in the vertical strategy but not in the horizontal one. The theoretical conclusion is that freer trade would promote vertical FDI but render horizontal FDI redundant. Cuevas *et al.* (2005) argue that because of the cost advantage of Mexico in the form of cheaper labor, NAFTA should promote FDI of the vertical type. The difference in size between Mexico and the larger partners, Canada and the United States, would suggest that the losses in horizontal FDI would be much smaller than the gains in vertical FDI.

Although Mexico experienced a major twin crisis in 1994–5 and the reform effort ceased, Cuevas *et al.* (2005) estimate that FDI may have been higher by two-thirds with NAFTA than would have been without the treaty. The difference in size between Mexico and its partners, Canada and the United States, is a factor of the significant impact on FDI. At a more general level, Cuevas *et al.* (2005) argue that FTAs have strong impact on FDI. The level of FDI into a country is influenced by world FDI flows. Domestic variables influencing FDI include stable macroeconomics and more educated workers because FDI and skilled labor are possibly complementary.

The multilateral negotiations within the WTO and the reduction of tariff rates worldwide caused increasing activity in antidumping and countervailing duties as forms of restricting trade by import-sensitive sectors. The United States has actively followed this restriction of trade and has resisted its elimination in the WTO negotiations and in FTAs. NAFTA finds a compromise by establishing binational panels to review antidumping and countervailing duty actions between members at the request of a party. There is an important research issue of whether this mechanism has been effective (Blonigen 2005). The review panels are limited to determining if a country follows its national laws in determining antidumping or countervailing duties. However, the appeals of US antidumping and countervailing duty actions by Canada and Mexico have been processed by the panels instead of the courts. Blonigen (2005) does not find evidence that the binational panels significantly reduced antidumping and countervailing duty activity of the United States against its NAFTA partners.

One of the major fears relating to NAFTA was the equalization of wages among the partners. Theory suggests that increasing trade and FDI would increase the demand for labor, raising wages in Mexico toward the level of the United States (Robertson 2005). There would be greater integration of labor markets among the members of NAFTA. Wages depend positively on demand and productivity. The rising productivity of the PTAs would raise wages in the country with lower labor cost. Wages did not converge between Mexico and the United States. Robertson (2005) uses three other aspects of labor market integration: the relation between US wage shocks and Mexican wages, the speed of relative wages in returning to a long-term differential and the rate of convergence of absolute wages. There are mixed results from using these three factors. Robertson (2005) uses trade, FDI and migration, concluding that trade and FDI affect labor integration positively. The increasing border patrol after NAFTA hides the positive effects of trade and FDI.

There are short-term effects of PTAs in the form of displaced workers and closed plants and long-term gains of efficiency by owners of competitive plants and consumers of final and intermediate goods (Trefler 2004). The conflict of the costs of these short-term adjustment and the long-term gains explains the difficulty in selling FTAs. In addition, the research on the gains of FTAs is mostly on developing economies with few studies on industrialized countries. Trefler (2004) finds significant employment loss in the Canada–US FTA. It caused the reduction of employment by 5 percent for manufacturing and of 12 percent for the import-competing industries that were most affected. The results are consistent in the econometric analysis of both plants and industries. Simultaneously, the FTA caused major gains in labor productivity, which increased by 14 percent at the plant level. In the import-competing industries with highest effects, labor productivity increased by15 percent but with one-half of this effect originating in the exit and/or contraction of plants with low productivity. Although most of Canadian manufacturing was duty free, labor productivity in manufacturing as a whole increased by 6 percent. There was more trade creation than diversion in the FTA and import prices possibly declined. There is not yet a resolution of the debate between short-term adjustment costs and long-term efficiency gains, which is of critical importance to the population. Analysis and empirical research should address these short-term and long-term conflicts.

An important change of perception was that NAFTA closed the return to an inward-looking economic model in Mexico. This new view of the country would be an important determinant of a larger inflow of foreign investment (Castañeda 2004, 51). Mexican policies would be viewed as more predictable, creating a better investment environment.

Other trade agreements and negotiations with the WTO reduced the advantages of NAFTA for Mexico and Canada. However, there is no doubt that trade and benefits increased during the agreement. The three countries have experienced significant change as a result of NAFTA. The quality of products has improved and prices declined because of higher competition, with major benefits to consumers. Producers also experienced benefits by market access with low or no tariffs. However, Castañeda finds difficulty in reconciling benefits and losses to different sectors. Specialization in agricultural products had adverse effects on Mexican agriculture. There was not a trend of growth of FDI but rather stabilization at the level of $14 billion of 1994. In agriculture, the United States reduced tariffs on manufactured goods and agricultural products but left them unchanged in sugar. Mexico maintained tariffs on crops such as corn and beans. Castañeda (2004, 53) argues that Mexico created 500,000 jobs in manufacturing but lost 1.3 million jobs in agriculture. Economic growth in Mexico has not been as dynamic as in the past, with rates well below the 6 percent per year obtained in 1940–70. Regional income inequality has worsened. Migration to the United States has increased. Castañeda (2004, 54) argues that "NAFTA has not been the win-win situation some of its supporters said it would be. Nor has it been the catastrophe its critics predicted." He believes that the full benefits would be only obtained with a North American economic community, sharing common policies, objectives, needs and values.

The effects of the entire liberalization effort of Mexico are questioned because of the low rate of growth after the reforms. Tornell *et al.* (2003) argue that the growth rates of Mexico do not imply that liberalization inhibits growth. Mexico had high rates of growth of exports and FDI inflows in the 1990s. There are two factors, according to Tornell *et al.* (2003), the lack of structural reforms after 1995 and the response of Mexico to the crisis. The credit crunch in Mexico was deeper and lasted longer than in most countries. The stagnation of exports at the turn of the Millennium can be traced to bottlenecks created by the credit crunch.

APEC

There is no FTA similar to APEC with its forum of consultations and voluntary agreements. The dimensions of APEC are the largest of any similar undertaking. It would concentrate more than 50 percent of world output and a significant part of its trade. The challenge of definitively creating APEC is as large as its dimensions. Table 1.4 shows the dimensions of APEC. It would weld into one trading bloc the entire North America and the largest countries in Asia, excluding India.

APEC is a unique form of dialogue and cooperation. It "operates as a cooperative, multilateral economic and trade forum" (APEC 2007). Its uniqueness consists of the lack of legally binding obligations. There is a commitment to reducing

Table 1.4 GDP, GDP per capita, exports and imports in APEC 2005

	GDP	GDP per capita	Exports	Imports
	US$B	US$	US$B	US$B
Australia	709	35,199	135	150
Brunei	6	16,800	6	2
Canada	1,131	35,073	519	467
Chile	111	6,833	48	39
China	1,981	1,533	655	604
Hong Kong	173	24,521	341	322
Indonesia	281	1,263	94	82
Japan	4,559	35,593	652	589
Korea	787	16,472	335	315
Malaysia	131	5,159	161	131
Mexico	768	7,180	250	264
New Zealand	109	27,209	307	334
Papua New Guinea	5	905	2	2
Peru	76	2,739	18	15
Philippines	97	1,176	45	46
Russia	766	5,349	270	164
Singapore	117	26,997	284	249
Taiwan (2006)	354	15,391	215	205
Thailand	177	2,749	130	133
United States	12,456	41,768	1,303	2,019
Vietnam	53	631	36	39
Total APEC less United States	12,591		4,233	4,152

Source: United Nations, http://unstats.un.org/unsd/snaama/countryList.asp.

trade barriers and increasing investment among its members. Dialogue is the vehicle for promoting trade and investment. The members engage in individual and collective actions designed to liberalize markets and foster economic growth.

There are yearly meetings of APEC in a host country. The host country acts as the chair of APEC and its various meetings. A diplomat from the member hosting the current year meeting is the Executive Director of APEC; a diplomat from the host of the next year meeting becomes Deputy Executive Director of APEC. Small contributions by members provide the budget of only \$3.4 million per year. Japan began to provide additional resources of \$2.7–4.2 million per year to fund projects supporting liberalizing trade and investment. The headquarters of APEC are located in Singapore.

The meetings of leaders provide the policy agenda of APEC. Prior meetings of ministers of foreign trade and the economy provide suggestions for the leaders. There are additional meetings on various sectors of interest. The council of business advice provides suggestions for improving the business and investment environment in the APEC region. There is a special committee to promote trade and investment among members.

The Osaka Action Agenda of APEC formulated general principles that must be followed in the entire agenda of liberalization of trade and investment. One of these principles is consistency with the principles of the WTO. The Bogor Goals of APEC provide for the more advanced members achieving free trade by 2010 and the less advanced members by 2020. The individual members provide yearly progress reports on achieving open trade and investment goals in the form of Individual Action Plans (IAP), with records of actions taken to attain the goals. The individual members determine their goals and timelines on purely voluntary bases. Reporting follows the Osaka Action Agenda of 15 issue areas, the first four of which are tariffs, non-tariff measures, services and investment (APEC 2007). On a yearly basis, several members volunteer to have a peer review of their IAPs. There is participation of the business council and experts in the peer review. The IAPs and the peer reviews are available online (APEC 2007). An important ingredient of the APEC process is to involve governments, academics, business, industry, research institutes and interest groups.

The process of APEC is open and wide. The Pacific Economic Cooperation Council (PECC) counts with the participation of government, business and intellectual circles. The objective of PECC is to provide a "forum for cooperation and policy coordination to promote economic development in the Asia-Pacific region" (APEC 2007). The spirit of partnership and cooperation is the basic principle of PECC. Berger (1999) provides a historical analysis of the origins of APEC and the initial role played by PECC.

There is sharp contrast between APEC and the EU (Langhammer 1999). The open regionalism of APEC consists of MFN liberalization by its members, on a unilateral and voluntary basis. Members in the EU engage in non-MFN, discriminatory liberalization. There are two recurring proposals within APEC: open regionalism and the Free Trade Agreement of Asia and the Pacific (FTAAP) (Bhagwati 2006b). In the open regionalism proposal, APEC would continue as a forum, with members liberalizing trade and extending it to the world via the MFN. APEC would exert its influence to conclude the Doha Development Round (DDR) of the WTO. The FTAAP would eliminate trade barriers among APEC members, maintaining discriminatory tariffs against the rest of the world. Bhagwati (2006b) finds political and technical difficulties with the FTAAP. There is a growing Asian identity in the Asian nations within APEC that differs from that around the Pacific Ocean. Bhagwati (2006b) finds that the FTAAP would worsen the spaghetti bowl of bilateral agreements with its discriminatory tariffs depending on origin.

In a study with panel data for 28 countries of the EU and APEC in four subperiods 1981–2000, Tang (2003) finds that the EU countries reduced their trade with NAFTA, ASEAN and the newly industrialized countries (NIC). Trade decrease accentuated in 1996–2000. In the subgroups of APEC, ASEAN countries appear to have a more stable rate of growth with the EU countries. Trade among the EU countries increased as a result of integration, which is also the case of trade within members of ASEAN and the NICs.

There is a survey probing the FDI environment in 14 Asia-Pacific economies (Han and Kim 2003). Market access is the most important motivation of FDI, especially in developing economies. The authorization process is significantly more difficult in developing economies. The authors used the inward FDI index of the United Nations' (UN) UNCTAD that consists of an unweighted average of three ratios that capture the propensity to attract FDI after adjustment for the weight of the host economy in the world. This index shows decrease in the capacity to attract FDI by the Asia-Pacific economies in the 1990s. Economies liberalizing FDI regimes show high indices. Han and Kim (2003) find that there were policy changes to attract FDI in most economies. However, the policy measures were not adequate for the problems revealed in the survey of investors.

ASEAN

The initial establishment of ASEAN was in the 1960s because of political interests. Eventually, economic motives reshaped ASEAN into an FTA and gradually into an intention of greater integration. Table 1.5 shows the diversity of members of ASEAN in terms of level of economic development, from the sophisticated Singapore to countries with relatively low per capita GDP. The ambition of ASEAN is to provide a framework for greater growth and progress to its members. There could be alliances with the United States, the EU and countries in Asia, such as China, India, Japan and Korea. The economic motives are mixed with political interests and the special nature of relations in Asia.

ASEAN was established by a treaty, the ASEAN Declaration, signed in Bangkok, Thailand, on August 8, 1967, by the foreign ministers of Indonesia, Malaysia, the Philippines, Singapore and Thailand (ASEAN 2007). Other countries subsequently joined ASEAN: Brunei Darussalam in 1984, Vietnam in 1995, Lao PDR and Myanmar in 1997 and Cambodia in 1999. The combined population of ASEAN is

Table 1.5 GDP, GDP per capita, exports and imports in ASEAN 2005

	GDP	GDP per capita	Exports	Imports
	US$B	US$	US$B	US$B
Brunei	6	35,199	135	150
Cambodia	5	384	3	4
Indonesia	281	1,263	94	82
Laos	3	485	0.8	0.9
Malaysia	131	5,159	161	131
Myanmar	10	217		
Philippines	97	1,176	45	46
Singapore	117	26,997	284	249
Thailand	177	2,749	130	133
Vietnam	53	631	36	39
Total	934		889	835

Source: United Nations, http://unstats.un.org/unsd/snaama/countryList.asp.

about 500 million. The goals of the Declaration of 1967 were the acceleration of economic growth, social progress, cultural development and regional peace and stability.

The goal of the ASEAN Vision 2020 is regional free flow of goods, services and investment with reduced poverty and social and economic differences by the year 2020 (ASEAN 2007). The ASEAN economic region would be dynamic and competitive. The strategy of ASEAN is to use the diversity of the region to form an ASEAN Economic Community, consisting of integration of the members to enhance economic competitiveness. The ASEAN Free Trade Area was established in 1992 to obtain the benefits of competitive advantage by creating a single production unit. The instrument is the elimination of tariff and non-tariff barriers, promoting efficiency, productivity and competitiveness. The average tariff for the ASEAN-6 has been reduced from an initial 12 percent to 2 percent. The newer members with lower GDP have reduced most of their tariffs to the 0–5 percent level. The complementary agreement in services is the ASEAN Framework Agreement on Services and the agreement on investment is the ASEAN Investment Area. The ASEAN has selected sectors for accelerated integration by 2010, including air travel, agribusiness, automotive, e-commerce and electronics. The community is also facilitating the movement of business persons, skilled labor and talent across the region. It is improving the ASEAN Dispute Settlement Mechanism to provide fast and legally binding resolution of economic claims.

ASEAN is planning integration in capital markets, currency cooperation and the liberalization of capital accounts and financial services (ASEAN 2007). There are also plans to develop the transportation network of the region, including air travel. Integration plans also cover telecommunications, energy, infrastructure, IT and tourism.

The highest level of decision of ASEAN is the yearly meeting of heads of state and government (ASEAN 2007). The meeting of leaders is typically preceded by meetings of foreign and economic ministers. The secretariat of ASEAN initiates and coordinates activities of the institution. There are various centers of excellence in ASEAN capitals.

The leaders of ASEAN have been following national and regional approaches to development of capital markets with the objective of promoting growth and avoiding financial crises (Plummer and Click 2005). Financial diversification is being pursued by correcting currency and maturity mismatches, pricing risk through better instruments, accessing new sources of long-term capital, better asset management and increasing the participation in world capital markets. To be sure, banking is a priority in ASEAN and other countries. However, Plummer and Click (2005) consider the returns and obstacles of developing internal bond markets and the benefits of issuing fixed-income securities through a regional market. There is a wide spectrum of bond market development within ASEAN, from the world-class market of Singapore through incipient markets and no market at all in several countries. This diversity dictates the use of individual characteristics in every country. Plummer and Click (2005, 141) argue that the significant policy reform effort in the individual countries may be as important as the actual establishment of a regional market. Capital market reforms should be complementary to banking development and reform.

Analysis of the emerging ASEAN MNCs proceeds on the basis of three management concepts (Bartels *et al.* 2006, 172):

1. *Strategic coherence.* The firm adapts to changing conditions in global business by designing and implementing the evolution of its organizational structure with operational clarity.
2. *Dispersed functionality.* The firm develops a structure dispersed geographically and economically by means of international development and joint international business associations such as M&As, joint ventures, strategic alliances and so on. Firms that are scattered geographically and have high levels of capitalization or ownership of assets possess higher dispersed functionality. Delegation of authority to subsidiaries enhances dispersed functionality.
3. *International management capability.* This is the capacity of the firm in managing international operations, depending on the extent and quality of its vertical integration. Within the transaction costs approach of the NIE, firms experience greater operational efficiency when they have the capacity to respond to markets.

The analysis postulates structural relation of strategic coherence, dispersed functionality and international management capability.

Bartels *et al.* (2006) tested the model with survey data on ASEAN MNCs. As expected in their hypothesis, dispersed functionality directly explains strategic coherence with an indirect effect by international management capability.

The United States launched in October 2002 the Enterprise for ASEAN Initiative (EAI) with the objective of creating an FTA between the United States and qualifying ASEAN countries (Naya and Plummer 2006). The EAI would consist of several bilateral FTAs between the United States and ASEAN countries that are members of the WTO and had a Trade and Investment Framework with the United States. The model for the bilateral agreements would be the US–Singapore FTA of 2002, considered to be one of the most advanced FTAs in existence.

A quantitative study by Naya and Plummer (2006) concludes that the United States is the most important trade partner of the ASEAN region. An agreement with the United States would foster structural change in the economies of the region. The agreement would recover the losses in MFN caused by the multiplicity of US FTAs. The use of the Singapore–US FTA as a model poses challenges of economic reform for the ASEAN countries and negotiation in sensitive labor and agricultural sectors issues in the United States.

There are multiple factors of the increasing interest of a trade and investment grouping of East Asian countries (Cai 2003, 388–9). The growth of the EU and NAFTA poses a challenge to East Asia that could feel left behind as a continent without a major trade agreement. The enlargement of the EU toward Eastern Europe and the possibility of the creation of the FTAA also contributed to a common interest in meeting the challenge of regional integration. Negotiations with blocs in the EU and NAFTA motivate the need of an East Asian bloc. There has been increasing integration of the East Asian countries in trade and investment, creating the interest in regional association. In addition, the EU and the United States are major markets for products of East Asia. The Asian financial crises also exposed regional fragilities leading to the belief that a union would strengthen the region and individual countries. There was also dissatisfaction that APEC and ASEAN would not effectively promote the interests of East Asia.

There have been three approaches to the creation of a regional grouping in East Asia (Cai 2003). In 1990, the Prime Minister of Malaysia, Mahatir Mohamad, proposed the creation of the East Asian Economic Grouping (EAEG). However, Mohamad created frictions with the United States and suspicion within East Asia. The second effort was the ASEAN initiative of the ASEAN plus Three (APT), leading to a broad agreement between ASEAN and the three strongest economies in East Asia – Japan, China and South Korea. The third approach is the negotiation of individual FTAs between ASEAN and the three strongest economies, ASEAN plus One (APO). The individual FTAs could eventually result in a broad regional agreement.

There are multiple factors of the increasing interest of a trade and investment grouping of East Asian countries (Cai 2003, 388–9). The growth of the EU and NAFTA poses a challenge to East Asia that could feel left behind as a continent without a major trade agreement. The enlargement of the EU toward Eastern Europe and the possibility of the creation of the FTAA also contributed to a common interest in meeting the challenge of regional integration. Negotiations with blocs in the EU and NAFTA motivate the need of an East Asian bloc. There has been increasing integration of the East Asian countries in trade and investment, creating the interest in regional association. In addition, the EU and the United States are major markets for products of East Asia. The Asian financial crises also

Table 1.6 Trade of ASEAN and China
US$B, 2005

	Exports	Imports
ASEAN	889	835
China	1,543	1,439

Source: United Nations, http://unstats.un.org/
unsd/snaama/countryList.asp.

exposed regional fragilities leading to the belief that a union would strengthen the region and individual countries. There was also dissatisfaction that APEC and ASEAN would not effectively promote the interests of East Asia.

The combination of ASEAN and China in an FTA would result in large dimensions (Cai 2003, 401). The combined GDP of ASEAN, Table 1.5, is $934 billion. Adding the GDP of China of $1981, Table 1.4, the total of the potential FTA would be $2911. The total trade of the potential FTA is shown in Table 1.6, about $2.4 trillion in exports and $2.3 trillion in imports. Cai (2003, 401) reports that the Secretariat of ASEAN estimates that the FTA would allow an increase of ASEAN exports to China by 48 percent with an impact on regional GDP of 0.9 percent, or US$5.4 billion. China could increase its exports to ASEAN by 55.1 percent and GDP by 0.3 percent, US$0.9 billion.

There would be the inevitable short-term adjustment costs. China and ASEAN would compete in similar labor-intensive products with low value added (Cai 2003, 401). The distribution of costs and benefits in similar FTAs has been uneven, with losses and gains by different firms and individuals. Industries would contract in one of the countries and expand in the other. Firms may relocate from ASEAN to China because of advantages of supplies of intermediate inputs, electronic components and processing equipment (Wong and Chan 2003, 510). The proximity of supporting industries may concentrate investment in China, creating internal redistribution among regions.

The expectation is that in the long term both economies would become more efficient and competitive, attracting FDI inflows (Cai 2003, 401). Moreover, a large joint market would benefit from economies of scale caused by increasing market size in the form of lower unit costs (Wong and Chan 2003, 509). Firms would become more productive because of more intensive competition. A first move by China would also create pressure for similar moves by the other strong regional economies of South Korea and Japan, perhaps leading to a more intensive and broader integration effort.

The Premier of China proposed in November 2000 the creation of an ASEAN–China FTA in ten years (Wong and Chan 2003). The gains from a China–ASEAN FTA would be higher if the two economies were complementary instead of competitive (Wong and Chan 2003, 516–7). In reality, the economies of China and ASEAN are competitive instead of complementary, with the possible exception of Singapore. China does not have a major market in the ASEAN economies. In

1980–2000, only 6.4 percent of China's exports on average had ASEAN-5 countries as destination, with 3.1 percent to Singapore alone (Wong and Chan 2003, 517). The imports of Singapore from China in 1980–2000 were only 4 percent of total imports on average. Wong and Chan (2003, 517) conclude from this low level of trade that the economies of China and ASEAN are competitive instead of complementary. The industrialized countries of Japan, the EU and the United States constitute the major market targets for exports of both China and ASEAN. The low FDI flows between the two regions confirms the lack of an interest in investment for vertical integration. Thus, China and ASEAN would compete with each other in selling traditional and non-traditional manufactures in the markets of advanced countries.

China has been gradually increasing the use of multilateralism in its foreign policy at the turn of the twenty-first century (Cheng-Chwee 2005). The initial attitude was one of caution and suspicion that multilateral institutions could endanger China's sovereignty and strategies. Policy changed toward viewing multilateral institutions as useful in fostering China's policy goals. Cheng-Chwee (2005) considers two important general principles. China perceives that multilateralism is complementary instead of supplementary in its bilateral relations with ASEAN. The motivation for this change is the ambition of China to shape the structure of regional cooperation. This is a major change in the old Chinese view of " 'never aspire to lead' in international affairs" (Cheng-Chwee 2005, 119). The change in policy toward regional agreements could signal similar approaches in the global relations of China.

There is an interesting concept of considering two views of whether the economies of China and emerging Asia are comrades or competitors (Ahearne *et al.* 2003, 184). According to the view of comrades, increasing trade among countries in Asia originates in sharing mutual benefits from growing incomes of consumers in China and the expectation of increasing integration of product lines throughout the region. The second view argues that China and emerging Asia are competitors in world export markets by their specialization in producing goods that are close substitutes. Ahearne *et al.* (2003) find that there are elements of both views in Asia's reality. The view of comrades is vindicated by growing imports of China from the rest of Asia as a result of high growth in China and its accession to the WTO in 2001. Countries such as Singapore, Taiwan and Malaysia have moved upward in the production of goods with higher value added using more sophisticated and less labor-intensive technology. The competitive view is also vindicated by an acceleration of the transition of sectors in other Asian economies as China has further integrated in the world economy. There is fear within Asia that manufacturing is relocating to China to benefit from low-cost labor and the growing domestic market. Asian economies are facing displacement of workers and industries that impose a burden of adjustment. There are also complaints that China's advantage is derived from its undervaluation of the exchange rate. Ahearne *et al.* (2003) do not find that exchange rate movements are the major determinants of export performance in Asian economies.

The correlation of Chinese export growth with that of the ASEAN-4 and the NICs is positive in most cases but not significant, leading Ahearne *et al.* (2003) to find possibility of complementary instead of competitive association. Exchange rates matter in explaining export performance but the strongest determinant is the income of the trading partners. China and emerging Asia depend on income growth in the advanced countries. There is evidence supporting the "flying geese" pattern with China and ASEAN-4 gaining share in product markets no longer served by the NICs that in turn moved to more sophisticated products. The competition for these "flying geese" markets causes adjustment burdens in some of the less advanced Asian countries.

The policy of Japan toward its major neighbors, China and Korea, and in relation to the East Asian community that ASEAN desires to create is not as clear (Hwee 2006). There is strong alliance between Japan and the United States, which is in part driven by the view of China as a security threat. Another view would see the participation of China in regional economic and political affairs as a form to guarantee that China's development is peaceful and beneficial to the region. The future of the APT is unclear until the roles of Japan and China are more precisely defined. Part of this definition will require peaceful and constructive solution to the North Korean nuclear situation. However, Park (2006) finds evidence that Japan has moved after the Asian crisis to develop regional institutionalism instead of ideas as the form of effective collaboration in East Asia. In this view, Japan has been proactive in developing institutionalism through APT. There may still be hurdles in the future because of the legacy of earlier historical events.

Although there have been significant liberalizing efforts, the share of intra-ASEAN trade is stagnant (Sally and Sen 2005). At the same time, trade and investment of ASEAN with China and India has grown much faster. There are benefits in closer cooperation of ASEAN with the large and growing economies of China and India. The gap in the liberalizing policy of China relative to ASEAN has diminished recently and a similar phenomenon may occur relative to India. The integration of China and India in the world economy exposes weaknesses in domestic sectors in the ASEAN countries. There is a challenge for these countries in liberalization and deregulation to accompany the more dynamic sources of growth from China and India.

The multilateral negotiations and bilateral regional agreements may not be enough for ASEAN countries to accompany the dynamism of China and India (Sally and Sen 2005). Progress in negotiating and implementing agreements may be too slow and likely to stall. Even implemented agreements face significant bureaucratic impediments and complex rules of origin. The changes from these agreements are considered to be as originating from above. Sally and Sen (2005) propose more aggressive change from within the ASEAN countries themselves. They argue that liberalization has to proceed unilaterally to accompany the similar process initially in China and then in India. The measures can be reinforced within regional agreements and the WTO but this should be secondary in priority to unilateral liberalization.

MERCOSUR

The beginning of MERCOSUR was merely a CU with four countries – Argentina, Brazil, Paraguay and Uruguay – with the interest that common negotiation would strengthen external negotiation. Venezuela joined in 2006 and other countries have become associate members. At points, Argentina and Brazil have used MERCOSUR in the efforts to gain strength in the negotiation of the FTAA. Table 1.7 shows that there is significant diversity in the size of GDP and level of development among the countries. Brazil has a significantly larger industrial sector that is competitive internationally in some areas together with a formidable agricultural sector that is the subject of intense negotiations for access to markets in developed countries. It is difficult to reconcile the interests of the members of the CU. Moreover, MERCOSUR has functioned in stop and go fashion. In past financial and macroeconomic crises, Argentina and Brazil have used trade restrictions that temporarily interrupt the treaty. Eichengreen (2004) concludes that macroeconomic policies and institutions are more important in Latin America than common currencies. The EU has been trying to negotiate an agreement with MERCOSUR for more than half a decade.

Argentina, Brazil, Paraguay and Uruguay signed on March 26, 1991, the Treaty of Asunción, creating MERCOSUR (Del Castillo 1993). On July 4, 2006, Venezuela became a full member of MERCOSUR. Bolivia, Chile, Colombia and Ecuador are associate members. The objective of creating MERCOSUR is the integration of the members by means of free exchange of goods, services and productive factors (MERCOSUR 2007). The intention is developing a common trade policy, coordinating macroeconomic and sector policies, harmonizing the pertinent legislation and establishing a common tariff for non-members. Thus, MERCOSUR

Table 1.7   GDP, GDP per capita, exports and imports in MERCOSUR 2005

	GDP	GDP per capita	Exports	Imports
	US$B	US$	US$B	US$B
Argentina	183	4,731	45	35
Brazil	799	4,289	132	102
Paraguay	7	1,248	3	3
Uruguay	17	1,187	49	46
Venezuela	132	4,949	44	24
Subtotal	1,138		273	210
Associate Members				
Bolivia	9	1,059	3	3
Chile	111	6,833	48	39
Colombia	122	2,673	26	28
Ecuador	33	2,499	9	9
Total	1,413		359	289

Source: United Nations, http://unstats.un.org/unsd/snaama/countryList.asp.

is closer to the initial EEC than to FTAs, at least in intentions. The meeting in Ouro Preto, Brazil, in December 1994, added an additional protocol, providing the institutional structure of MERCOSUR and giving it a juridical international nature. The Ouro Preto meeting adopted the instruments of the common trade policy in the form of a CU with a common external tariff. The objective was creating a common market.

The tenth meeting of the council of MERCOSUR on June 25, 1995 approved a declaration of democratic commitment. Bolivia and Chile adhered to that declaration. In 2000, the members of MERCOSUR launched the treaty again, restating the objectives of integration (MERCOSUR 2007).

The Ouro Preto protocol created in 1994 an administrative secretariat of MERCOSUR. Montevideo became the permanent seat of the MERCOSUR and its secretariat on May 29, 1997. The initial duties of the secretariat, until 2002, consisted of maintaining the archive of documents. It also published and divulged the decisions of the common market and organized meetings, informing the legal measures taken by each member. After 2002, the secretariat was transformed into a technical advisory organ. It consists of three sectors, technical advice, norms and documentation and administration and support.

There are various levels in the institutional structure of MERCOSUR (Vervaele 2005, 391–2). The council of MERCOSUR has a commission of permanent representatives and organizes the meetings of ministers and other consultative groups. The market group of MERCOSUR consists of various working groups and special meetings on the business of the common market. There is a trade commission of MERCOSUR consisting of various technical committees on tariffs, customs and so on. There is a proposal for a MERCOSUR parliament, strongly endorsed by Venezuela. Finally, MERCOSUR has an administrative and labor court and a permanent tribunal for revision of the treaty.

An important change in MERCOSUR was the Decision 18/04 of its council in July 2004 (Arieti 2006). This decision opened the access of associate members in the organizational institutions of MERCOSUR that were accessible only to full members. The freezing of the FTAA and the opposition by Venezuela and other countries to the United States has been motivating the creation of a common market of Latin American countries. The Andean Community of Nations (CAN) reached an agreement with MERCOSUR in 2002, which granted MERCOSUR associate status to its members, Bolivia, Colombia, Ecuador, Peru and Venezuela (Arieti 2006, 762). The broader objective is to create a South-American Community of Nations (CSN) departing from the base of MERCOSUR. With Venezuela as full member, MERCOSUR may be more aggressive in broadening its integration with other countries.

MERCOSUR has operated in stop-go fashion according to macroeconomic and exchange rate disruptions (Peláez and Peláez 2005, 28–42) that interrupt its functioning. Eichengreen (2004, 1–2) provides a revealing summary of the history of these interruptions. After Argentina implemented its convertibility plan in 1991, the overvaluation of the Argentinean relative to the Brazilian currency motivated Argentina to impose antidumping duties and safeguards against Brazilian exports to defend its currency. When the Brazilian currency became overvalued after the economic plan in Brazil in 1994, Brazil increased tariffs and imposed quotas on imports from Argentina to support its overvalued currency. The Brazilian fiscal and trade deficits significantly worsened as the country insisted in maintaining an unsustainable overvaluation (Peláez and Peláez 2007, 169–73).

Eichengreen (2004, 2) documents how Brazil imposed licenses on selected Argentinean products in 1997 in an effort to support its currency. The devaluation of Brazil in 1999 caused "Argentina to slap import quotas on textiles and to impose bureaucratic restrictions on imports of Brazilian machinery, and Brazil to retaliate by reintroducing subsidies for rice production and to demand limits on imports of footwear" (Eichengreen 2004, 2). The devaluation, default, political crisis and economic contraction of Argentina after 2001 had strong effects on MERCOSUR. There was a decline of intra-region trade by 10 percent in 2001 after increasing by 16 percent per year on average in the 1990s. Exports of Brazil to Argentina fell by one-half in 2002 while Argentina's exports to Brazil fell by 25 percent. Eichengreen (2004, 2) concludes that MERCOSUR was designed to increase trade among its members but actually caused trade tensions among them because of currency turmoil.

The experience with trade agreements suggests that their support is related to macroeconomic stability (Eichengreen 2004). Financial and exchange rate turbulence disturb RTAs. There is support for protectionism when currencies of member countries in a trade agreement are threatened. Eichengreen (2004) reminds that the unification of currencies would require a joint central bank. Political institutions such as a regional parliament take long periods of gestation and implementation. The common trade and investment interests of the member countries are not sufficiently strong, as the episodes of trade tension reveal. The adoption of the dollar as the currency of MERCOSUR is now politically unfeasible because of the membership of Venezuela. Moreover, the common dollar currency would eliminate entirely a role for monetary policy. The common macroeconomic problems of Argentina and Brazil are strongly related to recurring fiscal deficits. It has been extremely difficult to harmonize fiscal deficits even within the European Monetary Union (EMU) countries (Peláez and Peláez 2007, 127–35). Common monetary and exchange rate policies are unfeasible with diverging fiscal policies. There is no political strength within MERCOSUR for common fiscal policies.

Eichengreen (2004) finds that it is difficult to soften exchange rate turbulence in international agreements. His suggestion is that the MERCOSUR countries follow sound monetary policies, perhaps within an inflation targeting framework, together with prudential fiscal and debt policies. The resulting macroeconomic stability would diminish exchange rate fluctuation, providing the environment for regional integration. The development of hedge markets would contribute to effective financial and trade integration.

The new trade policy of the EU emphasizes FTAs based on the potential of markets, in terms of size and growth, and the protection against EU exports in terms of tariff levels and non-tariff barriers (Azevedo and Henz 2006, 438). MERCOSUR, ASEAN and Korea are priorities in the new EU agenda of FTAs. The new policy goes beyond elimination of tariffs to include liberalization of services trade, investment, public procurement and competition. Azevedo and Henz (2006) argue that MERCOSUR does not have the potential contemplated by the new EU policy because of recent disappointing growth, such as 2.5 percent per year in GDP for Brazil 2002–5, well below the average for emerging countries.

MERCOSUR is not negotiating with competitors of the EU because of the collapse of negotiations for the FTAA. In addition, meaningful negotiations would have to be reached on agricultural barriers, which would conflict with the preferences currently provided to developing countries partners of the EU. The main reason for negotiations is the high level of MERCOSUR tariffs against EU exporters. The motivation for MERCOSUR is that the EU is its main trading partner and the level of protection by the EU against its exports is relatively high. Azevedo and Henz (2006) argue that agricultural exports account for 48 percent of EU imports from MERCOSUR, in spite of strong trade barriers. On the other way, machinery and transport account for 50 percent of EU exports to MERCOSUR. The negotiations of MERCOSUR and the EU since their cooperation agreement in 1999 have not been successful. Both regions have excluded their vulnerable sectors from liberalization (Azevedo and Henz 2006). There may be slow negotiations in agricultural sectors because of the opposition within the EU; the heterogeneous nature of MERCOSUR countries generates opposition to negotiations in some goods (Martínez-Zarsoso and Nowak-Lehmann 2004).

There is an analysis of FDI in the four MERCOSUR partners in 1960–2000 by Bittencourt and Domingo (2004). FDI inflows in the MERCOSUR countries grew at the average annual rate of 5.9 percent in 1960–2000 while the rate of growth of MERCOSUR GDP was 3.8 percent. There was significant acceleration of FDI inflows in the 1990s as part of a worldwide event. FDI in M&As was 70 percent of the total inflow for Brazil in 1993–8 and 57 percent in Argentina in 1992–9. Econometric research shows that growth of the internal market, export performance and macroeconomic stability are important determinants of FDI inflows (Bittencourt and Domingo 2004, 113).

The success of MERCOSUR has been more evident in attracting FDI inflows than in improving the share of the group in world trade and output. Chudnovsky and López (2004) argue that the share of MERCOSUR in world FDI increased from 1.4 percent in 1984–9 to 5.9 percent in 1997–9. The share in world GNP was below 4 percent and in trade about 1.5 percent. An important event has been the replacement of state-owned enterprises (SOE) and to certain extent domestic conglomerates with MNCs. The FDI surge occurred simultaneously with liberalizing measures and privatization while integration accelerated within MERCOSUR. FDI inflows were viewed as complementary to the policy of financing the balance of payments and improving technological progress.

The motivations of inflows of FDI in MERCOSUR were similar to those of the import substitution period 1950–80, according to Chudnovsky and López (2004). In both cases, the strategy was to access the growing domestic market, with the incentive of extending operations into MERCOSUR in the more recent experience. Chudnovsky and López (2004) argue that the exports are low and destined to other developing countries or to MERCOSUR partners. The MNCs export to developed countries mostly products of natural-resource-intensive manufactures. They import inputs and final goods from developed countries. Most trade is within firms.

The average annual rate of growth of exports to MERCOSUR from Canada in 1990–9 was 7.5 percent and of exports to MERCOSUR from the United States 14.1 percent. The comparable rates of growth of imports from MERCOSUR were 4.4 percent for Canada and 4.8 percent for the United States. Jurn and Park (2002) argue that the growth of trade with non-members of MERCOSUR was dynamic. This could be preliminary evidence of lack of significant trade diversion.

The critical impact of PTAs on economic welfare is through relative price or terms of trade effects, according to Chang and Winters (2002, 892). They found that export prices of non-members of MERCOSUR decreased by about 15 percent in the years of initial creation of MERCOSUR 1991–6. The export prices of Argentina to Brazil increased in the same period. That is, MERCOSUR was successful in improving relative prices of its members and in deteriorating those of non-members. Chang and Winters (2002) construct a model of export pricing to guide their formal estimation. Their results confirm the hypothesis that tariff preferences in MERCOSUR decreased the export prices of non-members, deteriorating their terms of trade. The provisions of Clause XXIV of GATT indicate that non-members should not be harmed by PTAs. However, in practice the effect of PTAs that are successful in improving the economic welfare of members is to harm non-members through deterioration of their terms of trade.

OPEC

One of the major current vulnerabilities of the world economy is the rising price of oil. There has been an increase in oil prices to levels around $100 per barrel of oil (pbo). OPEC is not a PTA but rather an agreement of producers with evident intention to restrict trade to increase the price of crude oil and extract monopolistic rents from this behavior. The discussion below considers the institutional framework of OPEC, the economics of the oil market and the literature on what OPEC really accomplishes or not.

The US Energy Information Administration (EIA) prepares an annual energy outlook. Table 1.8 lists the price of oil and consumption of oil corresponding to the reference case of the EIA outlook for 2007 (EIA 2007). After 2004, oil prices have risen to levels above $60 pbo. The forecast is that by 2030 the nominal price of oil will reach $95 pbo in nominal dollars or be above $59 pbo in 2005 dollars. The projections assume that US GDP grows at 2.9 percent per year as a result of growth of the labor force and labor productivity. The projection assumes that OPEC increases production in such a way as to maintain prices within $50–60 pbo. The incentive for OPEC would be to avoid production in non-OPEC oil countries and development of alternative liquid fuels. The projection also assumes that non-OPEC oil producers increase output rapidly. In the reference case the demand for world liquid fuels increases from 84 million barrels of oil per day (mbod) in

Table 1.8 Projections of US oil price and consumption

	Oil price	Consumption of oil
	$ pbo	Quadrillion btu
2004	42	41
2005	56	41
2020	52	46
2030	59	52
2005–30 ppy	0.2	1.0

Notes: Oil price in US dollars pbo, oil consumption in quadrillion British thermal units (btu) per year (py) and rate of increase in average percent per year (ppy).
Source: EIA http://www.eia.doe.gov/oiaf/aeo/pdf/appendixes.pdf.

2005 to 117 mbod in 2030. OPEC production of liquid fuels would increase by 40 percent, from 34 mbod in 2005 to 48 mbod in 2030. Non-OPEC countries would increase production of liquid fuels from 50 mbod in 2005 to 70 mbod in 2030.

There are regular long-term forecasts of oil output and capacity by the US EIA and the International Energy Agency (IEA). Gately (2004) analyzed the feasibility of forecasts of growth of capacity until 2020 at 3.5 percent per year on average by the EIA and of 3.7 percent per year on average by the IEA. OPEC would increase capacity aggressively if it could gain more by that strategy than by increasing it more slowly. Gately (2004) does not find OPEC would have incentives to collectively increase output as fast as in the forecasts of the EIA and the IEA. The return from aggressive increases would be lower if OPEC attempts to increase its market share above the current 37 percent. Coordination of planning by OPEC is not likely. The doubling of capacity implied by the forecasts of the EIA and IEA is not likely to occur. OPEC's capacity has been relatively unchanged in the three decades after the oil producing countries withdrew control of facilities from the oil companies.

A widespread public perception that has influenced policy is that the world supply of oil will be exhausted. In reply to the date when this exhaustion will occur, Adelman (2004, 17) answers: "never." Oil is drilled from mineral deposits called reserves that have been identified and can be profitably extracted. There is a breakeven price of the operation of a well equal to the operating costs. Adelman (2004, 18) argues that "the well's proved reserves are the forecast cumulative profitable output, not the total amount of oil that is believed to be in the ground." The forecast of reserves requires complete knowledge of future science and technology. Reserves will change together with prices and scientific progress in a largely unpredictable fashion. Adelman (2004, 18) recalls that in the 1970s non-OPEC remaining proved reserves were 200 billion barrels of oil. In the following 33 years, those countries produced 460 billion barrels of oil and still have 209 billion of remaining reserves. These producers used inventories at the average rate of 7 percent per year while replacing them. In the same period, OPEC countries started with 412 billion of proved reserves, producing 307 billion and having remaining reserves of 819 billion. There are 80 known fields in Saudi Arabia but only nine are currently in production. There is no incentive for Saudi Arabia to find more fields because the discovery would reduce world oil prices. Adelman (2004) argues that the disruption of the oil market began and continues through the action of OPEC.

There were significant fluctuations of oil prices in 1966–2000 (Alhemoud and Al-Nahas 2003, 345). The price stagnated during the 1960s at $2.11 pbo. There was a yearly increase of 300 cents pbo in 1971–3. The oil embargo in late 1973 caused a jump in price from $3.14 pbo to $11.22 pbo, that is, a 257 percent increase. Then prices stabilized until 1970 when they increased by 126 percent to $29.22 pbo, rising during the Iranian revolution to $34.28 pbo in 1981. There were stable prices around $14 pbo until 1988. Prices began to increase again after 1999 to levels around $100 in 2007. Other sources of supply developed as expected in these type of producer attempts to maintain prices at high levels. About 37 producers not linked to OPEC expanded output or began commercial production. The price of oil rose above the marginal cost of production of these non-OPEC producers. The increase in oil prices has been accompanied by an increase in the elasticity of supply of these producers.

The Baghdad Conference of September 10–14, 1960 created OPEC as an intergovernmental organization (OPEC 2007a). There were five founding members: Iran, Iraq, Kuwait, Saudi Arabia and Venezuela. Other members joined in subsequent years: Qatar in 1961, Indonesia and Libya in 1962, UAE in 1967, Algeria in 1969, Nigeria in 1971, Ecuador in 1973–92, Gabon in 1975–94 and Angola in 2007. The headquarters moved from Geneva to Vienna, Austria, on September 1, 1965. The combined GDP and trade of OPEC members, Table 1.9, mask the significant impact of the oil trade in the world economy and politics. The objective of

Table 1.9   GDP, GDP per capita, exports and imports in OPEC 2005

	GDP	GDP per capita	Exports	Imports
	US$B	US$	US$B	US$B
Algeria	102	3,112	47	25
Angola	29	1,810	23	18
Indonesia	281	1,263	94	82
Iran	217	3,117	66	53
Iraq	33	1,159	34	37
Kuwait	74	27,621	49	19
Libya	37	6,351	29	12
Nigeria	113	863	63	26
Qatar	42	51,809	29	14
Saudi Arabia	314	12,779	193	86
UAE	134	29,751	113	79
Venezuela	132	4,949	44	24
Total	1,508		784	475

Source: United Nations, http://unstats.un.org/unsd/snaama/countryList.asp.

creating OPEC was to obtain stable and fair prices for oil producers by means of coordinating and unifying the petroleum policies of its members. Other objectives consist of maintaining regular, economic and efficient supply of petroleum to consuming countries. An added objective is to maintain a fair return on capital to investors in the petroleum industry.

The highest level of OPEC is the Meeting of the OPEC Conference that meets twice a year in March and September or in extraordinary sessions whenever required. Every member has a vote in the Conference and decisions must be unanimous. The main decision is the matching of oil production to the expectations of demand by OPEC. The decisions are communicated via a press release. The materials used by the Conference members evaluate current oil market conditions and the forecasts of fundamental variables, including the rate of economic growth and scenarios of petroleum demand and supply. The Conference decides on applications for membership to OPEC and on recommendations submitted by the Board of Governors. It elects the Chairman of the Board and approves appointment of governors and the budget submitted by the Board. The Conference uses the advice of an Economic Commission on how to promote stability in the oil market.

The 144th meeting of the OPEC Conference was held in Vienna on March 15, 2007 (OPEC 2007b). The participating members were the ministers of energy of OPEC members. OPEC expects world economic conditions in 2007 to remain stable but somewhat lower than in 2006 because of the impact of interest rates. The Conference finds that the supplies of crude oil are adequate for the market, with reasonable stocks in OECD countries. However, the Conference still expects volatility in oil markets.

OPEC monitors oil markets to maintain world economic growth and market stability. OPEC also releases crude oil production ceiling allocations by members in mbod. The history of these ceilings is in OPEC (2007c). A ministerial subcommittee monitors output and exports of oil by members. The production quotas consist of an instrument to influence prices. OPEC argues that it does not control oil prices because its share in world output of crude oil is only 43 percent and the share in trade of crude oil is 51 percent. This high share ensures a strong market impact of OPEC quota changes. OPEC argues that it has both decreased and increased quotas in accordance with market conditions. In 2005, OPEC members had proven oil reserves of 904,255 million barrels of crude oil, equivalent to 78.4 percent of the estimated total for the world of 1,153,962 million barrels (OPEC 2005).

The Secretary General is the chief executive of the Secretariat of OPEC and its legal representative (OPEC 2007a). The Secretary General acts in accordance with directions from the Board of Governors of OPEC. The governors are appointed by the member countries. The Secretariat has administrative, research and public relations divisions.

There are important reasons why oil is a primary source of energy (Stevens 2005, 19). There are major economies of scale in the oil business because it is a liquid flowing in three-dimensional space. These economies of scale result in lower costs relative to other fuels. Oil has 50 percent more energy content than coal on a weight basis and 170 percent more than natural gas on a volume basis.

Crude oil is the most traded item in international trade, in value and volume, and has key strategic and defense importance. Its price has political implications and influences central bank policy in the advanced countries and in many countries that do not produce oil. Oil is extremely important to the world economy. The concentration of production in the Middle East significantly affected politics during the Cold War and even in the new millennium.

OPEC typically complains that it does not control oil prices because they are determined in futures markets and the final price of oil derivatives is only a fraction of the crude oil price. There is heavy taxation of oil derivatives in the EU (Stevens 2005, 21). Demand for oil is inelastic, which means that the proportionate increase in price because of a tax is higher than the decrease in quantity demanded along an inelastic and negatively sloped demand curve. Thus, oil taxes have greater revenue than price impacts for the government, are simple to operate and almost impossible to evade. Stevens (2005, 21) quotes the OPEC 2003 statistical bulletin that in the European Union crude oil accounts for only 12 percent of the price of gasoline.

The constraints of OPEC are analyzed by Stevens (2005, 23–5). There are rents, or excess of price over the cost of replacement of a barrel, because of market manipulation or low production costs caused by economies of scale. There is continuing incentive for the owner of the reserves to develop production capacity. There are temporary shortages caused by political events. However, the situation returns to normal after some time. OPEC faces the difficult task of estimating the demand for its crude and allocating it among its members to effectively manage the market. This is as difficult as the determination of the price of public utilities by a government regulator. As Stevens (2005, 24) says, in estimating demand and allocation to members "the best OPEC can do is guess and hope." In addition, there is the problem of cheating by OPEC members, which consists of violating the commitments on production quotas. The importance of Saudi Arabia relative to OPEC and its willingness to use huge stocks to manage the market of oil has been widely discussed in the literature. The literature on the true market power of OPEC is also challenging, as Stevens (2005, 25) concludes: "In the best traditions of empirical testing in econometrics, the results are ambivalent and contradictory." The rise in demand and prices in recent years has reduced the interest in the actual control of OPEC. There are some countries, such as Venezuela and Indonesia, that cannot meet the quota but still want to hold to their share.

A common problem in economics is determining the direction of causality between two related variables and the possible presence of feedback. Granger (1969) proposes "testable definitions of causality and feedback" and illustrates them with simple models of two variables. Kaufmann *et al.* (2004) estimated an equation for real oil prices with quarterly data for 1986–2000. The objective of their research was to determine if OPEC affects oil prices. Their conclusion is that OPEC capacity utilization, OPEC production quotas, the difference between OPEC crude oil production and quotas and crude oil stocks in OECD countries "Granger cause" real oil prices but real oil prices do not "Granger cause" the OPEC variables and OECD stocks. The evidence shows that "OPEC plays an important role in determining oil prices" (Kaufmann *et al.* 2004, 68). The decision variables of OPEC to influence prices are quotas, production and operable capacity.

The behavior of option volatility around the meetings of OPEC is another indicator of the influence of their decisions on crude oil prices. Horan *et al.* (2004) analyze the behavior of the volatility of options on light sweet crude oil in each of the 48 OPEC meetings in 1989–2001. They consider also the behavior of volatility around the meetings of the Ministerial Monitoring Committee (MMC), which has significant influence on the decisions of the OPEC Conference. If OPEC has influence on oil prices, the implied volatility of oil options should rise in the days before the release of important market information and then drift downward after the release. Horan *et al.* (2004) find that the implied volatility increases before OPEC meetings and then declines by 3–4 percent on the first day following the meetings. They find a sharper decline of 11 percent following the MMC. Various parametric and non-parametric tests verify the robustness of the results. The results suggest that OPEC decisions have an impact on crude oil prices.

There is a comparison of market behavior after 50 meetings of OPEC in 1984–2001 (Wirl and Kujundzic 2004). There is merely weak association between the Conference decisions and subsequent market behavior, with perhaps stronger association for recommendations that imply price increases. There is also no support for the converse view that OPEC follows the market in its decisions. There are several reasons why the observations do not support the fact that OPEC affects world oil and energy markets. The information on decisions by the OPEC ministers may be leaked to markets in advance to the Conference. There may be better results with higher frequency data, say by the hour instead of by days. The Conference has also a credibility issue in by how much the members will cheat with their actual production relative to the decisions by the body of ministers.

The public perception and academic literature is concerned with the proper characterization of OPEC as showing behavior that could be competitive, collusive or monopolistic (Smith 2005, 52). It is difficult to model the behavior of OPEC with economic theory. Smith (2005, 42) finds that the evidence analyzed in this inquiry is consistent with a large number of conflicting models. The public perception is that OPEC engages in collusive conduct. The sample used by Smith (2005) covers 348 monthly observations from January 1973 to December 2001 for the output of each OPEC member. His tests on OPEC members and their rivals suggest that OPEC behaves more like a non-cooperative monopoly than a frictionless cartel. The traditional interpretations using economic models are rejected. The only surviving hypothesis is that OPEC behaves as a cartel limited by the costs of reaching and enforcing consensus among its members. It is difficult for the cartel to attain the common good. There was an increase in transaction costs as a result of the introduction of the quota system, further eroding the behavior as a frictionless cartel. There is not sufficiently strong evidence that Saudi Arabia has behaved as the leader of the cartel. The group consisting of Saudi Arabia, Kuwait and the UAE may have acted jointly to compensate for production behavior by other OPEC members. There are doubts on whether OPEC has the information to anticipate and act in response to market impulses.

Summary

The ideal policy for economists is the movement toward multilateral trade negotiations reducing trade barriers in general. Many of the proposals emphasize the importance of the DDR for developing poorer countries.

In reality, the world economy is divided into relatively tight compartments of PTAs. Trade economists are frustrated with the growing complexity of preferential arrangements and complex rule of origin. Unfortunately, most of trade in the world occurs through PTAs. Moreover, while the DDR stalls, the movement for more PTAs may gain momentum.

There is a tough theoretical and practical challenge of whether the system of PTAs could be managed in such a way as to movement toward multilateral trade negotiations with the rule of the MFN clause. The increase in world oil prices is becoming a potential issue of conflict between consuming and producing countries that is considered also in Chapter 5.

2
Poverty, Inequality, the Environment and Social Issues

Introduction

One of the most hotly debated issues is the actual path of world poverty and inequality and its relation to openness. The analysis of public goods of Chapter 5 of Volume I is extended in a specific section to regional, international and global public goods GPG.

An individual section considers the economics of analysis of the environment and its relation to openness. Climate change is allegedly the largest market failure in history, generating a debate on the types of required economic policies. There are major research efforts to uncover empirically the relationship between political regime, mostly democracy, and openness.

Global poverty and inequality

There is no conclusive evidence on the relationship of globalization to poverty and inequality among and within countries. There is no evidence that openness causes an increase in poverty. Theory suggests that economic growth diminishes poverty. Openness is one of various forms to increase economic growth. There are many factors operating on growth at the same time, preventing isolation of the effects of openness. The literature is vast and conflicting. In addition, various arguments are based on value judgments. The differences in judgments prevent comparisons. On a narrow definition of a poverty line, poverty has decreased. There is controversy on the definition of poverty that limits the research design and conclusions. A significant portion of the poor of the world concentrates in China and India because of the large population of these countries. The increase in the rate of growth of these two countries, especially in China, accounts for a major part of the reduction of world poverty. The issue of inequality is more complex. There appears to be a strong case for the argument that economic growth is the only way for the poor to escape poverty.

In their comprehensive and deep survey of the literature on trade liberalization and poverty, Winters *et al.* (2004, 72) claim that the accepted view by most economists is that open economies have better performance than closed economies and that policies of open exchange make significant contributions to economic development. They are aware of the concern of many analysts that the poor may suffer from liberalizing policies and that even in the long term some people remain in poverty. Distributional effects are likely to occur in shocks of openness. An important research issue is the nature and extent of these effects. If there were cases in which liberalization is the only shock, it would be possible to isolate effects of openness on distribution and poverty. As in all economics, many shocks occur simultaneously. Winters *et al.* (2004) propose the decomposition of the effects into multiple steps to analyze them individually.

A key result from systematic analysis of the empirical literature is that it is not possible to obtain a general conclusion on the relationship between trade liberalization and poverty (Winters *et al.* 2004, 106). According to theory, trade liberalization will alleviate poverty on average and in the long term, with broad supporting empirical evidence. There is no empirical support for the proposition that trade liberalization worsens poverty. However, the evidence does not indicate that trade liberalization is one of the key factors of reduction of poverty or that the static gains from trade always benefit the poor. The essence of the explanation is the familiar displacement of some people and firms in the short term, which may include some of the poor.

The empirical evidence surveyed by Winters *et al.* (2004) strongly supports the view that trade liberalization has significant positive effects on productivity. There is no strong empirical support for the view that liberalization has general adverse effects on employment or wages of the poor. However, there is insufficient evidence on transitions of employment and the transfer of price effects resulting from trade liberalization.

A distinguishing characteristic of the nineteenth century was innovation, consisting of the application of science to developing new goods and improving production (Becker 1994). This effort began in Great Britain during the industrial revolution and then spread to Europe (Cameron 1961). Becker (1994) calls the twentieth century the "age of human capital" because the success in improving a country's living conditions depends on its success in developing and using "the skills, knowledge, health and habits of the population." Human capital consists of education, on-the-job training, other training and health; it consists of about 80 percent of the capital or wealth of the United States and other developed countries. Becker (1994) argues that the countries in East Asia, such as Japan, Taiwan, Hong Kong and South Korea, compensated with human capital their lack of natural resources and the discrimination against their products in the West. Policies of improving human capital cut across cultural barriers, producing success stories in Latin America and Africa. Machines are important in this view but they require human capital to operate them and manage the firms.

It is difficult to separate in empirical research the effects of higher economic integration on poverty and inequality from other effects (Ravallion 2004, 3). There are diverse types of outcome of the impact of integration policies depending on the structure of countries. Generalizations are difficult for samples of many countries but disagreement may be less sharp when focusing on an individual country.

In addition, the various sides of the debate have different values on what should be a fair distribution of the gains from economic integration. There are different value judgments in how the gains should be measured. However, the differing ethical judgments are not necessarily discussed in the debate in explicit form.

There are three discrepancies on the methods of measuring poverty and inequality that, according to Ravallion (2004), depend on value judgments. The first discrepancy is in whether countries are weighted or not by population in measuring the change in poverty that could result from increasing economic integration. If countries are weighted by population, there has been significant decline in the inequality among nations in the past 50 years. This is the method advocated by the proponents of the benefits of globalization. However, if countries are not weighted by population, there has been a marked increase in inequality. This is the method used by those opposed to globalization. Ravallion (2004) argues that the significant decline in inequality in China and the large size of its population together with rapid growth and large population in India determine most of the outcome of the analysis based on weighting by population. If China and India are excluded, the decline in inequality disappears. Thus, most of the decline in inequality has occurred in China and India. There are arguments supporting both sides. It would appear that if the intention is to measure the behavior of inequality for the world as a whole, weighting by population provides a better measurement.

The world population could experience a decline in inequality but it would not be reflected in the method of not weighting by population (Ravallion 2004). If the intention is to merely consider the difference in inequality among countries, then giving all countries the same weight may be appropriate. The combination of both measurements leads to the conclusion that world inequality has declined but that differences among countries have increased. There is no convincing empirical result showing that these trends have anything to do with increasing integration in the world economy in the past quarter of a century. There is the additional issue of diversity of experience among nations with very different economic and social structures that have followed sharply different policies toward economic integration. In fact, the same policies have not been consistent for individual countries over long periods.

Economic integration, as all major policy changes, causes gains to some and losses to others. There is a revealing example of the concepts of vertical and horizontal inequality (Ravallion 2004, 20–1). China's accession to the WTO caused changes in prices of goods and factors. A GE model measures the impact on prices resulting from direct and indirect effects of initial tariff changes. The results show positive effects of WTO accession on mean household income. Inequality does not change and aggregate poverty increases moderately in the short term. This is the vertical result, showing little change in inequality. However, the variance of effects across households is significantly high, showing horizontal losses. The impact of the tariff reforms on regions is larger in some areas of China than in others and rural families lose while urban households tend to gain. The conventional measurements of welfare effects capture only the vertical effects but not the horizontal ones. The proponents of globalization focus on the vertical effects while the critics alert to the horizontal ones.

A final choice of measures on the basis of individual values is between relative and absolute measures of income inequality (Ravallion 2004, 23–7). The typical economic research uses measures of inequality relative to the mean. These measures do not show any relation between growth and inequality. Thus, to the extent that economic integration causes growth it does not increase inequality. Absolute inequality tries to capture the absolute differences in income. Consider the illustration by Ravallion (2004, 23–4) of an economy with two households, one earning $1000 per year and the other $10,000 per year. If growth results in doubling of income for both households, one would earn $2000 and the other $20,000, experiencing the same gain from growth. The mean is $5500 before growth, with the first household having a ratio of 0.182 relative to the mean ($1000/$5500) and the second household a ratio of 1.818 relative to the mean ($10,000/$5500). The mean jumps to $11,000, with the ratio of the first household being unchanged at 0.182 and the ratio of the second household also unchanged at 1.818. In terms of welfare relative to the mean, there is no change for either household. However, in the initial situation, the absolute difference in income was $9000 that jumps to $18,000 after the reform. The absolute difference of $18,000 instead of $9000 is interpreted as a doubling of deterioration in absolute welfare levels. The relative and absolute measurements are simply two ways of making calculations. The choice of one over the other is a value judgment.

Ravallion (2004, 27) concludes that his "paper has demonstrated that the factual claims one hears about what is happening to inequality in the world depend critically on value judgments embedded in standard measurement practices." Normative judgments are difficult to defend on the basis of not weighting countries by population. Those measurements would prevent the evaluation of well-being of large segments of the world population. Ignoring horizontal changes may not be a sound foundation for policy because of the high costs of displaced labor and firms. Absolute inequality is what everybody experiences in real life. It may be too much to ask for a policy that can erase in the short term historically accumulated absolute differences in income levels.

There is an unusually acute poverty problem in India. Bhagwati (1998b) argues that early literature unjustly claimed that pro-growth policies ignored poverty and inequality. Income redistribution was unfeasible in a country with many poor and hardly any wealthy from whom to redistribute. The growth of population in a stagnant economy would have almost immediately eliminated any gains from redistribution. Economic growth was the instrument to effectively draw the unemployed and underemployed into the productive sectors of the economy. The initial Indian approach of import substitution industrialization (ISI) in activities that were capital intensive did not contribute to employment generation. The reduction of poverty accelerated when the growth rate of the economy rose from 3–3.5 percent per year to 5 percent per year in the 1980s.

Increasing integration into the world economy by means of freer trade and FDI flows can also assist in eradication of poverty (Bhagwati 1998b, 35). External integration can also work with programs of privatization to further promote growth of the economy. The government requires tax revenue, increasing together with economic growth, to finance schools, infrastructure and health.

There are two static arguments in favor of the proposition that trade contributes to reducing poverty in developing countries (Bhagwati and Srinivasan 2002, 180). These countries specialize in labor-intensive economic activities. Thus, in accordance with the Stolper and Samuelson (1941) argument, the remuneration of labor would increase. Evidence from multiple countries confirms that trade benefits employment and wages in developing countries (Krueger 1983). The second argument is that trade promotion requires a stable domestic environment. Inflation hurts the poor in developing countries. The more careful attitude toward inflation resulting from external integration contributes to reducing poverty.

The dynamic argument is that trade promotes growth, which reduces poverty (Bhagwati and Srinivasan 2002, 180). The more general form of the argument is that trade has links with two fundamental causes of growth, accumulation of factors and innovation that discovers new and more productive use of resources. The increase and variety of imported inputs surmounts the limitations imposed by protection. There are opportunities in larger scale available under trade relative to the more limited scale under protection. External integration opens a much larger world market than under protection, increasing the marginal efficiency of capital. If there is plentiful supply of labor for the growing sectors of the economy, trade and growth will reduce poverty. There are extreme cases in which trade and growth may not affect the remote tribal areas that cannot supply labor to the new activities. Technological change may increase the output of larger farms, reducing prices that have adverse effects on poorer farmers working in small plots.

The best way to evaluate the impact of growth on poverty is by analysis of China and India where most of the world poor live (Bhagwati and Srinivasan 2002, 182). WB data show that China grew at the average yearly rate of 10 percent in 1980–2000 and India at 6 percent per year. China had the largest growth rate in the world and less than ten countries grew more rapidly than India. Bhagwati and Srinivasan (2002, 182) refer to data from the Asian Development Bank (ADB) and the government of India showing that the incidence of poverty declined in China from 28 percent in 1978 to 9 percent in 1998 and in India from 51 percent in 1977–8 to 27 percent in 1999–2000. In those 20 years, India and China increased their external integration. Poverty in India oscillated around 55 percent in 1950–80 when there was extreme intervention by the government in the economy.

Cross-country studies of the relation of growth and inequality encounter data and institutional hurdles (Wei and Wu 2004, 1–2). There are significant differences in the comparability of data on income inequality across countries. These data are also adjusted by purchasing power parity (PPP), which requires the construction of a basket of representative consumption. There are numerous differences in cultures, legal systems and other institutions that are difficult to quantify and control in cross-county regressions. Baghwati and Srinivasan (2001) propose that country studies may be more revealing. Wei and Wu (2004, 2) argue that country studies may complement the other cross-country research. In a short time period it may be possible to control culture, legal systems and other institutions. Data comparability problems may not be as critical as in cross-country research.

The choice of China is important beyond the size of the country (Wei and Wu (2004, 3–4)):

- *Trade openness.* The ratio of trade to GDP of China increased from 8.5 percent in 1977 to 36.5 percent in 1999. Large fluctuations permit better measurement of effects.
- *Regional variation.* The effective increase in openness varies across regions in China because some regions are too remote to actively participate in trade. It is possible to analyze the impact of openness on inequality, controlling numerous factors.
- *Large sample.* The large number of regions in China provides a large sample.
- *Limited migration.* Migration was discouraged during the sample period, making China more like a collection of countries for sample purposes.
- *Geography.* The geography of China prevents some regions from effectively participating in trade, allowing for the use of access to major seaports as an important instrumental variable.

There is presumption in the Heckscher (1919), Ohlin (1933) and Samuelson (1948, 1949, 1951, 1953) model that openness will lower inequality in China (Wei and Wu 2004, 4). The opening to trade would increase the remuneration to the factor of production that is abundant at home. China is evidently abundant in labor. Because labor has low remuneration before openness, external opening should reduce inequality. However, there is ambiguity in the theory as pointed out by Rodriguez and Rodrik (2001) and Baghwatic and Srinivasan (2001). This ambiguity dictates an appeal to data.

There are three major conclusions of the econometric research of Wei and Wu (2004). The rural–urban inequality of China declines as a result of trade openness. This is an important result because the largest inequality in China is between rural and urban areas. The inequality within the urban sector is modestly associated with increasing openness. The inequality within the rural sector is reduced by trade openness. The three results taken together are used by Wei and Wu (2004) to show a combined effect of trade openness in reducing inequality in a labor-abundant country.

Because of conflicting reports on the evolution over time of poverty data, Chen and Ravallion (2004) recalculated the numbers using consistent data and methods. The data originate in nationally representative surveys whenever possible. They use the conventional poverty line of $1 per day. There were 200 million fewer people in the world in poverty in 1998 compared with 1980, creating the controversy. Their new calculation shows that there were 1.1 billion poor people in 2001, close to 400 million less than in 1981. Chen and Ravallion (2004) show that the poor in China declined by 400 million. Most of the decline in the poor in China occurred in the early 1980s. The number of poor outside China increased slightly.

They project that the number of poor on $1 per day will be reduced by one-half by 2015. However, the reduction will be concentrated in East and Southeast Asia.

There are limitations in these studies of poverty reduction, acknowledged by Chen and Ravallion (2004, 4). There is concern about the welfare measures used in the surveys, their accuracy and comparability and various aspects of the data, such as the PPP exchange rates. An important problem with earlier studies was the choice of 1987 as starting point for the series because it coincided with much lower growth in China and India, countries with significant weight in population. Chen and Ravallion (2004, 4) use 454 surveys of 97 countries that account for 93 percent of the population of all low and middle income countries of the world. The surveys were conducted by government statistics offices. The measures of poverty are calculated from the primary survey data.

There is strong criticism of the measurement of the poverty line by Chen and Ravallion (2004, 8–10) in the work by Reddy and Pogge (2005, 4–9). The argument of Reddy and Pogge (2005, 5) is that the poverty line should provide a measurement of the resources required to satisfy basic human needs. They argue that the WB uses an international poverty line (IPL) that does not have relation to such resource needs. The WB IPL is defined in abstract monetary units and in domestic currency equivalents. The IPL was constructed in 1990 based on information for 33 countries for the 1980s. The domestic consumer price index (CPI) was used to calculate the IPL for 1985 converted into common units of real purchasing power equivalents using the 1985 PPP conversion factors. The chosen IPL was $31 per month and rounded to $1 per day. The IPL was converted into national currency units using the Penn World Tables (PWT) and inflated by the local CPI data obtained from the International Monetary Fund's (IMF) International Financial Statistics.

The IPL used by Chen and Ravallion (2004, 9) is $32.47 per month, equivalent to $1.08 per day. Reddy and Pogge (2005, 7) argue that the WB uses the United States as base country. The US CPI increased by 34.3 percent in 1985–93 while the increase in the IPL was from $30.42 in 1985 to $32.74 in 1993, implying CPI change of 8 percent. Reddy and Pogge (2005, 7) argue that this caused a lowering of US national poverty lines by 20 percent. They argue that examples of the resulting poverty lines show lowering by 30 percent for Nigeria and increase by 157 percent for Mauritania. Because of these and other methodological objections, Reddy and Pogge (2005, 9) contend that the IPL would have to be significantly higher to provide resources required for the nourishment of a human being. They also argue that the PPP concept is not well defined or appropriate for measuring poverty. A final criticism is that the WB extrapolates from limited data that suggest likely large errors that cannot be precisely estimated.

The transition of Russia and China during the 1990s was very dissimilar in terms of rates of economic growth. As Table 2.1 shows Russia experienced negative rates of growth during most of the 1990s for cumulative decline of 32.7 percent. Meanwhile, China had close to double digit growth rates through the decade with cumulative growth of 161.6 percent. Russia made the transition

Table 2.1   GDP growth in Russia and China 1991–2000 in %

	Russia	China
1991	−5.0	9.2
1992	−14.5	14.2
1993	−8.7	13.4
1994	−12.7	12.7
1995	−4.1	10.5
1996	−3.6	9.6
1997	1.4	8.8
1998	−5.3	7.8
1999	6.4	7.1
2000	10.0	7.9
Total Δ%	−32.7	161.6

Sources: China, National Bureau of Statistics of China, Russia, International Monetary Fund, World Economic Outlook Database, September 2006.

with a parliamentary regime and freer press. China merely made some economic reforms and maintained a centralized, closed and oppressive regime.

Surprisingly, Galbraith *et al.* (2004) find unusual similarities in income inequality in the same period for both countries. There was significant increase in inequality in both countries in the turmoil of 1991–8 and in China during the growth collapse of 1993–4. The rise in inequality was sharper at the regional than at the sector levels. The increase in relative income was sharper in the financial and political urban centers, Moscow, Beijing and Shanghai. The regions generating exports in hard currency, West Siberia and Guangdong, also experienced significant rise in relative income. Galbraith *et al.* (2004) suggest that rents in sectors with monopoly power in activities for the domestic sector, such as transportation and public utilities, were obtained from the liberalization process. Financial capitalism in both countries was able to obtain significant gains. The transition to market allocation was accompanied by decline in the relative income of the agricultural sectors. Education sectors made more gains in relative income than other sectors in China but experienced major losses in Russia.

It is difficult to measure inequality of household income and the data originate in unofficial surveys (Galbraith 2002, 15–16). There are accurate measurements of level of pay for many countries. The UN provides an industrial accounting framework that permits cross-country comparisons. Galbraith (2002, 16) argues that level of pay is only part of income but calculations are more accurate than for household income inequality. The UN provides data on the year 2000 on 3200 country/year observation in 1963–98. Galbraith (2002) calculates the Theil index of inequality. Conceição and Ferreira (2000) provide an intuitive description of the Theil index, explaining its superiority over the conventional measure of inequality, the Gini coefficient. For the purposes here, inequality is measured as the dispersion of the distribution of income among individuals.

The findings of Galbraith (2002) show lowest inequality of manufacturing pay in 1963–98 in the social democracies of Scandinavia and Australia and in the communist regimes in Eastern Europe, China and Cuba. This measure of inequality was also low in a second group of countries in Southern Europe and North America. Some of the wealthier countries in Latin America and Iran constitute a middle group. The highest inequality occurred in a broad group around the equator, including Peru, Brazil, central Africa and southern Asia. Manufacturing and production of capital goods was weakest in the highest inequality group. Galbraith (2002) argues that there is inverse association between inequality and the level of development of a country. He postulates that inequality declines with greater industrialization and the increase in income.

The findings of Galbraith (2002) indicate that inequality increased in the two decades 1980–2000. He considers the important events of that period to be the rise of neoliberalism and the end of Keynesian policies. The hypothesis preferred by Galbraith (2002) is that there is a global element in the world economy influencing the inequality of manufacturing pay. In this view, trade and the transfer of technology are not the major factors and the term globalization does not explain the rise in inequality. Galbraith (2002) claims that the process of integration on the basis of unsustainable finance caused the inequality. This process of indebtedness transferred wealth from poor to rich countries and to the richest class in the rich countries. The system divided the world into an advanced center composed of wealthy countries and a periphery of countries without the means to develop. The advanced countries did not assume any responsibility for the poor. There is no process for reversing the fate of the poorer countries and evident apathy to their fate. Galbraith (2002, 25) characterizes the process as similar to a "perfect crime."

In 1980–2000, the rate of growth of trade was twice that of world income (Dollar and Kraay 2001). The focus of research by Dollar and Kraay (2001) is the impact on growth and inequality in a group of 24 countries that experienced significant openness in 1980–2000. The ratio of trade to GDP doubled to 33 percent for this group of countries. Over one-half of the population of developing countries is in this group because it includes China and India. Dollar and Kraay (2001) reach four conclusions from the experience of this group of countries:

1. *Increasing growth rates.* The rate of growth of per capita income increased from 1.4 percent in the 1960s and 2.9 percent in the 1970s to 3.5 percent in the 1980s and 5.0 percent in the 1990s. There was strong growth performance in 18 of the 24 countries and the results are independent of the inclusion of China and India in the sample. The countries that did not globalize experienced lower rate of growth of per capita GDP from the peak of 3.3 percent in the 1970s to 1.4 percent in the 1990s.
2. *Sharing in the gains.* There is no evidence that inequality increases with growing trade.

3. *Declining poverty*. Growth with stable inequality contributed to lowering poverty incidence.
4. *Narrowing poor/rich gap*. The poorer countries in the sample lowered their gap relative to rich countries because of comparatively higher growth rates.

Criticizing the results of Dollar and Kraay (2002), Watkins (2002) claims that advanced countries with 14 percent of the world population held almost three-quarters of the income of the world at the beginning and end of the 1990s. Watkins (2002) claims that international trade reinforces income inequality among nations. The shares in world trade are reflected in the pattern of world income distribution. Exports have a strong influence on world income because of the faster rate of growth of exports than world GDP. Watkins (2002) argues that $0.75 of every $1 of exports is received by advanced countries. Poorer countries receive about $0.03. The gap between poor and rich countries can only close if the poorer countries can obtain a higher share of world exports. Watkins (2002) argues that globalization is increasing inequality in various ways with limited access of the poor to markets, productive assets and education. The rights of workers have eroded with various types of exploitation, in particular, gender deprivation. The policy according to Watkins (2002) should be the complete elimination of tariffs and restrictions of exports of developing countries. The benefits of the WTO on international property rights (IPR) only accrue to MNCs in advanced countries. The trade agenda does not include issues of true interest to developing countries.

In reply, Dollar and Kraay (2002) argue that openness by itself will not be sufficient to reduce poverty. Their only claim is that a more liberal trade regime is one of various instruments in a strategy to promote growth and reduce poverty. They dispute the claim of Watkins (2002) that globalization increased inequality. Dollar and Kraay (2002) argue that the only possible statement is that inequality stabilized after the 1980s and that the number of people living on less than $1 a day has declined. The high rate of growth of the countries in the sample contributed to narrowing the gap in living standards with the advanced countries.

Globalization may affect inequality within countries, which is a typical type of research. Another approach is to analyze inequality among individuals in the world as a whole, which is the objective of Milanovic (2002). The data consist of 216 country surveys, averaging 10.8 data points in 1988 and 11.4 data points in 1993. The data points are weighted by the population in which they originate. The quality of the surveys and the definition of income and expenditures vary from country to country. It is possible to standardize the definitions of income and expenditure. The sample covers about 84 percent of the world's population and about 93 percent of world GDP in 1988 and 1993. Milanovic (2002) uses this sample to estimate the world income and expenditure with household surveys.

The conclusion of Milanovic (2002) is that world income inequality is quite high. The Gini coefficient is 66 using income adjusted for purchasing power of countries and about 80 using current dollar incomes. He estimates that the Gini coefficient increased from 62.8 in 1988 to 66.0 in 1993. The most important factor of world inequality is the difference in mean income of countries, explaining

75–88 percent of overall inequality. The main reason for increase in the Gini coefficient was the growth of rural per capita income in China, India and Bangladesh in comparison with income growth of various countries of the Organization for Economic Co-operation and Development (OECD). The faster growth of urban China versus rural China and rural India was also an important determinant. World inequality is dependent on the relative position of China and India relative to the United States, Japan, France, Germany and the United Kingdom. Milanovic (2002, 88) argues that the richest 1 percent of the world receive the same as the 57 percent poorest. The total income of the 25 million richest Americans is equivalent to the income of about 2 billion poor people.

There is an estimate of the world distribution of wealth prepared with household data by Davies *et al.* (2006). Their data show significantly higher concentration in world wealth than income. Common shares of the top 10 percent in a country's wealth are about 50 percent. The share of the top 10 in world wealth in 2000 is 85 percent.

There is significant difficulty in defining poverty. It is a concept with multiple dimensions beyond income (Sala-i-Martin 2004). The adjustment for PPP is the subject of considerable debate. The welfare implications may vary with the measurement of either income or consumption poverty. Even if it were possible to solve the methodological discrepancies and obtain a monetary measurement, Sala-i-Martin (2004) argues that the drawing of the line of definition of poverty may be quite difficult. The existing lines are the extreme poverty line of $1 per day and the poverty line of $2 per day. They are as arbitrary as any other lines.

The research of Sala-i-Martin (2004) shows that in 1970–98 the rates of poverty declined: from 40 percent to 18 percent for the $2 per day line and from 17 percent to 6 percent for the $1 per day line. He also finds decline in the number of people in poverty in 1976–98: from 600 million to 350 million for the $1 per day line and from 1.4 billion to 1 billion for the $2 per day line. Moreover, Sala-i-Martin (2004) shows that poverty declined in 1970–98 for every conceivable poverty line. The debates on the choice of poverty line are fruitless. Any poverty line chosen will show a decline in poverty.

Another aspect of the debate is the argument that when China and India are excluded poverty increases. Sala-i-Martin (2004) provides calculations showing that poverty declined in China, in the rest of Asia and in Latin America. Poverty increased in Africa. There could still be an argument that globalization was stronger in East Asia, South Asia and Latin America compared with Africa. Sala-i-Martin (2004) follows the approach of Dollar and Kraay (2001), dividing the world in two groups, according to globalization after 1980. The conclusion of Sala-i-Martin (2004) is that poverty counts decreased by 309 million for the globalizing countries using the $1 per day line and increased by 79 million for the non-globalizing countries. The $2 per day line shows decline in poverty counts of 478 million for the globalizing countries and increase by 80 million of the non-globalizing countries. Sala-i-Martin (2004) argues, with significant value, that there is no precise definition of globalization that could permit cross-country regressions of poverty rates with globalization as the explanatory variable.

Sala-i-Martin (2002) calculates that worldwide income inequality increased in the 1970s, declining in the following two decades. There are disputes about the validity of using PPP-adjusted income and GDP per capita to anchor the mean. There is an important result that the Gini coefficient does not decline uniformly. That is, there are reversals of the improvement in income distribution. Sala-i-Martin (2004) argues that there should be caution in using inequality data for very short time periods such as the comparison of 1988 and 1993 by Milanovic (2002). Sala-i-Martin (2004) shows that inequality behaves in similar fashion with the use of many other indexes: Theil index, Atkinson index with coefficients 0.5 and 1.0, the variance of log-income, the coefficient of variation, the ratio of the income of the top-20 percent to the bottom-20 percent of the population and the ratio of the income of the top-10 percent to the bottom-10 percent of the population. There is significant variety in the cross-country econometric results of the relation of openness to growth and inequality. Sala-i-Martin (2004) argues that there is no empirical evidence in this vast literature that openness is inversely associated with economic growth. The critics of globalization are concerned and skeptical about the arguments that openness promotes growth. Sala-i-Martin (2004) contends that these critics should be more concerned and skeptical about the claim that openness restricts economic growth, for which there is no evidence.

Regional, international and global public goods

The need for collective action at various levels originates in the existence of regional, international and GPGs. The market may not supply these goods. There are also threats to nations such as financial instability and wars that require collective action. The discussion below consists of an analysis of the reasons contributed by various economists for the provision of public goods at the international level and the classification of those goods. Stiglitz (2006) strongly argues the need of providing public goods and finds that the current governance of international financial institutions is not conducive to an adequate provision of public goods.

Health is one of the earliest and most important concerns and involvement of many countries in public goods. A well-known example is preventing the spread of contagious diseases, requiring cooperation by nations and international organizations, such as the World Health Organization (WHO). The classic properties of public goods constitute the departing criterion of a taxonomy for activities of transnational nature (Sandler and Arce M. 2002, 198). These characteristics are that the benefits of public goods are non-rival and non-payers cannot be excluded. In the case of many nations, the consumption of one good is non-rival if consumption by one country does not diminish the consuming opportunities of other nations for the same unit of the good. The property of not being excludable means that once the good is supplied, the benefits are enjoyed by payers and non-payers alike. Sandler and Arce M. (2002, 198–206) argue that global and transnational goods in preserving health can have these two properties in various forms.

There are five different types of public goods according to the two basic properties of non-rival and non-excludable (Sandler and Arce M. 2002, 198–206):

1. *Pure public goods*. The two properties of public goods apply to many nations. Consumption does not diminish the benefit to other nations and once provided other nations cannot be excluded.
2. *Impure public goods*. There is one property and/or both that is not met entirely. The consumption of the good by one nation may partially detract from the consumption of another, breaking the non-rivalry condition. A country may enjoy the benefits of the good but that may not be entirely the case of another nation.
3. *Club goods*. The benefits are not excludable but there is rivalry in consuming them. It is possible for the users to create a club to provide the good.
4. *Joint products*. An activity can create two or more outputs that differ in the characteristics as public goods.
5. *Private goods*. There is rivalry among nations in consuming the benefits of the goods and nations can be excluded from consuming them.

The second form of classifying public goods used by Sandler and Arce M. (2002, 206–14) is according to the technology of public supply aggregation, or aggregation technology. The global supply of the public good is determined by the effort of nations in providing it. Pure and impure goods and also joint products can be classified into subcategories. The need of international public policy depends on the type of aggregation. Sandler and Arce M. (2002, 206–14) identify six different aggregation technologies:

1. *Summation*. The summation of individual provisions equals the aggregate level of the public good that is available. The individual provisions are perfect substitutes and thus do not depend on the nation providing them. There is a tendency for free riding by individual nations. The richer nations are likely to engage in provision of the public good. Multilateral organizations could have a role in supporting provision to compensate for the less than optimal national contributions.
2. *Weighted sum*. Individual weights are assigned to obtain a weighted sum of provisions. The technology of an individual nation may be more advanced than those of others.
3. *Weakest link*. The overall success of providing the public good depends on the nation providing the smallest effort. Sandler and Arce M. (2002, 17) provide polio as an example where the efforts of many countries with vaccination programs did not eliminate the disease because some nations did not make efforts of eradication.
4. *Weaker link*. There are some smaller gains in providing more than the smallest effort (see analysis in Arce M. and Sandler (2001)).
5. *Best shot*. The minimum required effort of supplying the good determines its provision. Provisions below the minimum do not add to the global or transnational supply of the good.

6. *Better shot*. Provision below the maximum required may still contribute to the overall level of the public good. There are likely several suppliers compared with the best-shot public good.

The large diversity of public goods leads to the policy implication that institutions and policies must adapt to the specific characteristics of public goods (Sandler and Arce M. 2002).

Economic openness has been associated with cross-border flows of goods, services, capital and labor. There are other cross-border flows: pollutants, diseases, terrorism, knowledge, culture, financial crises, political turmoil, medical discoveries, innovations and computer viruses and worms (Sandler 2006). Globalization and technology drive these flows, suggesting that collective action, sometimes influenced by international organizations, may be required beyond the boundaries of nations in controlling transnational public goods (TPG). TPGs can benefit people in two or more countries. When the benefits or costs have global effects the goods are called GPGs. There are benefits and costs of goods that affect two or more countries in a specific location, being called regional public goods (RPG). The taxonomy and policy implications can proceed with the same characteristics of public goods – non-rival, non-excludable and aggregation technology (Sandler 2006).

There are three key types of RPGs (Sandler 2006). Peace and security is an important regional concern. Regional conflicts have negative externalities that can be reduced by RPGs. Regional wars have very adverse effects on economic growth. According to Sandler (2006), knowledge is the archetype of best-shot or better-shot public good. The best results are obtained by concentrating efforts in research centers of excellence. Provision of knowledge as a public good requires coordination. Thus, knowledge that is specific to a region would be best developed by a global or regional institution. Governments give patents to these goods, in an exchange of a short-term monopoly for larger numbers of discoveries. There are short-term losses from the monopoly power given to a producer that must be compared with the long-term benefits of more active innovation. The third important RPG underscored by Sandler (2006) relates to the effects of communicable diseases. A disease such as avian flu (SARS) requires worldwide epidemic controls in the form of providing a GPG. There are region-specific diseases that require collective action in the form of RPGs.

The environment

The conservation of the environment is the classic case for public intervention considered by neoclassical economists. The problem is the lack of a price for clean air. The most promising approach is applied welfare economics or cost/benefit analysis. Unfortunately, the economic arguments are quite appealing but have not convinced decision makers. Other criteria are used in environmental legislation, requiring the analysis of the political economy of decisions. Empirical research has not made great progress because of the lack of a theory of economic growth and the role of the environment in such theory. The issue becomes even more intractable when trying to relate openness to the environment. Developing countries complain that the imposition of environmental standards in trade agreements prevents them from improving their living standards.

The basic regulation theory required for analysis of environmental policy is covered in Chapter 5 of Volume I in the section on the public interest view. A specific survey relating to environmental economics is provided by Cropper and Oates (1992). There is no observable price for clean air. Pollution causes an externality, such as in the classic example of the laundry soiled by the emissions of the factory. The market failure caused by the negative externality of pollution prevents the market from attaining a Pareto-optimal outcome. The marginal social cost of the output of the factory is higher than the marginal private cost. A tax in the sense of Pigou would attain the Pareto-optimum outcome. This is the case for regulation based on the public interest view.

Coase (1937, 1960) introduced transaction costs, arguing that they were not negligible. With negligible transaction costs, there could be an agreement between the company affected by the pollution and the polluting company. Cropper and Oates (1992, 680) make the important point that such an agreement would not occur in reality because of the large number of market players involved in environmental issues. The hurdle becomes one of finding the second-best outcome in the presence of major transaction costs. The case for government regulation is not as straightforward as in the theory before Coase (1960). The government also faces the same transaction costs as market players and regulation may cause government failure. An appeal to the methods of welfare economics, by calculating costs and benefits of regulation, was not incorporated in the early legislation on the environment (Cropper and Oates 1992, 675–6).

The criterion of Pareto efficiency is that an economic state is Pareto improving if at least one person is better off without anyone being worst off. There are few public policies that can meet this test (Stavins 2004, 1). The criterion of Hicks (1939) and Kaldor (1939) intends to identify simpler conditions. There is a Pareto improvement if the winners of a change could fully compensate the losers and at least one gainer would still be better off. This is the essence of applied welfare economics covered in Chapter 5 of Volume I.

The tools of applied welfare economics provide standard evaluation of environmental regulations in terms of the familiar net present value of net benefits (*PVNB*) as in (Stavins 2004, 2):

$$PVNB = \sum_{t=0}^{T} (Bt - Ct)/1 + r \tag{2.1}$$

Bt are benefits at time *t*, *Ct* are costs at time *t*, *r* is the discount rate and summation is from $t = 0$ to the terminal period at time *T*. If

$$PVNB = 0 \tag{2.2}$$

the project may yield a Pareto improvement, meeting the Hicks (1939) and Kaldor (1939) criterion. Equation 2.1 consists of a discounted sum, by an appropriate discount rate, of the net benefits in every period. The practical problem of the criterion is to obtain good estimates of the benefits, costs and the discount rate. There are other more complex approaches to the economics of regulation. Stavins (2004, 13) concludes that "economic analysis has assumed a significant position in the regulatory state. At the same time, despite the arguments made for decades by economists, there is only limited political support for broader use of benefit-cost analysis to assess proposed or existing environmental regulations."

The analysis of the gains from trade concludes that trade raises national income. An important issue in environmental analysis is the relation between the quality of the environment and higher income (Copeland and Taylor 2004, 10). An important early contribution is the inverse-U relation of inequality and economic growth discovered by Kuznets (1955). The economy is initially concentrated on agricultural activities with relatively low per capita income and not much inequality. The smaller industrial sector has relatively higher per capita income and possibly income inequality. Economic growth is driven by the industrial sector, increasing the inequality of incomes for the economy as a whole. Industrialization draws labor from agriculture and eventually overall income inequality diminishes. Barro (1999, 32) relates inequality and growth with a broad panel of countries, concluding that "The Kuznets curve – whereby inequality first increases and later decreases in the process of economic development – emerges as a clear empirical regularity. However, this relation does not explain the bulk of variations in inequality across countries or over time."

A significant body of empirical literature surveyed by Copeland and Taylor (2004, 10) finds an inverted-U relation between growth and the environment. This research is called the environmental Kuznets curve (EKC) because of the work of Kuznets (1955) on economic growth and inequality. The EKC shows the environment deteriorating with economic growth in developing countries and improving for countries with high levels of income. There is little theoretical development behind the changes in the EKC such that the results are open to various explanations (Copeland and Taylor 2004, 10).

One explanation of the EKC is based on the sources of growth (Copeland and Taylor 2004, 16). The process of growth is initially driven by capital accumulation and in later stages by acquisition of human capital. Environmental quality would deteriorate during the first phase and then improve with the composition of growth factors changing toward human capital. A second explanation focuses on income effects: demand for environmental quality rises with income (Copeland and Taylor 2004, 17–8). The willingness to sacrifice income to clean the environment increases with economic growth. A third possibility is that the quality of the environment deteriorates in the early stages of growth but improves after reaching a threshold.

Research on the EKC makes important contributions (Copeland and Taylor 2004, 23). The common uninformed view that economic growth necessarily results in deterioration of the environment is not supported by evidence. It also suggests the likely policy action at higher levels of income. The next step of research requires analysis of the causes of the EKC. Further theoretical research is required to specify the relationships.

There are two hypotheses on which countries attract industries that deteriorate the environment after liberalizing trade (Copeland and Taylor 2004, 29–34). According to the pollution haven hypothesis, countries with careless policies on the environment will specialize in production of goods that deteriorate the environment. There are multiple types of this hypothesis that assume that low-income countries are those with weak environmental controls. The factor endowment hypothesis postulates that there is no relation between trade and environmental policy. Trade is determined by differences in factor endowment or technology.

The pollution haven effect postulates that the weakening of environmental policy determines exports of goods that adversely affect the environment and the location of plants in the country with such policies (Copeland and Taylor 2004, 34–5). According to the stronger version, the pollution haven hypothesis, activities that adversely affect the environment relocate from more advanced countries with stronger environmental policies to poorer countries without such policies. In this extreme version, the lack of environmental policy determines the location of pollution-creating industries. Thus, pollution increases in the developing countries and decreases in advanced countries. The alternative hypothesis is that conventional factor endowment and technology determine the pattern of trade.

Data limitations restrict research on trade and the environment. Data on pollution are quite difficult to obtain. The hypotheses also involve data requirements of poorer countries, which are also of lower quality and restricted availability (Copeland and Taylor 2004, 35). The literature also suffers from more precise theoretical development of the hypotheses. Copeland and Taylor (2004, 66–7) find three major conclusions from the empirical literature. There is evidence showing that increasing income positively influences the quality of the environment. An earlier professional view that environmental policy does not affect trade and investment flows is not warranted. There is some evidence of pollution haven effects but not confirmation of the pollution haven hypothesis.

A common argument against environmental policy is the possible adverse impact on jobs and the rate of economic growth. Openness gives a new dimension to the issue because companies can relocate production to other countries without environmental policy. The loss of firms and investment could have adverse effects on the domestic economy. Schofer and Granados (2006) analyze the impact of environmental policy during the period of globalization 1980–2000, using a sample for 100 countries. Their results indicate that countries with positive policies toward the environment experience better economic results on various measures than countries with lax environmental policies. There is no exodus of firms, investment and production as a result of environmental policy or an adverse impact of FDI inflow. There are some limitations of these results. There is not conclusive evidence that every conceivable type of environmentalism is conducive to higher growth or that the observed relation will continue in the future. Economic activity could be affected by extreme forms of environmentalism. International institutions and regulation could better coordinate economic outcomes.

Distinguished economists are voicing strong complaints against the environmental and labor restrictions in trade agreements, depriving poor countries of the opportunity to develop. There is characterization of the green movement as ecological imperialism (Lal 2005b). The historical evolution would provide support for this view. Initially, the West depended on organic agriculture. The progress of the economies of the advanced countries was achieved by changing their production into the exploitation of minerals and energy. The supply of minerals and energy would be unlimited. The institutional transformation, according to Lal (2005b), was defended by Smith (1776). Productivity improved even in an organic economy. The physical transformation consisted of using the capital in energy derived from fossil fuels. The liberal world economy of the nineteenth century was partly dismantled by imperialism, which found a motivation in the "white man's burden" (Lal 2005b). Western values were imposed on the colonies by the force of imperialism.

A similar phenomenon occurs presently under the new values of ethical trading and foreign policies. Lal (2005b) claims that these policies are imposed in trade and investment agreements, preventing the development of poorer countries such as China and India. He argues that there is neither ethics nor logic in these ethical arguments that threaten to undermine the liberal world order that can bring progress to poorer countries. According to Lal (2000, 21), the Greens are opposed to the key forms of capitalism that can transform poorer countries – free trade as promoted by Smith (1776) and the continuing burning of fossil fuels. The elimination of these alternatives for development would simply condemn poorer countries to permanent poverty. Lal (2000, 29) recommends that developing countries resist the international treaties motivated by the agenda of the Greens. He sees the Green movement as part of Western cultural imperialism, a descendant of the spirit of Christian missionaries.

Climate change

Global warming because of greenhouse gas (GHG) emissions allegedly is the largest market failure ever invoked. There is no private solution for the problem and it would require global collective action. There are two reviews of the problem by the United Kingdom and by the UN, discussed below. There is strong criticism by economists of the use of near zero discount rates in the UK report. The comparison of welfare among individuals and over generations is quite challenging. The near zero discount rate would concentrate all the effort of adjustment in the current generation. Conventional economic analysis has used what Nordhaus (2006) calls the "ramp" approach. The adjustment would occur as in the rising slope of a ramp, allowing for economic growth to make the costs of the adjustment more amenable.

The HM treasury review

The critical scientific finding of the Stern review on the economics of climate change (HM Treasury 2006, 3) is that CO_2 concentrations increased from 280 parts per million (ppm) around 1750 to 380 ppm in 2006. The ppm is "the ratio of the number of GHG molecules to the total number of molecules of dry air. For example: 300 ppm means 300 molecules of a greenhouse gas per million molecules of dry air" (IPCC 2007Feb5, 2 note 3). The burning of fossil fuels, deforestation and other changes in the use of land are the main causes of these concentrations. There have been concentrations of other GHGs, such as methane and nitrous oxide. The greenhouse effect consists of the warming effect on the world's climate resulting from increasing GHGs that raise the infrared radiation, or heat energy, blocked by the atmosphere (HM Treasury 2006, 3). The radiation of the sun increases the warmth of the earth. However, a major part of infrared radiation moves back to outer space, cooling the earth. Part of the infrared radiation is blocked by GHGs, with resulting cooling of the earth. The net effect is a trend of warming of the earth. The warming caused by GHG emission of human activity is about 430 ppm of CO2, growing at 2.3 ppm per year. The levels of GHGs surpass the highest in 650,000 years of history.

Scientists use the concept of global mean surface temperatures to measure climate change (HM Treasury 2006, 5). The warming of the earth since 1900, measured by global mean temperature, has amounted to 0.7 °C. The rate of warming has been about 0.2 °C per decade, on average, in the past 30 years. The warmest 10 years on record have been experienced since 1990. HM Treasury (2006, 6–7) claims that "the rising levels of greenhouse gases provide the only plausible explanation for the observed trend [of global warming] for at least the past 50 years." The climate models surveyed by HM Treasury (2006) suggest that the doubling of GHGs could lead to an increase in global mean temperatures of 2–5 °C, in 2030–60. There has not been similar experience in the world since the last ice age to the present. By 2100, there could be warming of the world by 3–10 °C. The stock of CO2 would reach 850 ppm or four times higher than in preindustrial times (HM Treasury 2007a). Under the assumption of stabilization of annual emissions at the level of 2000 through the entire century, the concentrations of CO2e would reach 650 ppm by 2100.

There would be significant effects of global warming (HM Treasury 2006, iv–viii). There would be winners and losers of an increase of temperature of 1–2 °C. There would be economic gains from longer growing seasons in northern latitudes, lower mortality from cold phenomena and new activities in energy and tourism. However, there would still be impact on indigenous communities in the Arctic Circle and the need for evacuation in tropical islands at low levels. Coral reefs are vulnerable to changes in temperature and the intensity of droughts could increase. HM Treasury (2006, iv) argues that the difference between the present and the last ice age is 5 °C. An extra 5 °C could have major impact on the physical and human geography of the world. The damages increase sharply in accordance with the rise in temperatures. There would be a stronger El Niño and Siberia or the Amazon could experience forest fires. The decline in monsoon rains could affect agricultural production in Asia, Australia or Latin America. Food output could be threatened and there could be migration, misery and social disruption in areas of the world with high density of population. The rise in global temperatures would make these catastrophes more likely.

The Stern review (HM Treasury 2006, i) claims that climate change "is the greatest and widest-ranging market failure ever seen." The challenge of analyzing the economics of climate change is formidable. The analysis must encompass the entire world during very long periods. It requires elements of the economics of risk and uncertainty. There are likely non-marginal jumps in variables. The analysis must borrow from multiple areas of economics and even quite recent research. The framework of analysis is that climate change is caused by global actions and has global consequences. Thus, the approach is that the nature of the response and its dimensions require international collective action. Such response is the only type that could result in effects that are effective, efficient and equitable. It is difficult not to consider some of the similarities with the economics of mineral and fossil fuel analysis. In particular, the analysis of Adelman (2004) appears relevant. The long horizons of analysis of climate change probably require knowledge of the development of science in similarity to the analysis of oil reserves. If applicable, such analysis may be even more difficult than recognized in the economics of climate change that assumes that science is constant.

The Stern review (HM Treasury 2006, i) is careful in acknowledging that there is no certainty in the estimation of the consequences of climate change. However, it argues that the knowledge is sufficient to understand risks. Early mitigation of climate change can be viewed as an investment that could reduce the consequences of high risks in the future. Careful analysis of investment can limit costs, providing growth opportunities in the future. The objective of policy is to reveal market signals to conquer market failures. The core must consist of risk mitigation and equity.

The Stern review focuses on stabilizing GHG concentrations in a range of 450–550 ppm CO2e (HM Treasury 2006, ix). In the upper range of 550 ppm CO2e, global emissions would peak in 10–20 years and then fall at 1–3 percent per year, being below 25 percent of current levels by 2050. The world economy would be three to four times larger than currently. Thus, emissions per unit of GDP in 2050 would be 25 percent of current levels. Stabilizing the concentration at 450 ppm CO2e by 2050 would require a peak in 10 years and then decline by over 5 percent per year. In 2050, emissions would be 70 percent lower than currently. The reduction of emissions would consist of combinations of reducing demand for goods and services that are emission intensive, increasing efficiency to save money and emissions, increasing non-energy emissions and using technologies for power, heat and transportation that are low in carbon use.

The estimate of resource costs by the Stern review is 1 percent of world GDP by 2050 to stabilize concentrations at 550 ppm of CO2e (HM Treasury 2006, xiii). The range of forecasts is −1–3.5 percent of GDP. The review concedes that there are numerous difficulties in this estimation. The estimation requires the costs of various technologies in periods of half a century. It may be added that it could be impossible to foresee new technologies that are presently unknown. The estimates require trajectories of prices of fossil fuels over the long term when it is almost impossible to forecast them for short periods. Demand cannot be ignored because people will certainly have behavior responding to price changes that is difficult to foresee. The proposal is based on a carbon-price signal of difficult estimation. There are multiple other policies requiring effective regulation.

The UN IPCC

The World Meteorological Organization (WMO) and the UN Environment Programme (UNEP) created in 1988 the Intergovernmental Panel on Climate Change (IPCC). Membership is open to all members of the UN and WMO. The objective of the IPPC is to evaluate all aspects of climate change induced by human activities. The IPCC does not engage in original research or in monitoring climate data. Peer review and the technical and scientific literature constitute the elements for evaluation by the IPCC.

The structure of the IPCC consists of three working groups and a task force on national GHG inventories. Working Group I (WGI) evaluates the scientific aspects of the climate system and change. The role of Working Group II (WGII) is to evaluate how climate change creates vulnerabilities for natural, social and economic systems; it also assesses negative and positive effects of climate change and available adaptation alternatives. The evaluation of options to limit GHG emissions and mitigating climate change is the objective of Working Group III (WGIII). The IPCC national GHG inventory is the responsibility of the Task Force on National Greenhouse Gas Inventories (TFIPCC).

There is a plenary meeting of the IPCC every year where reports and work plans of the working groups and the task force are accepted, approved or adopted. The panel elects the chair of the IPCC and the members of the bureau. There are two-three meetings per year of the bureau, which supports the chair in planning, coordinating and monitoring work progress. The Secretariat manages the IPCC at the WMO in Geneva, with support by the UNEP and the WMO. There are technical support units for the working groups and task force. These units receive support from the government of the country acting as co-chair of the working group or task force. A research institution in the co-chair countries hosts the technical support units. The key output of the IPCC is the series of assessment reports begun in 1990. These four reports provide an assessment of the state of knowledge on the issue of climate change.

The WGI adopted a summary for policymakers of the fourth assessment report (AR4) on February 2, 2007 (IPCC 2007Feb2). There were 600 authors of this summary, originating in 42 countries. In addition, there were 620 expert reviewers and many government reviewers. Representatives from 113 governments reviewed the details of the summary before its adoption.

The summary for policymakers of the WGI of AR4 provides an explanation of the human causes of climate change together with observations of actual change, the process and attribution of climate change and projections of future climate change (IPCC 2007Feb5). The foundation of the WGI of AR4 is the building on earlier assessments and the new findings of research in the 6 years after the Third Assessment Report (TAR). The WGI of AR4 claims that there has been significant scientific progress in the 6 years since TAR (IPCC 2007Feb5, 2).

There is anthropogenic influence (by human beings) of the environment that has accelerated since the middle of the eighteenth century following the industrial revolution (IPCC 2001). The composition of the atmosphere is especially influenced by the combustion of fossil fuels for industrial or home use and burning of biomass. These activities generate GHGs and aerosols. The GHG absorbs radiation generated by the surface of the earth and clouds. Then it emits infrared radiation at a level colder than the surface of the earth. As a result, it traps part of the energy, warming the surface of the earth. The ozone in the upper atmosphere filters damaging incoming ultra-violet radiation. The main GHGs in the atmosphere of the earth are water vapor (H_2O), carbon dioxide (CO_2), nitrous oxide (N_2O), methane (CH_4) and ozone (O_3). Most of the GHG emissions of the United States originate in energy use. CO_2 emissions from petroleum and natural gas account for about 80 percent of US anthropogenic GHG emissions (EIA 2003, EPA 2004, ES-6). The US Environmental Protection Agency (EPA) (2004, ES-6) estimates that fuel combustion accounted for 94 percent of US CO_2 emissions in 2004. This share of fuel combustion grew slowly from 77 to 80 percent in 1990–2004. In 2002, the United States accounted for about 23 percent of the emission of CO_2 in the atmosphere in 2002. Aerosol consists of a collection of airborne particles that has no relation to commercial aerosol sprays.

The stock of GHG content in the atmosphere was relatively constant in the thousand years preceding the industrial revolution but has increased since then by more than 30 percent. Infrared radiation absorption and emission is strengthened by increasing concentration of GHG. As a result, the emission of the earth's radiation is processed at higher altitudes where less energy is emitted because of lower temperatures, causing climate warming. The effects of aerosols are less known but they tend to offset the GHG effects. Numerical models of the climate system are used by scientists to quantify climate response because of the nonlinear behavior of variables. These models are based on principles of physics, chemistry and biology and are combined with empirical and statistical methods.

The most important anthropogenic GHG is CO_2. The concentration of CO_2 in the atmosphere was 280 ppm in the pre-industrial period. That is, there were 280 molecules of GHG per million molecules of dry air. In 2005, IPCC (2007Feb5, 2) estimates the CO_2 concentration in the atmosphere at 379 ppm. This concentration exceeds the range of 180–300 ppm in the past 650,000 years. The concentration is a stock. The addition to the stock is the rate of growth that was on average 1.9 ppm per year, much higher than the average of 1.4 ppm per year in 1960–2005. The growth of the stock of CO_2 in the atmosphere resulted mostly from use of fossils, with a smaller contribution by land use. The other sources of GHG also increased. The range of CH_4 concentration in the atmosphere was 320–790 parts per billion (ppb) compared with 1774 ppb in 2005, significantly higher than the pre-industrial value of about 715 ppb. The IPCC (2007Feb5, 3) considers very likely that anthropogenic activities in agriculture and fossil fuel use were important contributors to increasing CH_4 concentrations but other contributing factors are less certain. The pre-industrial value of the atmospheric concentration of N_2O was 270 ppb, rising to 319 ppb in 2005. The growth rate remained constant after

1980. Anthropogenic activities in agriculture contribute about two-thirds of all N2O emissions.

The potential change in climate of a mechanism is measured by radiative forcing, which measures the effect in altering the balance of energy entering and leaving the earth's atmosphere (IPCC 2007Feb2). Negative forcing cools the earth while positive forcing warms it. The values of radiative forcing are expressed in watts per square meter (W m^{-2}). The conclusion of the WGI of AR4 is of high confidence that effects of human activities since 1750 contributed to warming the earth with a radiative forcing in the range of +0.6 to +2.4 W m^{-2}, with mean of +1.6 W m^{-2}. The combined radiative forcing caused by CO2, CH4 and N2O is +2.30 W m^{-2}. The radiative forcing of CO2 jumped by 20 percent in 1995–2005, the largest in any decade in the past 200 years.

The conclusion of the WGI of AR4 is that "warming of the climate system is unequivocal" (IPCC 2007Feb5, 5). There are multiple reasons for this conclusion, in the form of increases in global average air and ocean temperatures, snow and ice melting and an increase in the global average sea level. Temperatures increased by 0.76 °C from 1850–99 to 2001–5. The linear trend of warming per decade in the past 50 years of 0.13 °C is almost twice that of the last 100 years. The 100-year linear trend of temperature increase in 1906–2005 is 0.74 °C. The IPCC (2007Feb 5, 10) concludes that anthropogenic GHG concentrations are very likely the cause of the increases in globally averaged temperatures and other aspects of climate change such as ocean warming, temperature extremes and wind patterns.

The IPCC (2007Feb5, 12) projects warming of global average temperatures by 0.2 °C per decade; these projections are based on six scenarios and additional observations. The change in 2090–9 compared with 1980–99 is 1.8 °C in the best estimate for the lowest scenario with range of 1.1–2.9 °C and 4.0 °C in the best estimate for the worst scenario with range 2.4–6.4 °C. The sea level rise in the same period is in the range 0.18–0.38 meters in the lowest scenario and 0.26–0.59 in the worst scenario. The more confident projections on warming, wind patterns, precipitation and aspects of extremes and ice are not favorable. Stabilizing GHG concentrations would not prevent anthropogenic warming and rise of the sea level.

The report of the WGII of AR4 considers the effects of climate change on natural, managed and human systems as well as the adaptation and vulnerabilities of these systems (IPCC 2007Apr6). Temperature increases have been affecting natural systems. Some examples are the larger numbers and enlargement of glacial lakes, rock avalanches, ground instability and changes in Arctic and Antarctic ecosystems. Water quality and thermal structure have been affected by the warming of lakes and rivers. Rivers fed by glaciers and snow have experienced increasing runoff and peak discharge occurring earlier in the spring. Spring is coming earlier for leaf-unfolding, bird migration and egg-laying. There are changes in ranges in plant and animal species. Warming has increased in growing seasons with earlier greening of vegetation in the spring. Increasing water temperatures have affected marine and freshwater biological systems. The IPCC (2007Apr6, 3–4) concludes with "high confidence" that anthropogenic warming in the past three decades influenced many physical and biological systems.

There are disturbing projections by the IPCC (2007Apr6, 7–10) of various systems and sectors:

- *Fresh water*. The availability of water will increase by 2050 by 10–40 percent at high latitudes and wet tropics, decreasing by 10–30 percent in dry regions and mild latitudes and dry tropics. Droughts and heavy precipitations will increase while water from glaciers and snow will decrease.
- *Ecosystems*. The combination of climate change and associated disturbances will challenge the resilience of ecosystems.
- *Food, fiber and forests*. Changes in weather will affect crops and forest products in diverse forms.
- *Coastal and low-lying areas*. There are multiple vulnerabilities to areas around the coast and in low-lying locations resulting from changes in sea-level rise and similar disturbances.
- *Industry, settlement and society*. There will be significant changes varying by location, scale and the actual climate change.
- *Health*. Climate change will have strong adverse effects on health.

The WGIII of AR4 finds significant dynamism in 1970–2004 in the drivers of increasing energy-related CO2 emissions: population growth was 69 percent and global income growth was 77 percent (IPCC 2007May4, 3). The increase of GHG global emissions weighted by their global warming potential was 70 percent. CO2 emissions grew by 80 percent, representing 77 percent of total anthropogenic GHG emissions in 2004. The GHG emissions of the energy supply sector increased by 145 percent in 1970–2004. The growth of emissions for other sectors was slower: 120 percent for transport, 65 percent for industry and land use and 40 percent for land use change and forestry. A group of countries with 20 percent of world population and 57 percent of world GDP was responsible for 46 percent of GHG emissions.

Mitigation potential measures the reduction of GHG emissions by a given carbon price relative to emission baselines (IPCC 2007May4, 9). The market mitigation potential is measured using private costs and private discount rates. It takes into account current policy measures. The economic mitigation potential is measured using social costs and benefits and social discount rates (SDRT). It assumes improvements in market efficiency by policies and measures. The bottom-up studies evaluate mitigation options using specific technologies and regulations. The top-down studies measure the effects of mitigation options for an entire economy. The WGIII of AR4 argues that available bottom-up and top-down studies suggest that there is significant economic mitigation potential to reduce global GHG emissions relative to the projections without further policies. The estimated costs of stabilizing emissions in the range 445–710 ppm by 2030 are between a reduction of global GDP by 3 percent and a small increase of 0.2 percent, relative to the baseline. There are significant differences in the pattern of regional costs relative to the average (IPCC 2007May4, 15). The costs by 2050 of stabilizing GHG emissions in the range of 445–710 ppm are in the range of a 1 percent gain and a 5.5 percent loss of global GDP (IPCC 2007May4, 26).

The economics of climate change

There is disagreement by economists on the cost and benefit analysis of climate change, as analyzed by Wolf (2007Feb6). An important criticism of the Stern review is that it exaggerates the economic consequences of climate change. The worst outcome would be that income per capita increases in the future nine times instead of 13 times. The consensus of economists is that climate change would not be an economic catastrophe. There is also the argument about action and science: future generations will adapt much better than what the review could model. There is a counterargument that environmental losses have value to people, are difficult to predict and become irreversible.

Another difference of opinion among economists found by Wolf (2007Feb6) is that there is high uncertainty in the costs of mitigation. The Stern review uses risk and uncertainty, two words that evoke the suspicion of imprecision and error among economists, especially those engaged in financial transactions. The Stern review has a wide range of a gain of 1 percent of world GDP by 2050 to a heavy loss of 3.5 percent of world GDP by 2050. The only way to find out is by allowing climate change to occur. However, Wolf (2007Feb6) argues that there would be gains of new technology on using fossil fuel energy more efficiently. The argument centers on the costs and benefits of that technology.

The critical issue of disagreement among economists is the calculation of net present value (Wolf 2007Feb6). The net present value is the estimation of the upfront cost of making the adjustments, requiring inputs of benefits, costs and the most controversial, the appropriate value of the discount rate.

An immediate critical reaction to the Stern review was on the assumption of the discount rate. Wilkinson (2006) interprets the assumption of a discount rate of close to zero as resulting in high present value of the damages of climate change: "a new economic framework based on a vision of Armageddon could turn out to be a big waste of money."

Two of the academic authorities on the economics of the environment have expressed sharp disagreement with the Stern review. There are specific ethical values in the Stern review that cast the results in doubt, according to Dasgupta (2006, 3–4). The first value judgment is on the tradeoffs of welfare between future generations and the current one. The second value judgment is on the tradeoff of welfare among people no matter on what generation they appear on earth. The Stern review assumes that there should be high expenditures today for the well-being of future generations even if after adjusting for risk they were to be better off than the current generation. Dasgupta (2006, 7) illustrates the consequences of these ethical judgments in an economy with no population growth, no technological change and social rate of return of 4 percent per year. Under those assumptions, the current generation would have to save 97.5 percent of its output to pay for the future. In the United Kingdom, where Dasgupta resides, the savings rate is 15 percent. The tradeoff is that the current generation would have to starve in order to save to pay for the future generation. The model assumes that "starvation isn't all that painful!" (Dasgupta 2006, 7).

The problem with the economics of climate change is the rate of discount, r, used for the calculation of *PVNB* in equation 2.2. The rate of discount, as Nordhaus (2006, 7) emphasizes, is not the rate used in capital budgeting and cash flow discounting. The abridged term is the SDRT, measuring the welfare of future generations relative to the current generation. The key difference relative to the discount rate in other applications is that the SDRT discounts future welfare not future goods or dollars (Nordhaus 2006, 6). The Stern review uses a discount rate of 0.1 percent, which is about equal to zero. This assumption equalizes the welfare of future generations with the present generation. In the case of a positive SDRT, the welfare of future generations is discounted to the present generation by the SDRT.

Table 2.2 helps to illustrate the use of a zero or near zero discount rate. This table is similar to the discount tables used in financial calculations before the advent of the computer. The first column shows the discount factor assuming the rate of the Stern review of 0.1 percent. If the calculation were in finance, $1 in 50 years from now would be worth $0.99 today $1 times the discount factor of 0.99. The comment by Nordhaus (2006, 6) is appropriate: it does not matter to use 0.1 or 0 as the discount rate. There is no discounting: all future net benefits of a policy of environmental cleaning would be simply added at face value. The discount to present value of $1 received 200 years from now is $0.82. At a very low rate of discount of 1 percent per year, the present value of $1 received 200 years from now is only $0.14. The effect of the zero discount rate is to significantly inflate the cost of cleaning the environment to the present generation.

The dynamic integrated model of climate and the economy (DICE) is used by Nordhaus (2006) to illustrate the differences between the Stern review and a more conventional economic measurement. Table 2.3 shows the results of simulations by Nordhaus (2006, 147) using DICE. The carbon price of the Stern review is $311 per ton. The price of carbon per ton of the standard run of DICE is $17.2 rising to

Table 2.2 Discount factors of future values

	Percent discount rates					
	0.1	**1.0**	**2.0**	**3.0**	**4.0**	**10.0**
1 year	0.99	0.99	0.98	0.97	0.96	0.91
2 years	0.99	0.98	0.96	0.94	0.92	0.83
10 years	0.99	0.90	0.82	0.74	0.67	0.38
50 years	0.99	0.61	0.37	0.23	0.14	0.01
100 years	0.90	0.37	0.14	0.05	0.02	0.00
150 years	0.86	0.22	0.05	0.01	0.002	0.00
200 years	0.82	0.14	0.02	0.002	0.000	0.000

Note: The discount factors are equal to the inverse of 1 plus (discount rate/100) to the power of the number of years.

Table 2.3   DICE model simulations by Nordhaus (2006)

	Run 1	**Run 2**	**Run 3**
Carbon price $/ton			
2005	17.12	159	19.95
2050	84.00		
2100	270.00		
Optimal emission rate %			
2005	6		
2050	14		
2100	25		
Temperature increase 2000–100	1.8 °C		

Note: Run 2 uses the same assumptions as run 1 with SDRT of 0.1 percent per year. Run 3 maintains the 0.1 percent per year SDRT but calibrates the curvature of the utility function or elasticity of the marginal utility of consumption. *Source*: Nordhaus (2006, 14–7).

$270 in 2100. Run 2 uses the same assumptions as run 1 but uses the 0.1 percent SDRT of the Stern review, which raises the price of carbon to $159 per ton.

The literature on the economics of climate change finds that efficient economic policies of slowing climate change consist of lower rates of reduction of emissions in the short term followed by faster reductions in the medium and long terms. Nordhaus (2006) labels this policy as the climate-policy ramp. The policies become tighter as if climbing a positively sloped ramp over time. This model has survived intense scrutiny of assumptions and measurements. Nordhaus (2006) persuasively explains its rationality. The highest returns in investments are in physical capital, technology and human capital. R&D in the reduction of GHG emissions is one such investment. When economies prosper, becoming richer, it is rational to devote higher investments to reduction of GHG emissions. The decision on how to mix and time the reduction of emissions is determined by specific knowledge of costs, damages and the irreversibility of climate change and damages. The assumption of a zero SDRT simply flattens the policy ramp, concentrating all the costs of adjustment in the current generation. Nordhaus (2006) argues that the Stern review does not provide new analytical innovations with the exception of the zero SDRT.

There are three important requirements of an effective climate policy according to McKibbin and Wilcoxen (2006, 2–3). The policy must be widely adopted. In addition, it must be implemented indefinitely. The critical third condition is that there must be undisputed incentives in the policy for individuals and firms to commit investment resources that reduce emissions. McKibbin and Wilcoxen (2006) argue persuasively that individual countries can control policies within their borders only if they have the support of their citizens. Laws can be repealed or they can be imperfectly enforced until they become ineffective. The reduction of emissions requires major investment in capital and R&D. A carbon tax would be economically efficient but eventually will organize lobbying efforts for its repeal or for exemptions. A credible, long-term policy must have the incentives that are required for major investments by the private sector in reducing emissions. This alternative is more likely to be successful than creating another large international institution while control of emissions is mostly within national boundaries. Policies at the local level must focus on the incentives to the solution of the problem without political challenges.

The concern on global warming is not enough, according to Bhagwati (2006a). There have to be effective policies to solve the problem. The Kyoto Protocol (KP) has been ratified by 160 countries, except the United States. Bhagwati (2006a) argues that "the Kyoto Protocol is dead in the water: you cannot stage Hamlet without the Prince." The key hurdle in passing the KP is the exemption for two major polluters, China and India. In fact, China is closing in GHG emission to the United States. There was no support for these exemptions in the US Senate.

An important issue is that CO2 is a stock instead of a threshold pollutant (McKibbin and Wilcoxen 2006, 5–6). There are problems with threshold pollutants only after emissions reach a threshold but not when they are relatively low. The key target of policy is to keep emissions below the threshold. In the case of CO2, emissions remain in the atmosphere for decades. McKibbin and Wilcoxen (2006, 5) claim that "current annual emissions are equal to only about 1 percent of the total anthropogenic carbon dioxide in the atmosphere." The accumulated stocks of CO2 and GHG emissions create the risks of climate change. An additional ton of emissions raises the risk only slightly and there is no risk threshold for emissions. Every ton of new emissions, like cigarettes in causing cancer, causes the same damage as any other ton.

Although there are significant current emissions by China and India, the largest part of the accumulated stock that causes the risk occurred because of earlier emissions by advanced countries. Bhagwati (2006a) claims that "the accumulated damage attributable to India and China fossil fuel CO2 for 1850–2004 shows as less than 10 percent while the European Union, Russia and the United States jointly account for nearly 70 percent." The argument used by China and India in seeking no limits on their GHG emissions is that because they did not create the stock they should not be penalized for the flow.

The solution proposed by Bhagwati (2006a) is the spirit of the US Comprehensive Environmental Response, Compensation and Liability Act of 1980, typically called the Superfund. This act imposed a tax on the chemical and petroleum industries. In what Bhagwati (2006a) calls the "American fascination with torts actions" it provided for liability of people for "the release of hazardous waste at closed and abandoned hazardous waste sites." The Superfund is a trust that would receive payment for past damage and would correct the damage of actions that could not be attributed to a known party.

The Bhagwati (2006a) proposal is to apply the Superfund concept at an international level. The advanced countries that created the stock of CO2 in the atmosphere would collect damages into the global warming superfund. The damages would be assessed for a past period of at least 25 years by the estimated opportunity cost of cleaning the atmosphere in the next 25 years. However, cleaning the atmosphere is not feasible in the case of global warming. The collections at the global superfund would be used to develop technologies that save CO2 emissions and to subsidize the use of technologies by developing countries, including China and India, which are friendly to the environment. Bhagwati (2006a) expects that the advanced countries would accept the principle that they have already used and that business would also support it. The proposal would also include taxes on the flows under the principle of preventing significant deterioration. The market principle involved in the proposal is for every nation to pay for its share in total pollution. The tax would be a form of creating a missing market for clean air.

The FT (2007Feb) considers the forecast of the rise of global average temperatures of the IPCC to 3 °C by 2100. The difference is close to the change in temperature between the last ice age and today. Mitigation should aim to maintain the stock below 550 ppm, which would still be higher than the pre-industrial levels. The FT (2007Feb) finds comfort in the cost estimate of the Stern review of 1 percent of GDP but warns that the required mitigating investments have very long gestation. Thus, investment should be made immediately. Negotiations by 2010 should replace the KP that expires in 2012. Important discussions will take place between the advanced countries and several key developing countries – Brazil, China, India, Mexico and South Africa. The FT (2007Feb) argues that an agreement without the United States would not mean much. All that would be required from the United States is the implementation of an effective program for control of emissions that is linked to a global one. The developing countries would only join the discussion if the United States shows the will of action. However, developing countries are seeking lower emission controls than those that would be implemented by advanced countries.

The FT (2007Feb) proposes compensation to developing countries for the costs that would promote using the most efficient energy technologies. Another suggestion is for advanced countries to acquire emission rights issued by developing countries. A third proposal would be a common tax framework with cross-border transfers. The FT (2007Feb) argues that there must be a clear and predictable price for carbon. The lack of this price is the critical issue in traditional welfare economics a la Pigou (1932). A second important issue is investment in R&D of renewable sources of energy, nuclear power and methods of capturing and storing carbon. There would be a third requirement of disseminating the best technology around the globe. These three elements are all within the public interest view: incorporating the price of pollution in decisions, public policy of encouraging alternative technology and making that technology a GPG.

Political regime

Research on the relationship of liberalization, democracy and political regime has accelerated in the past few years. The major obstacle is the lack of precise theories. Research attempts to solve the issues by an appeal to data. Many contributions use the instrumental variables (IV) method. Unfortunately, economics is abundant in endogenous variables and scarce in IVs. There is a group of contributions discussed below by Rigobon and Rodrik (2004), Yu (2005) and Li and Reuveny (2003) that find an inverse relation between democracy and openness, using different methods. A second group of contributions subsequently discussed is more optimistic about the relationship of democracy and openness. Several authors have used long historical series of data to explore the relationships. Interesting work by Giavazzi and Tabellini (2005) tries to unveil the ideal sequencing of democracy and openness.

There are critical issues in the social sciences that have not been adequately explored, according to Rigobon and Rodrik (2004, 1). These issues are the relationship of income and quality of institutions, the role if any of democracy in development, the types of effects of openness on development, the quality of institutions and democracy and the role played by geography. The quantitative measurement of economic variables such as income is available but finding measurements of the quality of institutions, democracy and geography is challenging.

Proxies can be found for some of the variables. However, Rigobon and Rodrik (2004, 1–3) argue that the most difficult hurdle is the inference of causality of the variables in the right-hand side of the equation on the dependent variable on the left-hand side. Research using cross-national samples has tried to solve the problems with IVs. There are three properties of an adequate IV: it is exogenous, correlated with the endogenous variable and does not have any other influence on the endogenous variables. In practice, it becomes extremely difficult to find a suitable IV.

The problem of inference of the influence of institutional quality on income is explained by Rigobon and Rodrik (2004, 3) by means of the following two equations

$$Y = \alpha I + \varepsilon \tag{2.3}$$

$$I = \beta Y + \upsilon \tag{2.4}$$

Y is income, I institutional quality, α and β parameters and ε and υ random disturbances. This is the typical problem of identification. The system requires estimation of four unknowns – the two structural parameters and the variances of the disturbances – but the data only provide three moments – the variances of income and institutional quality and their covariance. The IV approach consists of finding a variable that enters into the equation of institutional quality but not in the first income equation.

The intuitive explanation of the method of Rigobon and Rodrik (2004, 3) consists of dividing the sample into two subsamples, A and B, in such a way that the variance of the disturbance in the equation of institutions, $Var\ (\upsilon)$, is larger in A than in B. Thus, the distribution of points of Y and I in subsample A is closer to the first equation than in subsample B. It would then be possible to solve the problem of identification.

There are two splits of the data into subsamples by Rigobon and Rodrik (2004). The objective is to obtain differences in structural shocks without altering the values of the parameters. The data are split according to colonization or not and geographical location and used to jointly estimate four endogenous variables: income measured as GDP per capita, economic institutions as rule of law, political institutions as democracy and economic integration as trade. Rigobon and Rodrik (2004) find a positive association between income growth and democracy and the rule of law, with the latter having a stronger effect. The impact of openness, measured as trade relative to GDP, has an inverse effect on income levels, controlling for geography and institutions. There is weak impact of income on the quality of institutions. There is mutual positive influence of rule of law and democracy but the effects are not very strong. Opening to trade positively influences the rule of law but adversely affects democracy. There is a significant negative effect of trade openness on democracy. Trade has significant positive effects on the quality of institutions in one specification but non-significant in another. There is a positive but weak effect of income on openness and negligible effects of democracy and rule of law on openness. Geographic variables explain 50 percent of the variance in openness. The sample contains 43 countries in each subsample.

There are arguments on both sides of whether trade liberalization promotes democracy, according to Yu (2005, 3–5). Theory is not conclusive on the effects of openness on democracy. Increasing democracy in labor-intensive countries may motivate politicians to relax trade barriers to increase labor rewards and thus obtain political power. The flows of trade, capital and ideas may disseminate democratic principles, creating more competitive domestic political systems. Yu (2005, 4) argues that in less democratic regimes the rulers may liberalize trade but maintain repressive conditions on labor. Growing GDP could become a means to strengthen political power by the rulers. Thus, Yu (2005, 4) claims that the issue cannot be solved without empirical verification.

The sample used by Yu (2005, 11–12) uses panel data for 157 members of the IMF in 1962–98. He uses a two-step method. First, there is a benchmark analysis of how democracy affects trade. The gravity equation expresses volume of trade in terms of size of country and geography. Yu (2005) adds measures of democracy to a revised gravity equation that also has several control variables such as environmental quality, WTO membership, socio-economic variables and members in RTAs. The possibility of reverse causality is analyzed by a linear system of structural form estimation (Yu 2005, 9). Judicial independence is the key variable for democracy. The results suggest that trade liberalization can promote democracy. However, democracy does not have a significant effect on trade.

There are three types of arguments in vast literature, including the philosopher Immanuel Kant in the eighteenth century and Joseph Schumpeter in the twentieth century, analyzed by Li and Reuveny (2003, 35–8). Two of the arguments claim that globalization promotes or obstructs democracy; the third argument claims that globalization has no effects on democracy. Proponents of the promotion of democracy by globalization emphasize the positive effects of globalization on economic development and multiple other factors such as the diffusion of democratic ideas. The argument that globalization prevents democratic progress claims that globalization results in public policies that benefit foreign investors instead of the population, creating more losers than winners in the short term. There are several additional arguments such as the unfavorable effects of financial crises and the increasing income inequality of countries allegedly resulting from globalization. The third group of arguments claims that the effects of globalization are vastly exaggerated and vary from one country to another.

The sample used by Li and Reuveny (2003, 39) consists of pooled time-series cross-sectional data for 127 countries in 1970–96. They find evidence that trade openness and portfolio investment have a negative effect on democracy. The trade effect remains constant over time but that of portfolio investment increases. There is a positive effect of FDI on democracy but it diminishes over time. The diffusion of ideas is persistent in positively influencing democracy over time. The results are similar for all countries and also for the group of developing countries. Li and Reuveny (2003, 53) conclude that "the economic aspects of integration into the world economy are beginning to cause a decline in national democratic governance." The prospects of democracy, according to their results, are eroded by economic globalization. Continuing trade liberalization adversely affects progress in democracy. FDI and foreign financial flows threaten democracy.

An important characteristic of a democracy is that the chief executive requires approval of a majority in the legislature to implement trade policy (Mansfield *et al.* 2000). The legislative ratification of commercial policy is a feature of parliamentary and presidential systems. The candidate for prime minister in a parliamentary system must negotiate trade policy before taking office. The legislature enforces its preference for trade policy through confidence votes. The presidential system is characterized by ratification of trade policy by the legislature after the candidate takes office. The chief executive in an autocracy has more independent power than in democracy. The legislature does not exist or simply ratifies pro forma the preferences of the autocrat. The research objective of Mansfield *et al.* (2000) is to analyze theoretically and empirically trade policy among pairs of countries according to political regime. They argue that pairs of countries with democratic regimes tend to agree on lower trade barriers than mixed pairs of a democracy and an autocracy because of the institutional difference in the role of the legislature. The preferences of the chief executives determine if trade liberalization among pairs of autocracies is stronger relative to pairs of democracies or mixed pairs.

The hypothesis of Mansfield *et al.* (2000) is that there would be lower trade barriers between a pair of democratic countries than between an autocracy and a democracy. They use a sample of pairs of countries in the period 1960–90. Two chief executives in a democracy will opt for significant trade liberalization because trade wars between two protectionist legislatures are worse than a trade war with only one protectionist legislature. The empirical results show that there is stronger trade between pairs of democracies than within mixed pairs of an autocracy and a democracy. There is 15–20 percent less trade in mixed pairs of a democracy and an autocracy than in pairs of democracies. They also find evidence that the relation becomes stronger over time. In the 1990s, trade of mixed pairs was 40 percent less than of pairs of democracies. Mansfield *et al.* (2000) do not find significant difference in trade within pairs of autocracies and within pairs of democracies, suggesting that preferences of politicians and officials making decisions determine the nature of trade policy.

Trade agreements have proliferated in such a way that the relationship of type of political regime to trade policy should be applied to trade agreements. Mansfield *et al.* (2005) argue that the type of political regime of a country, the number of veto players and the diversity of preferences among the veto players are critical in explaining the participation of a country in RTAs. They consider five different types of trade agreements among countries. The incentive to political leaders in engaging in RTAs is the potential gains. Democracies are less likely to enter into an RTA as the number of veto players increases. The type of trade agreement is dependent on the type of regime and the number of veto players. There are consequences in distribution of income and resources in full integration agreements. The increase in the number of veto players increases the possibility of development of a constituency against the RTA and the chances that it will be blocked. The depth of the type of integration raises the potential influence of veto players. Mansfield *et al.* (2005) use a sample of pairs of countries in 1950–2000 to conduct statistical tests. The conclusion supports the view that democracy and veto players have a major influence on the entering of states in RTAs and the types of agreement chosen.

There was significant change in trade policy of developing countries in 1970–99 documented by Milner and Kubota (2005, 161–3). Data for 85–90 countries shows tariff duties as percent of imports declining by 53 percent from 1973–99, reaching 10 percent of import value in 1997. The data of statutory tariffs also show decline to around 10 percent by the late 1990s. The decline in tariff rates was not offset by compensatory nontrade barriers. Trade as percent of GDP increased from 55 percent in 1970 to 85 percent in 1999. Milner and Kubota (2005, 162) conclude that there was significant reduction in trade barriers by many countries around the world.

The movement toward freer trade was accompanied by democracy. Milner and Kubota (2005, 158) find that the number of democratic countries in the world increased from about 30 in 1975 to 89 in 1992 and then 120 in 2002. They argue that democracy facilitated the movement toward freer trade. Many groups without representation in the period of ISI gained access to voting. These groups had more to gain from liberalizing trade than from continuing protectionism. Politicians experienced a reduction in their capacity to build political support with trade barriers. The relatively higher power of trade liberalization versus trade barriers in increasingly democratic countries became a new form of capturing political support.

The Heckscher, Ohlin and Samuelson theorem and the Stolper and Samuelson (1941) theorem provide an explanation of the distribution effects. Milner and Kubota (2005, 168–9) argue that the earlier regime of ISI benefited capital in the import-competing industries and the higher-paid unionized workers. This was the case in Brazil where the industrialists producing for the domestic market created an alliance with the labor unions to maintain protectionism. The concentration of benefits in a few facilitated the maintenance of the trade regime. The losers in this process were agricultural workers and urban dwellers that did not work in ISI activities. After some point the model exhausted the limits of the domestic market, coinciding with the return to democracy. The groups that had been disenfranchised during the period of ISI were the ones that would gain from an outward-directed export policy. Trade liberalization in agribusiness and labor-intensive activities shifted the relative power of the members of society that had relatively less interest in trade protection and more in increasing foreign trade. Voters preferring lower levels of protectionism were enfranchised by means of voting. Democracy thus benefited trade openness as a policy.

The hypothesis of Milner and Kubota (2005, 169) is that democratic countries are more inclined to trade liberalization, which increases with the degree of democratization. These authors use a cross-section of time-series of 179 developing countries in 1970–99. They control for the competing hypotheses of influence on trade liberalization by financial crises, pressures from the advanced countries and international organizations and changes in ideas. The conclusion is that more democratic countries are more likely to open to the international economy, controlling for other factors.

The position of a party in the ideological spectrum from left to right is significantly important in determining its position on trade policy, according to Milner and Judkins (2004, 101). They analyze this hypothesis for 25 developed countries in 1945–98. The argument finds support in the Stolper and Samuelson (1941) theorem. Protectionism could support the rewards to the scarce factor, labor; and freer trade would tend to support the rewards of the abundant factor, capital. Parties position themselves in the ideological spectrum of left to right to attract voters that share similar preferences. Parties tend to maintain support from similar groups of citizens during long periods. Milner and Judkins (2004) argue that the distributional effects of trade based on factor endowments determine the partisan position on trade or protectionism. In advanced countries, left-wing parties tend to support more protectionist policies than right-wing parties. Globalization in the sense of increasing openness is also important. There is less protectionism by parties in countries that are more open to trade. The effects of partisanship are diminished by exposure to liberalizing trade. Differences among parties on the position on trade policy decline with globalization.

Increasing democracy is likely to promote liberalizing trade in countries where labor gains from freer trade and more protectionist regimes in countries where workers benefit from barriers to trade, according to the hypothesis of O'Rourke and Taylor (2005). The distributional effects of the Heckscher, Ohlin and Samuelson and the Stolper and Samuelson (1941) theorems suggest that democratization should promote trade liberalization in labor-abundant countries while causing protectionism in labor-scarce countries. The Heckscher and Ohlin model was intended to explain the late nineteenth century. That period is ideal for testing the implications of the model.

The data used by O'Rourke and Taylor (2005) consists of country-level panel data for 35 countries, developed and developing, in 1870–1914. The power of democracy to influence free trade depends on the political economy of trade policy that is not the same for every country. The Heckscher, Ohlin and Samuelson model is powerful in explaining trade and politics in the nineteenth century. The effects of democracy on tariff levels are different in Europe and the poor New World. Democracy did not significantly affect tariffs in land-scarce regions that were relatively poor and in land-abundant regions that were relatively rich. The conclusion of O'Rourke and Taylor (2005) is that the relation between democracy and trade openness is complex. The relation of democracy with more general economic liberalization could be even more complex. There is no assurance that democracy will guarantee the adoption of market-friendly policies. However, democracy does not prevent those policies. The preferences of voters significantly vary across countries and over time.

There is skepticism by López-Córdova and Meissner (2005) that the empirical literature on democracy and globalization has adequately solved the key problem of the endogenous nature of the variables. They are cautious in assessing if the results are definitive. There are likely missing variables in the analysis that affect the results of Rigobon and Rodrik (2004). The theoretical literature provides a role for income and asset distribution in determining democracy. Openness and income distribution are likely mutually affected. The method of identification through heteroskedasticity may be affected by the omission of variables. The heteroskedastic method leads to conclusions that openness adversely affects income levels but other studies using that method show the opposite effect. The method also assumes that the effects of openness on democracy are the same for all countries. There is evidence that the effects vary across countries and even time. There is not yet a definitive empirical solution to the relationship of openness and democracy.

The challenge of research is finding variables that influence the level of trade and are uncorrelated with the determinants of democracy, serving as IVs to capture the effect of trade liberalization on political outcomes. López-Córdova and Meissner (2005) follow an approach used by Frankel and Romer (1999) to analyze the impact of trade openness on output per capita. The method uses geographic variables, such as distance from other nations, land area and waterway access, to estimate the openness of a country by the gravity equation. The first equation consists of ordinary least squares (OLS) regression of the ratio of exports plus imports to GDP on the geographical variables. The prediction of openness of this equation is the IV for the actual openness. The second step consists of an IV regression of income per capita on openness as an endogenous regressor. López-Córdova and Meissner (2005) develop an instrument for trade openness with the gravity equation and additional variables than those used by Frankel and Romer (1999). In the second step, they run a regression of democracy on the predicted openness measure as IV. There is a challenge that other variables in addition to openness influence democracy. The estimation would not be biased if the omitted variables are uncorrelated with the geographic variables.

The general finding by López-Córdova and Meissner (2005) is strong association between openness and democracy in 1895–2000. The relationship is constant over time. The effects are of long-term nature and there can be variations by region. The data may not reflect all characteristics of democracy. Openness increases competition and participation in the choice of the executive and also checks and balances. The determinants of liberalizing trade influence the construction and strengthening of democracy.

There is an argument that globalization and democracy are related as analyzed by Eichengreen and Leblang (2006). If openness has benefits, citizens would demand elimination of restrictions to freer international transactions. Political competitiveness increases because openness not only increases competition in markets of goods and services but also disseminates ideas. The higher availability of diverse ideas promotes political competitiveness. Market stability in economies open to financial flows requires transparency by financial supervisors and regulators. Transparency is not possible in autocracies. Eichengreen and Leblang (2006, 1) argue that the number of democratic countries increased fourfold in 1975–2000 while the IMF measured that the number of countries open to international capital flows increased from 25 to 38 percent.

The diverse results in the literature suggest the possibility of bidirectional causality that Eichengreen and Leblang (2006) analyze for the period 1870–2000 using data on trade, capital controls, democracy and IVs. The evidence suggests that there is a two-way positive relationship between trade and democracy, with exceptions in specific times and geographic locations such as in labor-scarce countries.

An important issue is the nature of the relationship and the sequencing of economic and political liberalizations. Giavazzi and Tabellini (2005) use a sample of 140 advanced and developing countries in 1960–2000 to probe this issue. The analysis faces the problem of reverse causality. The econometric strategy is to consider a sample with as many countries as possible. Some of the countries experienced reform and are called "treated." The countries that did not experience reform are called controls. In the case of economic liberalization, control countries were always liberalized so that they did not experience reform. Giavazzi and Tabellini (2005) then compare economic performance in the countries experiencing reform before and after the treatment in relation to the economic performance of the control group in the same period. They call the method "difference-in-difference" estimation. The method considers the variation within countries and also the comparison among countries. The concentration of economic and political liberalizations in the 1990s could confuse identification of effects in simple analysis of changes within countries alone. The high likelihood of omission of variables could confuse results in cross-sectional comparisons.

There are important conclusions on sequencing of reforms in the analysis by Giavazzi and Tabellini (2005). Growth and investment are positively affected by economic liberalization. Trade openness is only one of several other factors that must accompany economic liberalization. These factors include improvement of the budget surplus, diminishing corruption and enhanced protection of property rights. Moving toward democracy improves the quality of institutions but deteriorates macroeconomic performance and has limited effects on economic growth. There are key feedbacks and interaction effects. The chain of causality, as shown by the timing of events, appears to run from political to economic liberalizations but there are feedback effects in both directions. There are less frequent observations of political liberalizations preceding economic liberalizations. The interaction effects are confirmed by the observation that countries that implement both economic and political liberalization show better economic performance than those that implement only one type of reform. There is better performance by countries that first liberalize the economy and then the political system than the converse. Russia liberalized politics and then tried to liberalize the economy with less favorable economic performance than China that first liberalized the economy and is yet to liberalize the political system.

There are some explanations for the economic impact of the sequencing of liberalizations, according to Giavazzi and Tabellini (2005). The volume of trade rises during an initial reform consisting of economic liberalization and then continues to increase after political reforms. The effects on trade are weaker for countries that first reform the political system and then proceed with economic liberalization. The pattern of economic liberalization is less effective in democracies than in dictatorships. Dictators are not likely to open economic regimes but if they take the decision of opening it is easier for them to suppress the opposing interest groups. A democracy that starts with a liberalized economy is likely to strengthen democratic rule. Liberalization accelerates growth and increases competitiveness. Growth following economic liberalization may permit redistribution required in democracy. In practice, political reforms may be imposed on politicians by the frustration of the people and could even originate in weak economic performance. Optimal sequencing may not be an option.

The United States should assume its role as the current empire, according to Lal (2004, 2005a). He argues that the world has been more prosperous and politically stable under empires. Lal (2004, 2005a) claims that the United States should assume the role of empire based on its asymmetric military and economic power. The British and Roman empires used combinations of direct and indirect administration of the territories under their influence.

The system of multiple states requires a dominant empire, according to Lal (2004, 2005a). He argues that globalization links areas of diverse resource endowment in a common geographic unit. The best hope for world progress is through globalization. In addition, the fall of empires can be followed by long periods of economic and political turmoil, as it was the case of the 500 years after the fall of the Roman Empire. Lal (2004, 2005a) argues that Britain maintained economic dominance in the world from 1820 until about 1870 when it lost it to the United States. Instead of assuming its role as an empire, the United States followed the model of Wilson of the League of Nations. According to Lal (2004, 2005a), the UN and the League of Nations have been unsuccessful in maintaining peace by means of sanctions. Peace requires dominance by an empire, such as the United States, that has asymmetric military and economic strength. The failure of the United

States in Iraq is attributed by Lal (2005a) to not assuming the administration of the country after the war. He believes that because the United States does not assume its role, China or India may become the next empire.

Summary

The evidence on the issues discussed in this chapter does not lead to very solid conclusions that are widely accepted. Empirical verification of causality in economics leaves much to be desired. There is a theoretical case for the provision of regional, international and GPGs. The management of market failures by the government finds the same lack of information on prices of missing markets and major cost/benefit calculations and hurdles.

It is not possible to clearly relate deterioration of the environment to trade openness. Climate change is an important issue but the economics appears to be more promising in the ramp approach of Nordhaus (2006).

The evidence at this time appears to favor the existence of some relation of democracy and trade openness. There appears to be a sequencing of democracy and openness but it is difficult to influence the process with actual policies because of respect of sovereignty.

3
Financial Globalization

Introduction

Economists are in general in favor of the benefits resulting from greater global integration of trade. There is no agreement on the benefits of financial globalization. The gains from trade are derived from an extension to foreign markets of the benefits of the expansion of the market by specialization within the nation state. The benefits of finance for efficiency and growth constitute the basis of the argument for freer capital markets. The empirical evidence on the efficiency and growth effects of financial liberalization is still debated by the profession.

The first section considers the arguments in favor of increased efficiency and growth as a result of financial markets and institutions. Financial repression, in the form of intervention in financial markets, has been denounced as causing losses of efficiency and opportunities for growth. The new theory of financial restraint proposes controls in financial markets to attain Pareto efficiency because asymmetry of information prevents the market from attaining efficient outcomes. Financial liberalization consists of eliminating government controls of financial markets. There have been waves of financial liberalization in the past three decades.

A separate section considers the advantages and costs of liberalizing foreign access to domestic financial markets. The debate has focused on capital account liberalization, that is, unrestricted flows of capital among nations. The main argument against liberalizing capital flows is the incidence of financial crises with adverse effects on output and employment. The final section before the summary presents the innovative approach of the political economy of financial reversals.

Finance, efficiency and growth

Adam Smith referred to the role of finance in terms of a parable (Levine 1997, 701). Specialization was the driver of economic growth that Smith observed during the industrial revolution. The transition to specialization from a barter economy required a medium of exchange, provided by money. The early characterization of economic development was the movement away from the subsistence to the money economy, which is not far from the parable of Smith.

The parable of Levine (1997, 701–2) focuses on the need for the entrepreneur to escape the constraints of self-generating resources to obtain the appropriate risk, liquidity, intertemporal allocation and volume of resources provided by financial markets and institutions. External financing is the key opportunity and function provided by financial markets that permits individuals and even large corporations to escape the constraints of self-generated capital. External finance requires financial markets and institutions and makes a significant difference in modern technologically and organizationally driven economic growth. Levine (1997, 701–2) argues that the functions of financial intermediation cannot be considered in isolation, except for specific analysis, but rather must be taken together to identify how they promote the two channels of capital and technological accumulation. This section focuses on the relation of finance to efficiency in the allocation of resources and economic growth.

There is a view that financial development, both of markets and institutions, is an important part of economic growth (Levine 1997, 689). Empirical evidence shows that financial development successfully predicts future economic growth, capital accumulation and technological change. Evidence from cross-sections of countries, individual case studies and research at the firm and industry levels indicates that economic development is significantly affected by financial development in long periods. Financial crises cause significant losses of employment and output but the relation between financial development and economic growth is also of a long-term nature.

The perfectly competitive model of the first-best of efficiency assumes that there are no frictions or imperfections of information and transaction costs (Arrow 1951, Arrow and Debreu 1954, Debreu 1951). Financial analysis must add frictions to the standard economic model. Without the frictions there is no role for a financial system engaged in evaluating projects, monitoring managers, developing/applying risk-management systems and spending on systems to gather information and facilitate transactions.

The synthesis of financial theory of Levine (1997, 691) begins with the origin of financial markets and institutions to ameliorate the market frictions created by information and transaction costs. Financial markets and intermediaries perform numerous functions that are outlined in Table 3.1. These financial functions operate on two channels of growth: capital accumulation and technological innovation. The consequence of this interaction of financial intermediation with the channels of growth is economic growth itself.

There is no need of financial market intermediaries in the first-best model of perfect competition without market frictions and perfect knowledge (Becsi and Wang 1997, 47). Agents would be able to find optimum investment opportunities for their savings. Under uncertainty, there would still not be a need for financial intermediaries because markets would develop that would provide liquidity in one time period in exchange for payment in a future time period. The prices of securities would behave as in the efficient market hypothesis, reflecting all available information (Shleifer 2000). The propositions of Modigliani and Miller (1958) and

Table 3.1 Functions of financial intermediation

I. Permitting economies of scale

- Transforming securities from bonds and stocks into demand or savings deposits
- Mobilizing savings

  o Pooling large small funds of investors into the financing of large projects

- Facilitating risk management

  o Pooling concentrated risks into diversified risk instruments for smaller investors
  o Transferring/trading risks, permitting larger projects that diversify risks among many institutions

- Allocating resources

  o Facilitating intertemporal allocation: financing presently directly productive activities with long gestation/high return for future repayment

    - Creating liquid markets to securitize directly productive activities

      - Converting long-term, large-scale project financing into short-term liquidity for small investors

  o Screening risks of large projects, providing information at low cost

- Reducing transaction costs

  o Facilitating vertical integration to reduce transaction costs

II. Bridging asymmetry of information and incomplete markets

- Providing instruments that reduce the asymmetry of information

  o Hedging liquidity and credit risk
  o Hedging market risk

- Exerting corporate control

  o Lowering costs of discipline, enhancing monitoring and control
  o Providing take-over opportunities of inefficiently run companies

Source: Becsi and Wang (1997), Levine (1997).

Miller and Modigliani (1961) would be valid: real sector economic allocation is independent of the form of financing.

There were early contributions by Gurley and Shaw (1955, 1960), Cameron (1961, 1967, 1972), Cameron *et al.* (1992) and Goldsmith (1969). The relaxation of the assumptions of perfect competition creates important functions for financial intermediation. Modern technology requires relatively large investments that are indivisible. For example, it is impossible to construct a dam or a railroad with small, incremental investments. Thus, technology makes investments indivisible.

As analyzed in monopoly theory, there could be heavy sunk investments and the incumbent firm may produce at low costs relative to potential entrants. The analysis even applies in contestability theory when potential entrants have the resources to make the required heavy investments.

Financial intermediaries provide important services. They can transform the large-volume securities, stocks and bonds, issued by the firm into smaller investments demanded by investors. Thus, firms may have access to a large pool of investors. Underwriting of securities and loan syndications by banks constitute an important form of making large investments accessible to small savers. This technique actually helped to finance the new world as English portfolio investors financed the infrastructure of the United States and many other new countries. Accounting and auditing firms developed in response to the need to monitor and control the investments. Financial intermediation provides bridges of liquidity, risks and information that are essential to finance large investments. The asymmetry of investors not having sufficient information about borrowers can be bridged by financial intermediaries, providing lower cost monitoring and control in the form of privately issued contracts.

Banks provide monitoring functions as shown in II in Table 3.1. There is an interesting view of delegated monitoring by financial intermediaries proposed by Diamond (1984) and simplified in Diamond (1996). There are two doubts on the rationale for financial intermediaries. First, there is the issue of why investors do not lend directly to borrowers instead of lending to banks. Second, the nature of the financial technology of banks to serve as intermediaries must be clarified. Banks have the incentive of costly liquidation to coerce borrowers to repay their obligations. However, banks can selectively avoid inefficient (costly) liquidation of borrowers by monitoring. The function of monitoring could be extremely expensive if carried out by a multitude of potential inventors but it can be centralized in financial intermediaries such as banks. The nature of the contracts is important: banks issue unmonitored debt (deposits) and monitor loan contracts. The monitoring of loan contracts is required while that of deposits is not required because of the financial engineering technology of financial intermediaries made available by diversification. This financial engineering of diversification permits the mitigation of risk. Thus, banks provide "delegated monitoring." Diamond (1996, 65) concludes that "debt, monitoring and diversification are the keys to understanding the link between financial intermediation and delegated monitoring." The financial engineering of diversification is essential to institutions such as banks that use leverage of about ten times of capital such that bad loans can bankrupt the institution.

The modern focus on finance in economics originates in the works of Modigliani and Miller (1958) and Miller and Modigliani (1961). This work created a revolution in financial analysis not only because of the important propositions but also because of their inspiration: "The [Modigliani and Miller] theorems are a cornerstone also because they are an enlightening example of a research method that can still inspire scholars for many years to come" (Pagano 2005, 246). The Modigliani and Miller propositions focused the attentions of economists on finance (Stiglitz

1988, 121), led to questioning of the assumptions of theory (Stiglitz 1988, 122) and "Modigliani and Miller, in their brilliant papers, have set forth a research agenda which will occupy economists for decades to come" (Stiglitz 1988, 126). It is instructive to outline the contributions by Modigliani and Miller to show how the synthesis with subsequent work illustrates the control functions of financial intermediaries (Diamond 1994).

The first proposition of Modigliani and Miller (1958) is on the value invariance of financing the firm. The capital structure is the choice of debt versus equity to finance the firm, or the ratio of debt to equity. Under no costs of bankruptcy, the value of the firm is independent of the ratio of debt to equity. There has been voluminous research on the value of the proposition in reality. Miller and Modigliani (1961, 412) used the standard assumptions of perfect markets and rational behavior together with perfect certainty in some cases. Subsequent research has focused also on the change in the proposition resulting from modifying its assumptions. The proof of the proposition used arbitrage arguments that became popular in finance (Miller 1988, 99). The second Miller and Modigliani (1961) invariance proposition is that the value of the firm is independent of its dividend policy.

The proof of the first proposition is implicit in option pricing theory. Consider the expression of the put-call parity theorem (Miller 1988, 110):

$$S = C(K) + Ke^{-rt} - P(K) \tag{3.1}$$

The current price of the stock is S, $C(K)$ and $P(K)$ are the call and put prices at the same exercise price K, r is the riskless interest rate, t is time and exercise occurs at time T. There is an analysis of the capital structure in the option pricing contributions of Black and Scholes (1973) and Merton (1974). Default at time T occurs when the value of the assets, $A(T)$, is below the value of the firm's debt, D, or $A(T) \leq D$. The market value of the firm's assets follows a log-normal diffusion process (Duffie and Singleton 2003). Thus, the firm's equity is a call option on the total assets, A, with strike value at the firm's debt, D. The Black–Scholes formula can be used to obtain the value of the firm's debt by deducting the option price from the initial asset value. The value of the firm's debt without risk is Ke^{-rt}. If at maturity S were to be lower than K, the shareholders put the firm back to its creditors by appeal to limited liability. Thus, the present value of the debt less the put value of the shareholders, $Ke^{-rt} - P(K)$, is the actual market value of the debt. While the values of the equity and debt of the firm depend on the firm's leverage, the put-call parity theorem shows that their sum is independent of leverage. Miller (1988, 109) states that the option pricing results show new aspects of the Modigliani and Miller propositions that "is hardly surprising since [Modigliani and Miller] type arbitrage arguments were explicitly invoked by Black and Scholes in deriving their option valuation formula."

The main concern of Modigliani and Miller (1958) as recalled by Miller (1988, 101) was on the determinants of aggregate investment by business. The ultimate source of financing of capital formation by business is household savings. The conventional demonstration by economists was to show the T accounts of business and households. The assets of business consist of productive capital and the assets of household include debt and equity of firms, which are the liabilities of business. The liabilities of households consist of household net worth. The national accounts aggregate productive capital of firms as assets and household net worth as liabilities. The debt and equity securities disappear in the consolidation. The value of the capital underlying debt and equity securities consists of the value of business to its ultimate owners, the households. The debt and equity securities are "intermediate assets serving to partition the earnings (and their attendant risks) among the many separate individual households within the sector" (Miller 1988, 101). Modigliani and Miller (Miller 1988, 101) applied this macroeconomic intuition to microeconomic analysis of corporate finance. The essence of financial intermediation is to channel household savings into productive capital.

There is double taxation of corporate net income in the United States (Miller 1988, 111):

> The U.S. Internal Revenue Code has long been the classic, and by now is virtually the world's only, completely unintegrated tax system imposing "double taxation" of corporate net income. A separate income tax is first levied directly in the corporation and, except for certain closely-held corporations a second tax is then levied at the personal level on any income flows such as dividends

Subsequent work by Modigliani and Miller considered that with double taxation firms should not issue equity and "the optimal capital structure might be all debt" (Miller 1988, 112). The all-debt firm may default frequently but there was no default-cost assumption in the analysis (Diamond 1994, 12).

Further work focused on analyzing the capital structure of the firm by providing incentives to management or by granting control of the firm to outsiders. Another strand of research introduced bankruptcy costs. There are extreme cases according to the assumptions (Diamond 1994). The optimum firm has only debt if there are no costs of bankruptcy. The optimum firm has only equity if there are bankruptcy costs but no tax savings from debt. Diamond (1994) integrates the analysis for an intermediate firm that has both debt and equity. The model regards bankruptcy costs as including in some cases a control benefit. Bank debt is more expensive than public issue of securities because banks have significant operational costs. However, there is an important strategic advantage of banks because they could restructure outside bankruptcy firms that have feasible investment projects. Significant tax advantage may lead firms to rely on bank debt and avoid equity and public debt.

One of the original and most impressive contributions to understanding economic development was by Schumpeter (1911). It explained the process of development as long periods of disequilibrium of a model of perfect competition with shocks of technological innovation. In the analysis of Schumpeter, banks play a key role in the allocation of credit to the financing of the projects of innovations that cause economic growth (King and Levine 1993). Rajan and Zingales (1998, 1) trace back to Schumpeter the argument that the financial sector allocates resources to efficient economic activities. This allocation process does not have significant risk of losses due to moral hazard, adverse selection or transaction costs and constitutes "an essential catalyst of economic growth."

Empirical research on the association of finance and growth encounters the difficulty of establishing causality in economic reality. One problem is that theory is not very precise in what variables to include in regressions while several excluded variables may be in the disturbance term (Rajan and Zingales 1998, 560). For example, household saving may be an important factor of economic growth but may be reflected in econometric research simply as financial development. Another problem is that financial variables may anticipate economic growth, being the present discounted value of future cash flows. Financial development may be a leading indicator of growth but not its cause.

A route to circumvent the causality problem is to focus on the theory of how finance influences economic growth (Rajan and Zingales 1998, 560). The specific theoretical argument is that the financial sector, consisting of markets and institutions, helps firms to find external finance by ameliorating the problems of adverse selection and moral hazard. Thus, financial development should be significantly important in helping firms or industries that depend on external financing for their development. Technology is the cause of indivisibilities in investment.

Rajan and Zingales (1998) classify industries in the United States that have demand for external financing depending on their use of technology. These industries should grow at faster rates in developing countries. For example, the pharmaceutical industry has much larger technological investments than tobacco products and thus should have higher needs of external financing and should grow at higher rates in developing countries. The approach is within the center of the argument by Schumpeter (1911) that innovation drives economic growth and that banks finance innovating firms. There is significant evidence documented by Cameron (1967) on the facilitating role of banking in the early stages of industrialization. There is similar caution of the result by Rajan and Zingales (1998, 561) and by Cameron (1967, 2) that the approach mainly analyzes how firms escape the constraint of internally generated profits to finance projects rich in innovation that can augment the rate of economic growth. The approach of Cameron (1961) was to explain economic development in terms of institutional factors, with financial institutions playing a key role in the early stages of modernization.

The basic hypothesis of Rajan and Zingales (1998, 562) is that industries using external financing exhibit higher growth rates in countries with more advanced financial systems. An important feature of their research is the inclusion of accounting standards as a measure of financial development. The investigation used data for 41 countries, finding that industrial sectors with greater needs of external financing experience disproportionately faster development in countries with financial markets that are more developed.

An important policy conclusion is that improvements in accounting, disclosure and bankruptcy codes promote economic and financial development (Rajan and Zingales 2001). Political structure, perhaps modified to some extent by history of inherited structure, explains financial development.

Using the method and data of Rajan and Zingales (1998), Vlachos and Waldenström (2005) find that in countries with liberalized capital accounts or equity markets, industries that rely on external financing do not show higher growth in value added. There is positive association between the creation of new firms and output growth and liberalization of capital accounts and equity markets.

The complexity of the relationship between financial development and growth constitutes a hurdle to the design of policy (Manning 2003, 1). There is uncertainty as to whether empirical research has accurately measured the relationship. Finance and growth show stronger relation in the early stages of economic development with a more important contribution by banks in the process of industrialization, a fact observed in economic history (Cameron 1961, 1967, 1972). In addition, there are studies showing the relationship between finance and other social, political and legal factors, surveyed in the section on the view of disclosure in Chapter 5 in Volume I. The problem of identification could be present, camouflaging the relation of growth to those other social, political and legal factors instead of simply financial development. It is possible that finance and growth have stronger association in the early stages of development but that they may influence each other in higher stages of development, that is, finance leads growth that in turn requires more finance.

An important issue of research is the long-term relationship between economic growth and the development of the stock market relative to the banking system (Arestis *et al.* 2001). There is a second issue as to the direction of the causal relationship between banking system development and growth and stock market development and growth. Arestis *et al.* (2001) investigate these issues with quarterly data in the period of the 1970s to the 1990s for the United States, Japan, the United Kingdom and Germany. Their econometric research shows that there is a positive contribution of stock market development to economic growth but the contribution of the stock market is only a fraction of that of the banking system. They conclude that financial systems based on banks may provide stronger impulse to economic growth than those based on capital markets. Stock market volatility has adverse effects on real output in Japan and France, negative effects on output and financial development in the United Kingdom and non-significant effects on output in Germany.

Capital market imperfections, such as asymmetric information, distort the costs of internal and external financing of the firm. Love (2003) used firm data for 36 countries with different degrees of financial development. Financial development is associated with decreases in financing constraints, reducing asymmetry of information and imperfections of contracting.

There are many studies on finance, efficiency and growth, having all the difficulties of empirical research in economics. Nourzad (2002) uses three separate panels of developed and developing countries to show that financial development increases productivity. The effects are stronger in developed relative to developing countries. Rioja and Valev (2004) use panel data for 74 countries. There is a strong effect of finance on productivity growth, especially in developed countries. In developing countries, effects are processed through capital accumulation.

The effects of financial liberalization can be separated into a quantity effect, in which higher interest rates increase the volume of financial services and lower their prices, and a quality effect, in which credit flows to higher quality projects (Abiad *et al.* 2004). There is a model that shows that global financial diversification can improve resource allocation, leading to growth (Obstfeld 1994). Suppose that risky technologies have higher returns than safer ones. International trade in assets permits countries to have portfolios that are diversified in investments with higher risk and higher returns. Financial liberalization can then allocate resources from low-risk and low-return activities to high-risk and high-return projects (Obstfeld 1994). Abiad *et al.* (2004) conduct a test of the quality effect by proposing that efficiency of allocation caused by liberalization results in less variability in the distribution of marginal returns to capital. With a sample of firms for five countries, they find that the equalizing effect on credit access of financial liberalization lowers the variation in expected returns across firms. Financial liberalization and efficiency in allocation are positively related.

The "inequality-widening" proposition claims that financial development increases income inequality (Clarke *et al.* 2006, 580). Rajan and Zingales (2003a–c) include the argument that credit in developing countries requires collateral. Because the poor do not have collateral, financial development benefits only the rich. In addition, the rich have own capital irrespective of the level of financial development and could have higher gains when financial market imperfections erode (Clarke *et al.* 2006, 580). There is another hypothesis of inverted U or ∩-shaped relation in which inequality first increases with financial development but subsequently declines. There are important policy implications in evaluating the relative merits of these hypotheses. Clarke *et al.* (2006) analyzed these hypotheses with a large cross-section sample. They find some support for the hypothesis that inequality narrows with financial development and decisive evidence rejecting the inequality-widening hypothesis. There are less conclusive results on the ∩-shaped relation of inequality and financial development.

Financial repression and restraint

Various countries implemented legal restrictions on financial institutions that were considered detrimental to efficiency and development. McKinnon (1973) and Shaw (1973) argue that these restrictions were detrimental to development. These restrictions are grouped in the literature into the term "financial repression." A typical restriction was an interest rate ceiling on deposits and many times also on loans. There were excessive reserve requirements on bank liabilities as well as constraints on bank liquidity. Banks were required to lend to specific activities that the government considered to be strategic to economic development. In many cases, such as in Brazil, banks used official funds to lend to those activities at a fixed spread between the cost of the borrowing from the government and the loan to the protected economic activity. Brazil also had multiple state and federal commercial and development banks engaged in directed lending. Capital requirements were also used to constrain bank activities.

The effects of the policies instead of the policies are important in the characterization of financial repression (Giovannini and de Melo 1993). The typical policies are the price and quantitative restrictions described above. The policies do not work without complementary restrictions on the flows of international capital. Otherwise, offshore financial intermediaries could offset the policies by capital flight.

The effectiveness of the restrictions on international capital flows is suspect. Brazil had all the financial repression policies in the 1970s that can possibly be designed together with capital controls. Trade and multinational companies, both local and foreign, permitted the capital flight through underinvoicing and lagging exports, overinvoicing and leading imports, intercompany loans, dividend remittances and price transfer. Such technology of capital flight was internationally available and marketed. By the 1980s Brazil had a GDP of a few hundred billion dollars and Brazilian nationals held close to $100 billion in offshore deposits.

The policies followed to relax financial repression have included the elimination of controls on trading of international assets and the restrictions on volume and rates in domestic financial transactions. Giovannini and de Melo (1993) argue that the analysis of repression is correct but that the policies have not taken into account distortions in the economy, in particular the interaction between financial controls and tax policies. They treat the controls on domestic intermediation as a type of taxation. Because their estimate of the revenue obtained by national governments is quite substantial, it may be necessary to implement changes in taxation and government expenditure together with financial liberalization. The base of the tax for the calculation of government revenue from financial repression is central-government debt. The estimated revenue is equal to the difference between international and domestic interest rates multiplied by the stock of domestic government liabilities. The period of measurement is characterized by significant repression and government deficits in the 1970s and 1980s. There are significant differences among countries but the non-weighted average is 2 percent of GDP and 9 percent of government revenue excluding that from financial repression.

There is a distinction between financial and monetary mercantilism (Aizenman and Lee 2006). East Asian countries have promoted economic growth with an outward strategy of exporting. The tools of financial mercantilism have included preferential financing of export promotion, constituting a subsidy to directed lending, achieved by direct subsidies of state banks or by forcing private banks by means of moral suasion. Monetary mercantilism has consisted of reserve hoarding.

Bank balance sheets deteriorated as a result of financial mercantilism (Aizenman and Lee 2006). Thus, banks can experience crises during growth decline. In periods of crisis, competitive devaluations by several countries erode an individual country's competitiveness from devaluation. Aizenman and Lee (2006) provide evidence on Korea and Japan on the characteristics of financial and monetary mercantilism but caution that normative conclusions require careful evaluation of costs and benefits.

There is an index of financial sector repression covering 24 years for 35 countries, constructed by Abiad and Mody (2005). The components of the index include a broad collection of measures of financial repression of the domestic financial sector and of the foreign exchange market. These components show the imagination of policy makers in finding measures to repress financial markets. The index shows that financial liberalization made progress throughout most of the world even with stops, gaps and reversals. There was liberalization of all countries according to income level but it was stronger in higher-income countries.

Abiad and Mody (2005) analyzed the political economy of liberalization in terms of three approaches – shocks, learning and government ideology, institutions and structure. They conclude that the combination of learning and discrete changes explains liberalization. Countries with highly repressive financial systems are the least likely to change. Regional competition for funds motivated liberalization. There were events, such as a decline in US interest rates that stimulated liberalization but increases in US interest rates reversed it. The opening to trade and investment stimulated the pace of reform in countries with significant financial repression. There were no significant differences in the pace of liberalization between left-wing and right-wing governments.

There is a new theory proposing financial restraint to mitigate moral hazard resulting from financial liberalization (Hellmann *et al.* 2000). Table 3.2 shows a

Table 3.2 Interest rate liberalization and prudential bank behavior

---

Financial market liberalization:
   Reduced barriers to entry
   Entry of foreign banks
   Elimination of interest rate restrictions
     On deposits and loans
   Elimination of restrictions on
     Branches
     Real estate lending
     Trading derivatives and foreign exchange
   Unchanged:
     Capital requirements
     Capacity of regulatory oversight
     ↓
Increased banking competition
   ↓
Profit erosion
   ↓
Lower bank franchise value
(Lower expectation of discounted future profits)
   ↓
Lower incentives to provide quality loans
Higher moral hazard: incentive to gambling

Source: Hellmann *et al.* (2000).

schematic outline of this theory. The first stage is financial market liberalization as interpreted by the authors of the theory in relation to recent cases. The motive for liberalization is to increase banking competition that would result in higher volumes of financial assets at lower interest rates, providing the financing of sound projects required to accelerate development. A key ingredient is the reduction of barriers to entry, typically including the entry of foreign banks because of the monopolistic internal banking system. All sorts of restrictions are eliminated at this stage, in particular those on maximum interest rates on deposits and loans. Liberalization eliminates other restrictions such as those on branches, real estate lending and trading in derivatives and foreign exchange. However, capital requirements are typically left unchanged and the capacity of regulatory oversight is unchanged or diminished. In short, there is significantly higher risk in banking together with less control by the monetary authorities.

In the second stage, the liberalization has the desired result of increasing banking competition. The increased competition causes erosion of bank profits; banks become more fragile and are not adequately remunerating their capital. Bank franchise capital is the present value of future profits, the reason for existence of a capitalized bank. Competition erodes current profits and the expectation of remuneration of capital with future profits. Banks have lower incentives to provide quality loans and moral hazard increases.

Banks are faced with low returns on quality loans because of profit erosion caused by financial liberalization (Hellmann *et al.* 2000, 148). The typical bank has an incentive to "gamble" by taking high risks. If the bank is successful, it appropriates rents from gambling. If the bank is unsuccessful, it passes on to depositors the realized risks of the failure. Hellmann *et al.* (2000) argue that freely determined deposit rates prevent the banking system to reach the Pareto frontier. They consider two alternative policies: ceilings on deposit rates and increased capital requirements. There is high cost in capital requirements. Deposit-rate ceilings can equally move the banking system toward the Pareto-efficient frontier and are preferable. Financial liberalization increases moral hazard problems. Other possible policies to mitigate moral hazard include "asset-class restrictions, entry restrictions and enhancing direct supervision" (Hellmann *et al.* 2000).

Stiglitz (1994) summarizes an interpretation of the arguments against financial repression. The main proposition is that controls that maintain interest rates below their free-market levels lower savings. Economic growth is restrained because savings required to financing capital projects are constrained by financial repression. Financial institutions no longer allocate savings efficiently to their best uses because of the distortion of interest rates. Government restrictions of interest rates diminish available capital; whatever capital is available is not necessarily allocated to the most efficient activities.

There are important objections to the characterization of financial repression, according to Stiglitz (1994). The volume of savings is determined by different factors, such as convenience and safety: Japan Post, for example, was able to raise huge amounts of money at low interest rates. There is transfer of wealth from households to business because of low interest rates. However, the higher marginal propensity to save of business is higher than that of households in a world of credit and equity rationing, such that the transfer increases the aggregate volume of savings.

The argument that financial repression causes misallocation of resources, in analogy with the goods sector, is misleading, according to Stiglitz (1994). In conditions of credit rationing and bankruptcy, Stiglitz and Greenwald (2003, 59) show that: "The bank chooses an interest rate which is below that which maximizes the expected return, because further increases in the interest rate would increase the probability of bankruptcy." Higher interest rates adversely affect incentives and the pool of applicants, which could include many projects that would default. Free-market interest rates under asymmetry of information need not result in allocation of resources to the best available alternatives. Stiglitz (1994) argues that financial repression lowers the cost of capital to business. The lower interest rates decrease the cost of debt, making overall capital less costly, thus increasing the firm's equity. There is an added benefit in the decrease of the expectation of bankruptcy, according to Stiglitz (1994), which encourages firms to engage in projects with long gestation, high yield and risk. He concludes that "Indeed, financial repression can be used as the basis of an incentive scheme to encourage higher savings and more efficient allocation of capital" (Stiglitz 1994).

Another form of intervention in credit markets consists of directed credit by the government to certain activities. Stiglitz (1994) argues that without these programs there would not be allocation of credit to activities with the highest social returns. Technology is an important activity that should qualify for directed credit programs.

The rapid economic growth of East Asian economies before the 1997 crisis is called the "East Asian Miracle." Stiglitz and Uy (1996) contend that there were many causes of economic growth in this episode but that an important factor consisted of systematic government intervention in financial markets throughout every stage of development. They document the market failures targeted by the authorities, rationalize the theoretical justification for intervention in those failures and verify with data the impact of policy. The authorities abandoned ineffective policies, designed policies to improve the probability of success and reduce abuse and successfully changed policy courses to accommodate changes in economic conditions.

There is an important test of financial restraint. Arestis *et al.* (2002) constructed a sample for six developing countries in the period 1955–97. They included specifications for two quantitative measures of quantitative policy restraint: ceilings on deposit and lending rates as well as reserve and liquidity constraints. Using advanced econometric techniques, they conclude that (Arestis *et al.* 2002, 119):

> Interestingly, we find that while financial restraints in some cases have negative direct effects, there are also cases where their effects are positive. Thus, our empirical findings demonstrate that the main predictions of the financial liberalization literature do not receive full empirical support, a result which is consistent with the prevalence of financial market imperfections

Their research suggests that financial restraint may be beneficial in the presence of weak institutional quality in the form of inadequate prudential supervision and regulation. Further challenging research is required to obtain a complete picture of the interaction of financial restraint and the effectiveness of financial liberalization.

Financial globalization

Financial globalization can be defined as the process of integration of the financial system of a country with international financial markets and institutions (Schmukler 2004, 39). The integration is usually accompanied with liberalization, or freeing, internal financial markets and the flow of international capital, or capital account of the balance of payments. The liberalization of financial markets consists of the elimination of controls on financial institutions, such as interest rate ceilings on deposits and loans, reserve and liquidity requirements on deposits, restrictions on assets and conditions to allocate loans to certain economic activities. The liberalization of capital flows consists of the elimination of controls on exchange rates and quantitative restrictions on foreign international transactions by domestic agents or foreign agents. Cross-border movements of capital significantly increase during financial globalization.

Globalization is the result of the interaction of four agents – governments, borrowers, investors and financial institutions (Schmukler 2004, 44–6). Governments promote globalization by eliminating restrictions on domestic financial markets and institutions and by allowing free flows of capital. Borrowers and investors can borrow and invest overseas, respectively. The diversification of financial transactions can be very important to weather crises. Borrowers can enjoy lowers rates of debt obligations and improved terms. Investors can tailor their investments to their risk appetites. Financial institutions constitute another important agent of globalization. International financial institutions have actively engaged in financial sector FDI (FSFDI), with many favorable effects on host-country financial markets. Liberalization of domestic financial markets has increased the efficiency of services provided by financial institutions.

Works by Caballero (2000) and Caballero and Krishnamurthy (2001, 2004) identify two important characteristics of emerging markets: weak links with the private international financial sector and underdevelopment of the domestic financial sector. Caballero distinguishes between international financial liquidity that borrowers in the emerging market can pledge in intermediation of loans and domestic financial liquidity that borrowers can use as collateral in domestic loans. Because of fear of floating on mismatched balance sheets, once a sudden stop (SS) occurs, the monetary authority prevents adjustment via exchange rates with adjustment by increasing interest rates. That is, monetary policy during SS is procyclical. In addition, the government cannot fund in international markets and increases its funding in the domestic market, further magnifying the squeeze on domestic activity. During the SS, there is relatively little international financial liquidity. Domestic borrowers do not have "insurance," that is, they do not have credit to bridge their projects to the future. There is a decrease in prices of nontradables used as collateral in local loans. There is further deepening of the domestic crisis. Moreover, adverse selection prevents the economy from recovering.

Caballero proposes that central banks avoid defending currencies with higher interest rates during SS. Policy should begin during booms of foreign financing. The central bank should acquire abundant international financial liquidity with issue of bonds. Ideally, the exchange rate regime should be a flexible exchange rate with medium-term inflation targets on nontradables and active management of reserves. During SS, the central bank would provide international financial liquidity, contributing to smoothing the impact of the crisis. In addition, policy would be counter cyclical, avoiding increases in domestic interest rates, which would require tolerance with the inflation target. Success of this policy in practice requires a credible and autonomous central bank. In the long term, structural change would consist in deepening the financial sector.

There is a measurement of FSFDI in the Cumming Report by the CGFS (2004, 4, 7) using cross-border M&As with targets of banks in emerging market economies (EME). FSFDI increased from around $6 billion per year in 1990–6 to about $50 billion per year in 1997–2000 and the share of financial institutions from EMEs rose from 13 percent in 1990–6 to 30 percent in 1997–2000. There was high geographical concentration with Latin America receiving $46 billion or 56 percent of total cross-border M&As with banks as targets in 1990–2003. The United States accounted for 35 percent of the total FSFDI, Spain for 46 percent and the United Kingdom for 8 percent. Central and Eastern Europe (CEU) received 24 percent or $20 billion of all cross-border M&As and non-Japan Asia 17 percent, or $14 billion.

The study by the CGFS (2004, 6–7) analyzes the drivers of FSFDI. The banking systems in Latin America and CEU but not those in Asia provided high returns that could be realized by the first entrants. There were opportunities in local financial markets for the introduction of new products in derivatives, foreign exchange and securities. Many EMEs implemented financial reforms in the 1990s that liberalized financial markets, reducing controls on credit, interest rates and international transactions. There were parallel reforms of the legal, regulatory and market organization. IFIs promoted strong domestic financial sectors and growing integration in the world economy. Increasing competition in advanced markets motivated international banks to search for growth opportunities abroad. FSFDI contributed to trends of: "global consolidation, ownership of banking and other financial institutions at the parent level by private shareholders and the spreading of effective competition and market-based pricing" (CGFS 2004, 7–8). IFIs were drivers of financial globalization but their efforts interacted with numerous financial, economic and political factors. Thus, IFIs alone did not have the strength and means to create the financial globalization of the 1990s, which did not originate in ideas by economists in Washington.

There were important economic motives for FSFDI on the part of investors (CGFS 2004, 8–9). Banks emphasize risk-adjusted profitability as a criterion for investment. The expectation of investors was for markets with long-term growth potential, adequate scale and improving infrastructure. There were institutions motivated by entering markets with new products and remaining until excess profits were reduced by competition. Banks approached the new opportunities with the business strategies that they developed in advanced countries. They searched for opportunities in economies of scale in a variety of segments such as product development, systems and operations and also in risk management. Capital flowed into EMEs in pursuit of higher differential marginal returns. Financial institutions in mature countries decided to engage in FSFDI to maintain managerial control that would not occur in portfolio investment (Cumming 2006, 12). Emerging markets provided the opportunity for diversification of sources of revenue and the efficiency of larger scale of operation in contrast with more competitive and saturated markets in advanced countries. Technology and improved communication facilitated managerial control.

The benefits of FSFDI found in the Cumming Report (CGFS 2004) are outlined in Table 3.3. A group of benefits originates in institutional change of the acquired banks. There are multiple exchanges of resources between the parent and the acquired bank, including the deployment of managerial and human capital from head office and the training of local staff. There are benefits to the market as a whole in that the quality and availability of financial professionals increases. There are also benefits in infrastructure, financing during crises and in the reputation of the parent that enhances the marketing efforts of the acquired institution. The process of decision making improves because of the higher level risk-adjusted decision techniques as well as more sophisticated risk-management approaches. The integration with world finance drives efficiency because of the comparison with risk-adjusted returns worldwide.

The most important and controversial gains are in efficiency and capital allocation. Competition drives efficiency, which consists of reducing costs or its counterpart of increasing productivity. Higher productivity lowers prices and volumes of credit, augmenting the access to credit of the economy. There are complaints that subsidiaries of foreign banks engage in "cherry-picking" of the best clients, with adverse effects on domestic banks that are driven toward second-rate risk clients.

There are positive effects of financial globalization, especially FSFDI (Cumming 2006, 14). Foreign financial institutions introduce more rigorous credit-risk and portfolio management techniques. These enhanced tools increase competition and improve the quality of credit decisions. Prices and conditions of financial assets reflect the level of credit risk, reducing directed credit flows. In addition, FSFDI introduces new products such as derivatives and securities that develop local markets and provide alternatives to bank loans. Improved consumer loans benefit households. In addition, Cumming (2006, 14) argues that FSFDI contributes to the stability of local financial markets. Local institutions become integrated with larger international banks and have access to equity and funding that strengthen the domestic operation. Another advantage is the creation of an active market for M&As that enhances incentives to management as well as the opportunity to reduce nonperforming loans.

Table 3.3 Benefits of financial sector foreign direct investment

---

Institutional change of acquired banks

- Resources of the parent

  o Managerial and human capital from head office
  o Training of local staff
  o Infrastructure in back office, credit controls
  o Financing during crises
  o Reputation of the parent

- Decision-making

  o Techniques of overall decision
  o Risk management

- Integration with world finance

  o Risk-adjusted return comparison with other markets

Efficiency and capital allocation

- Competition driving efficiency

  o Declining costs, increasing productivity → lower prices, higher volumes of financial products, greater access to credit
  o Better credit allocation → lower moral hazard
  o Criticism of cherry-picking of best clients

- Development of local market

  o Dynamism in funding, derivatives and securities markets
  o Product innovation (over the counter (OTC) markets and structured products)
  o Hedging markets

Financial and macroeconomic stability

- Sounder domestic market

  o Credit-risk management processes
  o Solutions to asset quality deterioration
  o Transparency and information for domestic regulation

- Softening domestic credit cycle
- Crisis stabilization

Source: CGFS (2004, 12–5).

However, there are concerns by policy makers on the benefits of FSFDI (Cumming 2006). Conflicts of interest can develop between the domestic operation of a foreign financial institution and the policy objectives of the host country. In addition, there are new requirements of coordination of the supervisors in the host country and in the country of origin. The implementation of Basel II is trying to iron the issues of information not only with the Group of Ten (G10) members of the Basel Committee on Banking Supervision (BCBS) but also with supervisors of 16 non-members (BCBS 2006).

The transmission of foreign technology influences the development of local financial markets. FSFDI brings new products and markets such as in derivatives, foreign exchange and securities; it also brings new technology in the management of risks of these products. There are also gains in the development of hedge markets that serve to improve the function of transferring risks.

There is significant debate as to whether FSFDI contributes to greater financial and economic stability in the host country. The CGFS (2004) finds positive contributions in generating sounder financial markets in the host country because of the more advanced risk management and credit-risk based processes transferred to the local market. Stronger banks soften the adverse impacts of the credit market. In periods of crisis, institutions with strong foreign parents may contribute to diminish financial scarcities. However, if the evaluation of country risk by the parent deteriorates, the parent will engage in hedging country risk by all means, from reduction of exposures in credit portfolios to shorting country risk in derivative products, accentuating capital flight.

An important structural change is the increase in local lending through subsidiaries that increased from 25 percent in 2000 to 45 percent in 2005, reaching $1 trillion (Cumming 2006, 13). This change occurred in an environment of growth of both international and subsidiary lending. According to Cummings (2006, 13), the share of foreign assets in banking rose above 65 percent for Mexico, the Czech Republic, Hungary and Poland. There has been a worldwide increase in foreign ownership of assets in domestic banking systems. FSFDI has increased in financial markets as a whole and not only in banking. The United States is an example of a worldwide phenomenon. The assets of commercial banks had a share of two-thirds of assets of foreign-owned financial institutions in the United States with securities companies having a share of 25 percent (Cumming 2006, 14). The share of banking assets in total assets of foreign-owned financial institutions in the United States declined to 40 percent by 2005 while securities companies increased their share to 30 percent and other financial institutions to 30 percent.

The Committee on the Global Financial System (CGFS) organized workshops with 37 central banks of emerging Asia, CEU and Latin America to follow up on the CGFS (2004) report on globalization. The main benefit of the entry of foreign banks occurred as a result of increased competition in banking (CGFS 2005Jun, 1–2). Enhanced competition "improved availability and quality of banking services, technology transfer and easier access to capital" (CGFS 2005Jun, 1). The introduction of advanced risk management processes was highly beneficial. In Chile, there was a decline in the cost/income ratio. Risk management improved in the Czech Republic. There was less agreement on other issues such as the contribution to stability.

Capital account liberalization

While there is broad agreement among economists about the benefits of free trade, there is significant controversy on the convenience of freeing the capital account. Capital account liberalization consists of the elimination of restrictions on the movements of capital among nations. There are no exchange controls or restrictions on any type of transactions that require the remittance of funds abroad or the entry of foreign funds. The definition of the capital account below is followed by the controversy on the role of the IMF in capital account liberalization.

The current and capital accounts of the United States in 2005 are shown in Table 3.4. The accounts are prepared by the Bureau of Economic Analysis (BEA) of the US Department of Commerce. The original data are in millions of dollars but the table summarizes the most important items in billions of dollars. Minor errors of rounding remain. There are three accounts: current account (CA), capital account and financial account. Line 1 provides the goods and services sold by US residents abroad that are called exports of goods and services, plus income receipts from abroad. The income receipts include receipts from direct investment of the United States in other countries, other private receipts, US government receipts and compensation of employees.

Line 4 provides the purchase of goods by US residents from abroad that are called imports of goods and services and the income payments for foreign-owned assets in the United States. Line 7 is an important subject of analysis in economics, the trade account, or exports of goods and services less imports of goods and services, equal to lines 2 and 5. In 2005, the United States had a trade deficit of $716.7 billion because its exports of goods and services of $1275.2 billion were lower by $716.7 billion than its imports of goods and services of $1991.2 billion. The summary measurement of US foreign financial needs is the balance in CA, equal

Table 3.4   United States international transactions, 2005 US$ Billions

Current account		
1. Exports of goods and services and income receipts	1,749.9	
2. Exports of goods and services	1,275.2	
3. Income receipts	474.7	
4. Imports of goods and services and income receipts	−2,455.3	
5. Imports of goods and services	−1,991.2	
6. Income payments	−463.3	
7. **Balance on goods and services (2 and 5)**		− 716.7
8. Unilateral current transfers, net	−86.1	
9. **Balance on current account (1, 4 and 8)**		− 791.5
Capital and financial accounts		
Capital account		
10. **Capital account transactions, net**		− 4.3
Financial account		
11. **US-owned assets abroad, net**		− 426.8
12. **Foreign-owned assets in the United States, net**		1,212.5
13. **Statistical discrepancy**		10.4

Source: US Department of Commerce, Bureau of Economic Analysis, http://www.bea.gov/international/index.htm#bop.

to the exports of goods and services and income receipts (line 1) less the imports of goods and services and income payments (line 4) plus unilateral transfers (line 8). The United States experienced a CAD of $791.5 billion in 2005. The capital and financial accounts show the flows of capital that financed the CAD of the United States. That is, the United States borrowed from foreigners.

The national income accounts constitute the departing point for the relation between the fiscal deficits and CADs. National savings is by definition equal to private savings plus the government balance, which is government revenue less government expenditure. The CA equals national savings less investment or:

CA = national savings less investment = private savings plus (government revenue less expenditure) less investment

Thus, the CA is a dynamic process (Obstfeld and Rogoff 1996, 15–16). An excess of savings over investment will flow into foreign asset accumulation and an inflow of foreign debt will finance an excess of investment over savings. In the case of a budget deficit, government expenditure will exceed government revenue, subtracting from private savings. The foreign savings in the form of a CAD will finance the fiscal deficit.

Liberalization of the capital account is defined as the removal of prohibitions on transactions in the capital and financial accounts of the balance of payments, which consists mainly of eliminating controls on foreign exchange and foreign-capital (Eichengreen and Mussa 1998, Mussa *et al.* 1998). Some countries have restricted the net foreign open position, consisting of unhedged foreign currency assets less liabilities as percentage of the bank's capital. Other countries such as Chile and Colombia taxed short-term capital inflows. Reserve requirements of banks have also been used to restrict foreign-currency denominated or foreign-originated deposits.

An important requirement is the sequencing of capital account liberalization, correcting problems in the domestic financial system to avoid financial crises (Eichengreen and Mussa 1998, Mussa *et al.* 1998). An important difficulty is weak market discipline because of inadequate accounting and disclosure. There could be an encouragement to unsustainable capital inflow originating in government guarantees. Sound prudential regulation and supervision of the domestic financial sector is required to avoid excessive risk-taking by financial institutions. Concentration of capital inflows through the financial system poses another major risk; diversification, especially with direct investment, reduces the possibility of crises. The observed volatility of FDI is much lower than for short-term capital movements.

The Interim Committee of the IMF requested the IMF Executive Board in September 1996 to conduct an analysis of world capital markets and possible changes in the Articles of Agreement of the IMF to respond to the growth of international capital movements (Eichengreen and Mussa 1998, Mussa *et al.* 1998). The Interim Committee agreed in April 1997 that the IMF could amend the Articles to obtain the benefits from orderly liberalization of capital movements. In September

1997, the Interim Committee issued a statement during the IMF and WB annual meetings in Hong Kong reiterating the position on orderly liberalization of capital flows (Friedman 1997).

At the meeting in Hong Kong on September 21, 1997, the Interim Committee (1997b) adopted the liberalization of the capital account. The official communication states (Interim Committee 1997a):

> The Committee reiterated its view that an open and liberal system of capital movements, supported by sound macroeconomic policies and strong financial systems, enhances economic welfare and prosperity in the world economy. The Committee adopted the Statement on "The Liberalization of Capital Movements Under an Amendment of the Fund's Articles," and considered that an amendment of the Fund's Articles will provide the most effective means of promoting an orderly liberalization of capital movements consistent with the Fund's role in the international monetary system. The Committee requested the Executive Board to accord high priority to completing its work and submitting a report and a proposed draft amendment to the Board of Governors

However, the Interim Committee (1997a) states that the design and implementation of policy should maintain the consistency of aggregate policy, preventing large external deficits and limiting the dependence on short-term loans while maintaining consistent macroeconomic policies. Exchange rate regimes have to be consistent with large capital flows and consistent with macroeconomic policies.

The fiftieth meeting of the Interim Committee (1998a) occurred after the famous speech by Rubin (1998) that formally began a more ambitious reform of the IFA (Peláez and Peláez 2005). There was reiteration of the proposal to amend the articles of agreement to make "the liberalization of capital movements one of the purposes of the Fund and extending as needed the Fund's jurisdiction for this purpose" (Interim Committee 1998a). However, it added the conditions of sequencing the liberalization:

> the importance of orderly and properly sequenced liberalization of capital movements, the need for appropriate macroeconomic and exchange rate policies, the critical role of sound financial sectors and effective prudential and supervisory systems

The meeting of the Interim Committee (1998b) in October 1998 occurred after the Russian crisis, the Long Term Capital Management (LTCM) episode and the Brazilian overvaluation crisis. At that meeting, the Interim Committee (1998b) warns again that:

> The opening of the capital account must be carried out in an orderly, gradual, and well sequenced manner, keeping its pace in line with the strengthening of countries' ability to sustain its consequences

At the meeting on September 26, 1999, the Interim Committee (1999) states that "persistent and sizeable capital inflows can be highly destabilizing particularly if they are intermediated by poorly regulated and unsupervised financial institutions." Open capital flows can be beneficial to the world economy but must be sequenced with special attention "to the relationship between capital account liberalization and financial sector stability."

The Managing Director of the IMF argues that the problem with the Asian crisis was not the opening of capital accounts (Camdessus 1998). According to this view, the countries that were most successful in dealing with the crisis, Hong Kong and Singapore, had the most open capital accounts. The speed of reform was not a problem either because the countries that were most affected by the crisis, Korea, Indonesia and Thailand, had different types and speeds of capital account liberalization.

Camdessus (1998) argues that the problem was the institutional and macroeconomic framework in which the countries involved in the crisis implemented the measures to open the capital account and the sequence with other reforms. The core three countries pegged the exchange rate, attracting large capital inflow; they also maintained high domestic interest rates to stimulate foreign borrowing because of lower foreign-borrowing rates caused by the expectation of an indefinitely unchanged exchange rate.

Thailand and Korea channeled foreign capital inflow through the domestic banking system (Camdessus 1998). The management of the local banks was lax and their regulation inadequate. The past record of excellent economic performance and the opaqueness of policy misled the private sector in risk estimation. There were explicit or implicit government guarantees that encouraged overlending by foreign financial institutions and overborrowing by local companies.

The Asian crisis, according to Camdessus (1998), provided important lessons. The framework of policy must be sound, in particular the consistency of monetary, fiscal and exchange-rate policy. The financial system must be strengthened with sound regulation and supervision. Capital account opening has to be sequenced with the soundness of policy and institutional development. There is need for market discipline and transparency in government policy.

Numerous economists argue that international capital flows are destabilizing. The international monetary system functioned with fixed exchange rates determined in the Bretton Woods agreement that created the IMF and the WB. The flexible exchange rate system that followed in the 1970s was criticized because of excessive variation of exchange rates. Tobin (1978, 153) pointed to a different cause:

> I believe that the basic problem today is not the exchange rate regime, whether fixed or floating. Debate on the regime evades and obscures the essential problem. That is the excessive international – or better, intercurrency – mobility of private financial capital

Tobin argued that adjustment to "massive" capital movements caused sacrifices of output, employment and inflation in implementing national economic policies. Domestic economic policies cannot prevent the adversity caused by capital movements.

The essential problem, according to Tobin (1978, 154), is that prices of capital move much less rapidly than prices of goods. This fact occurs in either fixed or flexible exchange rate regimes. Tobin (1978, 154) proposed "to throw some sand in the wheels of our excessively efficient international money markets." His specific proposal "is an internationally uniform tax on all spot conversions of one currency into another, proportional to the size of the transaction" (Tobin 1978, 155). The objective of the tax is to discourage "financial round-trip excursions into another currency" (Tobin 1978, 155).

There is the claim that the benefits of free capital movements constitute a myth of inadequate comparison with the obvious gains from trade (Bhagwati 1998a, 1999). During the Asian crisis there was a sudden reversal of capital flows with detrimental consequences. Bhagwati (1998a, 1999) recalls that capital flows are characterized by panics and manias (Kindleberger and Aliber 2005). The costs of these crises have been significant. The efficiency gains from capital mobility would have to be reconciled with losses during crises. Bhagwati (1998a, 1999) argues that Wall Street dominates Washington institutions and the US Treasury, what he calls the "Wall Street-Treasury complex." Thus, bankers contributed to the implementation of free capital flows because of self-interest without regards to the risks and losses of financial crises.

Financial markets have been characterized by repeated boom-bust cycles (Rodrik 1998). There are significant differences between financial markets and those for goods and services. Asymmetric information can result in excessive lending for projects with high risks. The intertemporal mismatch of assets and liabilities can make banks vulnerable to runs. Financial asset prices may exhibit complex behavior, such as bubbles and devaluations. Models of financial markets change after every crisis. In short, Rodrik (1998) argues that there will continue to be financial crises and that there is no set of tools to effectively resolve them. Financial markets have the risks of herding, contagion and crises. The opening of the capital account has significant risks. The liquidity that is available to borrowers in a given country increases, thus magnifying the adverse consequences of a capital reversal. In addition, the spread of the crisis from one country to others, or systemic risk, increases. Rodrik (1998) argues that there is no verification of the benefits of freeing international capital flows.

The benefits of international trading of financial assets are well established in theory (Obstfeld 1998, 10). The pooling of risks by residents of several countries is more effective as risk insurance than only the more limited domestic resources. Foreign markets provide a borrowing opportunity for countries experiencing a recession. The limitations of capital for productive projects in developing countries can be overcome with foreign capital. This is similar to the opportunity of external financing to a company as compared with only self generation of profits. The international capital markets allocate savings to their most productive opportunities, no matter where they are located. The model of Obstfeld (1994) shows that risk diversification in financial markets allows producers to engage in opportunities that have higher yield and risk (Obstfeld 1998, 10).

There is another important role of international capital markets. Unsound fiscal and monetary policies may be disciplined by international capital flows (Obstfeld 1998, 10). Examples of such policies are excessive government deficit, causing borrowing, or deficient bank regulation. These policies would trigger capital flight and higher interest rates. The consequences of capital flight are tough and known such that governments would try to avoid them by not engaging in unsound policies.

Devaluations in developing countries could have a high personal cost. A sample of 103 developing countries in the period 1971–2003 shows 188 currency crashes (Frankel 2005). The position of chief executive changed in 27 percent of those crashes within 12 months. In normal times, the chief executive changed 21 percent of the time in 12-month periods. Devaluation increases by 32 percent the probability of chief executives losing their jobs. In normal times, the chief executive loses the job in 6-month periods in 11.6 percent of the time but in 19.1 percent of the time after devaluation. The difference is statistically highly significant. The probability of the minister of finance or central bank governor losing their jobs increases by 63 percent and is highly significant. The phenomenon concentrates in middle-income countries, being low for poor countries and having no cases for rich countries.

There is a pragmatic analysis of financial openness (Aizenman 2004, 65). Effective restrictions on financial opening are eroded by trade integration. Thus, Aizenman (2004) concludes that countries that are successful in trade integration will eventually open their economies financially. He finds a highly significant relationship between changes in financial and commercial openness in developing countries and a positive association in the OECD at a lower level of significance. Aizenman is careful in alerting that the statistical results only suggest the linkages between financial and commercial openness.

The linkages between financial and commercial openness originate in its association with public finance. Financial repression could be implemented with relatively low costs of tax collection in developing countries. The effect of financial repression is to permit the financing of the government at lower interest rates than those under financial integration and to tax savings in foreign currencies. The lower interest rate resembles a tax on domestic savings motivating capital flight in pursuit of higher remuneration of savings. Capital flight is commonly processed by overinvoicing imports and underinvoicing exports. Dividend remittances and transfer prices among MNCs also process capital flight. Aizenman (2004, 67) argues that trade openness creates the volumes and mechanisms for capital flight.

The neoclassical growth model clearly implies that capital will flow from rich to poor countries in pursuit of higher marginal returns to capital in the poorer country (Lucas 1990, 92). In the neoclassical model, with homogeneous capital and labor, higher capital per worker determines that output per worker is higher in the more advanced country. Diminishing returns to capital occur at a higher range of output when the increase in production is proportionately lower than the addition of an extra unit of capital to production. If there is free trade in capital and other goods, there will be investment only in the poorer country, because of the higher return to the use of an extra unit of capital in production, until the marginal rates of return of capital and wages are equalized in both countries.

The differences in productivity of capital occur in reality but there have been limited flows of capital from rich to poor countries. Lucas (1990) seeks an explanation in relaxing the assumptions of the model. Neoclassical growth theory assumes homogeneous labor inputs. In reality there are significant differences in the quality and stock of human capital of labor between rich and poor countries. There is still a significant difference in marginal products of capital even adjusting for the differences in human capital, maintaining the paradox alive. Lucas (1990) then specifies a production function in which output per worker depends on capital per worker and human capital per worker. The variable human capital per worker is an external effect of human capital. These external effects of human capital together with the difference in the quality of the labor input explain the paradox.

Alternative explanations of the weakness of rich-to-poor capital flows consist of variations of the expropriation risk (Reinhart and Rogoff 2004). Weakness in enforcement of financial contracts would deter capital flows to developing countries in spite of the higher marginal returns of capital. Reinhart and Rogoff (2004) pursue the thesis in Reinhart *et al.* (2003) on debt intolerance (DI). They argue that political risk and credit markets constitute the main factor of the weakness of capital flows from rich to poor countries. Credit risk is extremely important: countries that do not pay their debts do not receive credit.

There is a conceptual difference between financial globalization and financial integration (Prasad *et al.* 2003, 7). Financial globalization consists of increasing global relations originating in cross-border flows. Financial integration consists of the linkages of an individual country with international capital markets. In practice what matters is the difference in *de jure*, or legal, financial integration, consisting of policies on capital account liberalization, and *de facto* financial integration, which is what actually occurs in reality. Prasad *et al.* (2003, 7) argue that, for example, many Latin American countries are *de jure* closed to external capital flows while *de facto* they are significantly open. Indicators of restrictions on capital flows capture the *de jure* aspects while measures of openness to capital flows measure the *de facto* aspects. They also distinguish between pull factors of financial integration, consisting of changes in policies, such as liberalization of capital accounts and local stock markets together with major programs of privatization. The push factors originate in the business cycle and macroeconomic policies of advanced countries. Savings, demographic changes, development of institutional investors, depositary receipts and cross listings in advanced countries have contributed to steady globalization of capital even with interruption of business cycles. In practice, pull and push factors interact.

The group of economies that are more financially integrated had faster growth rates than the group of less financially integrated economies during the past three decades. Output per capita in 1970–99 increased three times for the group of more financially integrated economies, which is about six times higher than that for less financially integrated economies (Prasad *et al.* 2003, 26). This result occurred in each of the three decades and in growth of consumption and investment. Prasad *et al.* (2003, 26) caution about the interpretation of these results. Closer inspection of the results shows fragility. There is only an observed association of financial integration and growth without verdict on causal relationship. Financial integration could simply respond to faster economic growth, instead of being its determining factor. China and India grew rapidly without financial integration, showing that it is possible to grow without liberalizing capital flows. Jordan and Peru opened their capital flows but experienced declines, showing that it is possible to liberalize without growing. Prasad *et al.* (2003, 31) considered 14 empirical studies on the relation between financial integration and economic growth in developing economies. Although three essays find a positive association, most studies find either no effect or a mixed one. They conclude that if there is a relation it is not very strong.

It is convenient to separately consider the effects of financial integration on output and consumption to assess the impact of financial integration on macroeconomic volatility (Prasad *et al.* 2003, 38). There is an avenue for greater volatility. Increased capital flows may finance specialization in economic activities that may be subject to cyclical fluctuation because of the characteristics and linkages of those industries. Prasad *et al.* (2003) provide new evidence showing that opening can smooth fluctuations in consumption, which can result in significant gains for developing countries.

Macroeconomic stability provides the environment for benefits from financial integration (Prasad and Rajan 2005). Fiscal discipline and flexible exchange rates facilitate the possible stabilization and growth benefits of financial integration. The IMF had warned about moral hazard and excessive debt in emerging countries before criticism developed (Prasad and Rogoff 2003). The Fund also criticized fixed exchange rates without sound domestic policies during increases in capital flows. There is moral hazard in encouraging countries by high domestic interest rates or moral suasion of monetary authorities to borrow abroad at interest rates that are lower if there is an expectation of no future devaluation because the government would prevent it. Evidently, there is no causality of financial integration to macroeconomic stability but rather of unsound domestic policies to financial crisis. There was an element of this type of moral hazard in the crises in Mexico, Asia, Brazil, Russia and Argentina.

With the advantage of more research, Kose *et al.* (2006) reconsider the effects of financial integration. There is a stronger relationship between financial integration and economic growth when *de facto* integration is used but there is no evidence of a robust relationship between financial integration and growth. There are numerous theoretical and other types of claims that financial globalization was the cause of the emerging market crises in the past three decades but no empirical evidence to support those claims.

The traditional view proposed that financial globalization improves the allocation of capital and international risk-sharing, smoothing consumption volatility and increasing the rate of GDP growth. Kose *et al.* (2006) suggest a more complex view. Financial globalization has traditional effects. However, it influences and is influenced by "potential collateral benefits," including the development of the financial market, institutions, governance and macroeconomic discipline. The interaction of the traditional and the side effects increases GDP growth and total factor productivity (TFP), reducing the volatility of consumption. The catalyst role of these side benefits could have stronger impact on GDP growth, technological progress and reduction of consumption volatility.

The approach of Kose *et al.* (2006) emphasizes the importance of threshold effects in determining the macroeconomic consequences of financial globalization. The threshold conditions are financial market development, quality of institutions, governance, sound macro policies and trade integration. Countries engaging in financial globalization at or above the threshold conditions experience acceleration of growth, increases in TFP and lower vulnerability to crises. Countries with conditions below the thresholds may be more vulnerable to crisis and could not have the gains of growth and improved TPF. If a country has the threshold conditions, financial globalization may be a catalyst of progress. Countries that do not meet the conditions may not reap the gains and could be more vulnerable to SS of capital flows.

There are numerous difficulties in measuring the impact of financial integration on economic growth (Block and Forbes 2004, 3–6). It is difficult to find an accurate measure of capital account openness, because of *de jure* and *de facto* conflicts. The benefits of various types of capital flows – FDI, equities and debt – may be different. The threshold analysis illustrates the existence and interaction with various other factors. Microeconomic research is just beginning to find improved evidence on the benefits of freer capital flows.

Neoclassical theory postulates that capital flows from wealthier to poorer regions in pursuit of higher marginal returns to capital. There is a paradox in that capital tends to flow from the poorer to the wealthier countries and among the wealthier countries (Block and Forbes 2004, 10–12). In fact, the United States absorbs more than two-thirds of world financial savings (Peláez and Peláez 2007). Block and Forbes (2004, 10) argue that in 1865–1914 about two-thirds of world capital exports moved from wealthier European countries to poorer countries. In addition, there have been significant flows of FDI to several countries such as China, Mexico and Brazil. The reality of the weakness of capital flows to some countries is more complex, being a mixture of the lack of credit-contract enforcement and past defaults.

Alleged financial crises, such as that of Asia in 1997–8, constitute a major case against capital integration. Block and Forbes (2004, 13) argue that domestic policies, vulnerabilities and macroeconomic imbalances are more important factors of financial crises than opening of the capital account. The necessity of the argument is contradicted by profound crises in countries with strict capital controls such as the debt crisis in Latin America in the 1980s, India in 1991 and China in 1994. Capital controls erode after some time as shown by the collapse of the Bretton Woods system in the 1970s. The empirical evidence is dubious, with greater likelihood of crises in countries with capital controls. In fact, a vulnerable country is likely to implement capital controls. The supposed stability of capital controls could occur with a cost in the form of stagnation.

World capital flows increased rapidly in the past quarter of a century while IMF resources have not accompanied this growth. Another criticism of the present system centers on the capacity of the IMF to resolve crises. The measurement of the effectiveness of IMF resources is difficult but they may not be sufficient under extreme conditions (Block and Forbes 2004, 15). The relation of world capital flows to IMF resources may not be appropriate to measure the effectiveness of the IMF. A major share of world capital flows consists of equity financing and private debt flows that the Fund would not be able to support. The payments for debt service of developing countries may be a more reliable indicator of the needs for funds of the IMF (Block and Forbes 2004, 15) and there has not been much change since the mid-1990s.

An important policy issue at the time is how to deal with the capital account liberalization of countries in Asia that peg their exchange rate to the dollar. There are serious internal monetary problems in the form of the sterilization of the inflow of reserves. China is the more evident case. The monetary authorities withdraw the foreign exchange with the issue of currency that ends mostly in commercial banks, which invest it in government securities. Monetary policy becomes ineffective in the control of inflation. Prasad and Rajan (2005) propose the creation of a closed-end mutual fund. This fund would issue shares in local currency, using the money to buy foreign exchange that it would invest abroad. Domestic investors would have an opportunity to diversify their investments abroad and local financial markets would be stimulated. The central bank would have control on the timing and quantity of outflows. General economic policy could concentrate on domestic issues.

The report of the IMF Independent Evaluation Office (2005, 57) concluded that the Articles of Agreement were ambiguous about the involvement of the Fund in the issues related to the capital accounts of members. The rise in cross-border flows in the 1980s and early 1990s caused an increase in the involvement of the IMF in the capital account issue. The staff advocated capital account liberalization in internal documents. The issue was included as part of Article IV consultations, creating a vehicle by which the IMF could influence the opening of the capital account.

The focus of the IMF on capital account opening changed toward risk factors in the second half of the 1990s as reported by the IMF Independent Evaluation Office (2005, 57, International Monetary Fund (2004)). The emphasis shifted toward understanding the relation between policies of industrial countries and world capital flows, searching for the factors of crises. The policy analysis concentrated on what countries should do to deal with the volatility of capital flows, including macroeconomic and exchange rate policy, sounder financial systems and fuller transparency. The exchange rate regime became an important issue in the reduction of moral hazard in excessive lending by international institutions and borrowing by local companies. The IMF Independent Evaluation Office (2005, 57) exempted the Fund:

> From the beginning of the 1990s, the IMF's management, staff and Executive Board were aware of the potential risks of premature capital account liberalization and there is no evidence to suggest that they promoted capital account liberalization indiscriminately. They also acknowledged the need for a sound financial system in order to minimize the risks of liberalization and maximize its benefits

The policy suggestions of sequencing of capital account opening and reforms did not leave the design stage until the latter part of the 1990s. The proposal to reform the Articles of Agreement did not obtain sufficient support after the crises in Asia, Russia, LTCM and Brazil. The consensus that emerged was for an integrated approach (International Monetary Fund 2004, 6), in which capital account liberalization is part of "a comprehensive program of economic reforms in the macroeconomic policy framework, the domestic financial system and prudential regulations" (IMF Independent Evaluation Office 2005, 58). The integrated approach has not made progress because the complexity of the sequencing prevents the specification of a proper hierarchy of risks. In addition, the approach is unofficial because it has not yet received endorsement by the Executive Board.

It is a fact that the IMF encouraged capital account liberalization in its country work during the 1990s. The policy packages presented by countries to the IMF included capital account liberalization as formal conditionality. However, the IMF Independent Evaluation Office (2005, 58) finds that in countries that liberalized fully or partially, "the process was for the most part driven by the country authorities' own economic and political agendas." After the Asian crisis, the IMF staff was more cautious, providing a pragmatic approach, especially because the ambiguity of the IMF role in the capital account continued. There were no official guidelines on the issue.

There is no evidence that the IMF followed a dogmatic approach unique to the institution or to a school of thought in economics. The IMF Independent Evaluation Office (2005, 58) finds that:

> The staff's policy advice on managing capital flows did not deviate much from the policy conclusions typically derived from the scholarly literature on open economy macroeconomics. To deal with large capital inflows, it advocated tightening fiscal policy and greater exchange rate flexibility

Financial crises

There are differences in the objections to free flows of capital. Many economists argue that there are benefits in long-term investment, such as FDI, FSFDI and portfolio investment of a long-term nature in equities. The major differences in opinion originate in short-term capital movements. There is another problem here. Trade integration requires trade finance, otherwise trade will be restricted. It is a fact that short-term lines of trade finance were highly volatile in Korea and in Brazil during crises. These lines are mostly less than a year in term and provided by international banks to their subsidiaries or to local banks. Because trade finance matures in a few months, banks do not renew them and do not provide new credit when there are adverse events affecting credit risk. Deducting FDI and trade finance from capital flows there is hardly anything left except for investments in fixed-income and stock markets.

The main objection to free flows of capital is that they cause financial crises when there is a sudden reversal in the flows. In the Richard T. Ely lecture, Summers (2000, 1) summarized the dramatic experience with the crises of the 1990s:

> Hundreds of millions of people who expected rapidly rising standards of living have seen their living standards fall; hundreds of thousands if not millions of children have forced to drop out of school and go to work; hundreds of billions of dollars of apparent wealth has been lost; the stability of large nations has been called into question; and the United States has made its largest nonmilitary foreign-policy-related financial commitments since the Marshall Plan

Table 3.5 shows economic indicators for Thailand, Korea and Indonesia during the Asian Crisis. There was a dramatic reversal from high growth rates in 1996 to sharp declines in 1997–8. There were equally dramatic reductions in the CAD and in the fiscal balances. Mishkin (1999, 3) summarized the experience:

> In Mexico, GDP growth fell from above 4 percent in 1994 before the crisis to −6 percent in 1995. In Thailand, Malaysia, South Korea and Indonesia, GDP growth fell from above 5 percent in 1996 before the crisis to below −5 percent in 1998. These swings of over 10 percent in rates of GDP growth are of the same order of magnitude as what occurred in the United States during the Great Depression

Table 3.A as an appendix to Table 3.5 provides economic indicators for a group of countries involved in the crises. All countries had CADs, which is what would be expected in emerging countries. The swings from growth to contraction were quite high, on the order of 10 percent or more. There are extremes in this adversity in the crises in Russia and Argentina. Russia's economy declined throughout the 1990s with extremely high rates of inflation. There were contractions of GDP of 14.5 percent in 1992 and 12.7 percent in 1994. Argentina suffered a contraction

Table 3.5 Thailand, Korea and Indonesia, indicators during the Asian crisis

	1996			1997			1998		
	Thai	**Korea**	**Indonesia**	**Thai**	**Korea**	**Indonesia**	**Thai**	**Korea**	**Indonesia**
Percent									
GDP growth	5.9	7.1	8.2	−1.7	5.5	1.9	−10.2	−6.7	−14.2
Consumer prices	5.9	4.9	5.7	5.6	6.6	12.9	8.1	4.0	64.7
Percent of GDP									
Fiscal balance	1.9	0.0	1.2	−0.9	−1.7	−1.1	−2.4	−4.4	−2.2
Current account	−6.0	−4.4	3.4	−7.9	−1.7	−0.9	−2.0	12.7	4.4
External debt	−31.6	54.5	−	33.2	163.3	−	46.9	129.0	
Billion dollars									
External debt	90.5	164.4	127.4	93.4	158.1	135.0	86.2	148.7	149.9

Note: Thai is Thailand.
Source: International Monetary Fund Staff (2000).

Table 3.A Countries in financial crisis

	GDP % Growth	Current account % GDP	Inflation %
Mexico			
1990	5.1	−2.8	27.7
1991	3.6	−6.7	15.5
1992	4.2	−4.7	22.7
1993	2	−5.8	9.8
1994	4.4	−7	7
1995	−6.2	−0.6	35
1996	5.2	−0.8	24.4
1997	6.8	−1.9	20.6
1998	5	−3.8	15.9
1999	3.8	−2.9	16.6
2000	6.6	−3.2	9.5
2001	0	−2.8	6.4
2002	0.8	−2.1	5
2003	1.4	−1.4	4.5
2004	4.2	−1	4.7
2005	3	−0.6	4
2006	4	−0.1	3.5
2007	3.5	−0.2	3.2

Table 3.A   (Continued)

	GDP % Growth	Current account % GDP	Inflation %
S Korea			
1991	9.4	−2.7	9.3
1992	5.9	−1.2	6.2
1993	6.1	0.2	4.8
1994	8.5	−1	6.3
1995	9.2	−1.7	4.5
1996	7	−4.1	4.9
1997	4.7	−1.6	4.4
1998	−6.9	11.7	7.5
1999	9.5	5.5	0.8
2000	8.5	2.4	2.3
2001	3.8	1.7	4.1
2002	7	1	2.7
2003	3.1	2	3.6
2004	4.7	4.1	3.6
2005	4	2.1	2.7
2006	5	0.4	2.5
2007	4.3	0.3	2.7
Russia			
1990	−3		5.6
1991	−5		92.6
1992	−14.5	−1.4	1345.1
1993	−8.7	1.4	878.8
1994	−12.7	2.8	307.5
1995	−4.1	2.2	198
1996	−3.6	2.8	47.7
1997	1.4	0	14.8
1998	−5.3	0.1	27.7
1999	6.4	12.6	85.7
2000	10	18	20.8
2001	5.1	11.1	21.5
2002	4.7	8.4	15.8
2003	7.3	8.2	13.7
2004	7.2	9.9	10.9
2005	6.4	19.9	12.6
2006	6.5	12.3	9.7
2007	6.5	10.7	8.5
Argentina			
1993	6.3	−3.4	10.4
1994	5.8	−4.2	4.2
1995	−2.8	−2	3.4
1996	5.5	−2.5	0.2
1997	8.1	−4.1	0.5
1998	3.9	−4.8	0.9
1999	−3.4	−4.2	−1.2
2000	−0.8	−3.2	−0.9
2001	−4.4	−1.2	−1.1
2002	−10.9	8.9	25.9

2003	8.8	6.3	13.4
2004	9	2.2	4.4
2005	9.2	1.9	9.6
2006	8	1	12.3
2007	6	0.6	11.4
Brazil			
1990	−4.2	−0.8	2947
1991	1	−0.3	477
1992	−0.5	1.6	1022
1993	4.9	−0.1	1927
1994	5.9	−0.3	2076
1995	4.2	−2.6	66
1996	2.7	3	16
1997	3.3	−3.8	6.9
1998	0.1	−4.2	3.2
1999	0.8	−4.7	4.9
2000	4.4	−4	7.1
2001	1.3	−4.5	6.8
2002	1.9	−1.7	8.4
2003	0.5	0.8	14.8
2004	4.9	1.9	6.6
2005	2.3	1.8	6.9
2006	3.6	0.6	4.5
2007	4	0.4	4.1

Source: International Monetary Fund, World Economic Outlook Database, September 2006.

of 10.9 percent in 2002. The problem in attributing the crises to capital account liberalization is the elusive verification of causality in economics. The counterfactual experiment of performance without capital liberalization is quite difficult to specify and test.

The concept, analysis and empirical evidence of twin crises constitute a foundation of the interpretation of emerging market crises. A sample of 76 currency crises and 26 banking crises plus the Asian crisis out of sample shows that there were 18 twin crises of the domestic financial sector and the balance of payments in 1980–95 and one in 1970–9 (Kaminsky and Reinhart 1999, 474, 477). The occurrence of financial market and currency crises began in the 1980s after the liberalization of domestic markets. The analysis of Kaminsky and Reinhart (1999) suggests that the problems in domestic banking occur before those of the balance of payments. Subsequently, the currency collapse augments the problems of the domestic financial system, "activating a vicious spiral" (Kaminsky and Reinhart 1999, 474). The critical aspect of twin crises is that output and employment effects of a currency crash can be magnified by domestic financial crises.

Banking crises commonly precede currency crashes and then there is reverse causality. Kaminsky and Reinhart (1999) emphasize that what is truly important is the common causes of the internal financial and external currency crises. There is abnormally low economic growth or recession before both types of crises partly caused by deterioration of the terms of trade, overvaluation of the exchange rate and increasing cost of credit, with exports significantly declining. Unhedged liabilities of banks magnify the vulnerability of the financial system. There are few crises in which the fundamentals are sound. Twin crises are characterized by weak fundamentals, economic fragility and extremely severe real effects.

It is not feasible to provide a survey of the immense literature on financial crises. The only possibility here is to outline some important forms of economic analysis of the crises. The common characteristics of the six emerging-country crises of the 1990s were a significant variation of the CA, major real depreciation and significant decrease in real output (Summers 2000, 5). There were three common types of behavior in the six crises analyzed by Summers (2000, 5):

- *Reduction of the stock of assets by investors in response to worsening fundamentals.* There were individual types of weakening fundamentals but doubts on the sustainability of the exchange regime in relation to macroeconomic policies were common in all crises.
- *Evaluation by investors of behavior of other investors.* After the earlier first phase, there was a point when decisions by investors began to be made on what other investors were doing, creating a run for the last available dollars to exit.
- *Adverse interaction of devaluation, fundamentals and financial-market response.* Devaluation reduced real income and spending; expectations of further devaluation caused further capital flight; deterioration of dollar-adjusted financial assets reduced the creditworthiness of domestic financial institutions and their borrowers; lending and fundamentals worsened further.

The essence of the approach of Summers (2000) is that it is not possible to explain capital withdrawal without an explanation of weakening fundamentals. The large discontinuities, or jumps, in capital flows require an appeal to a change in expectations leading to runs. The major impacts on domestic output and employment and the lack of response of exports to depreciation require an explanation in terms of the strains to domestic financial systems. It is difficult to find an emerging market crisis without the weakness of fundamentals challenging the sustainability of inadequate policies. The key lesson is the need to strengthen core institutions and fundamentals.

The expectation of failure of a bank causes a run by depositors to withdraw their deposits. This sudden and large withdrawal may force the bank to liquidate a major portion of its assets. Depositors in other banks may also run to withdraw their deposits. The financial system experiences a banking panic with breakdown of its functions, contracting output and employment. The celebrated model of Diamond and Dybvig (1983) departs from the financial engineering function of banks allowing them to convert illiquid bank assets into liquid demand deposits. Different levels of confidence on banks cause multiple equilibriums, leaving banks vulnerable to runs.

Banks improve on competitive markets by providing financial contracts permitting risk-sharing by agents that consume at different time periods (Diamond and Dybvig 1983). The demand deposit contract of banks is the instrument of this risk-sharing and transformation of illiquid assets into liquid deposits. This demand deposit contract may have a bank run as an undesirable equilibrium. In such equilibrium, depositors rapidly withdraw their funds, including those that would have left them in the bank if the panic mood did not prevail. Even sound banks can fail during a banking panic. The frustration of external finance, with recall of loans and erosion of the risk-sharing among depositors, may reach extremes that cause termination of investment and profound effects on output and employment. A shift of expectations by the public may occur as a result of many factors but the common effect is the erosion in the confidence of the banks that leads to immediate withdrawal of deposits or a bank run. Runs on essentially sound banks can probably be explained only on the basis of irrational behavior. Competitive markets alone could not provide the liquidity insurance of bank deposits that could permit them to avert a run.

Governments bail out banks from difficulties by insuring their liabilities or by replenishing their capital. The issue of whether to bail out and what to bail out is the most difficult in safety nets of banks within national financial systems or of countries in the international financial system. There are costs of bailing out banks in the form of erosion of the long-term incentives for sound management. The short-term benefits consist of the prevention of adverse effects on real economic variables, output and employment. Diamond and Rajan (2002) analyze the changes in available aggregate liquidity in the economy caused by bank bailouts. The benefit is that a carefully structured bailout can avert the collapse of a banking system through systemic risk, having adverse real effects.

However, Diamond and Rajan (2002) argue that a poorly structured bank bailout can throw a banking system into a systemic crisis. The choice of the banks that are being bailed out can either increase or decrease aggregate liquidity. The government may start with those banks that have greater fragility and illiquidity. If the bailouts of these banks lead to an increasing number of bailouts, the resources of the government and its credibility may be exhausted. If excess demand for liquidity increases as a result of bailouts, more insolvency of banks occurs, causing spread of contagion through common sources of liquidity. The entire financial system may break down. The decision to bail out insolvent banks poses difficult choices as to whether a crisis may be averted or provoked.

Asymmetry of information occurs in loan markets when lenders have less information on the actual economic and financial situation of their borrowers than the borrowers themselves. As a result of this imperfect information lenders may choose borrowers that are willing to pay higher interest rates but have the worst economic and financial situation, a distortion known as adverse selection. In fear of lending to borrowers that may default, lenders may reduce the amount of lending such that projects that could contribute to efficient allocation of resources do not receive financing. Borrowers may take higher risks after they receive the funds than those of the original project for which they requested financing. If the risky activity is successful, the borrower appropriates high profits; if it is unsuccessful, the lender bears the cost. The existence of adverse selection and moral hazard because of imperfect information prevents efficient allocation by the free market. Mishkin (1999, 6) uses imperfect information in financial markets to define financial instability:

> Financial instability occurs when shocks to the financial system interfere with information flows so that the financial system can no longer do its job of channeling funds to those with productive investment opportunities

Banks perform important functions of monitoring, control and allocation of resources. Shocks to the financial system may worsen adverse selection and moral hazard, preventing banks from performing their functions. The breakdown of banking intermediation can have adverse effects on real economic activity, output and employment. Mishkin (1999, 6–8) identifies four factors of increases in asymmetry of information, contributing to financial instability:

1. *Deterioration of balance sheets of financial institutions.* Banks experience reduction of their capital and may reduce lending. Information asymmetry can result in withdrawal of deposits from banks, as depositors do not know their actual situation, which could cause a run on a bank that can spread to other institutions. Output losses in banking panics can be very high.
2. *Rise in interest rates.* Asymmetry of information can result in credit rationing when interest rates increase (Stiglitz and Greenwald 2003, 27, Stiglitz and Weiss 1981). Banks are typically short funded, that is, they borrow from depositors at lower interest rates for short terms and lend at higher interest rates for long terms. The balance sheets of financial institutions are typically sensitive to rises in interest rates. Interest rate increases combine the problem of asymmetry of information with deterioration of balance sheets, resulting in less lending and deterioration of real economic activity.
3. *Shocks of uncertainty.* Banks transform illiquid assets, loans, into liquid assets, demand deposits. Uncertainty can originate in many factors, such as government policy, a recession, a war and so on. The reaction of banks to uncertainty is to reduce exposures to risk, reducing loans, which can have effects on real economic activity.
4. *Deterioration of non-financial sector balance sheets.* The deterioration of the balance sheets of bank borrowers has a direct impact on the quality of the loans. It has a secondary impact in increasing adverse selection and moral hazard, with resulting reduction in loans by banks.

Financial reversals and the modified private interest view

Endogenous growth theories have incorporated various types of accumulation of knowledge – education, on-the-job training, scientific research, learning by doing and process and product innovations. An important source of knowledge accumulation consists of improvements in the quality of products by industrial innovations (Aghion and Howitt 1992, 323). Schumpeter (1942) proposed that change in capitalism originated from within by constantly creating a new structure with new goods, techniques of production and new markets that effectively destroyed the older one. Aghion and Howitt (1992) model economic growth with Schumpeter's concept of creative destruction: progress causes losses and gains because new products make older ones obsolete. The drivers of capitalism are product, technical and organizational innovations. Producers of the new products may enjoy new rents temporarily but destroy the rents of incumbent producers. Success of capitalism depends on maintaining the innovation driver active by exploiting the benefits of competition. Rajan and Zingales (2003a–b) have made an important contribution by analyzing the political economy of financial development in terms of a modified private interest view. The balance of this section focuses on the model of Rajan and Zingales.

Developed countries had a higher level of financial development in 1913 than in 1980 (Rajan and Zingales 2003b, 6). These countries only attained in the 1990s the levels of financial development of 1913. It is difficult to explain this variation over time. Structural theories explaining differences in financial development in terms of type of law (La Porta *et al.* 1997, 1998) are not sufficient. Rajan and Zingales (2003b, 6) argue that institutional factors should be time invariant. There is the same result when comparing countries over time. The stock market capitalizations of France and the United States as percent of GDP show the following behavior in the twentieth century:

Period	France	United States
1913	0.78	0.39
1980	0.09	0.46
1999	1.17	1.52

The indicators of financial development show declines for all countries after the Great Depression of 1929, recovering only after the 1980s. The economies of the advanced countries recovered from the Great Depression and World War II in about two decades. The objective of Rajan and Zingales (2003b) is to identify the factors of these reversals of financial development over time and across countries.

The structural theories have provided important insight but more is needed. A new variable factor is required to explain time and cross-sectional differences in financial development (Rajan and Zingales 2003b, 7). This new variable is the relative strength of political interests favoring financial development. There can be high benefits in financial development. The theoretical task is to identify the interests against financial development. The capitalists already established in finance, the incumbents, can oppose financial development because it introduces competition in financial markets. This competition reduces rents of incumbents in these markets.

Financial development will make progress with less opposition when countries are open to both trade and capital flows (Rajan and Zingales 2003b, 7–8). There is a political decision on opening a country to trade and capital flows. An important explanation is why some countries open to trade and capital flows. There may not be a choice. For example, a country may be too small to close capital flows. Trade opening can result in the erosion of controls by means of underinvoicing, over-invoicing, dividend remittances, transfer pricing and so on. The profitability of groups gaining from open cross-border flows may strengthen them versus those opposing openness as in Becker (1983).

There is the more difficult issue of identifying causality (Rajan and Zingales 2003b, 8). There is higher international capital mobility in the beginning and the end of the twentieth century. Rajan and Zingales (2003b) find positive correlation between financial development and the exogenous part of the openness of a country to trade in the beginning and the end of the twentieth century. In the intermediate period between the beginning and end of the century there is no association. They conclude that the combination of open products and financial markets is required to overcome the opposition of incumbents to financial development because of the low international mobility of capital.

The modified private interest view of financial development of Rajan and Zingales (2003a–b) can be analyzed by means of Table 3.6. They depart from the

Table 3.6 The modified private interest view of Rajan and Zingales

Incumbent interest group	Power	Use of power

Industrialists	• Rents	• Financial repression
		  o Directed lending
		  o Asset restrictions
		  o Interest rate controls

	• Related borrowing
	• Collateral
	• Political power
	  o Ease of organization
	• Alliances with:
	  o Labor
	  o Nationalists
	  o Unemployed
		• Restriction of entry
		• Subsidies
		• Protectionism

Financiers	• Information asymmetry	• Financial repression
		  o Fixed spreads in guaranteed loans
		  o Allocation of subsidized credit
		  o Assured bailouts and recapitalization
		  o Certain profits in financing the government

	• Rents • Political power o Ease of organization • Alliances	

Source: Rajan and Zingales (2003b).

proposition that financing risky innovations is the essential driver of efficiency and economic growth. The environment for innovation requires competitive markets. The political economy of financial development reveals the importance of competition.

There are two powerful groups of incumbents, industrialists and financiers (Rajan and Zingales 2003b). The industrialists enjoy rents from protected production of goods. Their companies are typically enterprises that are inherited and controlled by families. The industrialists do not have need for external finance because of their high internal profits or need simple forms of external finance. They may even appropriate the rents of innovations in other products because they constitute the only alternative for implementing projects. Incumbents benefit from financial repression in the form of directed lending to their activities, asset restrictions on banks and interest rate controls. Incumbents have collateral required in markets with relationship lending. They may even receive lending at subsidized interest rates, with the excuse that the activities promote national interest. Although they may influence regulation to prevent entry, financial repression is a less obvious and more attractive form of maintaining market power. To maintain the internal market captive, incumbents influence authorities to implement protectionist measures. Incumbents can organize effectively because they are small in numbers and have large financial resources (Olson 1965, Stigler 1971). Their political power is enhanced by the ability to successfully organize alliances based on mutual economic and political interests with labor unions, nationalists and the unemployed.

The second major incumbent group is composed of financiers (Rajan and Zingales 2003b). They enjoy significant benefits from asymmetry of information, being the only ones that know debtors through relationship lending. Incumbent financiers enjoy many benefits from financial repression. There are special returns with low risk in directed lending in the form of fixed spreads in government-guaranteed loans. There are lines of subsidized credit allocated through banks in many countries that have attractive returns. Funding financial needs of the government is another field of adequate returns with low risk. There are implicit guarantees of bailout of incumbent financiers, including generous recapitalization, with the excuse of preventing systemic crises. Incumbent financiers also enjoy the possibility of successful organization because of their limited numbers and financial strength. They also form various types of alliances but less successfully than industrialists because of the allegations that finance does not contribute directly to production.

The argument of Rajan and Zingales (2003a–b) is that trade liberalization or financial liberalization do not break the power of incumbents. The joint implementation of trade and financial liberalization is required to open markets to competition. If there is trade liberalization without free cross-border capital flows, incumbents will prevent financial development. The entry of foreign competitors may drive rents, creating the need for external finance. Instead of financial development, incumbents will influence more financial repression, subsidies and protectionism, with the interests of industrialists and financiers coinciding in preventing reduction of their rents. The financial system may not change. If there are free capital flows, incumbents will also prevent financial development. The existence of rents in domestic production is not altered because there is no competition in the goods markets. Asymmetry of information will ensure that only the large domestic incumbent producers can have access to foreign capital markets. Financiers may conflict with industrialists that would desire to prevent financial development, which could finance competitors and challenge their rents.

The interest group conflict is only solved in favor of financial development if there is liberalization of both trade and cross-border capital flows (Rajan and Zingales 2003b). The industrialists will have their rents challenged and require alternative forms of financing. The government's role in directing credit will erode with the alternative of foreign capital financing. Relationship banking will diminish with the new methods of credit risk evaluation and risk management used in FSFDI. Shocks of innovation will change incumbents of both types.

Rajan and Zingales (2003d) intend to provide a blend of approaches:

> The novelty in our approach is to ask how the government can be made to set rules in the interests of the people when it is so often captured by private interests. Our proposals in the book recognize that politics and economics cannot be kept separate in modern democracies (there is a reason why the field was once called political economy), and that some forms of intervention may be necessary in the greater interest of keeping the market free

There are four ingredients of an effective financial system, according to Rajan and Zingales (2003b, 18). Property rights must be defined and respected. The accounting and disclosure system must promote transparency and the resources for private monitoring. The legal system must enforce contracts effectively and with reasonable cost. The regulatory structure must be market supporting instead of market suppressing. Regulation must protect consumers, promote competition and control excessive risks. Development of institutions plays a role in preventing interests to shape policies for their self interest. Rajan and Zingales (2003b, 45) also propose a safety net to rescue individuals from extreme economic adversity (Rajan and Zingales 2003c, 139).

Summary

The benefits of financial globalization are open to significant debate among economists. The virtues of free financial markets are questioned by the claims of imperfect information that results in adverse selection and moral hazard. Economists that propose liberalizing trade oppose free capital flows. There is a valid question if the *de jure* controls are actually circumvented by *de facto* freer capital flows. Markets have experienced crises with significant losses of output and employment. The profession has developed imaginative models of how the crisis starts and propagates with various proposals of policies to prevent the crises and resolve those that occur. There is not yet a generally accepted model explaining the crises.

IFIs and many economists propose regulatory institutions that should precede liberalization of financial markets and capital flows. These reforms are not intended as a substitute of sound fiscal and monetary policy, in particular the sustainability of policy in regards to the exchange rate regime. The modified private interest view of finance casts a doubt on the feasibility of financial development by opening trade without free cross-border flows of capital.

4
International Economic Law

Introduction

The efforts by the G7 and the IFIs to promote convergence of standards and codes can be characterized as the provision of a GPG. There are numerous advantages of this so-called soft law process in terms of negotiation and the process of creation and implementation of the standards.

The paramount standard is the framework of capital requirements of Basel II. There are differences in the implementation of Basel II in the United States and in Europe that may affect the competitiveness of international banking. The last three sections focus on regulation of securities markets, the Sarbanes-Oxley Act of 2002 (SOX) and the highly debated issue of US competitiveness in capital markets.

Soft law, standards and codes

The emerging market crises of the 1990s, especially the crisis in Asia in 1997–8, motivated the Group of Seven (G7) to implement international standards and codes through the IFIs. The standards and codes constitute soft law, that is, they are not binding. However, Article IV surveillance by the IMF includes the compliance with these standards in the process of country evaluations by the IMF and the WB. A rationale for the international standards is that they increase the transparency of countries, contributing to maintaining capital flows and avoiding crises. Disclosure is essential for investors to commit funds to countries. This disclosure is also essential for the process of catalytic financing of the IMF. The material below provides the origins, standards, codes and the process of the IMF and WB. This process is also considered a GPG. There are advantages in adopting and implementing soft law because of less complex and conflicting negotiation.

Standards and codes

The main theme of the 1998 Birmingham meeting of the G7 (1998) was "Strengthening the Architecture of the Global Financial System." The phrase had become famous after a speech of US Treasury Secretary Rubin (1998) at the Brookings Institution, one month before the G7 meeting:

> Second, we need to fill a gap in today's international architecture to provide for international surveillance of countries' financial regulatory and supervisory systems, just as the IMF now carries out surveillance of macroeconomic policies. There are a number of different ways that this could be done – perhaps through a joint initiative with the IMF and the World Bank, with the use of existing expertise of regulators. But it is critically important to find an appropriate way to fill this gap … We should consider examining other incentives that could be brought to bear for strengthening financial systems. For example, authorities in major financial centers could consider conditioning access to their markets by banks from other countries on a strong home country supervisory regime, as demonstrated by adherence to the Basle Core Principles, plus whatever relevant additional standards are developed

The failure of financial regulation, supervision and transparency in the five countries involved in the Asian crisis of 1997–8 (South Korea, Thailand, Malaysia, Indonesia and the Philippines) motivated finance ministers and central bankers of the G7 to transplant financial standards and codes of the advanced countries to emerging market countries.

The G7 yearly meetings gave impulse to the view that deepening twin exchange and domestic financial crises could originate partly in deficiencies in internal financial institutions in emerging countries (Peláez and Peláez 2005). In a relatively short period, various institutions generated core principles for strengthening standards and codes with corresponding methodology for evaluation.

Table 4.1 shows the major institutions that are active in strengthening financial systems. The BCBS (BIS 2001Mar) contributed the Capital Accord or Basel I, the Amendment to include market risk and the New Capital Accord or Basel II, in process of implementation, the Basel Core Principles of Banking Supervision (BCP) and the corresponding Methodology and their revisions after Basel II. Extensive consultations with specialists and supervisors in multiple countries contribute to generating guidelines. The principles remain at a general level to obtain consensus that would lead to implementation by many countries. Regulators issue the principles with complementary methodology, instructing how to evaluate them in practice.

International institutions of insurance and securities issued standards, codes and their respective methodologies. The Joint Forum extended the work to financial conglomerates, compiled standards and codes and compared them for three groups – banks, insurance companies and securities companies. The Committee on Payment and Settlement Systems (CPSS) issued core principles of systemically important systems and recommendations for settlement of securities systems, jointly with the International Organization of Securities Commissions (IOSCO).

The IMF initiated the process of standardizing and disseminating data, standards for transparency in fiscal, monetary and financial policy and criteria for the

116

Table 4.1 Institutions of strengthening financial standards and codes

---

Basel Committee on Banking Supervision (BCBS)
  ·Capital Accord (1988)
  http://www.bis.org/publ/bcbs04a.htm
  ·Amendment of Capital Accord to Incorporate Market Risks (1996)
  http://www.bis.org/publ/bcbs24.pdf
  ·New Capital Accord (2004)
  http://www.bis.org/publ/bcbs107.htm
  ·Basel II: International Convergence of Capital Measurements and Capital
    Standards: A Revised Framework (2005)
  http://www.bis.org/publ/bcbs118.htm
  ·Basel II: International Convergence of Capital Measurement and Capital
    Standards: A Revised Framework – Comprehensive Version (2006)
  http://www.bis.org/publ/bcbs128.htm
  ·Core Principles for Effective Banking Supervision (BCP) (1999)
  http://www.bis.org/publ/bcbs61.htm
  ·Methodology of Core Principles (1999)
  http://www.bis.org/publ/bcbs61.htm#pgtop
  ·Core Principles for Effective Banking Supervision (BCP) (2006)
  http://www.bis.org/publ/bcbs129.htm
  ·Core Principles Methodology (2006)
  http://www.bis.org/publ/bcbs130.htm
  ·Principles for the Management and Supervision of Interest Rate Risk (2004)
  http://www.bis.org/publ/bcbs108.pdf

International Organization of Insurance Supervisors (IAIS)
  ·Insurance Principles, Standards and Guidance (2003)
  http://www.iaisweb.org/358compilation_documentwithrevisionp53.pdf
  ·Insurance Core Principles and Methodology (2003, 2007)
  http://www.iaisweb.org/index.cfm?pageID=39

International Organization of Securities Commissions (IOSCO)
  ·Objectives and Principles of Securities Regulation (2003)
  http://www.iosco.org/pubdocs/pdf/IOSCOPD154.pdf
  ·Methodology for Assessing Implementation of the IOSCO Objectives and
    Principles of Securities Regulation (2003)
  http://www.iosco.org/library/pubdocs/pdf/IOSCOPD155.pdf
  ·First Public Report of the Public Interest Oversight Board (2006)
  http://www.bis.org/publ/bcbspiob01.htm

Committee on Payment and Settlement Systems (CPSS)
  · Core Principles for Systemically Important Payments Systems (2001)
  http://www.bis.org/publ/cpss43.htm
  ·Recommendation for Settlement Systems of Securities (2001)
  http://www.bis.org/publ/cpss46.htm
  ·Recommendations for Central Counterparties (2004)
  http://www.bis.org/publ/cpss64.htm
  ·Central Bank Oversight of Payment and Settlement Systems (2005)
  http://www.bis.org/publ/cpss68.htm
  ·General Guidance for National Payment System Development (2006)
  http://www.bis.org/publ/cpss70.htm
  ·General Principles for International Remittance Services (2007)
  http://www.bis.org/publ/cpss76.htm

The Joint Forum (BCBS, IOSCO and IAIS)
  ·Supervision of Financial Conglomerates (1999)
  http://www.bis.org/publ/bcbs47.htm
  ·Core Principles Cross-Sectoral Comparison (2001)
  http://www.bis.org/publ/joint03.htm
  ·Trends in Risk Integration and Aggregation (2003)
  http://www.bis.org/publ/joint07.htm
  ·Operational Risk Transfer Across Financial Sectors (2003)
  http://www.bis.org/publ/joint06.pdf
  ·Outsourcing Guidance for Financial Services (2005)
  http://www.bis.org/press/p050215.htm

International Monetary Fund (IMF)
  ·Special Data Dissemination Standard, SDDS (1996)
  http://dsbb.imf.org
  ·General Data Dissemination System, GDDS (1997)
  http://dsbb.imf.org
  ·Revised Code of Good Practices on Fiscal Transparency (2001)
  http://www.imf.org/external/np/fad/trans/code.htm
  ·Code of Good Practices in Transparency in Monetary and Financial Policy (1999)
  http://www.imf.org/external/np/mae/mft/code/index.htm#goodtrans
  ·Criteria for Management of Public Debt (2003)
  http://www.imf.org/external/np/mfd/pdebt/2003/eng/am/120903.pdf
  ·Criteria for Management of International Reserves (2001)
  http://www.imf.org/external/np/mae/ferm/eng/index.htm

World Bank (WB)
  ·Principles and Criteria for Effective Systems of Insolvency and Creditors Rights (2001)
  http://www.worldbank.org/ifa/ipg_eng.pdf
  ·Revised Principles for Effective Insolvency and Creditor Rights Systems (2005)
     http://web.worldbank.org/WBSITE/EXTERNAL/TOPICS/LAWANDJUSTICE/GILD/0,,
     contentMDK:20774193~pagePK:64065425~piPK:162156~theSitePK:215006,00.html
  ·2004-UNCITRAL Legislative Guide on Insolvency Law
  http://www.uncitral.org/uncitral/en/uncitral_texts/insolvency/2004Guide.html

Organization for Economic Co-operation and Development (OECD)
  ·OECD Principles of Corporate Governance (1999, 2004)
  http://www.oecd.org/dataoecd/32/18/31557724.pdf

International Accounting Standards Board (IASB)
  ·International Financial Reporting Standards (2007)
  https://buy.iasb.org/timssecommerce/timssnet/Common/TNT_ShowDetail.cfm?
     subsystem=ord&related_prod_flag=0&primary_id=10093&action=long

International Federation of Accountants (IFA)
  ·International Standards of Auditing (2002)
  http://www.ifac.org
  ·Handbook of International Auditing, Assurance and Ethics Pronouncements (2007)
  http://www.ifac.org/Members/DownLoads/2007_IAASB_Handbook.pdf

Financial Action Task Force on Money Laundering (FATF)
  ·Forty Recommendations of FATF on Money Laundering (1996)
  ·Forty Recommendations of FAFT on Money Laundering (2003)

Table 4.1 (Continued)

---

http://www.fatf-gafi.org/document/28/0,2340,en_32250379_32236930_33658140_1_
  1_1_1,00.html#40recs
·Recommendations on Terrorist Financing (2002)
http://www1.oecd.org/fatf/SRecsTF_en.htm
·Nine Special Recommendations on Terrorist Financing (2004)
http://www.fatf-gafi.org/document/9/0,2340,en_32250379_32236920_34032073_1_1_
  1_1,00.html
·Initiatives by the BCBS, IAIS and IOSCO to Combat Money Laundering and
  the Financing of Terrorism:
An Update (2005)
http://www.bis.org/publ/joint11.htm http://www.iosco.org/library/pubdocs/pdf/
  IOSCOPD181.pdf

Financial Stability Forum (FSF)
  ·12 Key Standards for Sound Financial Systems
  http://www.fsforum.org/compendium/key_standards_for_sound_financial_system.html

---

management of public debt and international reserves. Other institutions, such as the WB and the OECD, and international associations of accounting, developed standards and codes on corporate governance, accounting, auditing and insolvency.

Consultations under Article IV of the IMF elaborated the Report on Standards and Codes (ROSC). Technicians of cooperating institutions join IMF missions and evaluate institutions. The results constitute part of the Financial Sector Assessment Program (FSAP). This is one of the most important documents on evaluation of a country by the IMF, with copy to its Executive Board. In theory, observance of standards, codes and core principles is voluntary. In practice, divergence of internal institutions with accepted practice by the international financial community could cause hurdles in official financing during crises of liquidity and insolvency. A major effort to unify standards and codes of G10 countries was an important consequence of emerging market crises, in particular the Asian crisis of 1997–8.

The Financial Stability Forum (FSF) is a forum of senior members of national financial authorities, IFIs, institutions of international supervision and regulation, committees of central bank experts and the ECB (FSF 2007a). The staff of the FSF is at the Bank for International Settlements (BIS) in Basel. The FSF (2007b) has been having biennial meetings in March and September since 1999. It engages in important consultations on sources of risk in the international financial system and measures to preserve its stability. The FSF (2007c) maintains a compendium of the 12 key standards listed in Table 4.1 that the FSF has determined to be critical to financial stability. These are the standards used by the IMF and WB (2005a–c) in their Article IV surveillance, elaborating the ROSCs. The compendium collects together critical information: the complete standards, supporting documents and the assessment methodologies. The standards are the product of the FSF and the standard-setting institutions that are represented in the FSF.

The 12 key standards of the FSF (2007d) specify the sound principles, practices and guidelines in various areas. Standards can be classified by the sector to which they apply, such as the government, central bank, banking, securities, insurance and the corporate sector. The functional method classifies standards by the areas they cover, such as governance, disclosure, transparency and so on. Standards are focused on principles, practices and methodologies. The principles are more general and can be adapted to the characteristics of countries, such as the BCP. The practices are more specific, centering on a narrower concept, such as the BCBS Sound Practices for Loan Accounting. The methodologies and guidelines provide the measures that have to be adopted or requirements of compliance, allowing an objective measure of the degree of compliance.

The objective of setting and implementing standards is to promote sound financial systems and international financial stability (FSF 2007e). The standards do not reflect national biases. There are national and international benefits resulting from adopting and implementing the standards. The national benefit is to strengthen national domestic financial systems, avoiding country crises. The international benefit is improving international financial decisions, limiting risks of crises and preventing their spillover to other countries and regions. Individual countries must have strong legal and enforcement institutions for the standards to be effective. Table 4.1 provides the standards by the standard-setting institutions.

The FSAP of the IMF and WB (2005b) was launched in 1999 in response to the concern by the G7 of the role of the soundness of domestic financial systems in emerging market crises (Peláez and Peláez 2005, 63–162). The essence of the analysis of the FSAP of the IMF and WB (2005b) is the relationship between financial stability and development. The IMF and WB (2005b, 4) define financial stability in terms of two characteristics. The first characteristic is that the financial system prevents the insolvency or failure of significant financial institutions. The second characteristic consists of conditions that promote the normal conduct of financial business, that is, financial transactions are processed without disruption. An effective process of financial development consists of the provision of financial services required for economic agents to promote economic growth.

There are three pillars in the assessment framework of the FSAP (IMF and WB 2005b, 5). Surveillance of prudential macroeconomic policies and institutions and analysis of financial stability provide Pillar I of the FSAP. There is special emphasis on the risk and vulnerabilities that may affect financial stability, originating in domestic and external macroeconomic and institutional factors. Pillar II focuses on the promotion of sound risk management and governance of financial institutions by means of prudential supervision and regulation. The standards and codes initiative is an important ingredient. The principles are those initially analyzed in the Rey Report (G10 1996) and evolving in accordance with experience and theoretical development. Pillar III concentrates on the strengthening of financial infrastructure. Financial system stability requires adequate legal institutions, systems for processing of payments and transparent governance in financial institutions and policy. The integration of financial stability and development requires a surveillance process of key interrelations of: conditions in nonfinancial sectors, aggregate policies affecting the financial system, financial risks and vulnerabilities, adequacy of financial structure and legal and institutional frameworks. The FSAP must maintain a balance between analytical rigor and specific characteristics of countries.

The expansion and improvement of the analytical tools used in the assessments is an important area of further development of the FSAP (IMF and WB 2005c, 6). Part of the effort has focused on the technical issues while other efforts are leading toward greater relation of financial stability with financial development. There are four broad analytical elements in the surveillance by the FSAP (IMF and WB 2005b, 36). Surveillance analyzes if shocks can affect the financial system and how they can be anticipated with early warning systems (EWS). The analytical core of the FSAP focuses on the probable impact of vulnerabilities on the financial system and the repercussions on the aggregate economy. The tools used include stress tests and monitoring of financial sector indicators (FSI) (Peláez and Peláez 2005, 101–63). Another key component of surveillance is the analysis of the transmission of shocks from the financial system to the aggregate economy. The effect of devaluation on the balance sheets of the government, business and individuals is an important issue in emerging market crises. The FSAP has also focused on the conditions of debt sustainability, an important concern during the crisis in Argentina at the turn of the millennium.

Between the launching of the standards and codes initiative and April 30, 2005, the IMF and WB (2005a) conducted 723 assessments in 122 countries. The initial assessments amounted to 592. The developing countries have shown less participation in the assessments than the advanced and emerging countries. The rate of publication has been about 75 percent.

The strongest benefit of the standards and codes initiative consists of the identification of vulnerabilities and priorities to strengthen domestic financial systems (IMF and WB 2005a). The implementation of reforms is a benefit of long gestation and is still not fully realized. There is evidence of progress toward the implementation of standards. There is not yet sufficient use of the ROSCs by market participants and proposals to make them more useful. The staffs of the IMF and WB (2005a) still find merit in the initiative and are taking measures to improve its effectiveness. The standards and codes are likely to remain at the current 12 because of the significant effort required to implement them. An important area of future improvement consists of the finding of priorities of implementation and incentives for countries to engage in cooperation. Greater use by market participants is also an important issue. Comparison of standards across countries and over time can be quite useful as well as relating the ROSCs to other areas of work of the IMF and WB.

A key limitation of the work of the IMF and WB is that member countries have their own sovereign interests and governance. The evaluation by the IMF Independent Evaluation Office (2006, 7) finds that the boards of the two institutions select FSAP assessments for countries that are considered to be systemically important and/or have vulnerable financial systems. However, even this selection has not prevented the application of the FSAP to a significant percentage of countries,

20–25 percent, which are considered to be systemically important and/or have vulnerable financial systems. Some of the FSAP assessments for these countries have become dated. The participation of countries in the FSAP process is voluntary, a fact that creates the discrepancy between what is prudent and what actually happens. The IMF Independent Evaluation Office (2006, 7) also finds another difficult goal of the FSAP process: financial stability is quite complex, with many tests and variables creating an inevitable conflict between comprehensiveness and focus.

The report of the IMF Independent Evaluation Office (2006, 13–14, 59–71) provides seven recommendations for improvement arranged around three areas. There is need to improve the incentives for participation. The IMF should strive to maintain and further improve the quality of the FSAP process. The IMF and WB joint effort should continue.

There are three major changes by the International Monetary Fund (2006) in the standards and codes initiative in response to the review by the IMF Executive Board (2005). The first set of changes is on country coverage and prioritization. The priorities of countries will be as follows (International Monetary Fund 2006, 3):

- Systemic and regionally important countries;
- Other emerging countries;
- Program countries with weakness in ROSC;
- Resource-rich countries for fiscal transparency.

The staff will provide views on priority areas in appraisals of Article IV staff reports. The ROSC reports will be more flexible in updates. The Article IV missions will use functional department experts to conduct factual updates but the yearly updates by area departments will be discontinued. Technical assistance and diagnosis will be provided to countries that do not desire to engage in ROSCs. There are three reasons for the usefulness of BCPs: worldwide acceptance as the standard of banking supervision and regulation, focus on the implementation of laws and regulations and separate assessments for the individual 25 core principles (Demirgüç-Kunt *et al.* 2006, 3). The methodology developed by the BCBS for the BCPs permits comparability among countries. The teams of the international financial institutions (IFI) and expert supervisors conduct the reviews.

The liberalization of financial markets and capital flows since the 1980s was accompanied by sharp twin exchange and domestic financial crises in emerging countries. The G7 meetings instructed the IMF to tighten surveillance of domestic financial systems to prevent crises and better resolve those that occur (Peláez and Peláez 2005 63–100). The supervisory principles of the BCPs constitute the state of the art in banking supervision. An important effort is to prioritize the reforms that will have the highest initial impact on the improvement of banking supervision. Demirgüç-Kunt *et al.* (2006) use ratings of banks for 39 countries to empirically assess if compliance with the BCPs results in sounder banks. The FSAP of the IMF and the WB provides information for many countries on a wide range of issues.

The comprehensive research of Barth *et al.* (2006) suggests that the optimum financial systems in the world are those that provide for timely and accurate disclosure of information for the market to monitor the financial soundness of banks. Demirgüç-Kunt *et al.* (2006) confirm this finding with strong empirical association between compliance with provision of information and bank soundness. The timely and accurate disclosure of information by banks permits more effective monitoring by both regulators and market participants. The policy recommendation is that countries desiring to improve their supervision should give priority to information disclosure. Excessive power to regulators does not appear to lead to sounder banks, a critical finding by Barth *et al.* (2006). Integrating the ROSC assessment with the work of the IMF and providing clarity and timeliness in the reports are important in the process.

The FSAP process of the IMF and WB uses stress tests. These tests are also used in key standards, such as Basel II capital requirements and are quite common in private financial institutions and other economic and business activities. A general definition is that stress tests consist of multiple techniques used in evaluating the strength of a system to extreme events (Čihák 2007, 4). Stress testing can help to assess the stability of a system or entity. The system or entities are shocked with extreme events to find out the results at or near breaking points. The initial financial applications tested the resilience of individual assets and portfolios of assets. However, the process has been extended to entire banks, banking systems and financial systems. A common framework departs from an external shock that affects the aggregate economy of a country with specifications that trace the effects to the country's banks. There is more complete discussion of stress tests in Chapter 4 of Volume I.

The activities of the IMF can be illustrated by use of the theory of GPGs (Joyce and Sandler 2007). GPGs can be purely public when the benefits are entirely non-rival and non-excludable for consuming countries. This is the case of the use of best practices by individual IMF members to prevent crises. The property of being non-excludable makes GPGs subject to free riding or failure to reveal "the marginal willingness to pay through a voluntary payment" (Joyce and Sandler 2007, 3). The collection of a price for a non-rival GPG would exclude nations for which the positive marginal willingness to pay is less than the price. If the provision of those goods to these nations is costless, there is a net social loss in the form of the net marginal gains.

The limited resources of the IMF can result in congestion costs, making GPGs impurely public (Joyce and Sandler 2007, 4). The costs of extending the ROSC assessments are not zero. In fact, the Executive Board instructed the staff to allocate the scarce available resources in the most effective way, giving priority to countries that are significantly important in terms of systemic potential (IMF Executive Board 2005, IMF Independent Evaluation Office 2006, International Monetary Fund 2006). The benefits of averting international systemic crises are realized by all members of the IMF. These benefits consist of the contribution of ROSC assessments to international financial stability, an important GPG. However, some countries may be excluded from the individual benefits of the ROSC assessments because of the pressure on resources of the IMF. The reduction of lending activities by the IMF has decreased the interest on loans, which was a traditional source of funding for the institution.

Impure GPGs are considered as club goods because the benefits are rival to some extent and can be excluded at nil cost (Joyce and Sandler 2007, 4). The provision of technical assistance by the IMF is a club GPG. This technical assistance is provided to members in various forms in the areas of expertise of the Fund, such as taxation, monetary policy, exchange rate regime and regulation of the financial system. The IMF can restrict this assistance according to its resources.

The collective activities of GPGs can result in joint products, which have been important in the work of the IMF (Joyce and Sandler 2007, 6). The products may differ in their characteristics with the possibilities of being purely public, private, club goods and so on. The ROSC assessments have two products, the specific report to a country and the benefits to the international financial system from any pre-vention of systemic crises. The transformation of the IMF is partly from catalytic financing to provision of services for fees. This transformation changes the nature of its goods toward club goods that are provided at a fee. There may be room for provision of some of these goods by regional institutions.

Soft law

The terms in soft law are not binding. Typically, soft law consists of declarations of desired norms of international conduct (Williamson 2003, 63). The adoption of soft law can be easier than negotiating and adopting treaties. There are constitutional and legal requirements for the entry of treaties in force. Nation states prefer the flexibility of soft law because of the difficulty in anticipating the consequences of treaties.

A common reason for entering into nonbinding international agreements is to manifest the will of the international community to solve a pressing world problem caused by one of the states (Shelton 2006, 319). Soft law is used to denote an international act stating principles, norms, standards or statements of desired conduct. Political consequences can result from breaching agreements of soft law. Soft law is used as regulatory tool when there is no option to develop a formal treaty (Hillgenberg 1999, 515).

The international legal system can be divided into normative and operating systems (Ku and Diehl 2006). There are cases in which the operating system cannot promote the effectiveness of various norms. The acceptance of different levels of compliance may be required to broaden the norms across countries.

The probability of compliance of an international agreement can be enhanced by means of what Guzman (2005) denominates "design elements." These elements are included to create costs of not complying with the agreement. In addition to making the agreement an enforceable treaty, the design elements include the creation of procedures for dispute resolution and monitoring mechanisms. The process of surveillance of standards and codes under Article IV of the IMF is an example of a monitoring mechanism. In a sense, the analysis of the country reports by the Executive Committee of the IMF is another element of monitoring and not a mechanism of dispute resolution.

The debate on regulation has focused on the public interest view that market failures require intervention. Even in the presence of transaction costs, the market may find efficient outcomes if trades occur after taking into account transaction costs. Giannini (2002, 128–9) argues, following Olson (2000), that market failure may be an oxymoron because the status quo obtained through the market is efficient. Some trades such as spot transactions are self-enforcing. The main issue is the enforcement by the government of commitments that are not self-enforcing. However, coercion by the government may result in unfavorable outcomes in two forms: the use of coercion to promote socially undesirable outcomes and actions by the private entities that lead to undesirable outcomes such as moral hazard. The ideal role for regulation is to be market augmenting instead of market substituting. The government must have the strength to create and protect property rights and enforce contracts. It is difficult for the government to engage in market-augmenting behavior in autocracies, according to Olson (2000). The application to finance is evident because of the existence of financial transactions that discount future cash flows to the present, requiring property rights and enforcement of contracts. A major difficulty in implementing market-augmenting regulation, according to Giannini (2002, 130), is the recurrence of financial crisis, requiring prevention and resolution that is more complex than simple enforcement.

Market-augmenting regulation developed out of the experience with preventing and managing financial crises in advanced countries in the twentieth century, according to Giannini (2002, 131–40). Financial supervision and regulation evolved into a greater role for discretion, creating challenges for the supervising agencies and the financial system. There is significant creative ambiguity, in particular in deciding what institutions to rescue during a crisis. The process has to provide for exit of institutions from the safety net or otherwise the costs of resolution may be intolerably high. There should be independence of supervisors from pressure groups because the unfavorable outcomes originate more in inadequate implementation than in the nature of the regulation. The regulation of banks should be inserted into the institutions and laws of the country. International consultation and coordination may prove quite useful in developing regulatory reform. Some of these principles were considered in the Rey Report of the G10 (1996) after the Mexican crisis in 1994 (Peláez and Peláez 2005, 77–9).

The emerging market crises of the 1990s posed a supervisory and regulatory challenge for the world. Giannini (2002, 140) finds significant value in the soft law approach by means of formal versions of the Basel guidelines. The standards and codes of this Basel process are nonbinding. They are the result of international cooperation, consultation and coordination. However, they are implemented by national authorities. The standards and codes do not have the strength of ordinary law but are stronger than international conventions. Giannini (2002, 142–5) argues that the approach has three fundamental strengths. The content originates in international forums that have technical excellence and tradition. The governance originates in the G10 and is periodically augmenting. The incentives, according to Giannini (2002, 145–6), can indirectly occur in the form of reactions by the markets to nonobservance or can arise from reactions of the IFIs. The latter appear to be stronger in the early phases because of the time required by market participants to identify and appreciate the standards. Giannini (2002, 148) recommends strong action by the IFIs to provide the right incentives that can occur in the form of peer pressure, public opprobrium and financial approval such as in the form of inclusion in IMF conditionality. Giannini (2002, 150–2) also finds value in opening domestic banking systems to greater foreign ownership and control. Significant strengthening of the soft law could occur in the form of a hard roof by recognizing the value of international mobility of capital and the desirability of international financial stability as a GPG.

Compliance is defined as the behavior of the state induced by international law (Ho 2002). The theory of compliance should consider international treaties, customary law, arbitration, adjudication and soft law. Soft law is not binding. An influential school claims that compliance increases in response to greater enforcement. However, in soft law there is no form of institutionalized enforcement. In cases of soft law, the option to adopt the convention without a specific commitment, treaty or accession mechanism is quite relevant. The importance is what countries and for what reasons implements a code or standard, that is, commit to soft law in regulation.

Relatively large and well-capitalized banks benefit more from capital requirements than smaller banks. These banks maintain high capital to enhance their reputation in the market as a form to attract business. Ho (2002) argues that the well capitalized banks that benefit from the adoption of Basel requirements lobby domestic regulators to implement the agreement. The international exposure of these banks positively affects the implementation and compliance with the international capital standard.

There is a cross-national study of over one hundred countries by Ho (2002) on the determinants of adopting the Basel Accord by a country. The likelihood of implementation of the Basel Accord depends positively on the country's wealth, savings, CA surpluses, democracy, lack of corruption and less divided government. Ho (2002) finds a strong effect of democracy: an increase of two standard deviations of the democratic system raises the probability of implementation of the Basel Accord by 37 percent. Lower wealth and less democracy causes weaker prediction of commitment to the Basel Accord. Ho (2002) presents another important result: countries that have banking crises are less likely to implement the Basel Accord. Another interesting result is that bank concentration, government ownership and foreign ownership do not have an impact on the likelihood of adopting the Basel Accord. There is no evidence supporting the view that use of IMF and WB resources has effects on adopting the standard. There are some of the problems of cross-country empirical research such as endogenous variables and data limitations. In terms of policy implications, Ho (2002) concludes that building institutions is quite important. Olson (2000) argues that it is very difficult to have a market-augmenting government in autocracies.

Basel II capital requirements

The BCBS framework of capital requirements is one of the most important international standards and also widely adopted by banks in most jurisdictions. The process of generating the framework took several years and the contributions of central bankers, academics, bank executives and technicians from many jurisdictions. The process was interactive with multiple consultative processes and quantitative studies of the possible impact of the change in the standard. It constitutes a marriage of central banking with actual practice in bank management.

The BCBS announced the Capital Accord in 1988 with implementation date by the end of 1992. In 1996, it published an amendment to include market risk (BCBS 1996a–d). The Committee issued consulting work for Basel II in June 1999 and a second set in January 2001 with deadline for comments by May (BCBS 1999a–b, 2001a–p, Santos 2000). It issued a third consultative paper in April 2003 (BCBS 2003a). In addition, it conducted three quantitative impact studies (QIS) (BCBS 2003b–c, 2001q). The BCBS reached an agreement on Basel II at the May 2004 meeting (BCBS 2004a–e). Finally, it published Basel II, or Framework, in June 2004 (BCBS 2004f).

The Central Bank Governors and Heads of Banking Supervision of the Group of Ten countries endorsed Basel II in June 2004. The BCBS expects member countries of the Group of Ten to proceed with the implementation of Basel II. The BCBS favored implementation as of year-end 2006. Nevertheless, implementation of more advanced approaches will require further QIS or parallel calculations and may not be available until year-end 2007.

The BCBS expects that Basel II may not be a priority for some countries outside the G10, which may still benefit from the framework to strengthen their financial systems. The central banks of the G10 – Belgium, Canada, France, Germany, Italy, Japan, Luxembourg, the Netherlands, Spain, Sweden, Switzerland, the United Kingdom and the United States – established the BCBS in 1975. Thus, Basel II will be the standard for countries contributing over two-thirds of world product and for banks accounting for over 75 percent of global banking assets.

The dual objective of Basel II is to strengthen domestic and international financial stability while at the same time preventing capital requirements from creating competitive disadvantages among banks in various jurisdictions. Since the Capital Accord in 1988, financial institutions innovated significantly in quantifying and controlling financial risk. Basel II incorporates this reality and intends to promote sounder risk management processes in financial institutions. An important principle in Basel II is to relate capital adequacy regulation to actual financial risks. Basel II can incorporate changes in risk management through its more advanced approaches to credit, following the industry dynamically. However, some features of the 1988 Accord still remain: regulatory capital ratio of 8 percent of risk-weighted assets, the 1996 Market Risk Amendment and the definition of eligible capital. Most of the innovation of Basel II is in the denominator or calculation of risk-weighted assets.

The Committee created an Accord Implementation Group (AIG) to foster consistency in implementation of Basel II. AIG also serves as forum for exchange of information on approaches to implementation. This group also bridges communication between the industry and supervisors.

The original Capital Accord focuses on a single measurement of risk, credit risk, while Basel II emphasizes internal methods of banks, reviews by supervisors and market discipline (or transparency in disclosure). The original accord consisted of a unique standard, applicable to all, while the new standard incorporates flexibility, a menu of approaches and incentives to improve risk management. The original structure resembles a wide brush, while Basel II incorporates greater risk sensitivity.

Basel II consists of three pillars:

- *Pillar I*: Minimum Capital Requirements
- *Pillar II*: Process of Review by Supervisors
- *Pillar III*: Market Discipline

A method of menus considers each category of risk:

- Menu of Approaches to Measure Credit Risk

  o Standardized approach (modified version of existing Capital Accord)
  o Foundation approach based on internal ratings
  o Advanced approach based on internal ratings

- Menu of Approaches to Measure Market Risk (unaltered)

  o Standardized approach
  o Approach of internal models

- Menu of Approaches to Measure Operational Risk

  o Approach of basic indicators
  o Standardized approach
  o Internal approach of measurement or Advanced Management Approach

Basel II seeks an appropriate capital approach based on sensitivity standards of risk and internal measurement by banks. New forms to treat credit risk and specification of capital requirements for operational risk constitute the most important changes in capital requirements. The Standardized Approach, the Foundation and Advanced Internal-Ratings Based (IRB) provide avenues for treating credit risk (BIS 2001Aug). The objective is to encourage banks to improve management and measurement of risk, to apply the most advanced techniques for risk sensitivity and to determine adequate capital.

The objectives of Basel II consist of (BCBS 2001e, k):

- Promoting safety and soundness of the financial system, maintaining existing minimum capital requirements;
- Strengthening equality in competition;
- Providing more extensive approach to risk;
- Implementing approaches to capital requirements that incorporate sensitivity to degree of risk and bank activities;
- Focusing on banks with international operations but applicable to different levels of complexity and sophistication.

Because the three pillars constitute an interrelated package, Basel II requires compliance with all three pillars for definitive implementation (Descamps *et al.* 2002). Partial implementation of pillars would compromise the safety and soundness of the financial system. Supervisors must observe at least Pillar I of minimum capital requirements. As in the Amendment for market risk, the BCBS provided an evolutionary process in Pillar I to guarantee a sound prudential requirement compatible with incentives and sensitivity to risk. Banks that comply with specified minimum requirements could use risk-sensitive methodologies in calculating regulatory capital.

Basel II incorporated explicitly more risk elements, quality of debtor credit, structure and maturity of transactions and concentration of obligations. In the internal ratings approach banks use progressively, after complying with minimum requirements, a wide spectrum of internal risk measurements.

Pillar I: minimum capital requirements

The BCBS intends that supervisors apply Basel II to international banks on a consolidated basis. Entities will include a holding company within a banking group to encompass the risk of the entire banking group or an entity engaged in banking activities. Supervisors will apply the approach at all levels of a banking group on a consolidated basis. Supervisors will also assure protection of depositors by requiring stand-alone capitalization of individual banks.

Consolidation includes securities companies, majority owned or controlled by banking groups. For purposes of capital adequacy, supervisors will deduct equity, regulatory capital, assets and liabilities of non-consolidated majority-owned securities and financial subsidiaries. There will be similar deduction of significant minority investments in banking, securities and financial entities. Supervisors will also deduct equity and regulatory capital investments in insurance subsidiaries. In certain cases, supervisors may recognize "surplus capital" of a majority-owned or controlled insurance entity. There will be similar deductions for investments in commercial entities above certain materiality levels. Deductions of investments will be at the rate of 50 percent from Tier 1 capital (equity capital plus disclosed reserves excluding goodwill) and 50 percent from Tier 2 capital (undisclosed reserves, asset revaluation reserves, loan loss reserves, cumulative preferred stock and subordinated term debt).

Basel II retained the capital ratio and the definition of capital of Basel I. The minimum capital requirement ratio continues to be 8 percent of risk-weighted assets. The following formula measures bank capital ratios:

$$\frac{\text{Total Capital (unchanged)}}{\text{Credit} + \text{Market Risk} + \text{Operational Risk}} = \text{Capital Ratio(8\%)}$$

The denominator of minimum capital requirement consists of three components:

- Average weighted sum of risk for all assets
- Plus 12.5 times sum of capital charges for market risk and operational risk

For example, if a bank has $875 of assets adjusted for risk, a charge of $10 for market risk and $20 for operational risk, the denominator of the ratio of minimum capital requirement equals (BCBS 2001e):

$$\text{US\$875} + [(\text{US\$10} + \text{US\$20}) \times 12.5] = \text{US\$1250}$$

The work by the BCBS concentrated on the denominator. Tier 2 capital cannot exceed 100 percent of Tier 1 capital. There were some minor changes. Basel II does not allow including general provisions (or general loan-loss reserves) in Tier 2 capital. Rules for these provisions depend on calculation of expected loss (EL), subject covered under the IRB below.

The consultations and work of Basel II constitute one of the most important contributions made to banking supervision, attempting to incorporate practical and technical knowledge of authorities, specialists, academicians and bankers. The BCBS will review capital ratio calibration before implementation of the framework. It will consider a scaling factor at the time of implementation, perhaps 1.06, to maintain the aggregate level of minimum capital requirements.

Basel II also imposed a 3-year transitional floor of capital, based on the 1988 Accord, for banks using IRB for credit risk or the Advanced Management Approach (AMA) for operational risk. If the floor is higher than the calculated capital, banks must add 12.5 of the difference (1/8). The calculation of the floor is as follows:

Floor = (adjustment factor) (8% of risk-weighted assets + Tier 1 and Tier 2

deductions − general provisions recognized in Tier 2)

The adjustment factor is 95 percent at year-end 2006 (or parallel calculation), 90 percent at year-end 2007 and 80 percent at year-end 2008. The calculation of capital is as follows:

Calculation = 8% of total risk-weighted assets − (general provisions

− expected loss) + other Tier 1 and Tier 2 deductions

Banks must add 12.5 times the excess of Floor less Calculation. These transitional floors may prove to be difficult to implement and BCBS advises that supervisors may flexibly apply bank-specific floors. The objective of the floors is to ensure adequate capital during the transition.

Basel II calculates assets adjusted for risk by two methods: standardized and IRB. The major change in relation to the existing Capital Accord consists of greater diversification of risk. Originally, the BCBS considered as criteria for sovereign assets: IMF's data dissemination standards, the BCPs and 30 principles of securities regulation by IOSCO. The BCBS preferred ratings published by credit export rating agencies, encouraging larger number of countries with recognized external evaluation.

The BCBS advises that supervisors should not permit that banks use risk weights based mechanically on external evaluations. Both supervisors and banks have responsibility for evaluating methods used by external credit evaluation institutions and the quality of ratings. Basel II determines criteria for eligibility of ratings. Supervisors should avoid criteria to reduce capital requirements that are inconsistent with risk management.

Pillar I: standardized approach

The standardized approach intends that banks calculate regulatory capital in accordance with the state of the art in risk management (BCBS 2001g). The objective is to avoid complexity while introducing greater differentiation in banking risk components, including techniques of risk mitigation.

The new approach considers same asset categories – sovereigns, banks and corporations – but eliminated origin in the OECD. The standardized approach uses external credit assessment for support. This approach consists basically of a revision of the 1988 Accord to improve measurement of risks of assets. National supervisors may apply a lower risk weight to bank exposures to their sovereign (or central bank) denominated in local currency and funded in that currency. Supervisors may approve country risk scores prepared by export credit agencies (ECA), which publish their scores and subscribe to OECD methodology, or ECAs participating in the "Arrangement of Officially Supported Export Credits." Claims on BIS, the European Central Bank (ECB) and the European Community may receive 0 percent weight. Public sector enterprises (PSE) may receive weights according to options 1 or 2 for banks, which are discussed below. There could also be decisions by domestic supervisors to treat PSEs in the same way as sovereign of PSE origin. The multilateral development banks (MDB) will receive weights under option 2 for banks except 0 percent for MDBs with high ratings satisfying criteria of the BCBS, on a case-by-case evaluation.

Basel II has two options for claims on banks. Option 1 assigns banks a risk category one level below that of the sovereign of the country of establishment. However, there is a cap of 100 percent for unrated countries and sovereigns rated BB+ to B−. Option 2 uses external credit assessments of the bank. There is a short-term option of weight of 20 percent for an original maturity of the claim of 3 months or less. There is similar treatment for securities firms if supervisory and regulatory frameworks are similar to those of Basel II. If frameworks are different, securities firms will receive the same treatment as corporations.

Corporations and insurance companies receive the same treatment in accordance with external ratings. These types of claims cannot receive treatment that is superior to that of the corresponding sovereign.

Basel II also provides risk weights of 75 percent for claims included in a regulatory retail portfolio. The criteria for including claims in this portfolio are exposures to individuals or small business, type of loans (revolving credits, personal term loans and leases and small business credit), "granularity" or risk-reducing diversification and low individual value.

There is a risk weight of 35 percent for mortgages on residential properties occupied or to be occupied by the borrower or rented. Supervisors must ensure that there is sufficient margin in the mortgages. National supervisors may increase the risk weight in accordance with past experience of default. BCBS determined that commercial real estate lending have a risk weight of no less than 100 percent because of troubled past experience.

BCBS determined that for all loans past due more than 90 days, except certain qualifying mortgage loans, there will be the following risk weights:

150% specific provisions < 20% of loan outstanding
100% specific provisions ≥ 20% of loan outstanding
100% specific provision ≥ 50% with supervisory discretion to reduce to 50%

Basel II also has higher weights for higher risk categories. These weights could exceed 150 percent. It includes claims rated below B− on sovereigns, PSEs, banks and securities firms, claims on corporations rated below BB− and past due loans. In additions, securitization tranches with ratings between BB+ and BB− will have risk weight of 350 percent. Supervisors may also apply weights of 150 percent or higher to risks of venture capital and private equity (PE) investments.

Basel II converts off-balance sheet items with credit conversion factors (CCF). Commitments with original maturity of less than 1 year have a CCF of 20 percent and those over 1 year of 50 percent. Lending of bank securities or posting of securities as collateral by banks have CCF of 100 percent. There will be a 20 percent weight for credit originating in the movement of goods. Basel II maintained other CCFs in the 1988 Accord.

Basel II provided six criteria to qualify an external credit assessment institution (ECAI). National supervisors will determine if an ECAI meets these criteria. Approval of ECAIs should be a public process to ensure credibility. Supervisors will assign ECAI assessments to the risk weights in the Basel II framework. There should be consistency in this assignment with the criteria used in Basel II. In case there are two assessments by different ECAI, the bank will use the higher risk weight. If there are three or more risk assessments, the bank will use the higher of the two lowest assessments.

Basel II treats short-term assessments as issue specific, that is, for use only in reference to the rated facility. The claims are mostly on banks and corporations as, for example, issue of commercial paper.

There are various techniques of credit risk mitigation (CRM), available to banks. There may be first priority claim on collateral in cash or securities and guarantees by a third party. Banks can also net loans against deposits by the same counterparty and can buy credit derivatives to hedge exposures. There must be "legal certainty." All documentation of the technique of CRM must be legally binding and enforceable in relevant jurisdictions. Moreover, banks must monitor the transactions to ensure legal certainty. Many CRM techniques create other types of risk: legal, operational, liquidity and market. Banks must have strong methods to control these risks.

Basel II allows use of a simple approach similar to the 1988 Accord, applying as risk weights to the collateral those of the counterparty for the collateral, with a floor of 20 percent. A comprehensive approach permits fuller deduction of collateral against exposures.

An example illustrates the flavor of Basel II. Consider use of collateral as CRM. A "haircut" is a reduction in the value of collateral to allow for possible fluctuations in its market value. For example, in a reverse sale and repurchase agreement (RSRA), the financing entity reduces the principal of the security, a haircut, because if the counterparty defaults and price declines, the market value of the security would be lower than the principal. Banks must use haircuts to adjust both the value of the exposure and that of the collateral in CRM. That is, CRM must adjust by volatility both exposure and collateral. In cases other than cash, adjustment by volatility will increase the value of the exposure and reduce the value of collateral. If there is currency mismatch, banks must adjust exposure and collateral for fluctuations in exchange rates. In the case of an exposure with eligible collateral, the formula for calculating exposure after risk mitigation is (BCBS 2004f, 32):

$$E^* = \max\{0,\ [E \times (1 + He) - C \, x \, (1 - Hc - Hfx)]\} \tag{4.1}$$

where:

E^*: exposure after risk mitigation
E: current value of exposure
He: haircut appropriate to the exposure
C: current value of collateral
Hc: haircut of collateral
Hfx: haircut for currency mismatch of exposure and collateral

Fluctuations in market valuations should not reduce capital requirements. The reverse haircut increases the value of the exposure, $E\,x\,(1 + He)$, and the haircut reduces the value of collateral, $C\,x\,(1 - Hc - Hfx)$. The risk-weighted asset amount for the transactions with collateral is equal to the exposure value after risk mitigation multiplied by the risk weight of the counterparty.

A new approach introduced a type of weights for banks, line Banks I in the BCBS table, lower in one degree to that of sovereign of origin. It stipulated a ceiling of 100 percent for credits lower than B−. The second bank type, Banks II, uses directly

Table 4.2   Process based on internal ratings (IRB)

Debtor risk
  Classification of debtor in credit risk categories
  ↓
  Estimates of probability of default for each category, *PD*
  ↓
  Estimate of percentage of loss given default, *LGD*
  ↓
  Estimate of exposure at default, *EAD*
  ↓
  Estimate of expected loss, *EL*:
  $EL = EDF^*EAD^*LGD$
  where *EDF* = expected frequency of default, derived from *PD*
  Classification of exposures to risk by categories
  (sovereigns, banks, corporations, etc.)
  Risk components, using standardized parameters or internal estimates
  Right weight function to estimate capital requirements, *K*
  Risk-weighted assets $= K \times 12.5 \times EAD$
  Special requirements for specialized lending

IRB
  Foundation
  Percentage of loss given default determined by supervisory rules
  Limits on collateral
  Advanced
  Percentage of loss given default determined by bank but complying with
  rigorous minimum requirements
  No restrictions on allowed categories of collateral

Guarantees and credit derivatives
  Foundation
  Uses methods similar to standardized
  Advanced
  Bank can adjust risk category of a guaranteeing entity and probability of default

---

Source: Basel Committee (2001g, 2001h, 2004c).

ratings by agencies for a specific bank, applying weight lower in one degree for
terms of three months or lower with a minimum of 20 percent.

The last line of the BCBS table shows weights for corporations, including
insurance companies. Weight of 150 percent applies to ratings of BB−. The standardized approach specifies weights for retail assets, debts guaranteed by real estate
or commercial purposes, higher risk categories and other assets and off-balance
sheet items.

Pillar I: IRB

The BCBS developed an IRB approach that reflects a bank's individual risk profile
(BCBS 2001l, 2004f). It developed IRB for use by more sophisticated banks, but

believes that the number and type of qualified institutions will increase. Every category consists of three elements:

1. Risk components, for which the bank must use its own estimates or those of supervisors;
2. Function of risk weight that transforms risk components in weights to adjust assets;
3. Minimum requirements for banks to be eligible for IRB.

The BCBS developed the IRB based on best existing practices in risk control. Table 4.2 shows the process followed by the IRB. Banks classify their debtors by risk categories. They estimate a probability of default, with higher precision in some banks. It is more difficult to estimate the percentage of loss given default (LGD).

The risk components of IRB are probability of default, *PD*, loss given default, *LGD*, exposure at default, *EAD*, and effective maturity, *M*. Table 4.3 shows risk components. In some cases, banks may have to use a measure of risk component provided by supervisors. In others, banks may use their own internally generated measures. An essential element of IRB is calculation of unexpected losses, *UL*, and expected losses, *EL*. The framework uses risk-weight functions to calculate capital requirements for *UL*.

Banks must classify banking-book exposures into classes of assets with different risk profiles: corporate, sovereign, bank, retail and equity. Banks must have

Table 4.3   Risk components of Basel II

Probability of default, PD	
Corporate and bank	Greater of *PD* of internal borrower grade or 0.03%
Sovereign	One-year *PD* of internal borrower grade
Default borrowers	100%
Loss given default, LGD	
Foundation approach	• Corporates, sovereign, banks: senior, 45%; subordinated, 75%
	• Additional eligible collateral: receivables, specified commercial and residential real estate. Methodology similar to comprehensive approach to collateral in standardized approach
	• Guarantees and credit derivatives follow standardized approach
Advanced approach	• Supervisors may allow banks to use internal estimate of *LGD* for corporate, sovereign and bank exposures. *LGD* is percentage of *EAD*
	• May adjust *PD* or *LGD* to reflect risk mitigating of guarantees and credit derivatives or use foundation approach

Exposure at default, EDA

On balance sheet netting	Loans and deposits same as standardized
Off-balance sheet items	• Foundation. Instruments and Credit Conversion Factors, CCF, same as standardized except: CCF of 75% for Note Issuance Facilities, NIF, and Revolving Underwriting Facilities, RUF • Advanced. Banks may use own estimates of CCF except when 100% under Foundation • Derivatives (FX, interest rate, equity, credit and commodity) on the basis of replacement cost plus potential future exposure
Effective maturity, M	• Foundation: 2.5 years for corporate exposures except 6 months for repos • Advanced: M is the greater of one year plus remaining effective maturity in years but less than 5 years. Effective maturity is by definition the sum of all cash flows (principal, interest and fees) weighted by time relative to the sum of all cash flows: $$\sum t^*CF_t / \sum CF_t \text{ where } CF \text{ is cash flow}$$

Source: Basel Committee (2004c, 62–8).

consistent methods for classifying assets showing supervisors the soundness of these methods. Basel II provides precise definitions of these assets classes and their sub-classes.

There are three basic elements for each asset class in IRB. Risk components are parameters, provided by banks or by supervisors. Risk-weight functions transform risk components into risk-weighted assets and capital requirements. In both foundation and advanced approaches, banks must use risk-weight functions published in Basel II to calculate capital requirements. Basel II specifies minimum requirements for a bank to use IRB for a specific asset class.

There is a foundation and an advanced approach for corporate, sovereign and bank exposures. Under the foundation approach, banks provide the probability of default, *PD*, but must use supervisory estimates of the other risk components, *LGD*, *EAD* and *M*. In the advanced approach, banks must calculate effective maturity, *M*, and provide their estimates of *PD, LGD* and *EAD*. However, there are five sub-classes of specialized lending in corporate lending: project finance, object finance, commodities finance, income producing real estate and highly volatile commercial real estate. Banks that do not qualify for the corporate foundation approach for specialized lending must use five supervisory categories. Banks that qualify to provide their own *PD* for specialized lending may use the foundation approach for all classes of specialized lending except highly volatile commercial real estate. There could be approval by national supervisors of a foundation approach for highly volatile commercial real estate. Similarly, banks that qualify for the advanced approach in corporate lending may use the advanced approach for specialized lending and may use an advanced approach for highly volatile commercial real estate on approval by supervisors.

In retail exposures, banks must furnish their own *PD, LGD* and *EAD*. There is no differentiation in foundation and advanced approaches in this category. There is a market approach and a *PD/LGD* approach for equity exposures not held in the trading book. Banks that use the advanced approach for other exposure classes can use the *PD/LGD* approach for equity exposures. There is a foundation and an advanced approach for qualifying corporate receivables but no difference in approaches for retail receivables.

Basel II has specific guidelines on implementation of IRB. The framework specifically rules out application of IRB in a class of claims to lower capital charges. A bank that applies IRB to part of its holdings must implement it throughout the entire banking group. The Committee recognized that a bank may not be able initially to implement IRB simultaneously throughout all asset classes and banking units.

Supervisors may permit implementation of IRB in phases. A bank could start by implementing IRB in banking units within the same business unit. It would then move to extend IRB throughout business units in the same banking group. In a third phase, the bank would move from the foundation approach to the advanced approach in certain risk components. Banks must develop plans of implementation and share them with supervisors. Banks must not use intra-group transactions to reduce capital charges. A bank that adopts IRB for any of the asset classes must adopt it simultaneously for its equity exposures. Supervisors will approve return to standardized or IRB approaches only in exceptional circumstances.

The transition period for parallel calculations is 3 years. Banks must have a minimum of 2 years of data for implementation of Basel II, increasing by 1 year for each year of the transition period.

Basel II provides risk-weight functions for three types of retail exposures: residential mortgages, qualifying revolving retail exposures and other retail exposures. Formulas use *PD, LGD* and *EAD* as inputs but do not have a specification for effective maturity, *M*. Banks must provide estimates of *PD* and *LGD* for every pool. They may adjust either *PD* or *LGD* for guarantees and credit derivatives. There are rules for *EAD* similar to those of corporates, banks and sovereigns.

The Basel II framework uses risk components – *PD, LGD, EAD* and, in some cases, *M* – to calculate risk-weighted assets. A formula obtains a correlation, *R*, using probability of default, *PD*. The framework specifies some cases in which there must be a maturity adjustment. A third formula derives the capital requirement, *K*, from the cumulative normal distribution and the inverse normal distribution, using *LGD, PD, R* and, when appropriate, *M*. Finally, there is a simple calculation of Risk-Weighted Assets (*RWA*) (BCBS 2004f, 59–60):

$$RWA = K \times 12.5 \times EAD \qquad (4.2)$$

Table 4.4 shows some risks weights for *UL* calculated by Basel II risk weight functions. Calculations assume *LGD* of 45 percent and maturity of 2.5 years.

Table 4.4   IRB risk weights for unexpected loss

PD	Corporate	Residential mortgages	Other retail	Revolving retail
0.03%	11.30%	4.15%	4.45%	0.98%
5%	112.27%	82.35%	125.45%	103.41%
10%	146.51%	113.58%	142.69%	158.47%
20%	188.42%	140.62%	189.41%	222.88%

Note: LGD = 45%, Maturity = 2.5 years, Turnover for corporates = €5 million.
Source: Basel Committee (2004c, 197).

There appear to be lower risk weights for residential mortgages, which has been a factor in commentary on Basel II. There is an evident sensitivity to probability of default, *PD*.

The framework has market risk capital rules for equity exposures in the trading book. Banks may opt for a "market-based" approach or a *PD/LGD* approach. The market-based approach has two choices: simple-risk weight method or an internal models method. The simple-risk weight method requires a weight of 300 percent for equities publicly traded in a recognized security exchange and 400 percent for all other holdings. Cash and derivatives are acceptable to offset equity positions as long as they have at least 1 year of maturity. Maturity mismatches have the same treatment as corporate exposures. IRB banks may use value at risk (VaR) models of 99th percentile, with a one-tail confidence interval of the difference between quarterly returns and a risk-free rate. The bank multiplies the capital charge by the inverse of 8 percent, 12.5, but capital charges cannot be less than a risk weight of 200 percent for publicly traded equities and 300 percent for others.

The *PD/LGD* approach for equities is similar to that for corporates, banks and sovereigns. However, banks must use an LGD of 90 percent to derive risk weights for equities.

Basel II has specific rules for treatment of expected losses and provisions. Banks calculate expected losses as:

$$EL = PD \times LGD \times EAD \tag{4.3}$$

for all exposures of classes (corporates, sovereign, bank and retail) not in default. Specialized lending may be subject to slotting criteria of risk weights ranging from 5 to 625 percent. Banks using the *PD/LGD* approach can calculate expected loss of equities by the formula above. There is no contribution to expected loss from securitization exposures. Expected loss is zero for all other exposures.

Basel II includes the following in total eligible provisions attributable to exposures under IRB: specific provisions, partial write-offs and portfolio-specific provisions (e.g., country risk or general provisions). However, eligible provisions do not include specific provisions for equity and securitization exposures. Supervisors must evaluate if expected loses reflect market conditions before they allow

Table 4.5 Minimum requirements for IRB entry and use

a. Significant differential of credit risk
b. Integrity and comprehensiveness in designing ratings
c. Monitoring of rating systems and processes
d. Rating system criteria
e. Estimate of probability of default, PD
f. Systems and data
g. Use of internal ratings
h. Internal approval and validation
i. Corporate governance and validation
j. Disclosure (under Pillar III)

Source: Basel Committee (2001f, 2001g, 2001l, 2004c, 81–112).

banks to incorporate into Tier 2 capital the excess of total eligible provisions over expected losses.

Banks must fulfill various requirements to enter and continue to use IRB (Table 4.5). Basel II focuses on a bank's ability to rank and quantify risk. The process must be consistent, reliable and validated. Banks must have internally consistent methods to differentiate and quantify risk. Requirements apply to all asset classes and to both foundation and advanced approaches. Basel II provides detailed principles of minimum requirements. Supervisors must adapt these principles to the realities of their institutions.

Treatment of operational risk is an important innovation of Basel II. Operational risk can originate in external events or failures of internal processes, people and systems. It includes legal risk but excludes strategic and reputation risks. The framework provides three incremental methods to calculate capital charges for operational risk: Basic Indicator Approach, Standardized Approach and AMA. Basel II encourages banks to upgrade toward AMA.

The Basic Indicator Approach computes capital charges as an average of 15 percent of annual gross income over the previous 3 years. The formula excludes years in which gross income is zero or negative. Gross income is net interest income plus non-interest income. The Committee estimated the 15 percent from the relation of operational risk in the industry to gross income.

The Standardized Approach to operational risk classifies bank activities into eight business lines. For each business line, the approach provides the ratio of industry operational risk relative to industry gross income. These ratios range from a low of 12 percent for retail brokerage to 18 percent for corporate finance. The capital charge is the average over 3 years of the maximum of zero and the weighted sum of a business line times its corresponding ratio of operational risk to gross income. There is no limit on offsetting positive capital charges in one business line with negative capital charges in another. However, total negative capital charges are zero.

A bank can use AMA depending on qualifying criteria: involvement of the board of directors and senior management in oversight of operational risk management, sound system implemented with integrity and sufficient resources for the approach in major business lines. The supervisor will monitor the AMA process by a bank for a period to determine if it is credible and appropriate. There are detailed qualitative and quantitative requirements.

A bank must seek expert opinion to use external data in scenario analysis of exposure to high-severity events. Internal data, extending back 5 years, provide measures of internal loss. In addition, the bank must evaluate the business environment and internal controls that could affect its risk exposure. This requires necessary anticipation of problems that could occur and that may not be captured by data. Basel II allowed use of insurance as risk mitigating techniques of operational risk but to a limit of 20 percent of the capital charge for operational risk under AMA. The framework sets specific qualifying characteristics of insurance policies. AMA is somewhat flexible in that a bank can choose partial use of AMA for various parts of its operations by complying with certain requirements.

Basel II refined the definition of the trading book. The trading book is a collection of positions that the bank intends to trade or use as hedge of other exposures in the book. Financial instruments in the trading book must not have restrictive covenants and the bank should be able to hedge them entirely. There must be frequent and accurate valuation of these financial instruments and active management of the portfolio. Financial instruments include cash instruments and derivatives. Trading intent consists of holding positions for short-term resale with the objective of benefiting from short-term price movements or arbitrage. Basel II has specific criteria for inclusion of exposures in the trading book: clearly documented strategy, clearly defined policies, procedures and monitoring for active management of the portfolio.

The framework provides detailed guidelines for prudent valuation. Banks must have and maintain adequate systems and controls. There should be daily mark-to-market (MTM) at transparent closing prices. When MTM is not feasible, banks may prudently mark to model. Supervisors should evaluate mark to model prudence. There should be independent verification of prices and validation of models. Banks must have procedures for determining valuation adjustments and reserves. In addition to capital charges for market and specific risk, banks must calculate counterparty credit risk for OTC derivatives, sale and repurchase agreements (SRA) and other transactions in the trading book. There are specific rules on the treatment of credit derivatives.

Basel II has a specific framework for treatment of capital charges for securitized exposures (BCBS 2004f, 113–36). Table 4.6 summarizes the securitization framework. Banks that use the IRB approach for underlying exposure must use IRB for securitized exposure. Basel II has very specific provisions for this growing segment of banking activities. The insurance industry transfers risk through reinsurance. Banks and securities firms transfer risk through securitization and derivatives. Securitization of credit by banks has grown rapidly and is an issue on how banks use capital adequacy standards.

Table 4.6   Treatment of securitization exposures

Requirement	Banks must hold minimum capital against all securitization exposures
Examples	Investment in asset-backed securities, provision of credit risk mitigants, retention of subordinated tranche, extension of liquidity facility or credit enhancement
Deduction	50% from Tier 1 and 50% from Tier 2
External credit assessment	Must meet operational requirements: • Encompass entire amount of credit risk exposure • Eligible ECAI recognized by national supervisor • ECAI must have expertise in assessing securitizations • Consistent application of external credit assessment across a type of securitization exposure • CRM to a specific special purpose entity must use the risk weight of the external credit assessment
Standardized	• Standardized approach to underlying securitized exposure requires standardized approach under securitization framework • Risk weight is amount of position times risk weight in tables, with CCF for off-balance sheet following specified criteria
IRB	• Banks approved for IRB of underlying exposure must use IRB for securitizations • For rated securitization exposures, banks must apply Ratings-Based Approach calculating risk-weighted assets as amount of exposure times risk weights in tables • When no external or inferred rating is available, banks must apply the Supervisory Formula, multiplying capital charge by 12.5 derived from five bank supplied inputs, or the Internal Assessment Approach, which uses credit quality of securitization exposures applied to asset-backed commercial paper subject to requirements

Source: Basel Committee (2004c).

Pillar II: review process by supervisors

The objective of the second pillar is to ensure that banks maintain adequate capital relative to risk and that they develop and use better risk management practices. Capital does not substitute for adequate internal controls and risk management methods. The BCBS has provided major contributions to supervisory guidance, in particular the BCPs. Pillar II of Basel II provides an additional four principles of supervisory review.

Principle 1 states that banks require a process to assess the adequacy of their capital in relation to risks and a strategy to preserve that capital. This process requires that banks determine the stage of the business cycle, conducting stress tests, rigorous and forward looking, which identify events or changes in market conditions that could have adverse effects on the bank. A sound process requires board and senior management oversight. Rigorous risk management would result in sound capital assessment. In an increasingly sophisticated financial market, banks must identify, quantify and evaluate all risks: credit risk, operational risk, market risk, liquidity risk and other less quantifiable risks such as reputation and strategy. Sound management requires careful monitoring and reporting risk exposures. Banks must have an effective structure of internal control review.

Principle 2 requires that supervisors evaluate internal capital adequacy assessments, strategies by banks and their compliance with regulatory capital ratios. Moreover, supervisors must take corrective action when unsatisfied with the process.

Review by supervisors of adequacy of risk assessment is essential but supervisors should not function as bank management. The review could combine on-site examinations or inspections, off-site surveillance, interaction with management, review of auditor work related to capital requirements and periodic reporting. Evaluation of capital adequacy should include analysis by the bank of the impact of unexpected events on capital. The complexity and sophistication of stress tests should be proportionate to bank business. Supervisors should examine the quality of bank information and reporting and compliance with minimum standards and qualifying criteria for various approaches.

Principle 3 specifies expectations by supervisors that banks maintain capital above minimum regulatory ratios. Moreover, supervisors should be in a position to request that banks maintain capital in excess of minimum requirements. Supervisors must analyze if strict compliance with Pillar I is sufficient for the peculiarities of their financial markets. They should encourage banks to exceed minimum requirements. Banks that desire higher external ratings to attract capital would maintain standards above the minimum. A buffer above the required minimum protects institutions and the system from unexpected events. Supervisors can rank banks as, for example, well capitalized and adequately capitalized, to encourage standards above the minimum.

Principle 4 is a sort of preemptive strike. Supervisors should intervene early to avoid capital from falling below what would be required by the bank's risk profile. In addition, supervisors should have the authority to impose remedial action to maintain and restore capital. There are numerous available measures of monitoring and requesting immediate subscription of capital.

The framework also considers special issues during review by supervisors. When supervisors find that interest rate risk positions of banks threaten capital, they should demand reduction of risks, increase of capital or a combination of both. If standardized tests of increase of 200 basis points in interest rates result in decline of 20 percent of the sum of Tier 1 and Tier 2 capital, supervisors should monitor the bank closely.

Supervisors must assess if banks have sufficient capital under Pillar I and if results of stress tests of credit risk of Pillar I comply with IRB minimum requirements. Supervisors should review results and the quality of these stress tests. In case of a shortfall, supervisors should require reduction of risks and/or additional

Table 4.7   Definitions in Basel II

Default:	The bank concludes that the obligor will not pay credit obligations in full without action by the bank to realize security or obligor is past due more than 90 days in credit obligations
EAD:	*EAD* is the expected gross exposure of the claim on default of the obligor

capital/provisions to ensure that capital is sufficient for regulatory ratios and recalculated stress tests.

Banks must use the definition of default of Basel II, Table 4.7, to estimate *PD* and *EAD*. However, supervisors will provide guidance on how the definition relates to their jurisdictions. Supervisors must require banks to have appropriate policies and procedures to control "residual risks," such as inability to seize collateral, delinquency by a guarantor to pay and inadequacy of documentation.

Risk concentrations are typically the major cause of difficulties in banks. Banks must have adequate processes to identify, measure, monitor and control risk concentrations. Banks must consider these concentrations in their assessment of capital adequacy within Pillar II. Supervisors must assess the quality of processes by banks on risk concentration and their consideration in capital adequacy, reviewing also stress tests.

According to Basel II, the supervisory function must be transparent and accountable. There must be close and continuing dialogue between banks and supervisors and among supervisors in different jurisdictions for cross-border supervision of large banking organizations. The home country supervisor is responsible for the consolidated review and the framework of banks in its jurisdiction. The host-country supervisor may accept the process of the home country supervisor if it meets the host-country requirements.

Pillar III: market discipline

Asymmetry of information of creditors and debtors, companies and investors and monetary authorities and financial institutions constitutes an important foundation of financial theory and policy. Surprises of distorted information generate adverse market events, such as lack of reserves and insolvency of banks in the Asian crisis and, more recently, accounting revaluations of Enron, WorldCom, Adelphia and so on. Financial markets are efficient in their functions of intermediation and monitoring when savers and investors have access to complete and transparent information.

The BCBS designed Pillar III to complement the minimum capital requirements of Pillar I and the supervisory review process of Pillar II. Banks must have a formal disclosure policy, approved by the board of directors, covering types of disclosure and required internal controls. Market discipline is disclosure by banks of significant information to market participants (BCBS 2001d). This disclosure would allow market participants to assess risks of banks and their capital adequacy.

Market discipline is part of the role of supervisors to ensure sound and safe markets.

Supervisors have authority to obtain information from banks in the form of regulatory reports. In some jurisdictions, supervisors may disclose all or part of this information to the public. There is a range of mechanisms available to supervisors to enforce disclosure: moral suasion, reprimands and penalties. The framework provides another alternative. Supervisors may deny lower risk weights or more advanced approaches to banks that do not provide sufficient disclosure.

The BCBS has an ongoing dialogue with accounting authorities to conform Pillar III to accounting standards. The Committee may eventually alter disclosure requirements in accordance with accounting developments. Banks may have to meet accounting and listing requirements of disclosure and should describe the difference with requirements under Basel II and where to find additional information.

The content of disclosure must meet criteria of materiality: a bank must decide if omission or misstatement could alter economic decisions by a user of the information. A "user test" is if the user would consider an item in question as material. In general, banks must disclose information on a semi-annual basis, with some exceptions. On a quarterly basis, banks must disclose Tier 1 and total capital adequacy ratios and their components. Banks should disclose material information as soon as possible and never after national legal deadlines. General qualitative information on risk management objectives and policies, reporting system, definitions and so on can be published annually. Banks must balance the need to disclose meaningful information and protection of proprietary and confidential information. Basel II provides disclosure requirements in tabular form (BCBS 2004f, 177–90).

Implementing Basel II in Europe and the United States

Prudential regulation and supervision of banks has been analyzed as more beneficial to markets and consumers than securities regulations.[1] The process of rule making in banking regulation is more inclusive of public participation. In addition, it considers more carefully costs and benefits. Banking supervisors are more sensitive to the impact of their actions on financial markets. There are no high-profile prosecutions and as little as possible leaking to the press. The EU is applying Basel II to all its financial institutions. The United States has a diversified banking system, with 11 large banks accounting for most international banking and thousands of smaller banks engaged in regional and local banking. US regulators and supervisors are applying the more advanced Basel II only to the largest banks.

The BCBS has evolved into what could be a model for designing and spreading international rules with enhanced accountability and transparency (Barr and Miller 2006, 17). In the early stages of banking crises in the 1970s, the meetings of the central bankers at the BCBS were not accessible to outsiders. In enhancing accountability and transparency, the BCBS process has significantly gained in legitimacy. The BCBS process, particularly in Basel II, has included requests for comments from a wide audience, QIS seeking and providing information and formal implementation guidance adapting to local conditions. Barr and Miller (2006, 17) argue that the significant interaction of international administrative procedures enhances the accountability and legitimacy in global administrative practice.

There is a strong case for international regulation according to Barr and Miller (2006, 21). National regulators and supervisors may experience conflicts that could result in inadequate domestic financial systems. The closer integration of the world economy creates the need for cooperation among supervisors and regulators in countries and regions. Harmonizing standards and codes of financial institutions can strengthen the world's financial architecture. The BCBS strives to harmonize standards of regulation and supervision of financial systems across countries and regions. Barr and Miller (2006, 221) also argue that the BIS and the BCBS provide GPGs of information and expertise. The central bankers of the world have a forum in which they meet and share experience and principles. The BIS is the center for collection and dissemination of international financial transactions and the management of central banks. The BIS is at the center of designing and developing international financial standards in a transparent fashion. The nature of soft law of the BCBS is an advantage because norms are reviewed to adapt them to national realities. Countries adapt the financial norms to their own circumstances, enhancing their ownership, implementation and preservation.

The strength of the BCBS process is illustrated by the administrative review in the United States (Barr and Miller 2006, 29–35). The transparency of the process is enhanced in the United States by the required issue of advanced notice of proposed rulemaking (ANPR). The comments are widely accessible, creating the interaction between the regulators and supervisors, on one side, and the financial and nonfinancial communities on the other. Additional requests of comments on individual issues are also part of the process. The regulators issue white papers with quantitative and qualitative analysis of the impact of Basel II. There is also the opportunity for different opinions by the various regulatory agencies in the United States. Finally, Congress exercises oversight of the process. Barr and Miller (2006, 35) conclude that "these national measures, embedded in the democratic politics of the United States, have served as important means to fulfill the promise of global administrative law." The process informs the public and legislators, enhancing desirable goals of transparency, participation and accountability.

The EU operates under the system of comitology. The EC is assisted by advisory, management and regulatory committees. The EC prepares and implements initiatives in legislation. The committees function as forums for discussion with representatives from member states under the chair of the EC. These committees create a dialogue with national administrations prior to adopting implementing measures. The purpose of the process is to ensure that the measures reflect the situation in the individual member states. Parliament can monitor the implementation of legislative instruments.

The EU ECOFIN decided in December 2003 to extend to banking and insurance the Lamfalussy approach of integration of securities. The EC established the Committee of European Banking Supervisors (CEBS) in 2003 (CEBS 2005) to obtain advice on issues of banking supervision. The CEBS is part of the legal framework of the EU and is entrusted with the task of promoting convergence of banking supervision in Europe. It is the only committee in the EU for the central banks of the 25 countries, including the ECB. The CEBS advises the EC on issues of banking policy, especially preparing draft measures for approval by the European Parliament. It also issues guidelines, recommendations and standards with the objective of implementation and application of the legislation of the EU. The CEBS also fosters cooperation and exchange of information of banking supervision and is accountable to the European Parliament and Council.

The CEBS finds an opportunity in Basel II to promote convergence in supervision within the EU. The vehicle for convergence is the Capital Requirements Directive (CRD) of Basel II (CEBS 2005). The role of the ECBS in Basel II and the CRD is to guarantee consistent implementation of Basel II and the CRD in members of the EU. Another desirable goal is to pursue convergence in supervision related to Basel II and cooperation of home and host authorities. Consultations are designed to maintain quality of standards of supervision. There is comparison of individual national choices of implementation of the CRD that are followed by the system of supervisory disclosure of the CEBS.

Consultations, QISs and the work by the CEBS led to the CRD. The EU Parliament and Council (2006a–b) approved the directive applying Basel II to all banks and securities firms in the EU beginning in January 2007. The CRDs are consistent with Basel II, including the schedule of implementation. The CEBS created a CRD Transposition Group to facilitate accurate and coherent transposition of the CRDs in the legislation of member states. This group will provide member states with interpretation of the CRDs, developing proposals on how to solve problems.

The CEBS (2006) conducted a 5th QIS in 18 EU countries. The results are for 51 banks and were received by the CEBS in the first quarter of 2006. The minimum required capital for the choice of most likely approach would decrease by 7.7 percent for group 1 (49 banks) and 15.4 percent for group 2 (2 banks). The reported data show significant incentives to measure risk by using more sophisticated risk management approaches as intended under Basel II. The minimum required capital is 6.8 percent lower under the advanced than under the foundation IRB for group 1 banks and 12.4 percent lower under the foundation IRB than under the standardized approach for group 2 banks. The data are still insufficient for operational risk but suggest the incentive to move to the advanced AMA.

The process of implementing Basel II in an individual country is illustrated by the case of Germany (Deutsche Bundesbank 2006). Basel II is not legally binding for Germany but it provided the initial background for the directives of the EU. The approval of the directives by the EU Parliament and the Council still required incorporation into the regulations of Germany. There was intensive consultation with the banking sector during the process of creation of the standard and consideration by the EU authorities. The objective of these consultations was to adapt the standard to the realities of banking in Germany.

The monetary authorities of Germany conducted a dialogue with banks and industry associations at the early stages of the process with a formal working group on implementing Basel II. The objective of the dialogue was to optimize the effectiveness of implementing the capital requirements in Germany. In November 2006, the amendments to the Banking Act of Germany were published in its Federal Gazette. Pillars I and III of Basel II were incorporated into the Solvency Regulation of Germany and Pillar II became part of German law by means of the minimum requirements for risk management (Deutsche Bundesbank 2006, 68–70). These changes implement into German law the directives of the EU. German monetary authorities still have to approve requests by individual institutions to implement advanced IRB and AMA methods. This approval will normally require some time, which is obvious because of the major change in regulatory scope. Pillar I requires a period of gestation and approval. The expectation of the Deutsche Bundesbank (2006, 87) is for slight reduction of 5 percent in regulatory capital for the standardized approach and of 8 percent for the IRB approach.

The US approach consists of implementing Basel II for the largest 11 banks and a modified Basel IA for the remaining banks (Dugan 2006a–b). An important concern of the US supervisors is the reduction in the aggregate minimum required capital and the dispersion of results across institutions and portfolio categories revealed by the fourth QIS. Effective minimum required capital decreases by 11.7 percent; the median decrease is 22.6 percent for all participants in the QIS. The United States is postponing the parallel run, or prequalification period, to 2008 instead of 2007. This is the period in which banks test the IRB and AMA methods but still do not use them to calculate capital requirements. The prequalification period will be followed by a 3-year period during which reductions in capital requirements will be limited by floors: 95 percent in 2009, 90 percent in 2010 and 85 percent in 2011.

The objective of US regulators and supervisors is to observe in reality capital standards that are not yet tested. On the basis of future assessment, the supervisors will decide on the possible elimination of the floors after 2011. The United States will also retain the prompt corrective action (PCA) and leverage capital requirements because they provide a cushion for banks to engage in prudent risk taking, innovation and growth (Dugan 2006a, 8). The objective of Basel IA is creating a capital requirement that is sensitive to risk but without increasing the cost burden to banks. The intention is to reduce the gap between Basel IA and Basel II.

The Office of the Comptroller of the Currency (OCC), the Federal Reserve System (FRS), the Federal Deposit Insurance Corporation (FDIC) and the Office of Thrift Supervision (OTS) issued a Basel IA notice of proposed rulemaking (NPR) on December 26, 2006 (US Treasury 2006b–d). The Basel IA NPR uses the responses to an earlier NPR of October 20, 2005. The objective is to obtain a balance between feasible operations and consideration of risk sensitivity. An important objective is to avoid unnecessary burdens of regulation (OCC 2006c). The deadline for response to the Basel II NPR and the Basel IA NPR was extended to March 26, 2007. The NPRs are addressed to the CEOs of national banks, department and division heads, all examining personnel and other interested parties. Modifications were requested on nearly all the important issues relating to the capital standards. An important request for comment is on the possible use of loan-to-value ratios to weight most residential mortgages.

Regulatory agencies are required by US Executive Order 12866 to provide a regulatory analysis to the Office of Management and Budget (OMB) for any rule that may have an impact on the economy of $100 million or more (OCC 2006a–b). The OCC (2006a–b) provided this analysis for the Basel II NPR and for the Basel IA NPR. The regulatory analysis provides comprehensive information on the impact of the proposed rules. It also must provide the costs and benefits of the rules and alternative scenarios of possible behavior.

The United States will implement a "bifurcated" system of capital requirements (OCC 2006a, 24–5). Large internationally active banks will implement the advanced IRB and advanced AMA. The second system based on current capital requirement rules will apply to the rest of the institutions. Institutions that are not in the mandatory category may opt to implement the advanced methods when complying with minimum standards determined by banking supervisors. The mandatory organizations are those with total assets of $250 billion or $10 billion in foreign assets. At the time of the call report, there were four organizations meeting both criteria; two had $250 billion in total assets; and five had more than $10 billion in foreign assets. The 11 organizations meeting the mandatory requirements had total assets of $4.6 trillion, equivalent to 44 percent of total US banking assets of $10.5 trillion, and about $978 billion in foreign assets, equivalent to 96 percent of US foreign banking assets of about $1 trillion. Basel II will not be mandatory for the remaining general organizations, about 7000, accounting for 56 percent of US total banking assets. The OCC (2006a, 25) believes that some of the general organizations may move into Basel II as they acquire experience and knowledge about the more advanced methods. The OCC (2006a) estimates the present value of total cost at $545.9 million of implementing Basel II in the mandatory organizations by 2011. The average cost for the mandatory organizations is $46 million. The data were obtained from the QIS 4. According to the OCC (2006a), it is difficult to estimate the benefits from Basel II. However, the agency is optimistic that the benefits will be higher than the costs and are likely to increase over time.

On July 20, 2007, the four agencies supervising and regulating banks in the United States (Federal Reserve Board [FRBO], FDIC, OCC and OTS) reached a formal agreement on the implementation of Basel II (FRBO *et al.* 2007Jul20). The agreement maintained the transitional floors for maximum cumulative reductions of capital of 5 percent in the first year, 10 percent in the second year and 15 percent in the third year. The agencies will publish an evaluation after the second transitional year of whether there are deficiencies and if there is need for changes. The statements of limit of 10 percent of aggregate reductions in risk-based capital requirements were eliminated. The earlier proposed rule of the Basel IA option was abandoned. The agencies will issue a new proposed rule to allow non-core banks to adopt a standardized approach under Basel II.

Banks need to concentrate efforts in developing internal models, which is what made Basel I obsolete, leading to Basel II. The benefits of Basel II consist of greater differentiation of risk compared with Basel I. The costs of Basel II are in the form of required documentation, validation and data systems development to collect data and conduct computations (Araten 2006). Basel II intends to strengthen bank soundness and stability. The framework also uses the criterion of competitive equality to prevent banks from gaining over others. The foundation of Basel II is providing incentives to continue the revolution in risk management. The models of economic capital are designed to measure risks prudently in relation to the revenues that they generate (Araten 2006). The soundness and success of banks depends on pushing forward the frontiers of knowledge and application of risk management that permits innovation in products and bank profitability.

Self-regulatory organizations, the SEC and the FSA

The private institutions operating in financial markets have their own regulation through self-regulatory organizations (SRO). The most conspicuous ones are the stock and futures exchanges shown in Table 4.9. The exchanges create governance, rules, conduct codes and a process of investigation, discipline, prosecution and enforcement. There are additional clearing houses that also have their own regulation. Securities regulators in turn impose supervision of the SROs. The two major systems of securities regulation are those of the United States and the United Kingdom. The discussion in this section serves as background to more detailed analysis of the loss of competitiveness in finance of NYC and the United States to London and other financial centers.

Several stock and futures exchanges are listed in Table 4.8. There are also associated clearinghouses for the processing and payment of transactions. There is a global process of consolidation of exchanges. Part of the motivation for this consolidation is the loss of competitiveness of the United States, which could be viewed as the rise of the volume of exchanges in other countries. An important development is the rise of the Chinese stock market following China's accession to the WTO. China is restructuring its capital organization beginning with the opening of the financial system to foreign ownership and competition. A significant if not the major part of transactions in securities occurs in OTC markets. Associations of trading firms perform self-regulation in these markets. Supervisors of financial institutions also oversee these transactions. Banks also serve as custodians of securities, requiring norms of conduct and rules. There is a large sector of SROs worldwide linked online by electronic connection.

The self-regulation of the securities industry under Securities and Exchange Commission (SEC) supervision was consolidated during the New Deal (Seligman 2004). There were two factors that generated this system. It was impractical to directly supervise thousands of broker-dealers and business corporations. In addition, the industry preferred to avoid disruption of business, applying its

Table 4.8   Selected stock and futures exchanges

Stock exchanges
  NYSE Euronext http://www.nyse.com/www.nyseeuronext.com
  NASDAQ http://www.nasdaq.com/
  London Stock Exchange http://www.londonstockexchange.com/en-gb/home.htm
  Tokyo Stock Exchange http://www.tse.or.jp/english/index.html
  Frankfurt Stock Exchange http://deutsche-boerse.com/dbag/dispatch/en/kir/gdb_
    navigation/about_us/20_FWB_Frankfurt_Stock_Exchange
  Hong Kong Stock Exchange http://www.hkex.com.hk/index.htm
  Singapore Exchange http://www.sgx.com/

Futures exchanges
  Chicago Board of Trade Chicago Mercantile Exchange http://www.cbot.com/
  New York Mercantile Exchange http://www.nymex.com/index.aspx
  Chicago Board Options Exchange http://www.cboe.com/
  London Metal Exchange http://www.lme.co.uk/
  LIFFE http://www.euronext.com/home_derivatives-2153-EN.html
  Tokyo Commodity Exchange http://www.tocom.or.jp/

enhanced practical knowledge of the markets. Seligman (2004, 1377–84) finds four alternatives to the supervision of SROs:

1. *Maintain the 2003 NYSE restructuring.* The NYSE reorganized by creating an independent not-for-profit company, NYSE Regulation, Inc., to conduct the self-regulation under the SEC supervision. This structure is discussed below in detail. There are several deficiencies in this system, according to Seligman (2004, 1378–9). Earlier reorganizations in 1938 and 1964 focused on preventing the conflict of interest in NYSE disciplinary mechanisms instead of on the more critical conflicts of interest of rulemaking and advocacy such as the specialist system, quote competition and market linkages. Previous reorganizations of governance have deteriorated in periods of less concern by Congress and the SEC because conflicts of interest still remain. The 2003 reorganization did not correct the critical problem, which is the excessive concentration of power in the NYSE Chair. There still remain constitutional mechanisms that limit the authority of the Board of Directors.
2. *Separation of NYSE regulation from the exchange.* The creation of NYSE Regulation, Inc. partly meets the requirements considered by Seligman (2004). There are differences in the actual structure discussed below and the analysis of Seligman (2004).
3. *Establishment of an industry regulator.* The advantage of this system would be the elimination of conflicts of interest. However, Seligman (2004) finds a hurdle in conciliating diverse interests in the formation of rules.
4. *Regulation by the SEC.* The issue is again the two reasons used during the New Deal to develop self regulation: cost and complexity.

The objective of the SEC (2006) "is to protect investors, maintain fair, orderly and efficient markets and facilitate capital formation." The SEC is especially concerned with investor protection to ensure that citizens have a fair chance to preserve their resources. The SEC (2006) believes that the laws and rules that govern securities in the United States derive from the simple principle that all investors, large or small, should have accessible information about an investment before buying it and during holding and selling it. This basic right is ensured by requirements of disclosure of meaningful information, financial and otherwise, to the public. Investors can make adequate investment decisions only if they have the required information.

The SEC prevents fraud and ensures disclosure by overseeing major actors in the market of securities such as securities exchanges, brokers, dealers, investment advisors and mutual funds. The enforcement authority of the SEC empowers it to engage in civil enforcement actions for violation of securities laws, including fraud and misleading the public with erroneous information about securities and the companies issuing them. The SEC interacts with other areas of government such as Congress, federal departments and agencies, the SROs or stock exchanges, state securities regulators and private sector organizations. The President's Working Group on Financial Markets (PWGFM) includes the Chairs of the SEC, the FRBO, the Commodities Futures Trading Commission (CFTC) and the Secretary of the Treasury.

Congress passed the Securities Act of 1933 and the Securities Exchange Act of 1934. In the exegesis of the SEC (2006), the intention of Congress was to restore confidence by investors in the stock market by means of "more structure and government oversight." In this view, the securities laws are based on two common sense principles. First, the issuing companies must inform the public about the securities, their business and the risks. Second, the distributors and traders of securities – brokers, dealers and exchanges – have to give fair and honest treatment to investors, placing the interests of investors above everything. In 1934, Congress established the SEC with the objective of enforcing the new laws, promoting market stability and protecting investors.

There are five commissioners of the SEC appointed by the President subject to advice and consent by the Senate. The appointments are for 5 years and staggered in such a way that the term of one commissioner ends on June 5 of every year. There is a maximum limit of three commissioners from the same political party. The President also designates one of the commissioners as the chief executive or Chairman of the SEC. In meetings open to the public, the commissioners interpret federal securities laws, amend existing rules, propose new rules and enforce rules and laws.

The objective of the Division of Market Regulation of the SEC (2006) is to establish and maintain standards "for fair, orderly and efficient markets." Its main instrument to attain this objective is the regulation of broker-dealer firms, SROs (stock exchanges and clearing agencies) and other market participants. The definition of an SRO by the SEC (2006) is as follows:

A self-regulatory organization is a member organization that creates and enforces rules for its members based on the federal securities laws. SROs, which are overseen by the SEC, are the front line in regulating broker-dealers

The SEC (2006) operates by making rules. Rulemaking is the instrument for implementing legislation passed by Congress and signed into law by the President. The framework of oversight of the SEC consists of the Securities Act of 1933, the Securities Exchange Act of 1934 and the Investment Company Act of 1940. The statutes are quite broad in nature, consisting of basic principles and objectives. The evolution of securities markets requires rules by the SEC (2006) "to maintain fair and orderly markets and to protect investors by altering regulations or creating new ones." The process of rulemaking may start with a specific proposal or with a concept release in which the SEC requests views of the public on a given issue. The SEC then elaborates a rule proposal for the consideration of the Commission. After approval of the proposal by the Commission, the SEC presents it to the public for a period of time of 30–60 days for review and comment. The final rule takes the replies by the public as input into consideration for the final draft. The final draft is presented to the Commission; if adopted it becomes part of the official rules governing the securities markets. A major rule may require congressional review and veto consideration before it becomes effective.

The world's largest and most liquid exchange group is NYSE Euronext, which started on April 4, 2007. It is the result of the consolidation of the NYSE Group Inc. and Euronext N. V. NYSE Euronext consists of six cash equities exchanges in five countries and six derivatives exchanges. It provides listings, trading in cash equities, equity and interest rate derivatives, bonds and distribution of market data. The listed companies have a capital market value of $28.5 trillion, about twice the GDP of the United States.

Euronext N. V. is a limited liability Dutch public company with registered office in Amsterdam. It has subsidiaries in Belgium, France, the Netherlands, Portugal and the United Kingdom. The corporate governance of Euronext consists of two pillars of confidence by stakeholders and supervisors. The shareholders have approved its corporate governance structure and policy. Euronext has a Supervisory Board composed of independent members and a Managing Board. The Supervisory Board exercises power of oversight over the Managing Board and is governed by a code of rules and procedures and adopted a code of conduct. There is at least one member of the Supervisory Board that is knowledgeable on finance and at least another one that is knowledgeable on human resources.

The members of the NYSE include about 400 of the largest securities firms in the United States that service 92 million customer accounts. These firms handle 90 percent of the public customer accounts of broker-dealers with total assets of $3.28 trillion. The NYSE is an examining authority, as approved by the SEC, of its members and member firms. The merger of the NYSE and Archipelago Holdings, Inc. created a publicly traded company, NYSE Group, Inc., that is the sole owner of New York Stock Exchange LLC, a NY limited liability company. New York Stock Exchange LLC is the successor with registered securities exchange status of the NYSE. There are two subsidiaries, NYSE Market, Inc., a Delaware corporation, and NYSE Regulation, Inc., a NY Type A not-for-profit corporation.

The objective of the organizational structure of the two subsidiaries is to conform to the major changes in architecture completed in 2003. An independent commission headed by former Citigroup Chairman John Reed conducted the architecture reform work. An important feature is to insulate NYSE Regulation from the potential conflicts created by public ownership.

The primary responsibility for the regulatory oversight of the exchange subsidiaries of the NYSE Group is exercised by the CEO of NYSE Regulation, reporting only to the board of directors of NYSE Regulation. The board of NYSE Regulation is composed of six independent directors with no relation to the member organizations and listed companies. It also has three directors that are simultaneously directors of the NYSE Group. The CEO of NYSE Regulation is the sole management director in the board. The CEO of NYSE Group is not a member of the board of NYSE Regulation. The management of NYSE Regulation does not report to the NYSE Group CEO.

NYSE Regulation has a major role in monitoring the activities of its member firms and listed companies and in enforcing compliance with NYSE rules and federal securities laws. The SEC oversees the self-regulatory activities of NYSE Regulation. The rules of NYSE cover in detail the operations of its member organizations, on and off the trading floor. There are additional rules of adoption of first-class standards of financial and corporate accountability and transparency.

NYSE Regulation consists of four divisions:

1. *Market surveillance.* This division conducts surveillance on real time and after trades to detect market abuse and manipulation and insider trading. It produces rules and evaluates specialists. The staff has a presence in the trading floor and uses sophisticated electronic technology and human judgment of analysts. It recommends discipline and can refer matters to the SEC.
2. *Member firm regulation.* This division engages in surveillance of NYSE members for compliance by member firms of practices of finance, operations and sales with NYSE rules and SEC regulations.
3. *Enforcement.* This division investigates and prosecutes violations of NYSE rules and federal securities laws.
4. *Listed company compliance.* The objective of this division is to maintain original listing standards that are of first world class.

The approach of the United Kingdom is a unitary authority of regulation, the Financial Services Authority (FSA). According to the Director of Enforcement of the FSA, Margaret Cole (2007, 266), the London philosophy consists of a "light touch." This flexible approach has permitted London to become a "leading center for mobile capital." The FSA does not consider itself to be a regulator driven by high-profile enforcement. The leading aspect of regulation is the use of supervision and relations with the regulated firms. It has implemented a deliberate move to principles-based regulation.

The philosophy of the FSA could be criticized, according to Cole (2007, 267), by a contrast with US regulation. Cole argues that there is no evidence of high-profile prosecution of violation of securities laws in the United Kingdom. On the contrary, the approach consists of selective messages and "allows some illicit activity to go unpunished" (Cole 2007, 267). However, the FSA claims that it has created an innovative and extremely effective system.

The FSA is independent of the UK government (Cole 2007, 267). Its origin is in the Labor administration taking office in 1997 and it was created after giving independence to the BOE in the conduct of monetary policy. The FSA was the successor organization of ten predecessor UK regulators. It is now the only regulator of financial services in the United Kingdom. The funding of the FSA originates in fees paid by large and small firms that it regulates. Its responsibility of supervision encompasses wholesale and retail markets, equities and derivatives trading, banking and insurance. It is also the listing authority of securities in the United Kingdom. The regulation of mortgages and insurance has been recently added to the FSA. The population of the United Kingdom is about 60 million people of whom one million are in the industries regulated by the FSA that generate 7 percent of GDP. The staff of the FSA consists of 2800 employees and the current annual budget is £266 million. The FSA regulates about 30,000 firms. The objective function of the FSA is attaining maximum benefits subject to a cost restraint.

The legislation creating the system is the Financial Services and Market Act of 2000 (FSMA). The FSMA provides the FSA important powers of rulemaking, investigation and enforcement (Cole 2007, 268). The prevention of market abuse and the prosecution of insider trading are a key responsibility of the FSA under the FSMA. There are four statutory objectives of the FSA within the FSMA:

1. Market confidence in the financial system;
2. Public understanding of the financial system;
3. Consumer protection;
4. Reduction of financial crime.

The FSA endeavors to limit the potential for a business enterprise to be used with the objective of committing financial crime. The four objectives govern the operation of the FSA and its public, political and legal accountability. The FSA reports yearly to Parliament and can be challenged in the courts on the interpretation or negligence of implementing the objectives.

There is significant difference in the approach of the FSA and regulation in the United States. Cole (2007, 269–70) argues that the FSA does not target a system of perfection where there are no failures. The principle enunciated by Cole (2007, 269) is that "although the idea that regulation should seek to eliminate all failures may be appealing in theory, in practice it imposes prohibitive costs on the industry and on consumers." The regulation by the FSA (2007) is based on "an acceptance that a regulatory system neither can nor should aim at avoiding all failures." There is analysis in the following section of the recent regulation of SOX that centers on the proposition that eliminating all imperfections has unbearable costs. The costs of enforcement are minute compared with the costs of foregoing business and employment because of the heavy costs of compliance imposed on firms and markets.

The approach followed by the FSA, according to Cole (2007, 270) and FSA (2007), is to determine the amount of risk that the regulator is prepared to tolerate, given its objectives, and then to concentrate efforts on the risks that may be more important in terms of potential harm. There is minimization of risks with respect to a constraint of four objectives provided by the FSMA. The FSA (2007) restricts "regulation to those circumstances where the market does not provide adequate answers and where regulation has the prospect of doing so at reasonable cost." The objective of the FSA (2007) is of "regulation working with the grain of the market rather than against it." The US approach appears not to be focused on risk but rather on the elimination of every possible form of misconduct, large or minor.

Another important contrast between the US and UK approaches is in the attitude toward "market failure." The analysis of market failure is covered in detail in Chapter 5 of Volume I. In general terms, there is market failure when the market cannot deliver the optimum welfare and maximum efficiency, which could be provided with government intervention. Monopoly is a classic case of market failure because the market would deliver less output at a higher price than under perfect competition. Cole (2007, 270) reveals an interesting approach:

> Even when empirical analysis shows that there has been a market failure, we are not always convinced that regulatory intervention is the most efficient and cost-effective form of correction

In these cases, the FSA considers competition policy or the use of moral suasion with firms to change their behavior but, according to Cole (2007, 270), "without reaching for the heavy-handed tool of the regulator's rule book." Allegations of market failure trigger cost-benefit analysis and regulation in the United States.

The FSA (2007) enunciates principles of good regulation that orient its work:

- *Efficiency and economy.* The Treasury can commission value-for-money reviews of the FSA as a form of controlling its efficiency and economy.
- *Management responsibility.* The non-executive committee of the Board of the FSA oversees excessive intrusion into the business of regulated firms. Senior management in firms is accountable for their risk management.
- *Proportionality.* The FSA must balance the proportionality of costs relative to benefits of regulation. It conducts professional cost-benefit analysis of measures.
- *Innovation.* The FSA considers alternative ways of compliance to avoid restricting innovation of financial products and services.
- *International view and competitiveness.* There is focus on the international nature of financial services and in maintaining the competitive position of the United Kingdom.
- *Competition.* The FSA diminishes the impact on competition of its regulatory measures and analyzes the need for competition among the regulated firms.

Cole (2007, 270–1) argues that the outcomes-based approach of the FSA enables it to enhance its performance in improving markets. The regulatory dividend of less intervention by the regulatory body is an incentive for firms to deliver compliance. The focus on compliance with rules detracts from sound judgment and enhanced knowledge of the business. The lack of flexibility and resulting opportunities causes a flight of skills out of an industry. The objective of the FSA is to maintain competent professionals in the financial services industry. Cole (2007, 271) argues that standards based on rules and authoritative enforcement do not prevent dishonesty. The acceptance of risks by the regulators and the regulated firms may create a range of outcomes of judgments that can enhance market efficiency. Delivering the lecture in New York City (NYC), Cole (2007, 271) provides the results of the work of the FSA:

> By the end of September this year [2006], companies had raised more capital on the main market of the London Stock Exchange, $26.7 billion, than the New York Stock Exchange and NASDAQ combined, $26.4 billion – and this didn't even include the $6.7 billion raised on the London Stock Exchange's alternative investment market

International IPOs, according to Cole (2007, 272), even provide sharper contrast. The London Stock Exchange (LSE) attracted 59 deals with combined value of $15.9 billion. In the same period, the NYSE and NASDAQ jointly had 17 deals in the combined value of $5.9 billion. The following sections elaborate the debate on the loss of competitiveness of the United States, in particular NYC, to foreign financial centers and the measures required for reversing this loss.

Sarbanes-Oxley

There are numerous concerns with the consequences of SOX. The discussion below begins with an analysis of the structure of SOX. The various concerns are then discussed in turn. The SOX legislation was rushed in an election year after the WorldCom scandal. The costs of implementation are much higher in reality than anticipated and the benefits are difficult to measure. There is more emphasis in the literature on the excess of costs over benefits than the contrary view. The critical issue is whether SOX will affect governance in such a way as to create risk aversion in the management of public companies. If SOX were to affect the taking of risk by entrepreneurs it could retard the rate of economic growth of the United States, causing major damage to the country's competitiveness. There is growing literature showing that SOX can have stronger impacts on small and foreign companies. Finally, a significant part of SOX centers on gatekeepers, attorneys and auditors, generating also differing views on the act.

The structure of regulation

There were major declines of stock prices at the turn of the Millennium but more pronounced in Europe than in the United States. Coffee (2005) seeks to explain

Table 4.9 Corporate scandals according to Coffee

Ownership	Concentrated ownership	Dispersed
Ownership	Controlling shareholders	Many shareholders
Disclosure standards	Lax	Rigorous
Transparency	Opaque	Transparent
Share turnover	Low	High
Securities markets	Weak	Strong
Management compensation	Cash	Equity options
Interest in stock market Price	Low	High
Shareholder control	Command and control	Profit incentives
Disciplinary mechanisms	Banks, non-controlling shareholders	Markets after restatements
Incidence of scandals	Low	High
Perpetrators	Controlling groups	Corporate managers
Victims	Minority shareholders	Shareholders
Type of fraud	Appropriation of benefits	Manipulation of earnings
Examples	Parmalat	Enron, WorldCom
Gatekeeper failures	Benefit expropriation	Inflated earnings

Source: Coffee (2005).

the high incidence of corporate scandals in the United States relative to very few in Europe. Restatements of financial reports soared in the United States in the years 1999–2002 preceding SOX. Coffee (2005) provides an explanation for the differing behavior in the concentrated ownership of companies in Europe versus the dispersed ownership prevailing in the United States.

Table 4.9 has some of the elements of the theory proposed by Coffee (2005). There is much less market participation in concentrated than in dispersed ownership systems. A key difference is that there is no incentive in equity prices in the concentrated system because controlling shareholders exercise command and control over management. Management is paid according to stock price performance in dispersed ownership systems. Thus, the type of fraud occurs in the expropriation of benefits of minority shareholders in the concentrated system versus anticipation and/or fabrication of earnings in the dispersed system. Coffee (2005, 202) provides an example of a company with price/earnings ratio of 30 to 1, paying 2 million shares to its CEO. An increase in earnings by $1 causes an increase in price of $30 that can result in a payment to the CEO of $60 million. The difference in incentives explains the soaring restatement of earnings following stock market declines. The market has caused significant declines in the price of the stocks of companies engaged in this conduct. The gatekeeper failures in the analysis of Coffee (2005) occur in the form of expropriation of minority shareholders in concentrated systems and in inflated earnings in the dispersed system. The solution given by SOX is to make auditing accountable to an independent auditing committee.

The US President signed SOX into law on July 30, 2002 (US 107th Congress 2002). SOX created the Public Company Accounting Oversight Board (PCAOB) to oversee professional accounting in the United States. The objective of SOX was to strengthen corporate responsibility and financial disclosure, preventing corporate and accounting fraud. It was a reaction to the corporate scandals that followed the decline of the stock market after the high-tech collapse. The US SEC issued numerous interpretations of rules and reports on SOX (SEC 2007).

The structure of SOX as it originally entered in force is in Table 4.10. There are 11 titles in SOX. The objective of the law is to generate rules of conduct for the principal participants in publicly issued securities. Title I is directed to the auditing and

Table 4.10   Structure of SOX

Established PCAOB 15 USC 7211 Title I

- Nonprofit corporation under the District of Columbia Nonprofit Corporation Act
- Not "an agency of establishment of the United States Government" Sec. 101(b)
- Duties of the PCAOB, Sec. 101(c):

  - "Register public accounting firms that prepare audit reports for issuers"
  - Determine standards of "auditing, quality control, ethics, independence and other standards relating to the preparation of audit report for issuers"
  - "Conduct inspections of registered public accounting firms"
  - "Conduct investigations and disciplinary proceedings" of registered public accounting firms and associated persons
  - Promote high professional standards by registered public accounting firms and associated persons
  - Mandatory registration of public accounting firms that prepare, issue or participate in the preparation of any audit report to any issuer
  - Enforce compliance with SOX

Auditor independence title II

- Auditor reporting to audit committees, including communications with management
- Prohibited activities such as services to management
- Rotation of lead auditor after five consecutive years

Corporate responsibility title III

- Creation of corporate independent audit committee, Sec. 301, by amending 15 USC 78f Sec.10A
- Objective: prevent management to mislead and influence public auditors
- Composition: entirely independent membership
- Role: hire the public auditor and communicate with it
- Complaints: procedures to receive complains of the public and anonymous complaints by employees
- Recommendation: one member should be a financial expert with knowledge of GAAP and financial statements
- Corporate responsibility for financial reports I: signing officers must certify reviewing the reports, that they do not have material misrepresentations and omissions and that they are complete
- Corporate responsibility for financial reports II: signing officers must certify their responsibility for internal controls, that such controls are adequate to ensure disclosure of all material information, that they have evaluated the effectiveness of the controls, that they have disclosed to the auditors and audit committee any deficiencies in the controls and frauds and that all changes in the controls are disclosed

Table 4.10   (Continued)

- Forfeiture of bonuses and compensation: the CEO and CFO forfeit bonuses and profits received in the 12-month period after filing of a report that requires restatement
- Prohibition of insider trading during pension fund blackouts periods. Rules of professional conduct for attorneys: attorneys appearing before the SEC must report material violations of securities law, breach of fiduciary law or similar violation to the chief legal counsel or the CEO. If the counsel or CEO does not respond to the evidence, the attorney must report to the audit committee, another committee of the board of directors composed solely of independent directors or to the board of directors Sec. 307

Financial disclosures title IV

- Disclosure of all off-balance sheet transactions, arrangements, obligations and other relationships with unconsolidated persons or entities
- Prohibition of personal loans to executives
- Disclosure of transactions of management and shareholders
- Assessment of internal controls by management
- Corporate code of ethics for senior financial officers
- Disclosure of financial expert in audit committee

Conflicts of interests of analysts title V

- Objective: increase public confidence in analyst reports
- Rules of conflicts of interest by analysts
- Public disclosure of conflicts of interests by analysts

Accountability of corporate and criminal fraud title VIII

- Stiff penalties

Enhancement of white collar crime penalty title IX

- Stiff penalties

Corporate tax returns title X

- Signature of corporate returns by the CEO

Corporate fraud accountability title XI

- Increased criminal penalties

Source: http://www.sec.gov/about/laws/soa2002.pdf

accounting profession. It creates the PCAOB as a nonprofit institution, entirely separate from the federal government. The PCAOB regulates the profession of public accounting firms to enforce compliance with SOX. Public accounting firms involved in financial reports of issuers are required to register with the PCAOB, which will determine standards, conduct inspection, investigations, disciplinary processes and issue rules and take actions designed to promote high professional standards.

Title III introduces important measures of corporate responsibility. An important complaint that led to SOX was that management anticipated and/or fabricated earnings with the objective of receiving bonuses and higher compensation. Section 301 created the corporate independent audit committee. Criteria have been introduced to ensure the independence of the members. The role of the audit committee is to directly hire the public auditors and to communicate with them. There is the recommendation that one member should be a financial expert with knowledge of Generally Agreed Accounting Principles (GAAP) and interpretation of financial statements. SOX enhanced corporate responsibility of financial reports by senior management signing financial reports. In addition, it made signing officers accountable for establishing and maintaining internal controls, disclosing to auditors and the public deficiencies and fraud. SOX provided for the forfeiture of bonuses and profits from sale of corporate stock during the 12-month period following a financial report that is subsequently restated. It prohibited insider trading during pension fund blackout periods.

The disclosure requirements of financial reports are provided in Title IV. A critical provision is the disclosure of all off-balance sheet activities with unconsolidated persons or entities. In particular, this covers the special purpose entities (SPE) that surfaced during the Enron events. SOX prohibits the loans of corporations to executives. It requires a corporate code of ethics for senior financial officers.

There were complaints about information by stock analysts after the end of the high-tech boom and during the restatements of balance sheets and the wider corporate scandals. SOX intends to improve the confidence of the public in the reports of analysts. It requires the public disclosure of potential conflicts of interests that analysts may have in their reports on stocks. Several titles of SOX provide enhanced penalties for violations and fraud.

The events around Enron and Andersen triggered a first version of SOX prepared by Sarbanes. Whalen (2003) claims that the events of WorldCom before an election made SOX truly draconian. Bipartisan support originated in political convenience. The result, according to Whalen (2003), is more expensive regulation that is not necessarily more effective in preventing future corporate scandals. Whalen (2003) consulted legal experts who claimed that legal expenses for most public companies were likely to double because of SOX. These same sources calculate that independent directors may require 250 hours of work per year to carry out their new duties. The liability insurance of these independent directors is likely to increase significantly. Whalen (2003) also quotes a former staff member of the banking committee arguing that the law simply tries to make stock markets safe investments for everybody.

Costs and benefits

The critical issue in the evaluation of SOX is whether the costs merit the benefits (Braddock 2006). Some of the proposed benefits are questionable. The creation of a code of ethics in corporations need not deter dishonesty. Braddock (2006, 175) finds that Enron had a code of ethics but that did not prevent dishonesty. There can also be high costs in defending the corporation from frivolous law suits based on provisions of the code of ethics. The defense and settlement costs could be quite onerous. SOX does not address another problem that is related to risk in prolonged upswings of markets that end in disappointment such as the high-tech crash. There is immense pressure on corporations and pension plans to beat the market, which leads to corporate behavior that is almost impossible to control by regulation. Braddock (2006) also contends that corporate scandals were not the cause of the decline in US stock prices in 2000. In fact, as Coffee (2005) argues, the decline in foreign stock market prices were more pronounced. It is unlikely that Enron had any impact on the decline of the US stock market. Braddock (2006, 174) argues that SOX was an overreaction to the corporate scandals.

The costs of SOX are significant. Braddock (2006, 175) finds that Section 404 alone caused about $7 billion during the first year. These are recurring yearly costs. AIG warned investors that the compliance costs could be as high as $300 million. The impact of the costs on smaller companies is proportionately much higher. Braddock (2006, 175) finds that an industrial company paid $15 million in a 6-month period to comply with SOX, which represented about one-third of its profits. Such a large proportionate cost could significantly reduce the market price of a company. The second impact on corporate costs derives from the time required by directors to deal with the work burden of SOX. This cost is multiplied by the consultants and attorneys required in fear of the draconian penalties of SOX. Another high expense according to Braddock (2006) is the opportunity cost of resources spent in complying with SOX that could otherwise be used for development of the corporation.

Smaller and foreign companies bear significant indirect costs of SOX (Braddock 2006). These companies chose the option of delisting to avoid the costs of SOX. Investors lose in lack of transparency of companies. The exodus of foreign companies deprives investors of attractive opportunities to diversify their portfolios. The costs of SOX reduce profits and thus returns to investors. It is an open issue if SOX produces benefits that exceed its costs.

SOX could be the "final act in regulation of corporate disclosure," according to Carney (2006, 141). There is a critical issue if the costs of regulation have become sufficiently high to drive honest small and foreign companies from public registration. Carney (2006, 141) argues that the costs of entirely eliminating fraud could be more expensive than allowing some fraud to exist. Fraud should be prevented until the marginal cost of prevention is about equal to the returns from prevention. There is a social loss if the cost of prevention exceeds the returns. The main cost increase from SOX originates in Section 404 that is strictly confined to financial statements. The remaining aspects of corporate disclosure are left unchanged, according to Carney (2006, 142). Most of the controls in SOX already existed and did not prevent episodes such as Enron and WorldCom. Concerted action by employees can defeat such controls. Section 404 is merely due diligence instead of protection against fraud. The impact of SOX is to impose procedures that would not be selected otherwise.

Section 404 is creating a cottage industry of consultants. The implementation of internal controls involves management at all levels that contract outside consultants (Carney 2006, 145). CEOs head teams to operate these controls. Another structure of bureaucracy is being created in companies around a compliance officer. Auditing committees may retain counsel. SOX compliance also absorbs the time of the CFO. The opportunity cost of compliance could be extremely high as the company abandons the focus on business development in favor of avoiding the penalties imposed by SOX. Risk aversion could have highly detrimental effects on the corporate culture of the United States, currently leading ahead of Europe and Japan in innovation. A culture of risk aversion could jeopardize the future growth of the US economy.

Some of the costs of complying with SOX will not be reported in the income statement (Carney 2006, 147). These are the opportunity costs of complying with executive certification of financial statements, Section 302, and the certification of internal controls, Section 404. There are multiple direct costs of specialized staff required for compliance with these items. The available surveys of increases in costs caused by compliance with SOX show higher costs for every new survey (Carney 2006, 148). Most of these surveys are for larger companies. It is difficult to find accurate estimates for smaller companies. According to Carney (2006, 151), there are about 16,000 companies requiring compliance with SOX. Assuming a conservative estimate of $500,000 per company, the costs of complying with SOX are at least $8 billion per year. The estimates of losses of investors in Enron and World-Com are about $100 billion. These were highly unusual losses and it is fair to argue that a part would not have been prevented by SOX. Carney (2006, 151) estimates the present value of the costs of compliance at $266 billion, using a 3 percent per year discount rate and assuming that the costs are as certain as death and taxes. He refers to a study of the loss of $1.4 trillion in market value from the most significant rule-making events. There is evidence mentioned by Carney (2006, 152–3) of regulatory arbitrage with companies choosing other markets where to issue their stock.

There are multiple advantages for a company to become private (Carney 2006, 154–5). The private structure avoids numerous costs of public registration, including costs of litigation, higher directors and officers (D&O) insurance and higher legal and accounting fees. In addition, a leveraged buyout (LBO) provides the opportunity to sell large holdings that would obtain lower prices in thin markets. The total disclosed buyout transactions increased from $23.1 billion in 2001 to $136.5 billion in 2004. However, there are many factors determining LBOs that cannot be separated from the motivation of higher costs of compliance under SOX.

Governance and performance

The analysis of research literature and data by Romano (2005a, 1529) is used to support the view that SOX will not improve corporate governance or performance. The emphasis of SOX on independent directors and independent audit committees is based on the presumption that independent directors receive fees as compensation instead of bonuses based on performance. Thus, independent directors will not feel tempted to falsify financial reporting. There is no empirical evidence in the research literature surveyed by Romano (2005a, 1529–33) in support of the proposition that independent directors and audit committees improve corporate performance. Congress did not match the problem of the corporate scandals with a solution.

Another measure of SOX is the banning of public corporations of purchasing non-audit services from their auditors. The rationale for this measure is that management could possibly bribe the audit firms into misstatements by purchasing of non-audit fees. Empirical research finds no relation of audit quality and the purchase of non-audit services from the auditors. Romano (2005a, 1536) concludes that "SOX's prohibition of the purchase of nonaudit services from an auditor is an exercise in legislating away a nonproblem." The result of no relation between audit quality and purchase of non-audit services is the conclusion of the majority of scholarly research and the unanimous conclusion of the studies using the most advanced techniques. Moreover, the Panel on Audit Effectiveness does not find even one instance of compromise of an audit because of the purchasing of non-audit services from the auditor by the audited company (Romano 2005a, 1537).

SOX prohibits corporations, by Section 402(a), of extending loans to executive officers or directors. Corporate loans surfaced during the scandals of Enron, WorldCom, Tyco International and Adelphia Communications. The objective of the prohibition is avoiding the repetition of similar cases. Romano (2005a, 1538–9) finds that the effectiveness of the measure is dubious. Attempts to restrict the compensation of corporate executives typically result in different forms to maintain the compensation required to retain desired talent. Moreover, Romano (2005a, 1538–9) argues that SOX conflicts with the state law approach. Most of the loans are used to facilitate the conversion of stock ownership provided in remuneration packages. Thus, the loans merely serve to align the interests of shareholders and managers. In this sense, Romano (2005a, 1539) argues that the prohibition "is self-evidently a public policy error." The issues have been settled for decades by means of state laws.

The difficulty in providing an optimum model of corporate governance is an important issue regarding SOX (Fisch 2004, 43–5). The structure of SOX favors a board of independent directors engaged in policing fraud. It is not necessarily valid that an independent board is the best model of governance. There is the competing model of board composition in which the directors are appointed on the merits of their business knowledge. The board members contribute to the development of the corporate business model in ways that are far superior to policing fraud. Moreover, it is doubtful that board members could protect shareholders from fraud by management. SOX constitutes an intrusion in the ideal corporate governance. It appears more likely that Congress and regulators will be inferior to the actual selection of work of the board and its relation to the corporate business. Contributions of the board to business development are likely to bring more returns to investors than independent boards engaged in policing misconduct by management. There is here the recurring theme with SOX that it interferes with the strengthening of US business competitiveness. Fisch (2004, 49) argues that "the increasing intrusion of federal law into how corporations go about their business threatens to sacrifice the prime objective of corporate productivity." Federal intrusion shifts the focus of corporations away from innovation, creation of jobs, efficiency and global competitiveness.

An important characteristic of the federalist system of corporate law is its responsiveness to changing business conditions (Fisch 2004, 47–8). An important example is how the Delaware courts created legal standards on takeovers, protecting the board in its oversight of control changes. Simultaneously, the courts of Delaware protect the market for corporate control. Federal intrusion in the process of state development of corporate law would restrict the process.

The focus on the internal controls provided in Section 404 of SOX has detracted attention from the burdens imposed on the CEO and CFO by Section 302 as reminded by Langevoort (2006, 954–5): certification of the accuracy of disclosures, responsibility for internal controls, design of controls to ensure material information, evaluation of internal controls in the prior 90 days, reporting conclusions about effectiveness, changes and corrective actions. Audit Standard No. 2 (AS-2) of the PCAOB is expensive on the requirements of auditing internal controls. It intrudes into the corporate governance process and requires "every input that goes into the process of financial reporting, as well as the mechanisms for translating those inputs into the financial reports" (Langevoort 2006, 956). This includes all base data originating in daily operations of a corporation. The evaluation of the control environment requires the assessment of the effectiveness of the audit committee. The ineffectiveness of the audit committee could be a failure of internal controls. The view prevailing before SOX, according to Langevoort (2006, 956), was that the evaluation by an audit of the internal controls was not fraud prevention but rather a form of increasing the confidence in the data of the company.

The standard is the more than remote probability of misstatement that can be more than inconsequential. Langevoort (2006, 957) focuses on the issue of depth of the inquiry, double-checking and surveillance of the control environment in the compliance with the standard of more than remote likelihood. The issue of the costs and benefits of SOX centers on the need for state intervention. Langevoort (2006) argues that the two main reasons are the principal-agent problem and the aging of systems that may not work in current environments. Addressing these problems requires much less effort than the instructions in AS-2, which create an extremely laborious search throughout the entire firm. The net result is an increase in personnel and paperwork.

A fundamental flaw of SOX is that it does not address the essential problem relating to episodes such as Enron, which is the complexity of transactions in the current business environment. Romano (2005b, 214) points to the complexity of financial derivatives and the intangible nature of assets, both of which are bona fide vehicles of business. Basel II was the result of almost a full decade of contributions by authorities in central banking, commercial and investment banking, the financial sector, academics, legal scholars and critiques of every occupation. Romano (2005b, 214) argues that SOX will not prevent future scandals because it does not focus on the accounting failures of complex transactions. It is arguable that regulators and legislators may not be more adept to the task of solving the accounting hurdles than the private sector.

Small and foreign companies

The formation of an independent audit committee appears easier for US companies than for foreign entities seeking registration in the United States (Lansing and Grgurich 2004, 293–4). Foreign issuers have a two-tier board system such that the supervisory directors may not qualify as independent for the audit committee. In addition, many of these issuers have cross-share holdings in other companies, disqualifying potential members of the committee under the test of non-affiliate. Independence tests are difficult for foreign issuers. The SEC has created important exemptions for these foreign issuers (Lansing and Grgurisch 2004, 294). The complex cross-holding relations of European companies may require significant changes in accounting to incorporate all SPEs, deterring those companies from registration in US stock exchanges.

There is significant concern if SOX has interrupted the cross-listing of foreign companies in US exchanges and if it has caused an exodus from US capital markets in the form of delisting (Zhu and Small 2007). Most foreign companies cross-list in the United States by using American Depository Receipts (ADR), which are issued by a US bank on the basis of a number of shares held in a custodian bank (Zhu and Small 2007, 32). ADRs have the same investor rights as the original shares issued by the foreign company and are quoted in dollars and considered US securities. The purpose of ADRs is to facilitate the purchase, holding and sale of foreign securities by US investors. The trading of ADRs rose to 40.1 billion shares equivalent to $877 billion in 2004 from 4.3 billion shares equivalent to $125 billion in 1992, according to Zhu and Small (2007, 32). There are benefits to US investors of diversifying their portfolios in the equities of foreign companies without investing abroad. Foreign companies can enjoy multiple benefits of the large depth of US financial markets, lower transaction costs, higher coverage by analysts and protection of minority shareholders.

There are four different levels of ADRs issued in US markets that differ by compliance with SOX (Zhu and Small 2007, 33–4). Levels II and III ADRs are negotiated in the major exchanges in the United States, requiring full compliance with SOX. Level I ADRs are negotiated OTC and Level IV ADRs are private placement, requiring compliance with criminal provisions of SOX. The SEC extended the SOX compliance dates for non-US issuers and had to consider foreign laws and regulations.

The data of J. P. Morgan Chase are used by Zhu and Small (2007, 36–7) to assess if SOX has caused a "chilling" in cross-listing in the United States by foreign issuers. These authors provide caution that more analysis and longer periods are required for definitive conclusions. However, the preliminary information and analysis does show the chilling effect. There were only 12 new cross-listings in 2003 in the major exchanges, the lowest number since 1989. New cross-listings of Levels I and II ADRs in 2004 and 2005 were at the lowest level since 1992. The delisting of ADRs increased while the delisting of US issuers began to decline in 2005. Zhu and Small (2007, 36–7) calculated the listing ratio, consisting of new ADR listings to new US listings, and the delisting ratio, consisting of delisting of ADRs to delisting of US issues. The listing ratio attained a maximum in 2001, dropping to a 10-year low in 2005. The delisting ratio increased yearly in 2002–5, doubling from 0.047 in 2000 to 0.085 in 2005. Zhu and Small (2007, 37) conclude that the evidence shows "that Sox has weakened the competitiveness of US as a cross-listing venue." Further analysis and longer periods could confirm this trend.

Gatekeepers

On January 29, 2003, the SEC (2003) approved the final rule on implementing standards for corporate responsibility of attorneys under SOX. Part 205.3(b)(1) requires reporting of evidence of a material violation for an attorney representing an issuer. The evidence on the material violation can be obtained from any officer, director, employee or agent of the issuer. The attorney shall report the evidence to the chief legal officer (CLO) of the issuer or to both the CLO and the CEO. Vu (2006, 211–12) finds that SOX requires internal reporting of the evidence of material violation but only voluntary reporting to the SEC. Vu (2006) argues that the courts should protect unclear whistleblower rights of reporting attorneys. Part 205.3(b)(2) requires that the CLO conduct an inquiry to determine if a material violation is ongoing, has occurred or is about to occur. The CLO would then advise the reporting attorney of the determination reached and shall engage in all reasonable steps to have the issuer adopt a proper response. The CLO will also advise the reporting attorney of this effort. The CLO also has the option of referring a report of evidence of a material complaint to a qualified legal compliance committee (QLCC). Part 205.3(b)(3) provides that the reporting attorney continue reporting the evidence of material violation unless satisfied with the response of the CLO. The secondary reporting will be to the audit committee of the issuer's board of director, another committee of independent directors or the board of directors. Part 205.3(c) provides that the response to the reporting attorney can be conducted by a QLCC and then is no longer required to evaluate the response of the QLCC.

The SEC encourages the use of QLCCs because they would constitute effective corporate governance (Volz and Tazian 2006, 449). An important benefit to the reporting attorney is that there is no need to evaluate the response of the QLCC as in reporting to the CLO. Volz and Tazian (2006, 450) find the arrangement a convenient option that benefits the companies and their attorneys. If the CLO receives the complaint, it can be referred to the QLCC, which will evaluate it. The SEC has provided significant flexibility in the composition of the QLCC. It can be the audit committee or another committee composed exclusively of independent directors. The QLCC must have at least one member from the audit committee and at least two independent members of the board of directors. Volz and Tazian (2006, 451) find it interesting that no member of the QLCC is required to be an attorney or have a law degree. The confidentiality of the inquiry should not conflict with SOX. An attorney can provide the confidential report to the SEC to prevent unlawful activity when involved in an investigation for potential violation of reporting requirements. The QLCC has authority to notify the SEC if the issuer fails to implement a proper response recommended by the QLCC.

The main issue with the QLCC and SOX is the reconciliation of costs and benefits. According to Volz and Tazian (2006, 460–1), the SEC believes that the costs are not significantly above the administrative expenses of establishing the committee. The members of the QLCC are already members of the audit committee and the board. There are additional administrative costs. However, Volz and Tazian (2006, 461) argue that the costs of liability insurance of committee members may increase because of the additional service in the QLCC. As in similar cases, it is easier to estimate costs than potential benefits.

Aggressive accounting consists of premature recognition of earnings in financial statements. Lobo and Zhou (2006, 57) refer to a study by the US General Accounting Office (GAO) finding aggressive earnings management in 39 percent of the 919 financial restatements in 1997–2002. SOX created the expectation that penalties will be more severe for misrepresentation of facts in financial statements, increasing to as high as $5 million and 20 years of imprisonment. The research issue is if SOX created disincentives for management to use its discretion in overstating earnings, becoming more conservative under uncertainty and increased liability. Lobo and Zhou (2006) find that US firms are more conservative in financial reporting in the first 2 years after SOX than in the 2 years immediately preceding SOX.

The objective of Section 404 of SOX is to prevent false financial reports by mandating management and independent auditors to report on the effectiveness of internal controls. Lin and Wu (2006) argue that the objective is misguided. The internal controls contemplated in SOX were not designed to prevent frauds. In addition, such controls were already unsuccessfully mandated in the Foreign Corrupt Practices Act of 1976 (FCPA). There is nothing new in requiring independent auditors to evaluate internal controls. Lin and Wu (2006, 52) analyze the definition of internal controls of the PCAOB as being centered on the objective of the reliability of financial reporting. This definition does not take into account crucial aspects of the objective and design of internal controls.

The more appropriate process to internal controls, according to Lin and Wu (2006), is enterprise risk management (ERM). This risk analysis must cover all business activities. The critical risk is that resulting from the management process. Corporate frauds originate in strategies and objectives of management that corrupt the accounting process. Another activity that requires care is information. Most internal controls are designed to prevent errors not deliberate falsification of data. The other areas of activity are operation and compliance. Errors in operation and compliance can generate data errors. Compliance is part of the operational risks of Basel II. Internal controls should not be viewed as preventing or detecting major business problems. The effectiveness of internal controls simply assures that strategies and objectives designed and directed by management are attained.

The reporting required under Section 302 of SOX of the effectiveness of internal controls on financial reporting cover two dimensions, materiality and likelihood. The deficiency or combination of deficiencies must result in material misstatement in the financial report. In addition, the likelihood that the failure of the controls is not reported must exceed a remote possibility. Ge and McVay (2005, 141–2) constructed a sample using the 10-K filings from August 2002 to November 2004 of 261 companies that reported 493 distinct deficiencies of internal controls. There are interesting descriptive aspects of the sample. While the segment of computers accounts for 13.7 percent of firms, it accounts for 21.4 percent of the firms with material weakness in the sample. Banks account for 22.1 percent of the firms within the industry but account for only 9.2 percent of the firms with material weakness within the industry. The explanation for the latter case is that banks must file a yearly report with supervisors on the effectiveness of their controls. There is potential for the experience of banks to be useful in compliance with Section 404.

Lack of sufficient employees and insufficient training are important deficiencies that can cause misstatement of financial reports (Ge and McVay 2005, 143). These problems are significant in reporting complex accounts; derivatives and income taxes constitute the most important cases of complex accounts. There are major specific account deficiencies in the case of accounts receivables, accounts payable and inventory accounts. The statistical research of Ge and McVay (2005) provides evidence of positive association between material weakness disclosures and profitability. There are numerous research issues in explaining this relationship. Material weakness is positively associated with complexity of business measured by the number of operating segments and foreign currency translation. There is inverse relationship between material weakness and firm size. The audit by a large audit firm is positively related with reporting material weakness.

The market for audit reports can be analyzed by means of the information asymmetry model (Kaplan *et al.* 2006). The public accounting firms are sellers of the audit report and investors and creditors are the buyers. The two conditions of Akerlof (1970) are present in this market, according to Kaplan *et al.* (2006). The first condition is the difference in quality of the product. There are high quality audit reports that truly represent the financial position of the audited firm in accordance with Generally Agreed Auditing Principles (GAADP). However, there are also lemons or low-quality audit reports that do not represent the actual financial position of the audited firm. The second condition is asymmetry of information: the auditing firms may have information that the reports are substandard while the investors and creditors believe that the reports are of high quality. There is thus market failure or in this case auditing failure requiring government intervention.

The deterioration in the quality of reports by Andersen, culminating in the Enron episode, illustrates the needs for "counteracting mechanism," according to Kaplan *et al.* (2006, 366–8). The theoretical model of information asymmetry provides these mechanisms in the form of licensing, regulation and concerns for reputation. The licensing and regulation of the auditing profession by the states and professional institutions did not prevent the Enron episode. There are incentives for producing low quality auditing reports, according to Kaplan *et al.* (2006). The remuneration of management with performance-linked stock options could have caused deterioration in the accuracy of the information provided by audited firms to their auditors with the purpose of artificially inflating stock prices.

Consolidation created similar pressures in auditing firms to retain clients at all costs, lowering standards and accommodating management.

The incentives of SOX are in the form of independent auditing committees in firms, prohibition of sale of products by auditors to the audited firms and so on. SOX also created the PCAOB to oversee the auditing business. The specific proposal by Kaplan *et al.* (2006, 370) is that the PCAOB "include assessments of the control environment and the ethical climate as part of their annual inspections of public accounting firms." They place special emphasis on the need of reviews of the ethical climate of auditing firms.

US competitiveness in capital markets

There is an important episode in financial history illustrating that US regulations can shift markets abroad, according to Hubbard and Thornton (2006a). Reserve requirements in the United States in the 1960s caused significant costs of marginal bank funding. Interest-rate ceilings diminished bank revenues. London provided the opportunity for lower cost funding, motivating an exodus of transactions by US banks to the new Eurobond market. The experience is alarming. US regulators abolished Regulation Q ceilings on interest rates and permitted international banking facilities with lower reserve requirements. Meanwhile, the London market had already taken off. The interest equalization tax of the United States also encouraged the rise of the Eurobond market. The changes in taxes and regulation did not slow the relative growth of the Eurobond market. There is the troubling suspicion of whether the current trends in securities markets are a repetition of the loss of banking markets to London by the United States five decades ago.

There are several institutions analyzing the loss of competitiveness of the United States and proposing measures to reverse this loss: the Committee on Capital Markets Regulation (CCMR 2006, 2007a–b), McKinsey and Co. (MKC 2007) conducting research for NYC and the US Chamber of Commerce (USCC 2006, 2007a–b). The CCMR (2007a) is an independent and bipartisan group. There are 23 members in leading positions in investment, business, finance, law, accounting and academia. The CCMR was established in 2006. The major work of the committee focuses on enhancing the competitiveness of US capital markets. It is active in communicating with regulators, policymakers and the private sector the recommendations that can recover the competitiveness of the United States, and New York in particular, as the center of the world's capital markets. Research and policy advice on capital markets and shareholder rights will be complemented with analysis of the competitiveness of mutual funds and derivatives markets. The CCMR is issuing reports on current affairs as well as recommendations on policy, participating in the public discussion on these issues.

There are three issues in this effort: the actual loss of competitiveness, the causes of the loss of competitiveness and proposals to solve the problems. These three issues are discussed below in turn.

The loss of competitiveness

In early April, 2007, the 24 stock markets of Europe, including Russia and emerging Europe, increased the combined market valuation of the stocks listed in their exchanges to $15,720 billion, which was above $15,640 billion for US exchanges (Tassell 2007). This is the first time that the market value of stocks in Europe exceeded the market value of stocks in the United States. An important factor of this change in relative market value is the deterioration of the dollar relative to European currencies during most of this period. European stocks have also been more dynamic. The market value of European stocks increased by 160 percent in 2003–6 compared with 70.5 percent for the United States. At the same time, the euro gained 26 percent relative to the dollar. Part of this result reflects the definition of Europe, including Russia and Turkey. Authers (2007) also points to the indices used. The MSCI index, which adjusts for government ownership of companies, shows the US stock market value higher than Europe by 37 percent.

There are two reasons why New York will not regain its supremacy in financial markets, according to Gapper (2006). The first reason is that companies were attracted to the concentration of money in New York but that is no longer true. Estimates by Oxera for the LSE quoted by Gapper (2006) show that London had $7600 billion in equity assets under management (AUM) in 2005. New York had only $3100 billion and the total for all centers in the United States was $8200 billion. US money has flowed overseas instead of the opposite. US investors held $3100 billion in foreign equities in 2005 compared with $700 billion in 1995. The second factor analyzed by Gapper (2006) is the exporting of US investment banking knowledge to the world. As a result, London is equal in know-how to the United States. The study by Oxera shows that underwriting fees for international initial public offerings (IPO) in London average 3.5 percent on the LSE compared with 7 percent on NASDAQ and 5.6 percent on the NYSE. Gapper (2006) argues that SOX merely accentuated a trend already in effect. Only one of the top IPOs in value in 2005 was launched in New York.

The dimensions of the US and NYC capital markets are shown in Table 4.11 together with some of the worrisome details of the loss of competitiveness to overseas markets. The financial services industry of the United States is about 8 percent of GDP, the third largest sector in terms of GDP contribution. Moreover, it has been growing at a high rate of 5 percent per year in the past 10 years and generates a significant portion of employment, 6 million individuals. There are multiple contributions to capital formation in the form of financing of opportunities, monitoring and so on. The securities industry contributes 17 percent of the US financial services industry. MKC (2007, 32) measures a broad aggregate, the financial stock, comprising equities, bonds, loans and deposits. The value of the US financial stock in 2005 is an extremely high $51 trillion, still much larger than the values in the Euro Area of $38 trillion and $20 trillion in Japan. However, the growth rate of the US financial stock in the past 10 years has been 6.5 percent on average, lower than the high 8.4 percent of the United Kingdom, which is the true center challenging US competitiveness.

Table 4.11 The loss of competitiveness of US capital markets

US dimensions
  Financial services industry
    GDP: $1 trillion, 8.1% of GDP in 2005, third largest sector
    Employment: 6 million, about 5% of total private sector employment in 2005
    CCMR (2006, 23)
    Growth rate 1995–2005: average of 5% per year
    MKC (2007, 35)
  Securities industry
    $175 billion, 17% of financial services industry
    CCMR (2006, 23)
  Financial stock: equities, bonds, loans and deposits
    2005 US: $51 trillion, Euro Area: $38 trillion, Japan: $20 trillion
    2001–5 growth rates at constant exchange rates: US, 6.5%, Euro Area, 6.8%, UK, 8.4%,
      Non-Japan Asia, 15.5%
    MKC (2007, 32)

New York City (NYC) and New York State (NYS) dimensions
    Employment: 194,000 in 1/2006, 89.5% in NYC, 24.5% of US securities industry
      employment
    Employment: 2.2% of NYS, 4.7% of NYC
    Wages: 2.5% of NYS, 20.7% of NYC
    Annual gross income: 9.2% of NYS, 14.1% of NYC
    Tax payments: $2.1 billion in 2005, 11% of non-property taxes
    CCMR (2006, 27–9)
    NYC financial services growth rate 1995–2005: 6.6% per year
    Share of NYC business income tax revenues in 2005: 36%
    MKC (2007, 36)

Initial public offerings
    US global share: 37% in 2000, 10% in 2005
    CCMR (2006, 29)
    Mega IPOs > $1 billion, US exchanges, 57% of the world in 2001, 16% in first 10
      months of 2006
    MKC (2007, 43)

Investment banking
    Global advisory and underwriting fees
    US global share: $27 billion, 58% in 1996, $59.1 billion, 42% in 2005
    Compound growth rate 1996–2005: 4% for US, 10% for Europe
    CCMR (2006, 33)
    6 of the top 10 financial institutions by market value are in NYC
    Capital markets and M&A: 2006, US firms are in top 5 in combined capital markets
      and M&A;
    3 of top 5 in European deals
    Investment banking sales and trading: US $109 billion (45% of the world), Europe
      $98 billion (40%)
    Capital market revenue, 2005: US $92 billion, Europe $85 billion
    MKC (2007, 34, 40–1)

Foreign listing in the US
    2000: 100 foreign companies listed in the US for $55 billion
    2005: 34 foreign companies listed in the US for $5 billion

Costs: loss of $50 billion in funding raising equivalent to loss of $2.8 billion in
underwriting fees and yearly loss of $3.3 billion in trading revenue
CCMR (2006, 33)

Going private
Percent of private in public takeovers: 2.2% in 1995, 13% in 2001, 26.3% in 2005
CCMR (2006, 35)
Rule 144A: $83 billion in 186 equity issues in 2005 compared with $5.3 billion in 35
public offerings
Change: Rule 144A accounted for 90% of foreign issues in 2005 compared with 50% in
1995
CCMR (2006, 46)

Venture capital
Exits 2001–5: VC/PE exits $94.9 billion in 2005, VC/IPO exits $12.1 billion in 2001
Secondary buyouts (financial sponsors on both sides): 279 deals in 2005 for $33.2
billion
CCMR (2006, 36–7)

Small cap companies
Since 2001: 870 companies listed at AIM, 526 at NASDAQ
Companies raising similar capital in 2006 at AIM, $10.4 billion compared with
NASDAQ, $11.9 billion
MKC (2007, 50)

Derivatives and debt
OTC derivatives market notional amounts in $ trillions: $258 in 2004, $370 in 6/2006
Average annual growth rate: 27%
Share in foreign exchange derivatives: London 49%, US 16%
Share in interest rate derivatives: London 34%, US 24%
MKC (2007, 56)

There is high concentration of the US financial industry in NYS and in particular in NYC. The state and the city are extremely important in terms of size in the United States and also in terms of cosmopolitan visibility, being the host of the UN. The financial industry of NYS and NYC is very dynamic, growing at 6.6 percent per year in the past 10 years. It makes significant contributions to employment, taxes and income.

The IPOs constitute a dynamic and visible part of the equities segment. The data assembled by the CCMR (2006) and MKC (2007) show an exodus of the issue of IPOs from the United States, in particular NYC, to other stock exchanges. The US global share has declined from 37 percent in 2000 to 10 percent in 2005. This decline is continuing. Moreover, the share of the United States in mega IPOs, with value over $1 billion, collapsed from 57 percent of the global issue in 2001 to 16 percent in 2006.

Six of the largest ten financial institutions in the world are located in NYC. US investment banks continue to dominate the business worldwide. However, the location of the business has been shifting away from the United States to markets overseas. US financial institutions continue to dominate technology and talent in financial markets but a significant part of the business has migrated to other financial centers.

One of the most dramatic facts is the continuing decline in foreign listing in the United States. In 2000, 100 foreign companies listed in the United States with total issue value of $55 billion. In 2005, 34 foreign companies listed in the United States with issue value of $5 billion. The effect of this decline in listing is a significant decrease in underwriting fees and yearly trading revenue. Companies have continued to obtain capital in the United States but through the private route of Rule 144A that does not require public listing. Rule 144A provides a safe harbor from registration and disclosure requirements. Private financing in public takeovers increased from 13 percent in 1995 to 26.3 percent in 2005. There is a broad movement of going private. Foreign issues of equity in 2005 amounted to $83 billion or 90 percent of the total compared with 50 percent in 1995. The exit from venture capital is now mostly through PE. Small cap companies are now aggressively raising capital in the AIM market in London.

The most lucrative part of the derivatives market is in OTC deals. The growth rate in 2004–6 is 27 percent per year. London dominates the market compared with the United States that is losing ground. The foreign exchange OTC derivatives market is dominated by London deals. There is only remaining strength in the United States in commodities.

Causes of the loss of competitiveness

The key New York exchanges (NYE) are the NYSE, the American Stock Exchange (AMEX) and NASDAQ. In 1998, there were 894 foreign listings in the combined NYEs for 30 percent of total foreign listings in the world of 2978, according to Doidge *et al.* (2007, 1), on the basis of data of the World Federation of Stock Exchanges (WFE). The London exchanges (LE) consist of the LSE's Main Market (LSE) and the Alternative Investment Market (AIM), accounting for 16 percent of the world's foreign listings in 1998, 466 foreign listings at the LSE and 21 at the AIM. There was no other exchange with more than 7 percent of the world's foreign listings in 1998. In 2005, the LEs accounted for 19 percent of the foreign listings of the world. Doidge *et al.* (2007, 7) argue that most of the growth of the LEs occurred in the form of an increase of foreign listings at the AIM, 220 listings for 8 percent of global listings compared with 2 percent or 18 listings in 1998. In 1998, the foreign listings in the NYEs were 92 percent higher than in the LSE. In 2005, the NYEs had 165 percent more foreign listings than the LSE. The NYEs combined had only 60 percent more foreign listings than the combined LEs in 2005. The gain by the combined LEs in the 1998–2005 period occurred mostly as a result of gains by the AIM from 21 to 220 foreign listings while the LSE declined from 466 to 334 foreign listings.

The decision to list in the United States by a foreign firm depends on an evaluation of costs and benefits. Doidge *et al.* (2007) focus on the premium of listing in the NYEs relative to the LSE. Differences in listing motivation would be reflected in that premium. The attractiveness of listing in the United States for a foreign firm is determined by the superior governance. Controlling groups of foreign firms may find a cost in listing in the NYEs in the form of a loss of the capacity to expropriate corporate benefits from minority shareholders because of the stricter governance of US regulation and enforcement. There must be a significant net benefit in the form of raising capital at more attractive terms to fund growth projects. This net benefit increases the valuation of the cross-listed firms, resulting in a cross-listing premium.

Doidge *et al.* (2007) find that the companies that list in AIM are not attracted to cross-listing in the NYEs. The cross-listing peaked at the LSE and the NYEs at the turn of the century and declined in both markets. It is difficult to explain this simultaneous decline in terms of enhanced regulation such as in SOX. The econometric research provides evidence that firms continue to make their cross-listing decisions after SOX on the basis of the same reasons as before. Doidge *et al.* (2007) used various econometric techniques to uncover a listing premium for cross-listing in the United States but no such premium for listing in London. The listing premium in the United States is robust, exists every year and is permanent in event time. There is no evidence that the premium declined after 2001. They conclude that there is an observable governance benefit for foreign companies to cross-list in the United States that is not present in cross-listing in London or outside the United States. The research does not provide evidence of a weakening of this governance benefit over time.

The premium of listing in the United States is the difference between the value of the company in the market and its book value or accounting value of assets between cross-listed and non-cross-listed stocks (Ip 2006, CCMR 2006, 47). The CCMR (2006, 47) shows that this premium declined by almost one-half for a large sample of cross-listed companies from multiple countries. The premium for listing on both US and foreign markets was 51 percentage points in 1997–2001, declining to 31 percentage points in 2002–5 (Ip 2006). The decline of the premium was sharper for companies in countries with better corporate governance, such as Japan, Hong Kong, Canada and the United Kingdom. Investors perceive little extra benefit after 2002 from listing in the United States. There was little decline in the premium for countries with weaker governance. The decline of the premium for countries with good governance could be the result of excessive regulation under SOX (CCMR 2006, 47). The stability of the premium for countries with weak governance suggests additional benefits from listing in the United States (Ip 2006). Another measurement is the calculation of the control premium, consisting of the ratio of the market-to-book value of assets in transactions of controlled companies. The control premium is inversely related to the quality of governance in a country because it measures the ability of the company's controlling group to expropriate assets from minority shareholders. The CCMR (2006, 47–8) provides evidence that the decline in the listing premium is lower for countries with larger control premium.

Proposals

There are about 15,000 public companies in the United States with market value of around \$37 trillion (USCC 2006). The public companies are owned indirectly through pension funds or directly through individual investments and 401(k) plans by 84 million individuals in the United States and around the world. The USCC (2006, 3) finds that this vast market is required to ensure the liquidity and transparency that assure a fair price as well as reasonable cost of capital for companies. A survey concludes that 57 million US households participate in capital markets through stocks or mutual funds (USCC 2007a).

There is a delicate balance of regulation that maintains transparency and fairness without impeding free enterprise and innovation, according to Greenberg (2006, 30). The advantage of the United States depends on creating products and markets that are better than those overseas. Excessive regulation is eroding that advantage. The costs of excessive regulation, according to Paulson (2006), occur in the form of slowing innovation, administrative costs, restriction of competitiveness and lower job creation. The race to the bottom in standards of fairness and transparency should be avoided in the effort of reducing regulatory costs. Paulson (2006) proposes that "the right regulatory balance should marry high standards of integrity and accountability with a strong foundation for innovation, growth and competitiveness."

Paulson urges the United States to follow more principles than rules in financial market regulation and more flexible approaches as in the United Kingdom (Grant and Guha 2006). These changes would be required to maintain US competitiveness in financial markets. The innovations in capital markets, consolidation of stock exchanges and more flexible regulation are eroding the advantage of the United States. The US Treasury Secretary argues that the US system is prescriptive, not allowing compliance flexibility in accordance with regulatory principles. Grant and Guha (2006) argue that the issue is the less prescriptive approach of the UK FSA and European accounting standards. The United States is attempting to develop a safe haven based on rules. Paulson (2007) defends the use of principles. The reconciliation of the US GAAP and the international Financial Reporting Standards (IFRS) statements would not be attractive in terms of costs and benefits for a foreign company cross-listing in the US market. International cooperation can lead to a system in which US companies can list in Europe on the basis of GAAP and foreign corporations can list in the United States on the basis of IFRS (Paulson 2006).

Costly and complex rules do not create the accurate and timely information that companies need to maintain global competitiveness. According to Paulson (2006), the United States has four different banking regulators and added regulation in the securities and commodities markets. Regulatory philosophies and statutory responsibilities are different together with various degrees of preempting state law. Paulson (2006) argues that the consequence "is an ever-expanding rulebook in which multiple regulators impose rule upon rule upon rule. Unless we carefully consider the cost/benefit trade-off implicit in these rules, there is a danger of creating a thicket of regulation that impedes competitiveness." Past rules are currently deficient and current rules will be deficient in the future unless they are based on sound principles. Enforcement of regulations is required. However, Paulson (2006) argues that in the US multiple jurisdictions and entities engage in simultaneous enforcement, reducing the efficiency of the process. The regulated entities are fearful and feel threatened. The system should punish violations without disrupting honest and capable business leaders, shareholders and employees. Combining enforcement and guidance may be more reliable and effective than mere enforcement.

The reasons for concern in the United States, according to Paulson (2006), are the significant litigation risk, the complexity of the structure of regulation and its enforcement and the costly implementation of the SOX accounting and governance rules. A principles-based approach, according to Paulson (2006), is developed on the basis of tight ideas or concepts, constituting a framework of thought. Its advantage is in the form of flexibility to deal with new or special situations. The system of prescriptive rules provides more specific guidance than the principles-based approach but at the cost of rigidity. An important advantage of the United States is in its legal system, protecting property rights, providing contract law and dispute resolution together with compensation for injured parties. This system is required to protect business, investors and consumers. However, Paulson (2006) argues that the US legal system has moved beyond protection. The US tort costs were around $250 billion in 2004 or about 2.2 percent of GDP, twice the value in Germany and Japan and three times that in the United Kingdom. Compensated injured plaintiffs receive only 42 cents per tort dollar with the remainder going to administration, attorneys' fees and defense costs. Paulson (2006) argues that these tort costs constitute the equivalent of a tax ultimately paid by shareholders, employees and consumers. He argues that "the broken tort system is an Achilles heel for our economy." The issue is not political but rather of a social nature, affecting US competitiveness.

The strength of the United States in the twentieth century was the result of its dominance of the financial services industry, according to Bloomberg and Schumer (2007). Continuing long-term economic success will depend on the ability to meet the challenge of NYC as the world's financial capital. Bloomberg and Schumer (2007) argue that the threat to the United States is accentuated by the complex rules of regulation in contrast with understandable principles behind regulation in competing countries. The situation is aggravated by heavy costs imposed by SOX and the insistence that foreign companies comply with complex US GAAP. There is room for the United States to implement reforms while protecting investors and consumers.

A second problem according to Bloomberg and Schumer (2007) is the onerous US legal system compared with those in other countries that has created "a perception that penalties are arbitrary and unfair." This perception diminishes the competitiveness of the United States. The solution is legal reforms that maintain solutions for meritorious actions without creating the impression of arbitrary justice. The third area for reform proposed by Bloomberg and Schumer (2007) concerns the skilled workers required to maintain the US competitiveness. The solution requires reforms to increase the production of workers with the required quantitative background for financial employment together with the ability to attract foreigners. The agenda of Bloomberg and Schumer includes reforms at the level of NYC and the federal government.

The research of MKC (2007, 62) included interviews with major participants in the financial markets worldwide, including industry leaders, executives, regulators, attorneys and politicians. This research confirmed that the principal concerns of senior executives on the working of financial markets are the availability of skilled workers, a legal environment that is fair and predictable and a friendly regulatory framework. Moreover, the response to the surveys confirmed the view that NYC has become less favorable to financial markets than London in the 3 years after 2002. The three major reasons for the relative decline of NYC are the threat of availability of skilled workers, the unpredictability and unfairness of the US legal system and the constraining regulatory framework.

The business leaders interviewed by MKC (2007) find that the regulatory environment of London is more relevant to current business than that in the United States, which has deteriorated in recent years. The US system is complex, costly and lacking in responsiveness. US regulation has failed to keep pace with financial innovation. Business transactions and communications with regulators are easier in London than in the United States. The United Kingdom has a single regulator in the FSA. The US system is complex and fragmented with multiple federal regulators and overlapping federal and state regulators. Innovations are frustrated by the lack of responsiveness in US regulations. The United Kingdom's FSA functions within two principles. There are 11 high-level principles that incorporate what is expected from regulated firms (MKC 2007, 82, 90–1). There are seven guidance principles for the regulators to chart their course of action, including rigorous cost and benefit analysis of new regulations. In contrast, the United States has a system of rules and compliance with various missions, structures and mandates at the federal and state levels. There is no universal regulatory framework based on common principles. This disorganized approach creates significant uncertainty and doubts about fairness and effectiveness. The lack of common principles forces regulators to rely on legislative mandates that may be quite old. A common observation is that the US Securities Act of 1933 is closer in time to the Civil War than to the present.

US compliance costs have increased significantly. MKC (2007, 82) provides estimates of the Securities Industry Association that compliance costs reached $25 billion in 2005, which is almost twice the value of $13 billion in 2002. In the view of market participants, SOX stifles innovation. There is much less favorable perception of US compliance than that of the FSA in the United Kingdom. There is less dialogue in the United States, high-profile prosecutions and fear of measures such as the Thompson memorandum, which recommends prosecution for companies failing to waive attorney client privilege. The aggressive style of prosecution in the United States is also a factor of distrust.

Recent regulatory measures in the United States are reducing the capacity of the United States to compete in financial markets, according to the survey by

MKC (2007, 86). Industry leaders appreciate the environment of transparency and accountability intended by US regulators and legislators. However, the costs of SOX are deemed to be excessively onerous relative to the benefits. Section 404 in particular is considered to be arbitrarily expensive. Another reservation is in the higher capital requirements for large US banks contemplated in the revised approach to Basel II by US regulators.

The US equities markets do not experience yet the full consequences of the decline in US financial competitiveness because of several factors that CCMR (2006, 49–50) has identified. It does not appear likely that the United States will lose the listing and IPOs of US companies. IPOs are more likely to list in the market of origin instead of in the most competitive market, a factor that is very strong in the United States. The foreign companies that list in the United States cannot exit if there are 300 or more US shareholders. The proposed relaxation of these standards by the SEC would benefit only 10 percent of foreign companies listed in the United States (CCMR 2006, 49). A US company engaging in an overseas IPO may be covered by US regulations if it is owned by more than 500 investors worldwide. It is quite difficult for a US company to meet the test to deregister in order to move abroad with the purpose of avoiding US regulations. The CCMR (2006, 50) considers these impediments as a form of capital controls. An unfavorable consequence is that they delay the effects of the loss of financial competitiveness and thus the pressure for effective reform.

The proposals of the CCMR, MKC and the USCC are summarized in Table 4.12. Significant part of the proposals is concentrated on SOX Section 404. This is the

Table 4.12 Proposals for enhancing US competitiveness in financial markets

---

SOX Section 404
    Redefinition of material weakness CCMR (2006, 19)
    Enhanced guidance of SEC and PCAOB CCMR (2006, 19–20)
    Reconsideration of small companies CCMR (2006, 20–1)
    Do not duplicate Section 404 to foreign companies with equivalent home regulation
        CCMR (2006, 21)
    Obtain more data on costs and benefits CCMR (2006, 21)
    Clear guidance for implementation MKC (2007, 97–100)
    Make SOX part of the Securities Exchange Act of 1934 USCC (2007a–b)

Securities litigation
    Resolution of uncertainties in Rule 10b-5 Liability CCMR (2006, 12)
    Prohibition of double recoveries CCMR (2006, 12–13)
    Prohibition of pay to play practices CCMR (2006, 13)
    Indictment of entire firms only in extraordinary cases CCMR (2006, 13)
    Modify criteria to indict firms on factor four of the Thompson Memorandum CCMR
        (2006, 13–14)
    Reform with immediate impact MKC (2007, 100–4)

Uniform regulation
    Cost/benefit analysis for the SEC and SROs CCMR (2006, 8)
    Principles-based rules for SEC and SROs CCMR (2006, 8)

Table 4.12   (Continued)

Regulation of securities firms by SEC similar to prudential bank regulation CCMR (2006, 50)
Cessation of ad hoc rule-making by states and federal/state coordination CCMR (2006, 50)
Shared regulatory vision and principles MKC (2007, 106–7)
Reform/modernize federal regulatory approach to financial markets USCC (2007a–b)

Supply of skilled workers
Less restrictive entry of foreign professionals MKC (2007, 107–9)

Gatekeepers: Auditors and outside directors
Congressional consideration of protecting auditing firms from catastrophic loss CCMR (2006, 14)
Clarify Section 10A Liability CCMR (2006, 14)
Modify SEC Rule 176 and SEC Indemnification Policy of outside directors CCMR (2006, 14)
Domestic and international avoidance of catastrophic litigation USCC (2007a–b)
Allow auditing firms to raise capital from private shareholders other than partners USCC (2007a–b)

IFRS and GAAP
Permit IFRS without reconciliation MKC (2007, 109–11)
Promote international convergence of auditing and accounting standards MKC (2007, 109–11)

Shareholder rights
Allow shareholders of corporations with classified boards to vote on poison pills CCMR (2006, 17)
Alternative procedures for solving disputes with companies CCMR (2006, 17–18)

Basel II
Maintain US banking competitiveness MKC (111–13)

---

area where many are doubtful that the benefits compensate the costs of compliance. Material weakness requires precise definition. Small companies and foreign companies must be considered more carefully. Guidance for implementation is still lacking. There are not sufficient data on costs and benefits.

The second block of proposals focuses on the legal system of securities litigation. The CCMR is proposing the resolution of uncertainties in Rule 10b-5 liability, which is the common rule for most litigation. MKC is proposing reforms that have immediate impact. High-profile litigation in the United States is creating a feeling of fear and threat in US and foreign firms. This environment is not conducive to efficient investment decisions.

There are business leaders and policymakers desiring a uniform regulatory framework for financial markets such as the FSA. This is unlikely to occur. The various regulatory agencies operate in relation to various committees in Congress. There may not be political capital to unify this system into one agency reporting to one committee in Congress, even divided into multiple subcommittees. An important measure with rapid impact would be the development of cost/benefit analysis in the SEC and the SROs. Such process already exists for most regulators and the model of prudential regulation of banking may be appropriate. Many in the United States also desire a system with principles instead of rules and compliance. This is another difficult task because of customs of long tradition. There should be an end of ad hoc rule-making by state prosecutors in high-profile prosecution. The regulators should establish a framework of shared vision and principles. NYC is concerned with the migration of quantitatively trained finance professionals to other centers. Immigration policy could create incentives for foreign professionals.

In the case of gatekeepers, Congress should prevent another catastrophic loss of an auditing firm. This would result in excessive concentration in the industry. The USCC is proposing relaxation of the rules of capitalization of auditing companies. Strong auditing companies are required for the system of transparency and disclosure that has been a US tradition. There is much merit in the international-ization of accounting standards. The United States could pursue in the G7 and G10 the convergence of standards. Shareholder rights should be strengthened because of the traditional competitive advantage of the United States in protecting rights of minority shareholders. It would be wise to develop alternative solutions for disputes of shareholders with companies. The United States requires a strong banking system and regulators should prevent the erosion of that strength with excessive capital requirements under the modifications of Basel II.

Summary

The financial crises of the 1990s motivated the G7 to promote the international convergence of standards and codes. The belief behind this effort was that lack of transparency and disclosure, especially in the Asian crisis of 1997–8, adversely affected prevention of the crises and accentuated their effects. These standards and codes are voluntary. However, the surveillance under Article IV of the IMF has created a possible element of enforcement of compliance.

It took nearly a decade of major efforts to develop the new Basel II capital framework for banks. Implementation will differ between the more strict application in Europe and the modified one in the United States. The SEC and the FSA implement different approaches to regulation of securities markets. SOX, complex regulation, unpredictable litigation and the rapid growth of foreign securities markets are undermining the competitiveness of the United States as the center of world finance. The maintenance of competitiveness requires that the United States streamline its system of regulation, move toward principles instead of rules, curb frivolous litigation and strengthen its auditing firms. The Glass-Steagall Act illustrates that it is easier to pass restrictive litigation than to reverse it. The US competitiveness will continue to deteriorate unless there is strong, decisive action and change.

5
Vulnerabilities of the Global Economy

Introduction

The most critical vulnerability of the world economy is the possibility that housing events in the United States could create a broader credit contraction. Such an event or a similar shock could erode the perceived quality of US debt, causing disorderly exit out of dollar assets.

The theory of the financial accelerator of Bernanke *et al.* (2000) and Bernanke and Gertler (1995, 1999) analyzes the existence of a premium of external financing by business and households. Internally generated resources of business and households are cheaper relative to external resources obtained by borrowing. The recent contribution by Bernanke (2007Jun15) on the association of the financial accelerator and the credit channel is closely related to the current environment:

> Household borrowers, like firms, presumably face an external finance premium, which is lower the stronger their financial position. For households, home equity is often a significant part of net worth. Certainly, households with low mortgage loan-to-value ratios can borrow on relatively favorable terms through home-equity lines of credit, with the equity in their home effectively serving as collateral

Bernanke (2007Jun15) analyzes how the erosion of home values adversely affects borrowing and spending by households, especially because of two important implications. The first is that households with low equity in their homes experience much sharper reduction of their potential spending after a decline in home values. The second is that households exposed to mortgage contracts with variable rates suffer an immediate impact on their cash flows from rising interest rates. There are some adjustable rate mortgages (ARM) in the United States and also in the United Kingdom. Bernanke (2007Jun15) believes that further research is required to assess the impacts of these two factors.

A complementary analysis is the possible transmission of credit contractions through the bank lending channel. Financial conditions of banks may deteriorate if their earnings and assets are affected by shocks to their borrowers. Bernanke (2007Jun15) argues that even nonbank lenders may also experience increases in their cost of borrowing if there are adverse effects to their financial conditions, such as impacts on their net worth, leverage and liquidity. The contraction of credit by banks and nonbanks would adversely affect the real sector of the economy. A possible housing event in the United States is analyzed by Rogoff (2006b, 11) as a stress test of the continuing financing of the US CAD:

> Any discussion of the implications of globalization on monetary policy would be incomplete without noting the risks posed by the global imbalances, a euphemism for the humongous US current account deficit. Financial globalization is clearly an important driver of this process, particularly in inflating asset prices, which have in turn been an important driver of current accounts. Whereas one can argue that the effects until now have been relatively benign, it remains very much an open question of what will happen if the system is stress tested, say by a combination of housing price collapse in the United States combined with a sharp slowdown in growth in China

The probable impact of the collapse of housing prices on US international borrowing is a central concern in Peláez and Peláez (2007, 223–9). Unfortunately, there is ongoing unintended and undesirable stress test of these events. The best outcome would be that economic models lack predictive accuracy. The cost of calibrating, specifying and estimating new models is nil compared with the costs of employment and output of a global recession. The crucial vulnerabilities deserving analysis are those with high losses even if the probability of their occurrence is low.

The risk of the unwinding of dollar debt may have risen somewhat because of the events originating in real estate in the United States. The proposition of disorderly devaluation of the dollar is not sufficiently specific for testing. Various types of research by central banks, IFIs and the April 2007 *World Economic Outlook* and *Global Financial Stability Report* of the IMF fail to find historical cases that correspond to the proposition of disorderly devaluation of the dollar. Nevertheless, there are few economists that believe that US external imbalances can be sustained indefinitely. The fact that disorderly adjustment has not occurred before does not preclude its occurrence in the future. This does not negate the possibility of relatively benign adjustment in the United States as in the 1970s and 1980s. The risk of less benign adjustment and resulting global slowdown or contraction warrants the flood of research by academics and official institutions.

An important concern of this chapter is the issue of external imbalances and its relation to the real estate weakness and economic conditions of the United States. The first section below focuses on the risks and policy proposals on the US external deficits.[1] The second section analyzes the challenge to the IFIs and the G7 posed by the credit contraction and its possible impact on the real economy. The final section considers the fear of regulation, trade and devaluation wars. A summary concludes the chapter.

US external deficits and the global recession risk

The extreme version of the proposition of disorderly correction is that the overshooting of devaluation of the dollar would raise inflation and interest rates throughout the world, crashing stock markets. The recession would spread throughout the world economy. The US CAD was 6.1 percent of GDP in 2006, approaching $1 trillion. It absorbs more than two-thirds of world CA surpluses. The policy proposals can be classified into the savings and investment approach, the revived Bretton Woods approach and the analysis of global financial flows. The G7 has adopted the concern of the disorderly correction and is coordinating through the IFIs a doctrine of shared responsibility in which all regions would contribute to orderly adjustment of global imbalances. The final subsection focuses on the policy lags of the official doctrine, evaluating the fundamentals and risks of the United States for allocation of financial investment.

The US external imbalance

The data to illustrate the concern with the CA of the United States are shown in Table 5.1. The first block of numbers shows account balances that compose the CA: the sum of the balances in goods and services, income and unilateral transfers. There are small rounding discrepancies.

The United States has been running a trade deficit for many years and a CAD since 1997. However, there was acceleration of the trade deficit in 1999 and 2000, when it reached $379 billion, or 3.9 percent of GDP. The behavior of the CA mirrors that of its main component, the balance of trade in goods and services. The CAD jumped from $302 billion in 1999 to $417 billion in 2000, or 4.2 percent of GDP, and then to $640 billion in 2004, or 5.4 percent of GDP. The CAD for 2005 is $755 billion or 6.1 percent of GDP and $811 billion for 2006 or 6.1 percent of GDP. The CAD in the second quarter of 2007 was $190.8 billion, lower by 7.2 percent than a year earlier and $197.1 billion in the first quarter, lower by 1.7 percent than a year earlier. A simple extrapolation of the CAD in the first half of 2007 yields $774 billion or 5.6 percent of GDP of $13,893 billion. This would constitute the first reversal of increases in the ratio of the CAD to GDP since 1997.

The net international investment position (NIIP) of the United States followed the deterioration of the trade balance and CA. There was again a large jump from 1999 to 2000, reaching $1381 billion, or 14.1 percent of GDP, and then $2140 billion, or 19.5 percent of GDP, in 2003. In 2004, the NIIP reached $2294 billion or 19.6 percent of GDP, $2238 billion in 2005 or 17.9 percent of GDP and $2539 billion in 2006 or 19.2 percent of GDP.

The fiscal balance of the United States shifted from surplus in the late 1990s to a deficit of $413 billion in 2004, or 3.5 percent of GDP, declining to 2.6 percent

Table 5.1 US, current account, NIIP, fiscal balance, debt and nominal GDP $ Billions

	1998	1999	2000	2001	2002	2003	2004	2005	2006
Goods and services	−166	−265	−379	−365	−424	−497	−612	−714	−758
Income	4	14	21	32	27	45	56	48	36
Unilateral transfers	−53	−50	−58	−52	−63	−71	−84	−88	−89
Current account	−215	−302	−417	−385	−457	−522	−640	−755	−811
Nominal GDP	8747	9268	9817	10128	10469	10960	11712	12456	13246
CAD/GDP %	−2.5	−3.3	−4.2	−3.8	−4.4	−4.8	−5.4	−6.1	−6.1
NIIP	−895	−766	−1381	−1919	−2088	−2140	−2294	−2238	−2539
NIIP as % of GDP	−10.3	−8.3	−14.1	−18.9	−19.9	−19.5	−19.6	−17.9	−19.2
Exports of goods & services & income	1194	1259	1421	1296	1256	1338	1559	1788	2096
NIIP as % of exports	−75	−61	−97	−148	−166	−160	−147	−125	−121
Fiscal balance, FB	69	126	236	128	−158	−378	−413	−318	−248
FB as % of GDP	0.8	1.4	2.4	1.3	−1.5	−3.4	−3.5	−2.6	−1.9
Internal debt, ID	3721	3632	3410	3320	3540	3913	4296	4592	4829
ID as % of GDP	44	41	36	33	33	35	37	37	36

Note: NIIP is net international investment position with FDI at market value. Fiscal Balance is revenues
less outlays. Internal debt is debt held by the public.
Sources: GDP, http://www.bea.gov/national/xls/gdplev.xls
Current account and exports: http://www.bea.gov/international/xls/table1.xls
NIIP: http://www.bea.gov/international/xls/intinv06_t2.xls
Fiscal balance and debt held by the public: http://www.cbo.gov/budget/historical.pdf

of GDP in 2005 and 1.9 percent of GDP in 2006. However, the debt held by the public stabilized close to 36 percent of GDP.

These external and internal imbalances are termed "twin deficits" in the literature on the United States in the 1980s. Adjustment of similar deficits has been sharp and painful in terms of loss of output – ranging from around 5 percent for Mexico and Argentina in 1995, through average 7.2 percent for the Asian Five in 1998 and 15 percent in the first quarter of 2002 for Argentina. Evidently, emerging market crises are less relevant to the largest economy in the world whose currency, the dollar, is the standard reserve. The United States does not have a currency mismatch because it borrows on its own currency. Nevertheless, there is concern if eventual adjustment of the United States would have an impact on economic conditions globally because of its high share in world output. As typical, economists disagree on the risks and policies required for adjustment.

The US external deficit is commonly called the problem of global imbalances. For the world as a whole, deficits and surpluses cancel each other. There are surplus countries and deficit countries. Table 5.2 shows the estimates of global imbalances prepared by the *World Economic Outlook April 2007* of the IMFWEO (2007Apr) and revised in October 2007. The main projection is solid growth of 4.9 percent for the world as a whole in 2007 and 2008, changed in October 2007 to 5.2 percent and 4.8 percent, respectively. In this outlook, the US economy grows at a much lower rate of 2.2 percent in 2007 but recovers to grow at 2.8 percent in 2008, revised to 1.9 percent in 2007 and 2008. The Euro Area would continue its business cycle upswing, growing at 2.3 percent, revised to 2.5 percent in 2007 and 2.1 percent in 2008. Japan would expand at 2.3 percent in 2007 and at 1.9 percent in 2008, revised to 2.0 percent and 1.7 percent, respectively. The slower growth in the advanced countries would contrast with very high growth in emerging markets of 7.5 percent in 2007 and 7.1 percent in 2008, revised to 8.1 percent and 7.4 percent, respectively. Asia, the Middle East and the fuel-exporting countries would grow at very high rates. Newly available information is repeatedly changing forecasts because of the more accurate evaluation of the US credit and housing event.

The problem of the imbalances is shown in the columns on the CA and the balance in goods and services. The US would experience CADs of more than $800 billion in 2007 and 2008. Japan, other advanced countries and the emerging countries would experience significant surpluses. The US absorbs more than two-thirds of the surpluses or savings of the world.

Table 5.2   Global imbalances $B and %

	Current account		Goods and services		GDP growth	
Region	2007	2008	2007	2008	2007	2008
World					4.9	4.9
Advanced	−500	−550	−341	−356	2.5	2.2
USA	−784	−788	−721	−715	1.9	1.9
Euro Area	−21	−49	161	148	2.5	2.1
Japan	196	1195	74	71	2.0	1.7
Other adv	110	92	201	207	3.7	3.1
Emerging countries	593	624	609	615	8.1	7.4
Asia	389	446	303	349	9.8	8.8
Middle East	227	247	223	232	5.9	5.9
Fuel exporting	367	381	439	452	7.0	6.9
China	379	453			11.5	10.0

Source: IMF, *World Economic Outlook October 2007*, Statistical Appendix various tables.

Risks

The scenarios of "disorderly correction," according to Croke *et al.* (2005), describe the CAD adjustment by profound depreciation of the dollar with a run on the bond market, in the form of increases in interest rates and crash in the stock market, with resulting declines in equity prices. A disorderly correction would threaten the economic growth of the United States and possibly of the rest of the world. Croke *et al.* warn that interest rates would increase even if there is smooth adjustment because higher export activity would be compensated by lower domestic consumption and investment. The conventional wisdom consists of a set of policies designed to strike preemptively the disorderly correction of global imbalances.

The authors consider 23 cases of CAD adjustment of industrial countries over a period of 30 years. They analyze the sample as a whole and into two groups: an expansion group with the seven best cases of GDP growth and a contraction group with the seven worst cases of GDP performance. The results are shown in Table 5.3. Croke *et al.* (2005) warn that they do not test the theory of disorderly correction, partly because it does not have testable specifications. Their more pragmatic approach is to examine the CA adjustment of industrial countries to verify if there were empirical regularities similar to those of the disorderly correction. The CAD adjustment of industrial countries has not been characterized by empirical regularities of inflation, interest rate increases and collapse of equity prices similar

Table 5.3   Summary of results by Croke *et al.* (2005)

Indicator	Total sample	Contraction group	Expansion group
Inflation	No evidence	Increase but no surge	Steady decline
Real exchange rate	Moderate (8%)	Unchanged	Depreciation
Interest rates	Up before, then down and stable	Up before, down after Long-term rise before then down	Up before, down after Long-term rise before then down
Stock market price	Down before, then flat, then up	Decline before then decline and rebound	Decline before then increase
Savings/investment	Both decline before and after, but investment more	Inv > Sav rates then adjust with decline of investment	Both decline before then adjust with both higher sav, lower inv
Real imports/exports	Exports pick up after, adjust via imports	Export growth then adjust via imports	Export growth then less adjust via imports
Budget balance	Widen before, then Tighten	Surpluses rising then declining	Increase in deficits then balance
NIIP	Average 18% of GDP, flat in adjust	Worsens	Stable

to those of a disorderly adjustment. Naturally, these findings do not preclude the existence of such a correction. They merely indicate that such a phenomenon has not occurred over a large number of countries in the past 30 years.

Croke *et al.* find positive correlation between exchange rate depreciation and real economic growth. Moreover, there is positive correlation between long-term interest rates and economic growth, contradicting the disorderly description of lower growth because of increases in long-term interest rates. Apparently, higher GDP growth caused increases in long-term rates after the adjustment began. Finally, there is no correlation between the NIIP and the change in GDP growth.

There is still a possibility of recession in the sample used by the authors. In the seven contraction cases, median fourth quarter GDP growth was 1 percent in the first year after adjustment began and −1/2 percent in the second year. However, the economies were overheated, with actual output moving toward potential while the CAD worsened.

The role of relative external adjustment through the exchange rate and economic growth in advanced countries is analyzed by the IMFWEO (2007Apr). The sample includes episodes of swings in the CA balance of 2.5 percent of GDP of at least 50 percent of the initial CA imbalance. CA imbalances are defined as persistent and large when they remain above 2 percent of GDP for more than 5 years. The IMFWEO (2007Apr) identifies 42 cases of such episodes of large and persistent CA imbalances in advanced countries in the past 40 years. The average CAD at the year of reversal for the 42 countries was 4.1 percent, the average size of adjustment was 5.7 percent of GDP, the duration was 4.6 years, the average change of GDP growth was −1.4 percent and the real exchange rate change was −12.2 percent. The adjustment involved both depreciation of the real exchange rate and reduction in the rate of economic growth. The real exchange rate depreciation is lower than what would be expected of such significant adjustment.

The IMFWEO (2007Apr) also considered 13 cases of advanced economies CADs that were on average about 5 percent of GDP and lasted 11 years. The reversal of these CADs has occurred in seven of the countries while six still experience high CADs. In these 13 cases, growth of GDP and consumption was slower than in other periods while credit growth and the stock market had stronger performance. The IMFWEO (2007Apr) finds that the CADs were a normal macroeconomic consequence of productivity increases. The adjustment could occur by the movement of savings and investment ratios to new equilibrium levels. The decline of GDP growth was not sharper than in the 42 episodes of the complete sample and the adjustment time was not longer. The IMFWEO (2007Apr) concludes that the large and persistent CADs in advanced economies were the consequence of internal developments within the domestic economies instead of external events.

There is a classic characterization of policies to adjust the balance of payments by Johnson (1958). Expenditure-switching policies consist of depreciation of the currency that makes imports relatively more expensive than domestic goods and exports relatively cheaper in foreign markets. Relatively more expensive imports reduce the quantity of imported goods demanded and relatively less expensive exports increase the quantity of exported goods demanded. The expenditure-switching policies could improve the trade account through changes in relative prices. Expenditure-reduction policies would reduce aggregate demand, lowering as well the demand for imported goods. The reduction in demand could also improve the trade account. The role of expenditure-switching policies is also considered within the Mundell–Fleming model (Obstfeld 2001).

Discussion of the effects of depreciation has focused on the rate of exchange pass-through, which is the rate at which depreciation of the currency actually impacts on the actual prices of import and export transactions. Goldberg and Dillon (2007) argue that there is much weaker pass-through of depreciation to import prices than to export prices in the case of the United States. Thus, depreciation could have significantly lower effects on affecting US imports than US exports. There is a significant gap between the value of exports of goods and services of the United States, $1445 billion in 2006, relative to imports of goods and services, $2204 billion. Exports would have to increase by 52 percent to eliminate the trade deficit. The policy obstacle to depreciation is the significantly lower responsiveness of imports to depreciation.

The pass-through measurements used by Goldberg and Dillon (2007) consist of an OECD average of an impact of 0.64 percent on imports resulting from 1 percent depreciation. The pass-through to import prices after 1 year in the United States is only 0.42 percent per 1 percent depreciation. There are three factors that insulate import prices in the United States from the effects of depreciation of the dollar. Most of the imports of the United States are invoiced in dollars. These prices are set periodically. Thus, an increase in the domestic currency value of the dollar need not result in a lower price in dollars in the United States. In addition, the United States has a larger and far more diversified economy than most countries. Exporters to the United States try to maintain market shares in the competitive US market. It is likely that these exporters absorb depreciation of the dollar in the form of lowering profits but without changing their dollar prices. A third factor analyzed by Goldberg and Dillon (2007) is the domestic component of US imports in the form of distribution, shipment, storage and retailing costs after the good arrives in the US frontier. The domestic component of the goods may absorb some of the depreciation of the dollar, leaving the price relatively unchanged.

The analysis of Goldberg and Dillon (2007) leads to the conclusion that import prices may not be significantly affected by depreciation of the dollar but export prices, which are almost fully invoiced in dollars, immediately carry lower domestic currency prices into foreign markets. The expenditure-switching policy of depreciation will be processed largely through an increase in exports with mild effects on import reduction. There is a major hurdle because the elimination of the deficit would require an increase of exports by 52 percent without any change in imports. Even the reduction of the deficit by one-half, as proposed in discussion by the IFIs, may be significantly difficult.

The behavioral assumption of firms maintaining their competitiveness by managing their markups is used by Gust and Sheets (2007) in simulations with a dynamic GE model. Even if there are not nominal rigidities, this assumption permits incomplete pass-through. Under the assumption of unitary trade-price elasticities, the partial-equilibrium results show improvement of the trade balance regardless of the extent of the pass-through. There are two GE effects. First, the effect of the adjustment of the nominal trade balance is reduced by the lower pass-through effects on the real economy resulting from depreciation. With low pass-through, the exchange rate does not significantly affect import demand. Second, there is diminished impact on domestic prices and output from the depreciation because of low pass-through resulting in more limited increases in domestic interest rates. The decline in the exchange rate tends to be larger under low pass-through, leading to greater nominal adjustment of the trade balance. If there is slow adjustment of import demand, there may be more significant depreciation of the exchange rate and resulting improvement in the nominal trade account.

There are two types of biases in estimating trade elasticities for the United States, according to the IMFWEO (2007Apr). There is aggregation bias in that measurements of price elasticities for individual sectors are typically higher than those obtained for aggregate data. The diversity of price responses of individual sectors raises the doubt if there is bias in measuring the elasticities with aggregate variables. The second bias is the result of ignoring vertical integration. US imports have a component of US-made intermediate products and a component of value-added in other countries. The effect of depreciation is to reduce the demand for imports and to increase the demand for exports of intermediate products used in production of imports into the United States. As a result, the price elasticity of US demand for imports would be an underestimate of the true elasticity.

The IMFWEO (2007Apr) measured the price elasticities by correcting for the two sources of bias: measuring elasticities across 17 categories of US imports and 16 categories of US exports and adding intermediate products as a variable in the specification of the United States import demand. The new estimate by the IMFWEO (2007Apr) also includes fixed costs of entry into trade. The typical estimates of econometric models of the United States show that decreasing the CAD/GDP ratio by one percentage point requires real depreciation of the dollar of 10–20 percent. The IMFWEO (2007Apr) measurement of trade elasticities correcting for either aggregation or vertical integration bias suggests real depreciation in the range of 10–15 percent. The correction of the elasticities for both biases suggests that real depreciation of less than 10 percent would result in reduction of the CAD/GDP ratio by one percentage point. The IMFWEO (2007Apr) warns that these are partial-equilibrium considerations. The adjustment of the US CAD will likely require a combination of real exchange rate depreciation with slower growth of demand in the United States and rising demand in surplus countries. The rebalancing of demand in the United States would proceed in the form of return to savings rates prevailing before the decline beginning in the 1990s resulting from high asset valuations. Fiscal consolidation to face the increasing demand of population aging would also contribute to the adjustment.

The policy solution to the US CAD, according to Feldstein (2006), is to change policy away from a strong dollar to a competitive dollar abroad and a strong dollar at home. The domestic strength of the dollar would maintain its purchasing power at home, that is, its purchasing power would not be eroded by inflation. Feldstein

Table 5.4 US, exports, imports and trade balance $ Million

Period	Exports	Imports	Balance	Exports as % imports
1960	25,940	22,432	3,508	115.6
1965	35,285	30,621	4,664	115.2
1970	56,640	54,386	2,254	104.1
1975	132,585	120,181	12,404	110.3
1980	271.834	291,241	−19,407	93.3
1985	289.070	410,950	−121,880	70.3
1990	535.233	616,097	−80,864	86.9
1995	794.387	890,771	−96,384	89.2
2000	1,070,597	1,450,432	−379,835	73.9
2005	1,283,070	1,997,441	−714,371	64.0
2006	1,445,703	2,204,225	−758,522	66.0

Source: http://www.bea.gov/international/index.htm#trade.

(2006) recalls the experience of the United States in the 1980s. The trade-weighted value of the dollar rose by 40 percent in 1980–5 but declined by 23 percent in 12 months after April 1985 and by 37 percent by the beginning of 1988. This devaluation was accompanied by an average CPI rate of only 3.1 percent.

Table 5.4 shows the trade account of the United States since 1960. Consider the IMF sustainable deficit of 3 percent or about $397 billion. For the 2006 trade account, that would require exports to be about $1807 billion, increasing by 25 percent without compensatory growth of imports. These jumps in variables are not common in reality. There would have to be major worldwide redistribution of wealth, resources and competitiveness to attain even a trade deficit of 3 percent of GDP in the United States. To be sure, a movement toward a sustainable US external imbalance could dissipate the market fears that could cause disorderly adjustment. However, such initial movement would have to be prompt and significant. A policy failure or its anticipation could trigger the disorderly correction.

However, there may be some hopeful evidence in the adjustment during the second half of the 1980s. Exports increased by 85.2 percent from 1985 to 1990 while imports increased by 49.9 percent. The trade deficit declined by $41 billion or 34 percent. The CAD decreased from about 3 to 1.4 percent of GDP in 1990. The economy performed at capacity. In an earlier episode, exports increased by 134 percent from 1970 to 1975 while imports increased by 120.9 percent. The trade surplus jumped from $2.2 billion to $12.4 billion while the CAD moved from a slight deficit to a surplus of 1.1 percent of GDP.

Analyzing the US experience, McCormack (2007) finds that the United States will require significant devaluation as in 1971 and 1985. The solution to the US CAD would not be sustained unless there is an adjustment of multiple structural problems in the world economy. There are vulnerabilities in all regions, according to McCormack (2005, 2007). Some of these vulnerabilities are as follows. There is a crisis of leadership and employment in Europe. The prolonged effort to eliminate deflation left an extremely high internal debt in Japan. China requires many internal reforms, including restructuring of the banking system and more effective monetary and exchange rate policies.

Savings and investment

The reversal of the CAD requires a decrease in demand of US nontraded goods to generate the necessary increase in savings and an increase in foreign non-traded goods (Obstfeld and Rogoff 2005a). These authors argue that even a further 20 percent depreciation of the trade-weighted dollar exchange rate would only reduce the CAD of the United State by one-third. Their calculations suggest that most of the adjustment will come in the form of increased savings and productivity change.

An important consideration by Obstfeld and Rogoff (2005a–b) is the slow pass-through of depreciation to prices of goods and services. Thus, slower depreciation of the dollar may allow for effective pass-through, resulting in a cumulative lower depreciation of 16–26 percent in their model. In case of an overshooting, a depreciation of the dollar of 40 percent may be required to effectively change relative prices and reallocate productive factors. In terms of historical parallels, Obstfeld and Rogoff believe that the current adjustment of the CAD of the United States may resemble more the disruption occurring after the end of the Bretton Woods system in the early 1970s than the benign adjustment after 1987. They point to complications in the current environment such as high security expenditures, increasing energy prices, escalating retirement costs and the need to increase real rates of interest.

According to Obstfeld and Rogoff (2005a), the financial globalization argument may be a "double-edged sword." They observe that the United States is highly sensitive to increases in interest rates because it borrows on bonds at lower short-term interest rates, such as those paid on reserves held by foreign central banks, and lends on equity, appropriating the equity premium. Their calculations show that an increase of 1.25 percent in the short-term debt compensates for the revaluation of net positions with foreigners caused by dollar depreciation. They argue that concentration of risk has increased counterparty risk. In sum, Obstfeld and Rogoff (2005a) doubt that the valuation of the net foreign position of the United States can proceed in an orderly fashion with continuing deterioration of the CAD.

Financial flows

A phrase attributed to Charles Degaulle, "exorbitant privilege," which actually originated in his finance minister Valéry Giscard D'Estaing, is used by Gourinchas and Rey (2005) to characterize the exceptional advantage of the United States in international finance. In the1960s, the French claimed that the United States had a privilege in borrowing short term by issuing dollars held by central banks to run large investment surpluses. In the scholarly view, England became the banker of the world, borrowing short term and lending at long and intermediate terms, financing capital in the world economy. The United States replaced England as the banker of the world. In the recent deepening and integration of global financial markets, the United States has become the venture capitalist (VC) of the world, issuing short-term fixed-income liabilities and investing in equity and direct investment abroad.

Gourinchas and Rey argue that a depreciation of the dollar has two beneficial effects on the CAD: an increase in net exports and an increase in the net external asset value. This benefit derives from the reserve currency status of the dollar.

However, Gourinchas and Rey define the "tipping point" when the ratio of gross liabilities to gross assets results in negative net asset returns. That is, the tipping point is the ratio of *L/A* when

$$r_aA - r_1L < 0 \qquad (5.1)$$

where *A* is gross assets, *L* gross liabilities, r_a nominal return on assets and r_l nominal return on liabilities. The tipping point has increased continuously: 0.3 in 1952, 0.73 in 1973, 1.09 in 1991 and 1.34 in 2004. The exorbitant privilege helps to reduce significantly the magnitude of the depreciation of the dollar required to adjust the CAD. However, Gourinchas and Rey affirm that the United States is reaching the point when net asset income may become negative. Adverse expectations could develop in financial markets about the sustainability of continuing borrowing by the United States. Thus, the authors argue that investors in dollar assets may shift to other currencies, requiring a much higher premium on dollar assets because of perception of risk. They fear that there would be substantial depreciation of the dollar, a rise in rates and yields and possibly a global recession.

There are econometric estimates of the thresholds of CA adjustment in G7 countries by Clarida *et al.* (2005). The thresholds of the United States, in particular for deficit adjustment, were much wider than for other countries and the speed of adjustment slower after crossing the thresholds. In addition, the CAD has exceeded for many years the threshold of adjustment by a large magnitude. They consider two alternatives. The US CAD could be sustainable. In a second alternative, the authors identify current unusual factors that could slow adjustment:

- *Low international real interest rates*. Current low real interest rates would encourage investment while discouraging savings.
- *Slower and discontinuous depreciation of the dollar*. In contrast with the experience during the late 1980s, the dollar has depreciated in lower magnitude and more sporadically.
- *Exorbitant privilege*. Gross assets net of liabilities of the United States receive an excess return on interest, dividends and profits.
- *Compensatory effects of dollar depreciation on the foreign liability position*. For example, in 2003, the depreciation of the dollar compensated for 80 percent of the CAD.

Bernanke (2005) quotes a study at the FRBO showing that a $1 reduction in the fiscal deficit reduces the trade deficit by only $0.20. Thus, eliminating the fiscal deficit would only reduce the CAD by 1 percentage point, relative to the target of 3–4 percentage points of GDP. The reduction of the fiscal deficit would lead to desirable downward pressure on interest rates, which would work in the way of preventing an improvement in the CAD by encouraging consumption and investment.

The view of Bernanke (2005) is that external factors are more important in explaining the CAD than internal ones. An important policy effort could consist of showing developing countries that they should become borrowers instead of lenders of capital to invest in attractive domestic opportunities. The promotion of macroeconomic stability is essential to avoid the crises of the 1990s. It could be added that the elimination of international moral hazard may be important in preventing those crises. Structural reforms are also quite important such as stronger property rights, standards and codes in bank regulation and supervision, transparency of economic information and removal of impediments to international capital flows. Macroeconomic stability and a better business environment would permit lower levels of precautionary international reserves.

The G7, the IMF and the doctrine of shared responsibility

The statement of the meeting of finance ministers of the G7 (2007Feb9) in February 2007 included the issues of global imbalances, currency realignments and hedge funds (HFs). There are two warnings in the statement by the G7 (2007Feb9). The first is with respect to the need of exchange rates to reflect fundamentals and the second on HFs. Economic growth could be jeopardized by exchange volatility and "disorderly movement." The G7 (2007Feb9) continues to monitor exchange markets, engaging in cooperation whenever necessary. This cooperation can mean concerted intervention in currency markets. There is strong advice for one emerging country: "in emerging economies with large and growing CA surpluses, especially China, it is desirable that their effective exchange rates move so that necessary adjustment will occur." The Dow Jones Newswires (2007Feb10) finds the direct reference to the exchange rate movement stronger than in previous statements. The continuing depreciation of the dollar versus the euro is also creating a conflict between Europe and the United States. The G7 (2007Oct19) also insists in the appreciation of the renminbi:

> We welcome China's decision to increase the flexibility of its currency, but in view of its rising current account surplus and domestic inflation, we stress its need to allow an accelerated appreciation of its effective exchange rate

The Managing Director of the IMF proposed to update the 1977 mandate of surveillance over exchange rate policies. De Rato (2007Jun18) analyzes these changes in IMF surveillance (see Chapter 2). China joined the meeting of the G7 for discussion of the global economy (Reuters 2007Feb10). Representatives of Brazil, China, India, Mexico and South Africa joined the G7 finance ministers for another working dinner. There have been discussions for broadening the G7 with the inclusion of various countries. However, there are no formal proposals or announcements.

The IMF Staff (2007Apr) considers multilateral surveillance to be a GPG. The information, policy discussion and collaboration of the consultations with the IFIs would not be forthcoming by the private sector or even by the individual countries. The effort is also within the more general GPG of international financial stability, which is the very purpose in the creation of the Bretton Woods institutions. The IMF Staff (2007Apr) finds the use of multilateral consultation as an effective means of focusing on key issues affecting international financial stability. There is probably no more important current issue than global imbalances.

The IMF Staff (2007Apr) engaged the major systemically important countries and groups of countries in focused consultations on how to adjust global imbalances. The consultations resulted in an analysis of current policies and policy plans shown in Table 5.5. The essence of the US effort consists of reducing the budget deficit and encouraging domestic savings to diminish its dependence on foreign savings. There is a major challenge for the United States in reallocating resources toward export activity and increasing its international competitiveness in key sectors. This is a structural reorganization that cannot be expected to be completed in the short term.

Table 5.5   IMF regional policies of shared responsibility

United States
  Reducing the budget deficit
  Fiscal consolidation eliminating the unified budget deficit by 2012
  Tax incentives to savings
  Constraining budget spending
  Reforming entitlements
  Increasing capital market competitiveness

Euro Area
  Labor market reforms
  Increasing labor productivity
  Increasing product market competitiveness
  Integrating financial markets in the EU
    Reducing regulation
    Improving business environment

Japan
  Fiscal consolidation
  Labor market reforms
  Increasing competitiveness in product markets
  Promoting inward FDI

China
  Financial reform
  Flexibility of the exchange rate
  Increasing domestic consumer demand

Saudi Arabia
  Increasing investment in oil and infrastructure
  Increasing government spending in social programs

Source: IMF Staff (2007Apr); International Monetary Fund (2007Apr14).

The Euro Area also faces structural challenges in the form of reforming labor markets, increasing labor productivity and creating a more competitive environment in product markets. Japan is facing the need of fiscal consolidation as entitlements increase. Japan is recovering growth and eliminating the deflation of the lost decade. There are similar structural problems in Japan of increasing productivity. China is still engaged in reforming financial markets and creating greater flexibility of its exchange rate. There is also the challenge for China of finding a new paradigm of a large state sector coexisting with a growing and more productive private sector. The oil-producing countries can gain from the high oil prices by increasing investments in infrastructure and social programs. The policies designed to promote adjustment of the global imbalances also would improve the domestic economies of the regions and countries. There is a challenging effort to jump from policy design to implementation that depends on domestic political processes.

The International Monetary and Financial Committe (IMFC) reviewed the multilateral consultation on global imbalances (International Monetary Fund 2007Apr14) at the IMF/WB meetings in April 2007. The Managing Director of the IMF proposed the new multilateral consultation as part of IMF surveillance in April 2006 (De Rato 2006Apr5, 3), which was accepted by the IMFC. It is now up to individual regions and countries to implement reforms that could solve the issue of global imbalances. There is meager political capital for most of those reforms.

The challenge to the international financial system

Regulation of international finance and the resolution of crises developed during the postwar period by reaction to the crises that occurred instead of by an established theory based on empirical verification. The limitations of economics dictated this approach. The regime established in the past three decades consists of two types of institutional arrangements, the IFA and central banks. The objective of this section is to outline the current institutional arrangements to show how they have been nearly dismantled by the financial crisis originating in the collapse of the US real estate sector. The process of finding and implementing new, more solid arrangements may spread over several years in the future.

IFA: emerging market crises and soft law

The first arrangement originated in the reaction to emerging market crises by the finance ministers and heads of central banks of the G7 after the Mexican crisis in 1994 in the process known as IFA (Peláez and Peláez 2005). There were three mechanisms in this system.

First, the Rey Report of the G10 in response to the Mexican crisis of 1994–5 sanctioned the lending in arrears in the process of catalytic financing by the IMF as the form of *crisis resolution*. Balance of payments crises spread to domestic financial sectors, causing sharp contractions of credit and output. The second mechanism consists of *crisis prevention* by means of the FSAP process of the IMF-WB designed to use Article IV Surveillance of the financial sectors of members of the IMF. Third, the Asian crisis of 1997–8 exposed the lack of transparency of financial systems as well as the lack of standards and codes similar to those prevailing in the G7. Economic research suggests that transparency is required for adequate private and regulatory monitoring of financial systems. The G7 instructed the IFIs to develop *standards and codes* of best practice and to evaluate them through the ROSC program of the IMF-WB. These standards and codes constitute soft law, which is easier to implement through the moral suasion of the IFIs. The Basel II capital requirements constitute the most accomplished work on international codes and standards.

G7 central banks

The second arrangement originated in what Rogoff (2006a) considers being the "Great Moderation," or decline of the volatility of output, and the volatility of asset prices, including equities, housing and real trade-weighted exchange rates. The measurements of the volatility of quarterly seasonally adjusted output growth by Rogoff (2006a) show that it has significantly declined for the most advanced countries since the 1970s. In the United States, this measurement of output growth volatility declined by 50 percent from the 1970s to the 1990s and 2000s. There are important structural breaks in output volatility, for example, in the United States and the United Kingdom. Measurements using annual data show lower output volatility in the 1960s but declining in the 2000s. Rogoff (2006a) concludes that globalization is not a complete explanation of declining output volatility.

The "Great Moderation" has not spread to the volatility of stock price returns. The volatility of the S&P index appears to have increased after March 1988. Housing prices are quite difficult to measure. However, Rogoff (2006a) argues that they remain highly volatile in a longer-term horizon. There is similar evidence for continuing volatility of bond returns. Real exchange rates can be conceptualized as an asset price depending on real interest rate differentials at home and abroad and also as a goods-market price or the relative price of the home and foreign baskets of consumption (Rogoff 2006a, 17). The asset price role appears to dominate short and medium terms. The evidence shows some moderate decline in exchange rate volatility but much less than the decline in output volatility. The evidence shows more significant decline in the volatility of the terms of trade.

The second more informal mechanism is the primary role of individual central banks, especially the FRBO, the ECB, the Bank of England (BOE) and the Bank of Japan (BOJ), in the management of crises in countries in the G7. Cooperation among central banks would be informally used as required to prevent crises from spreading regionally.

The approach to central banking is particularly influenced by the experience of the BOE. The United Kingdom found its framework of financial system regulation after a troubled period in 1970–92. The average yearly growth rate of the United Kingdom declined from 2.8 percent in 1950–69 to 2.0 percent in 1970–92 while the average yearly rate of inflation rose from 3.9 percent in 1950–69 to 9.6 percent in 1970–92 (BOE 2007Q1, 26). However, there was similar experience in the United

States, Japan, Germany and France of lower growth and higher inflation. The United Kingdom maintained an average yearly rate of growth of 2.8 percent in 1998–2005 and of 2.5 percent in inflation. This was performance comparable with 3.0 percent growth in the United States and inflation of 2.5 percent and better performance than 0.8 percent growth with inflation of −0.3 percent in Japan, 1.3 percent growth with inflation of 1.4 percent in Germany and growth of 2.2 percent in France with inflation of 1.5 percent.

The United Kingdom has experienced continuing growth during 58 consecutive quarters since 1992. The unemployment rate declined from over 10 percent in 1993 to below 5 percent in 2005, the lowest rate in about three decades. The initial target for 1992–7 was inflation of the retail price index excluding mortgage payments (RPIX) of 1–4 percent and a point target of 2.5 percent until the end of 2003 when it was changed to 2 percent CPI inflation, which has typically been 0.75 percentage points below RPIX inflation. Inflation has never deviated from the target by one percentage point, avoiding a letter requesting explanation from the Treasury to the BOE.

The BOE (2007Q1, 25) argues that the policy framework is a combination of an understanding of the functioning of the economy with lessons of experience. In this analysis, the level of output and employment in the short term is affected by changes in the nominal demand for goods and services in the economy. Monetary policy operates on nominal and real interest rates that in turn change assets prices, including the exchange rate, influencing nominal demand that changes output and employment. Monetary policy is the primary tool of demand management (Bean 2007). The long-term level of output and employment depends on the capacity of the economy that is determined by productive resources such as capital, labor, land and their use in production by applying technology. Monetary policy can have only a long-term impact on the rate of inflation. There is concern of formulating monetary policy to avoid excessive short-term fluctuations of output that can have adverse effects on investment.

The BOE (2007Q1, 27) finds a significant role of institutional arrangements in the stability of growth and inflation of the United Kingdom. Reforms of product and labor markets were crucial (Bean 2003, 2). The framework of anchoring inflationary expectations consists of the explicit target for inflation, significant transparency and the independence of the BOE. The United Kingdom departed from anchoring to the exchange rate to floating its exchange rate and targeting domestic inflation. The EMU fixed the exchange rates of its member countries and the ECB provided common monetary policy. Eichengreen (2000) finds this to have been a key policy choice in the international financial system, sustainable pegged exchange rates in the EMU and sustainable floating rate with inflation targeting in the United Kingdom. The delegation of policy to the Monetary Policy Committee (MPC) withdrew political influence from the decision process, enhancing the credibility of the framework. The process of forming the view of inflation by the BOE is transparent, avoiding adverse expectations. The accountability of the members of the MPC by release of their votes and the announcement of the cycle of meetings add accountability and predictability to the system. The announcement of the target and the release of information through the inflation report make the process open, helping in the general effort of anchoring inflationary expectations.

The disruption of the system

The breakdown of the regulation and crisis arrangements of the world financial system occurred because the central banks created the crisis; the regulation of risk-based capital requirements is inadequate to deal with the crisis; and the central banks did not respond timely and effectively to the development of the crisis. These issues are discussed below in turn.

The FRBO, the central bank of the United States, created the current crisis by lowering its policy rate, the fed funds rate, to 1 percent in 2003 and maintaining it at that level for about a year. Fear of deflation, which had occurred unexpectedly in Japan, was the reason for lowering the policy rate to almost zero. Economic agents extrapolated similarly low interest rates for the future, causing a housing and consumption boom, sealing the bias of Americans against saving.

Monetary policy at the Fed under Greenspan (2004Jan3) combined two types of analyses. The environment of monetary policy is characterized by uncertainty, defined as lack of knowledge of the probability distribution, and risk, defined as events in a known probability distribution. The FRBO has used a risk management approach to identify the sources of risk and uncertainty, quantifying them whenever possible and analyzing the costs of these risks. In addition, the FRBO has accumulated knowledge over the years of the influence of a small set of variables on policy decisions and developed models to analyze their impact statistically. At the end, there is still a tough choice among many alternatives and a significant degree of imprecision. Greenspan (2004Jan3, 5) describes the technical limitations of policy:

> However, despite extensive efforts to capture and quantify what we perceive as the key macroeconomic relationships, our knowledge about many of the important linkages is far from complete and, in all likelihood, will always remain so. Every model, no matter how detailed or how well designed, conceptually and empirically, is a vastly simplified representation of the world that we experience with all its intricacies on a day-to-day basis

Greenspan was the archetype of the omniscient central banker, designing policy on the basis of views for the next 6 months. The technical central banks, such as the BOE, follow a more rigorous process of analysis and inflation targets. Both approaches have been seriously challenged by the financial crisis of 2007. There are hopes for improving the technical approach but the omniscient central banker may be part of history.

The second challenge to the current system consists of the failure of the central banks to anticipate the crisis and the inadequacy of the risk-based capital standards of Basel II. The major central banks of the world injected liquidity on August 9 and 10, 2007 (Perry and Ip 2007Aug11). The FRBO injected \$62 billion, the ECB \$213.6 billion and the BOJ \$8.39 billion. There were injections by other central banks: $1.7–2.5 billion by the Swiss National Bank, $4.2 billion by the Reserve Bank of Australia, $1.6 billion by the Bank of Canada and $0.9 billion by the Monetary Authority of Singapore. The press release by the FRBO (2007Aug10) states:

> The Federal Reserve is providing liquidity to facilitate the orderly functioning of financial markets. The Federal Reserve will provide reserves as necessary through open market operations to promote trading in the federal funds market at rates close to the Federal Open Market Committee's target rate of 5-1/4 percent. In current circumstances, depository institutions may experience unusual funding needs because of dislocations in money and credit markets. As always, the discount window is available as a source of funding

The interventions by the central banks were designed to maintain the policy rates at the target levels and not to lower interest rates.

The fed funds rate moved above 6 percent relative to its target level of 5.25 percent on August 9 and 10, 2007, prompting the large SRAs of the Federal Reserve Bank of New York (FRBNY) open market desk (Ossinger 2007Aug10). In the week ending on August 10, the FRBNY injected $90 billion by means of SRAs. The difficulty in trading mortgage-backed securities (MBS) is identified as one of the major reasons for the injection of liquidity (Ossinger 2007Aug10). On August 9, the French bank BNP Paribas suspended three funds with exposure to US credit markets (Lobb 2007Aug12). The suspension triggered significant uncertainty in world financial markets.

The FT (2007Aug10) argues that the structured investment vehicles (SIV) may be part of the reason for the injections of liquidity by central banks. These SIVs raise money in the commercial paper market to invest it in credit derivatives with long-term maturity. The SIVs use programs in banks to capture the difference between short-term borrowing rates and structured product investments (Tett *et al.* 2007Aug12). The FT (2007Aug10) quotes Moody's Investors Services that the SIVs account for $200 billion of outstanding commercial paper. The original value has been changed to around $400 billion, declining to $320 billion.

The transaction is as follows. The SIV issues commercial paper with a commitment line of credit from the bank, in the case of conduits, and engages in an SRA of its commercial paper. Most SIVs are registered in jurisdictions such as Grand Cayman and managed out of London (Mollenkamp *et al.* 2007Oct18). The funding rate on the SRA would be close to the policy rate of the central bank, a little over 4 percent in Europe and over 5.25 percent in the United States. The funds obtained from the SRA would be invested in structured credit products (SCP) such as collateralized debt obligations (CDO) and asset-backed securities (ABS) that with leverage yield closer to 10 percent at the original buying price. At maturity of the SRA, the SIV would renew it. At one point the market turned against this type of financing. The SIVs or conduits of German banks were not able to renew the SRA and the banks did not have sufficient liquidity to honor the commitment line of credit. If the SIVs did not honor the commitment to repurchase the commercial paper at maturity, the counterparty would hold CDOs and/or MBS that probably would not have the same market value as the SRA loan. The pressure originates in financing of the SIVs by banks because commitments have increased significantly. The banks finance the SIVs when they cannot obtain financing in the short-term commercial paper market. The realization of these tough facts caused the drying of financing for asset-backed commercial paper (ABCP). The central banks faced a situation in which short-term liquidity in money market funds, which invest in ABCP, could be adversely affected, probably causing significant withdrawals from financial institutions.

The FRBO (2007Aug17) lowered the rate for the primary rediscount window facility by 50 basis points to 5.75 percent, on August 17, 2007. The FRBO also announced "a change to the Reserve Bank's usual practices to allow the provision of term financing for as long as 30 days, renewable by the borrowers. These changes will remain in place until the Federal Reserve determines that market liquidity has improved materially." The lowering of the fed funds rate would probably not be as effective in financing illiquid ABCP markets. The FRBNY, according to Ip (2007Aug24), "clarified its discount window rules with the effect of enabling banks to pledge a broader range of commercial paper as collateral." The verbal rules of the FRBNY allow the use of ABCP that is guaranteed by lines of the credit of the bank borrowing from the fed. Outstanding commercial paper in the United States declined from a seasonally adjusted $2182 billion on August 8, 2007 to $1883 billion on August 15, or by $299 billion, equivalent to change of −13.7 percent (FRBO 2007Aug16). ABCP outstanding declined from $1174.3 at the end of July to $888.3 billion on October 17, by $286 billion, or change of −24.3 percent.

The US Treasury coordinated the creation of a super fund, the Master-Liquidity Enhancement Conduit, by the three largest US banks, Citigroup, J P Morgan and Bank of America (Mollenkamp *et al.* 2007Oct18). The simple calculation of the required financing by the super fund is $100 billion, about a third of the estimated maturity in 6–9 months of some $320 billion of SIV holdings. Citigroup found financing for its $80 billion in SIVs for the final quarter of 2007. The SIV sells its holdings to the super fund at 2 percent discount, receiving payment in cash and 4 percent in junior notes that are responsible for the first defaults in the assets. The super fund borrows money from investors by the issue of short and medium debt. There is a promise by the banks behind the super fund to pay the investors the borrowed funds in case the debt cannot be refinanced. The objective of the super fund is to prevent a fire-sale of the assets of SIVs that could disrupt markets of ABS, causing also losses in bank balance sheets. There is still the issue of the $1.5 trillion of mortgages with high rates of 300 basis points above the corresponding treasury. Defaults in these mortgages would not be covered by the mechanism of the super fund and could threaten financial markets.

The central banks were surprised by the crisis, with the FRBO focusing on inflation on August 7 while the mechanism of job creation of the United States had experienced significant erosion after June. The ECB and the BOJ were considering increases in interest rates. There are no mechanisms of anticipation of inflation, technical or by omniscient central bankers.

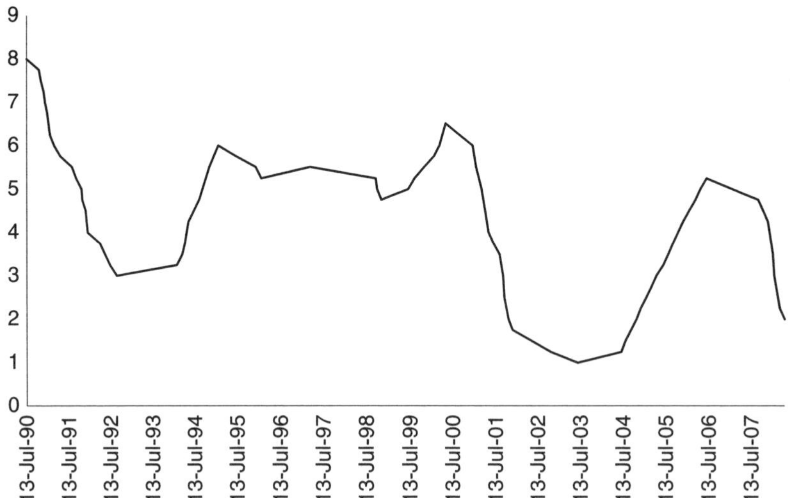

Chart 5.1   Fed funds rate 1990–2008
Source: Board of Governors of the Federal Reserve System.

The role of subprime credit in the crisis has been exaggerated. The value of risky real-estate loans at high rates of 300 basis points above the comparable treasuries amounts to $1.5 trillion, around 10 percent of GDP, across all social classes and regions in the United States (Brooks and Ford 2007). Chart 5.1 shows the fed funds target rate by the FRBO in 1990–2007. There have been capricious episodes such as the unexplainable increase in the fed funds rate in 1994 that caused a global loss of financial wealth of $1 trillion while the FRBO pursued a non-existing inflation threat. This rate increase contributed to the sovereign crises of Mexico and Argentina in 1994–5.

There are valid doubts as to the effectiveness of policy impulses by the US central bank. After the collapse of the high-tech stock market boom, the FRBO lowered rates in an effort to prevent a non-existent deflation threat. The 1 percent fed funds rate and the willingness to lower rates to 0 percent because of errors in price indexes created the impression that interest rates and inflation would be low forever, encouraging borrowing in excess of income and capacity to repay, for prime and subprime borrowers alike. Income, Y, is a flow obtained by a rate of return r from a stock of wealth W:

$$Y = rW, \quad \text{or} \tag{5.2}$$

$$W = Y/r \tag{5.3}$$

As $r \to 0$, $W \to \infty$. The US central bank misled borrowers that their wealth in real estate had experienced a significant permanent increase, also misleading lenders that there was no risk because collateral in the form of houses would always cover the values of the loans. Families purchased houses and lenders provided financing under the illusion that even if the adjustable rates increased monthly payments by 50–100 percent after 2–3 years, the borrowers could exit by selling the houses at a profit. There was failure in Congressional oversight of FRBO policy. It is difficult to accept that lenders and borrowers knowingly destroyed their lives in the value of 10 percent of GDP merely on their carelessness and not that of the central bank in creating the impression of low interest rates and resulting increasing personal wealth forever. The necessary subsequent increase in interest rates doomed borrowers and lenders and caused a global recession risk (Peláez and Peláez 2007, 206–9, 220–5). There is the possibility of a recessive wealth effect because as $r \to \infty$, $W \to 0$.

There is no standard of credit-risk pricing. As a result, various models provide different prices. A product without price becomes illiquid. The formula for calculating EL, 10.3, is not operational. There was also failure of another foundation of Basel II, credit ratings. Evidently, there is need to reconsider and improve existing arrangements of central banking and codes of capital requirements. As documented by Barth *et al.* (2006), worldwide experience in regulation of banking is more consistent with the private interest view than with the public interest view.

The credit/dollar crisis

The central banks followed the near zero interest rate with rapid increases to 5.25 percent. There was a resulting collapse in home sales and prices. Unsold inventories of houses rose toward the equivalent of 1 year of sales. Record levels of foreclosures added more houses to unsold inventories, further depressing prices. Banks were eventually forced to write down structured credit products. Losses in financial entities climbed toward half a trillion by mid-year 2008. Defaults spread throughout the financial production chain, beginning with home-equity loans and eventually affecting all types of personal loans. Credit spreads of junk bonds increased, paralyzing the market of loans of leveraged buyouts. Bond insurers suffered losses from the issue of CDS affected by widening credit spreads. Local government and small entities, such as hospitals and museums, were squeezed by increases in flexible auction rates from 4 percent to as high as 20 percent. Banks were forced to raise capital. The major problem was an increase in the perception of counterparty risk because of asymmetry of information. Banks were uncertain of their own balance sheets and of those of other financial entities. LIBOR rose dramatically over the 3-month Treasury bill. Some banks began to report fake lower rates to the British Bankers Association. Derivative transaction began to be affected by the decline in credit ratings of financial institutions.

The central banks showed significant creativity in using old and new tools to prevent the spread of the crisis to the real sector of the economy. The fed lowered the fed funds rate from 5.25 percent to 2 percent. However, funds did not reach the segments of the credit market that had become illiquid, that is, that could not find funding in SRAs. The central banks resuscitated the rediscount window, increasing its financing and widening the range of papers that could be rediscounted. Non-depository institutions such as investment banks were allowed to use the rediscount window. The central bank also brokered the sale of Bear Stearns, subsidizing potential losses of $29 billion just before the opening of equity markets in Tokyo. It is also considering a perfectly elastic supply of money by paying interest on deposits.

The price of oil doubled in an incredible generalized rise in all commodities. The marketing of this increase in commodity prices was that supply had been declining for years while demand increased in the global boom led by Brazil, Russia, India and China. This explanation would require an almost perfectly inelastic supply of all commodities, shifting to the origin, while demand jumped incessantly. This argument fails to explain why the boom in commodity prices coincided with the aggressive injection of liquidity by central banks beginning in August 2007 instead of occurring throughout the global expansion after 2004. A competing explanation is that the liquidity injected by the central banks was used in a "carry trade" of shorting the dollar/euro and going long in commodity futures and options. Positions were sporadically reversed to long dollar/euro and long the US stock market.

Government intervention also prolonged the crisis with efforts to prevent the cleansing of balance sheets with proposals such as the super SIV to avoid MTM of structured credit products and measures of impeding necessary foreclosures. Credit markets will not recover until counterparty risk perception diminishes to normal levels. The devaluation of the dollar would not have been as sharp had there not been a major US CAD. Efforts to intervene in currency markets will frustrate the adjustment of global external imbalances.

Central bank management

The IFIs and many countries adopted the model of inflation targeting of the BOE as the most adequate framework. The separation of powers and accountability of the system of the United Kingdom became the desired standard of financial regulation. It also partly collapsed during the financial crisis of 2007.

The FT (2007Sep19) summarizes the erosion of credibility of the BOE. The BOE raised suspicions that it was being overruled by Treasury. The division of responsibilities among Treasury, the FSA and the BEO has become confusing. The crisis of Northern Rock was not managed in proper form.

The system of central bank independence and technical inflation targets appears fragmented, at least temporarily. There is need for major work on repairing the system at both the individual banks and within the BIS. The G7 (2007Oct19) requested the FSF to:

> Analyze the underlying causes of the turbulence and offer proposals in the areas of liquidity and risk management; accounting and valuation of financial derivatives; role, methodologies and use of credit rating agencies in structured finance; and basic supervisory principles of prudential oversight, including the treatment of off-balance sheet vehicles

The BCBS should also address these issues and the need for strengthening Basel II.

The carry trade

The departing point in the carry trade is whether there can be actual profits in borrowing in the funding country currency at a lower interest rate, converting into the currency of the target country, investing into the higher interest rate of the target country and then at maturity reconverting into the currency of the funding country to repay the loan.[2] A simple textbook proposition in economics is the existence of interest parity. Suppose that i_j is the funding country's (Japan) proportionate interest rate, i_u is the target country's (US) proportionate interest rate, $i_j < i_u$, F is the units of target country currency required for buying a unit of funding country currency at the date of maturity of the borrowing and investment contracts and S is the target country units of currency required to buy a unit of funding currency at the initial date of the contracts. The borrowing cost per unit in the funding country is $(1 + i_j)$ and the investment return in the investment country is $(1 + i_u)$.

The initial step is to convert the funding country borrowing value into units of target country currency, that is, for every unit borrowed divide by S. If the funding country currency is the Japanese yen (JPY) and the target country currency the US dollar (USD), S would be JPY/USD, such that dividing the JPY principal of the loan by S would convert it into USD. At the maturity of the investment in the USD, the proceeds would have to be reconverted into JPY by the forward rate contracted, F, expressed as JPY/USD. For breakeven,

$$(1 + i_u)(F/S) = (1 + i_j) \tag{5.4}$$

Which is equivalent to:

$$(1 + i_j)/(1 + i_u) = F/S \tag{5.5}$$

This is the uncovered interest parity (UIP) condition equation (2) obtained by Burnside *et al.* (2006, 2–3) from the maximization of utility subject to a budget constraint. If the risk is the same in both currencies, arbitrage would ensure that the ratio of the interest rates, or interest rate differential, is equal to the ratio of the forward to the spot exchange rate. Burnside *et al.* (2006, 2–3) also derive the covered interest arbitrage (CIR) condition in their equation (3):

$$(1 + r_j) = (1 + r_u)[E_t(S_{t+1}/S_t + \text{cov}_t(S_{t+1}/S_t, \lambda_{t+1})/E_t(\lambda_{t+1})] \tag{5.6}$$

The expectation operator is E_t, taken at time t, cov_t is the covariance at time t and λ is the Langrange multiplier from the maximization of utility subject to a budget constraint that has the meaning of the marginal utility of a unit of foreign currency. The expression is identical to the common formula for CIR except for the inclusion of the risk factor in addition to the expected change in the spot interest rate.

The equations for the UIP together with that for CIR imply (Burnside *et al.* 2006, 3):

$$F = E_t(S_{t+1}) + \text{cov}_t(\lambda_{t+1}, S_{t+1})/E_t(\lambda_{t+1}) \tag{5.7}$$

In words, the forward rate is the expected value of the future spot rate plus a risk premium. If the covariance is zero, the forward rate is an unbiased predictor of the spot rate.

The data used by Burnside *et al.* (2006, 4–5) covers the period 1976–2005 for nine advanced countries. They estimate the regression of the percentage change of the spot rate on the percentage difference between the forward and spot rates. The slope coefficient should be equal to unity but they find that, consistent with the literature, it is significantly different from unity. If the forward rate were an unbiased predictor of the future rate, the currency with a forward premium, $F_t > S_t$, should appreciate. The evidence shows the existence of a "forward-premium puzzle," in the form of depreciation of the target currencies with forward premium or relatively higher interest rates and appreciation of the funding currencies with a forward discount or relatively lower interest rates.

The objective of Burnside *et al.* (2006) is to estimate the profits from exploiting deviations in UIP. The carry trade of funding in the low-interest currencies and investing in target currencies with high interest rates, without hedging exchange risk, is a strategy to capture deviation in reality from UIP. The payoff of the carry trade is:

$$YB[(S_{t+1}/S_t)(1 + i_u) - (1 + i_j)] \qquad (5.8)$$

The term S_{t+1}/S_t is the percentage change of the exchange rate from the initial date of borrowing to the maturity of the transaction and YB is the JPY borrowing. Depreciation of the JPY occurs when

$$S_{t+1}/S_t > 0 \qquad (5.9)$$

That is, the JPY depreciates, or the number of JPY required for buying one USD increases. If the borrowing is converted into USD at 100 JPY/USD and the rate changes to 110 JPY/USD, the carry trade has two gains, the higher interest rate earned in USD plus an exchange gain of 10 percent in JPY. If the rate appreciates to 90 JPY/USD, the carry trade has a loss of 100/90 or 11.1 percent more JPY required to repay the principal borrowed.

Burnside *et al.* (2006) and Cavallo (2006) consider an alternative carry trade strategy, consisting of selling forward the currency with the forward premium and buying forward the currency with the forward discount. The payoff of this strategy is the percentage of the forward rate relative to the spot rate at the maturity of the transaction. This strategy has the advantage of lower transaction costs. The tests of Burnside *et al.* (2006) confirm major statistical failure of UIP. However, the calculations of Burnside *et al.* (2006) for the individual nine currencies and for an equally weighted portfolio show that the payoffs of currency speculation via the carry trade are low. In the equally weighted portfolio with transaction costs, earning an average annual payoff of UK pound (GBP) 1 million requires the speculator betting GBP 33.3 million per month. The importance of the carry trade in financial instability appears to have been exaggerated.

Regulation, trade and devaluation wars

The actual loss of economic activity and employment after 2007 will be known with precision only when the National Bureau of Economic Research makes its judgment, if any, on the dates of beginning and ending of recession. There has been significant concern about the adequacy of regulation. This concern extends beyond the national level, encompassing the world. There are likely to be profound changes in financial regulation and in the institutions and policy of the international financial system. There is risk of regulatory, trade and exchange wars, depending on the existence and depth of a global economic contraction. International relations in general could be compromised by economic struggle among countries and regions.

According to a distinguished macroeconomist (Bernanke 1995, 1):

> To understand the Great Depression is the Holy Grail of macroeconomics. Not only did the Depression give birth to macroeconomics as a distinct field of study, but also – to an extent that is not always fully appreciated the experience of the 1930s continues to influence macroeconomists' beliefs, policy recommendations, and research agendas

The Great Depression of the 1930s consisted of a unique phenomenon in terms of economic contraction worldwide. Its impact was particularly strong in the United States. Table 5.6 shows US GDP in current dollars, or without adjusting for changes in prices, and in constant dollars, or adjusting for changes in prices. The decline in real or price adjusted GDP in 1930–3 accumulated to 25.7 percent. The decline in GDP in current dollars or without adjusting for prices in 1930–3 accumulated to 44 percent. It is possible that there was recovery in employment and dynamism in the US economy only after the beginning of the effort to win World War II.

The synthesis of research on the depression is based on the importance of domestic monetary policies and the instability of the international monetary system (Eichengreen 1996, 2002). The initial research proposed an autonomous role for tightening monetary policy in the United States that induced or accentuated an already ongoing milder contraction (Friedman and Schwartz 1963). Comparative research finds that there were similar policy mistakes in Germany and of a different form in France (Eichengreen 2002). The international monetary system of fixed exchange rates facilitated the transmission of the depression among countries in the form of rising interest rates to prevent depreciation of the currency. The tightening of monetary policy accentuated banking crises in many countries but perhaps not as much as in the United States.

Under the gold standard, a country would fix the content of its currency, the dollar, to its stock of gold with conversion at a fixed rate, or dollars per ounce of gold, at the central bank. The objective was to create a mechanism of adjustment to inflation and recession without need of economic policy. If there were inflation, the rate of exchange would depreciate to that of the gold export parity.

Table 5.6 US GDP growth 1930–45%

	Current dollars	**Constant dollars**
1930	−12.0	−8.6
1931	−16.1	−6.4
1932	−23.2	−13.0
1933	−4.0	−1.3
1934	17.0	10.8
1935	11.1	8.9
1936	14.3	13.0
1937	9.7	5.1
1938	−6.2	−3.4
1939	7.0	8.1
1940	10.0	8.8
1941	25.0	17.1
1942	27.7	18.5
1943	22.7	16.4
1944	10.7	8.1
1945	1.5	−1.1
1946	−0.4	−11.0

Source: US Bureau of Economic Analysis, Department of Commerce.

There would be conversion by the public of dollars into gold, that is, dollars would be withdrawn from circulation in exchange for gold. The lower quantity of dollars in circulation would increase the interest rate, which would decrease demand for goods and services, reducing inflation. The rate of exchange would appreciate below the gold export parity.

If there were recession, the rate of exchange would appreciate to the gold import point. There would be conversion of gold into dollars. The higher quantity of dollars in circulation would reduce the rate of interest, which would increase the demand for goods and services, alleviating the recession. The exchange rate would depreciate to a point between the gold export and import parities.

The countries that maintained the gold standard contracted the money supply to arrest an outflow of gold, appreciating the exchange rate. This was the policy of major central banks in defending the relative strength of their currencies. Exchange appreciation made exports more expensive to foreigners, reducing internal economic activity. For example, Brazil abandoned the gold standard almost immediately because of the collapse of the prices of its major export, coffee, depreciating the exchange rate and imposing exchange controls. The large trade balance resulting from exchange rate depreciation combined with fiscal stimulus from an internal revolution in São Paulo in 1932 and a drought to recover the Brazilian economy (Peláez 1968, 1972).

Implementation of stabilizing monetary policy required lowering interest rates, resulting in depreciation of the exchange rate. The abandoning of the gold standard permitted the pursuit of recovery by liberal monetary policy that restored stability to banking and finance (Eichengreen 2002). The banking crises and monetary policy errors were more important in the case of the United States while the breakdown of the gold standard was more important in other countries.

An important change in economics during the Great Depression was the introduction of the concept of involuntary unemployment and the creation of the field of macroeconomics (Keynes 1936). Involuntary unemployment is a continuing situation in which resources, such as labor, cannot find employment at prevailing wages. There were changes in attitudes about policies. The classical theory of international trade breaks down if the assumption of full employment of resources is replaced by involuntary unemployment. Full employment can be attained by national policies. The government can promote domestic consumption by increasing domestic investment or use an excess of exports over imports, or trade surplus, in attaining its objective. According to a distinguished economist with sterling contributions (Robinson 1946, 112):

> The more a country makes use of home investment (or reduced thriftiness) the smaller its surplus of exports (or the greater its deficit) and the more it helps to provide employment in other countries. The more it makes use of wage cutting (or exchange depreciation) or of protection, the harder is employment to maintain in the rest of the world. The situation of each country is affected by the policies of the rest, and any number of permutations and combinations are possible

The use of trade and exchange policy to promote employment at home at the expense of foreign employment was coined by Robinson (1937) as "beggar-my-neighbor remedies for unemployment." A distinguished economist also recognized as the ideal social scientist analyzed protection during the Great Depression (Schumpeter 1940, 5):

> But in times like the present one, in which conditions of underutilization of resources prevail, there is reason to believe that, even in those cases and in the long run, a policy of protection does more good than harm, while it is clear that in the short run discontinuance of protection would create most serious difficulties of adjustment

An important event during the Great Depression was the imposition of the Smoot-Hawley tariff on imports by the US Congress on June 18, 1930. Economic principles and the analysis of economists did not play a role in the discussion of the Smoot-Hawley tariff. An economist who accompanied the debates concluded that even if economics had been considered, the decision depended on the national opinion in the United States in 1929–30 (Fetter 1933, 427):

> The tariff situation was but one manifestation of a general post-war psychology, of a tacitly accepted belief that the way to promote the national welfare was to give each group what it wanted to make its members individually prosperous,

without any consideration of the relation of such action to larger problems of national policy. The dominant congressional opinion on the tariff, and the resulting legislation, was merely a reflection of this state of mind

There was a decline of US imports by 41.2 percent from the second quarter of 1930 to the third quarter of 1932 (Irwin 1998). However, real US GNP declined by 29.8 percent in the same period, likely accounting for a major part of the decline in imports. Americans reduced their purchases of all goods, imported or not, as their income collapsed as in no other recorded period of history. Ad valorem, or percentage tariff rates, increased from 21.08 percent in the Act of 1913, to 34.61 percent in the Act of 1932 and finally to 42.48 percent in the Act of 1930, the Smoot-Hawley tariff (Irwin 1998, 327). Many of the tariff duties were specified on a dollar value, being subject to the curse of deflation. The fixed nominal value represents a higher percentage of the declining price. Suppose that the price of an imported good is \$10 and the nominal tariff is \$1. After a decline of the price to \$8, the \$1 duty is equivalent to 12.5 percent of the price. That is, deflation increases the ad valorem or percentage tax rate, in the example by 2.5 percentage points.

It is quite difficult to analyze the Smoot-Hawley tariff because it requires the specification and measurement of a counterfactual. This counterfactual is what would have happened to imports and economic activity had there not been a tariff increase. This would resolve the issue of whether the tariff was detrimental or not and by how much. A sophisticated attempt to measure the impact of the tariff results in the following conclusions (Irwin 1998). There was an increase of US import prices of 5–6 percent resulting from the actual increase of imports duties by 20 percent caused by the Smoot-Hawley tariff. The combined effect of the increase of the tariff directly or through the deflation effect reduced imports by 12–20 percent. Approximately 22 percent of the 40 percent reduction in the volume of US imports is explained by the combination of the higher tariff and the deflation effect. Imports accounted for only 4 percent of GNP during the Great Depression. Thus, the impact of the combined tariff and deflation effect could not explain the brutal contraction of income.

The British Parliament passed the Abnormal Importation Act in November 1931 and the Import Duties Act in February 1932. Other countries implemented retaliatory measures against trade as a reaction to the Smoot-Hawley tariff (Jones 1934). The macro tariffs, or tariff duties divided by imports, nearly doubled in that period (Madsen 2001). The United States was the largest creditor in the world during the Great Depression. The interruption of credit by the United States to the rest of the world forced the reduction of imports by debtor countries that could not continue borrowing.

In 1929–32, the volume of exports and imports of industrialized countries declined by approximately 30 percent (Madsen 2001). It is difficult in economics to separate the effects of various variables because they are not observed in isolation. The available measurement shows that world trade declined 13 percent because of the contraction of income, 8 percent because of increases in tariffs,

7 percent because of physical barriers to trade and 5 percent because of the increase of tariffs by deflation. There was an additional feedback effect of up to 2 percent in the form of declines in income caused by the tariff that in turn caused decreasing trade. Thus, the increase in tariffs may have accounted for almost 10 percent of the reduction of trade, close to the 13 percent caused by the contraction of income.

Regulation is typically an overreaction to economic events rushed through Congressional approval. There are three identifiable factors of the repeal of the Glass-Steagall Act (Barth *et al.* 2000). Academic research demonstrates that the combination of banking and securities underwriting in the same corporate group did not cause the banking problems of the Great Depression (Kroszner and Rajan 1994, 1997). The limited securities activities allowed to banks in the 1990s did not result in banking problems. Finally, new technology allows the rapid use of information from one company to benefit another; there was an increase in the profitability of selling insurance and securities products to households and business. The Gramm-Leach-Bliley Act of November 12, 1999, reformed the restrictions imposed by the Glass-Steagall Act of 1933 and the Bank Holding Company Act of 1956 (Barth *et al.* 2000). However, American banks still lack the full flexibility of their competitors in other advanced countries.

There are significant grounds for concern on the basis of this experience. International economic cooperation and the international financial framework can collapse during extreme events. It is unlikely that there will be a repetition of the disaster of the Great Depression. However, a milder contraction can trigger regulatory, trade and exchange wars. Legislation is rushed through Congress that provides political solutions to economic problems. It is easier to pass harmful legislation than to repeal it. The Glass-Steagall Act lasted 67 years before its repeal. The loss of banking and foreign exchange by the United States originated in temporary ceilings on interest rates and costly, unnecessary reserve requirements. That loss has not been reversed.

Summary

The external imbalance of the United States is experiencing a real market stress test of credit conditions. The events originating in US real estate increasingly cloud the global economic environment. The IMF argues that these events are still not correlated with the economies of other countries. Moreover, the US economy appears only to be slowing instead of experiencing a recession. There are no signs of an exit out of dollar debts.

The strongest link between the United States and the rest of the world is through financial markets. The share of the United States in global finance is quite high and adverse events in US financial markets do have the risk of spillover to other regions. The problems have been recognized for many years but consultations have not yet yielded strong concrete action. The proposed solutions face significant political hurdles. If there is a correction it is more likely to be processed by the markets such as in the form of sharp depreciation of the dollar.

There is potential for significant confrontation in international economic affairs. That confrontation could gain momentum if there is a slowdown in global economic growth. The analysis of the doctrine of shared responsibility is not very specific on the distribution of the burdens of adjustment. Nation states are likely to protect their economies and levels of domestic employment. There is risk of increasing protectionism and reversal of trade and financial liberalization. In a more benign economic environment in which there is no contraction or prolonged slowdown, international economic negotiations may be more tranquil and further reform and integration of the world economy could proceed.

Conclusion

The Credit/Dollar Crisis

On the basis of monumental sample of world banking, Barth *et al.* (2006) conclude that the private interest view of regulation is superior to the public interest view. The credit/dollar crisis provides interpretations along these views of regulation.

There are two main approaches in economics to state intervention. The differences in these views are illustrated below with the credit/dollar crisis after 2007.

The *public interest* view claims that market failures in attaining the first-best allocation of perfect competition predict the entry of the government into regulation. The government moves the economy toward a Pareto optimum. There is regulation in about every economic activity in the world. Financial markets are among the most regulated, in particular in the United States, where the credit/dollar crisis began. Thus, the application of the public interest view requires the recognition that existing regulation was inadequate. Regulatory changes would be needed to prevent the repetition of the crisis.

The public interest view provides an interpretation of the origin of the credit/dollar crisis. Lending standards of mortgages were relaxed in the rush of increasing sales of mortgages. Borrowers with weak credit histories were offered products with teaser rates. For example, the initial monthly payments of $400,000 mortgages were reduced for the first 2 years to those corresponding to $250,000. In 2 years, interest rates and principal payments were adjusted to reflect the actual dollar commitment of the debtor, increasing sharply monthly payments above capacity to pay them, resulting in a wave of foreclosures. The mortgages were sold by individuals and entities that earned commissions on sales but did not participate in future default risk. Thus, there was not due diligence on the income and credit histories of the debtors to verify their creditworthiness and ability to pay relative to income. This was the case of both subprime debtors with weak credit histories and alt-A ones with reasonable credit scores but no verification of actual income. There was also fraud by debtors misrepresenting their income and assets.

Financial institutions, such as commercial, mortgage and investment banks, repackaged the mortgages in securities. There was not due diligence of verifying the quality of the underlying mortgages in the rush to increase sales and earn higher commissions. Mortgages were also combined in highly leveraged CDOs. Banks hid the CDOs in SIVs off the balance sheets. There are no adequate methods to value these structured products. Bank balance sheets did not reflect their actual financial weakness, misleading investors, depositors and supervisors.

The crisis magnified through the entire financial production chain. There were lax standards in the origination, securitization and distribution of mortgage products. The initial weakness of mortgages and their securitization eroded the confidence in banks. Similar problems developed in all forms of asset-backed securities. The interbank market paralyzed because of an unprecedented rise in the perception of counterparty risk. Banks did not trust their own balance sheets and would not lend to other banks to avoid absorbing their bad loans.

There are numerous proposals within the public interest view of preventing the next crisis perhaps because of the failure of solving the credit/dollar crisis. These proposals all lead to tightening regulation and supervision. Government agencies would ensure that lenders apply strict standards in originating and securitizing mortgages. Regulatory agencies would be reformed and strengthened. Supervisors would actively police transparency of bank balance sheets, inspecting the prudence of risk practices. The SEC and state authorities began to investigate violations with the objective of high-profile prosecutions.

The *private interest view* would argue that the credit/dollar crisis originated in government failure. The purpose of central banks and financial regulators and supervisors is preventing the market failure of financial crises with resulting output contraction and unemployment. However, the central banks created the credit/dollar crisis and are failing in its resolution. The lowering of the fed funds rate to 1 percent in 2003–4 and the expressed willingness of lowering it to zero eroded the risk discipline of banks and borrowers. The lowest interest rates in five decades created the impression that house prices would increase forever. Borrowers did not perceive risk in the known future increase in monthly payments because the worst that could happen would be to live in a better residence for 2 years and then sell it for a capital gain after repaying the mortgage. Lenders also believed that the downside would be early repayment of the mortgage or sale at market value in foreclosure. Supervision and regulation encouraged the expansion phase of the business cycle with unprecedented debt. The flood of money at low interest rates encouraged borrowing and lending without prudence, eroding the calculations of risks and returns by creditors and debtors.

There is eventually an unavoidable solution of the credit/dollar crisis. There is no relief in subsidizing a debtor to keep a house that will never be worth the principal in the mortgage, after allowing for taxes, improvements, amortization and broker fees. It is also unfair to transfer the subsidy to taxpayers that exercised caution in their financial decisions. Unprecedented moral hazard would jeopardize housing and general finance. Numerous plans to avoid MTM financial assets, such as the super SIV and the deep rediscount window of any security by central banks, merely perpetuate the credit/dollar crisis with higher eventual costs of output and employment. The recovery of the monitoring and intermediation function of finance requires MTM of all depreciated financial assets. Such a cleansing of balance sheets will reduce counterparty risk to normal levels. Delays and expediencies may merely magnify the crisis.

Past experience is revealing. A current interpretation emphasizes the flexibility of exchange rates in the more rapid recoveries of some economies in the 1930s. The devaluation of the dollar is a necessary adjustment in the current situation. The Glass–Steagall Act was based on erroneous analysis and distortion of experience but survived seven decades, undermining finance in the United States. Subsequent errors in regulation moved banking and FX permanently from NYC to London. SOX and frivolous litigation are transferring the remainder of the financial industry away from NYC.

International economic cooperation breaks during hard times. There should be a forward approach to regulation, trade and capital flows instead of the rush of regulatory shocks based on inadequate interpretations of the credit/dollar crisis that may create a different crisis and other problems of efficiency in the future. The emphasis should be in solving the current problems before embarking in regulatory, trade and devaluation wars. According to the NIE, both markets and government can fail. Pragmatic policy should balance regulation with the need to maintain economic incentives and property rights for future growth.

Notes

4 International economic law

1. A comprehensive analysis of the implementation of Basel II in Brazil is in Peláez (2007).

5 Vulnerabilities of the global economy

1. Other references in vast literature include Caballero *et al.* (2007), Cooper (2004), Cline (2005), de Rato (2006Apr5), Dooley *et al.* (2003, 2004), Eichengreen (2006), G7 (2006), O'Neill (2007), Plaza Accord (1985), Rogoff (2006b, 2007), Roubini and Setser (2004) and references in Peláez and Peláez (2007).
2. References include BIS (2004, 2007May, 2007Jun, 2007Jun24), Edison (2007), IMF (1998WEODec) and IMF (2006GFSRSep). On overshooting, see Dornbusch (1976), Obstfeld and Rogoff (1996) and Rogoff (2002).

References

Abiad, Abdul and Ashoka Mody. 2005. Financial reform. What shakes it? What shapes it? Washington, DC, IMF, Economic Issues No. 35, Jun.

Abiad, Abdul, Nienke Oomes and Kenichi Ueda. 2004. The quality effect: does financial liberalization improve the allocation of capital? Washington, DC, IMF WP/04/112, Jun.

Adelman, M. A. 2004. The real oil problem. *Regulation* 27 (1): 16–21.

Aghion, Philippe and Peter Howitt. 1992. A model of growth through creative destruction. *Econometrica* 60 (2): 323–51.

Ahearne, Alan G., John G. Fernald, Prakash Loungani and John W. Schindler. 2003. China and emerging Asia: comrades or competitors. *Seoul Journal of Economics* 16 (2): 183–213.

Aizenman, Joshua. 2004. Financial opening and development: evidence and policy controversies. *American Economic Review* 94 (2): 65–70.

Aizenman, Joshua and Jaewoo Lee. 2006. Financial versus monetary mercantilism: long-run view of large international reserves hoarding. Washington, DC, IMF WP/06/280.

Akerlof, George A. 1970. The market for "lemons" quality uncertainty and the market mechanism. *Quarterly Journal of Economics* 84 (3): 488–500.

Alhemoud, Abdulla M. and Abdulkarim S. Al-Nahas. 2003. Behavior of prices of oil and other minerals over the last few decades: a comparative analysis. *Journal of American Academy of Business* 2 (2): 343–8.

APEC. 2007. About APEC. http://www.apecsec.org.sg/apec/about_apec.html

Araten, Michael. 2006. Economic versus regulatory credit capital. *RMA Journal* 88 (7): 42–7.

Arce M., Daniel G. and Todd Sandler. 2001. Transnational public goods: strategies and institutions. *European Journal of Political Economy* 17 (3): 493–516.

Arestis, Philip, Panicos O. Demetriades and Kul B. Luintel. 2001. Financial development and economic growth: the role of stock markets. *Journal of Money, Credit and Banking* 33 (1): 16–41.

Arestis, Philip, Panicos O. Demetriades, Bassam Fattouh and Kostas Mouratidis. 2002. The impact of financial liberalization on financial development: evidence from developing economies. *International Journal of Finance and Economics* 7 (2): 109–21.

Arieti, Samuel A. 2006. The role of MERCOSUR as a vehicle for Latin American integration. *Chicago Journal of International Law* 6 (2): 761–73.

Arrow, Kenneth J. 1951. An extension of the basic theorems of classical welfare economics. In *Proceedings of the Second Berkeley Symposium on Mathematical Statistics and Probability.* Berkeley: University of California Press, reprinted as Cowles Foundation Paper 54.

Arrow, Kenneth J. and Gerard Debreu. 1954. Existence of an equilibrium for a competitive economy. *Econometrica* 22 (3): 265–90.

ASEAN. 2007. About ASEAN. http://www.aseansec.org/13103.htm

Authers, John. 2007. European stocks top US. *Financial Times*, Apr 2.

Azevedo, André Filipe Zago de and Renato Antônio Henz. 2006. The EU new trade policy and the perspective for an EU-Mercosur agreement. *Aussenwirtschaft* 61 (4): 437–46.

Baldwin, Richard E. 2006. Multilateralising regionalism: spaghetti bowls as building blocks on the path to global free trade. Geneva, Presented as the 2006 World Economy Lecture, Oct 2.

Barr, Michael S. and Geoffrey P. Miller. 2006. Global administrative law: the view from Basel. *European Journal of International Law* 17 (1): 15–46.

Barro, Robert J. 1999. Inequality and growth in a panel of countries. Cambridge, MA, Harvard University, Jun.

Bartels, Frank L., Ha Nam Khanh Giao and Tim J. Ohlenburg. 2006. ASEAN multinational enterprises: a structural model analysis of strategic coherence. *ASEAN Economic Bulletin* 23 (2): 171–91.

Barth, James R., Dan Brumbaugh, Jr. and James A. Wilcox. 2000. The repeal of the Glass-Steagall and the advent of broad banking. *Journal of Economic Perspectives* 14 (2): 191–204.

Barth, James R., Gerard Caprio, Jr. and Ross Levine. 2006. *Rethinking Bank Regulation.* Cambridge: Cambridge University Press.

BCBS. 1996a. Amendment to the capital accord to incorporate market risks. Basle, BIS.

BCBS. 1996b. Modifications to the market risk adjustment. Basle, BIS.

BCBS. 1996c. Overview of the amendment to the capital accord to incorporate market risks. Basle, BIS.

BCBS. 1996d. Supervisory framework for the use of "backtesting" in conjunction with the internal models approach to market risk capital requirements. Basle, BIS.

BCBS. 1999a. A new capital adequacy framework. Basle, BIS, Jul.

BCBS. 1999b. Capital requirements and bank behavior: the impact of the Basel Accord. Basel, WP 1.

BCBS. 2001a. Asset securitization. Basle, BIS, Jan.

BCBS. 2001b. Pillar 2 (supervisory) review process. Basle, BIS, Jan.

BCBS. 2001c. Principles for the management and supervision of interest rate risk. Basle, BIS, Jan.

BCBS. 2001d. Pillar 3 (market discipline). Basle, BIS, Jan.

BCBS. 2001e. Overview of the new Basel capital accord. Basle, BIS, Jan.

BCBS. 2001f. The internal ratings-based approach. Basle, BIS, Jan.

BCBS. 2001g. Consultative document, the standardized approach to credit risk. Basle, BIS, Jan.

BCBS. 2001h. The new Basel capital accord: an explanatory note. Basle, BIS, Jan.

BCBS. 2001i. Conducting a supervisory self-assessment, practical applications. Basle, BIS, Apr.

BCBS. 2001j. Essential elements of a statement of cooperation between banking supervisors. Basle, BIS, May.

BCBS. 2001k. Consultative document, the new Basel capital accord, issued for comment by May 31, 2001. Basle, BIS, Jan.

BCBS. 2001l. Working paper on the IRB treatment of expected losses and future margin income. Basle, BIS.

BCBS. 2001m. Update on work on the new Basel capital accord. Basle, BIS.

BCBS. 2001n. Working paper on the internal ratings-based approach to specialized lending exposures. Basle, BIS, Oct.

BCBS. 2001o. Working paper on the treatment of asset securitizations. Basle, BIS, Oct.

BCBS. 2001p. Potential modifications of the committee's proposals. Basle, BIS, Nov.

BCBS. 2001q. Results on the second quantitative impact study. Basel, BIS, Nov 5.

BCBS. 2003a. Consultative document, overview of the new capital accord. Basel, BIS, Apr.

BCBS. 2003b. Quantitative Impact Study 3 – overview of global results. Basel, BIS, May 5.

BCBS. 2003c. Supplementary information on QIS3. Basel, BIS, May 27.

BCBS. 2004a. Basel II: significant progress on major issues. Basle, BIS, Jan 15.

BCBS. 2004b. Principles for the home host recognition of AMA operational risk capital. Basel, BIS, Jan.

BCBS. 2004c. Changes to the securitization framework. Basle, BIS, Jan 30.

BCBS. 2004d. Modifications to the capital treatment for expected and unexpected losses in the new Basel accord. Basle, BIS, Jan 30.

BCBS. 2004e. Consensus achieved on Basel II proposals. Basle, BIS, May 11.

BCBS. 2004f. Basel II: international convergence of capital measurement and capital standards: a revised framework. Basel, BCBS Publications No. 107, BIS, Jun.

BCBS. 2006. Home-host information sharing for effective implementation of Basel II. Basel, BCBS, Jun 2.

Bean, Charles. 2003. Inflation targeting: the UK experience. Zurich, German Economic Association Meeting, Oct 1–3.

Bean, Charles. 2007. Is there a new consensus in monetary policy? In Philip Arestis, ed. *Is There a New Consensus in Macroeconomics*. Basingstoke, UK, and New York: Palgrave Macmillan.

Becker, Gary S. 1983. A theory of competition among pressure groups for political influence. *Quarterly Journal of Economics* 98 (3): 371–400.

Becker, Gary S. 1994. Human capital and poverty alleviation. Washington, DC, World Bank, Dec 16.

Becsi, Zsolt and Ping Wang. 1997. Financial development and growth. *Economic Review – Federal Reserve Bank of Atlanta* 82 (4): 46–62.

Berger, Mark T. 1999. APEC and its enemies: the failure of the new regionalism in the Asia-Pacific. *Third World Quarterly* 20 (5): 1013–30.

Bernanke, Ben S. 1995. The macroeconomics of the Great Depression: a comparative approach. *Journal of Money Credit and Banking* 27 (1, Feb) 1–28.

Bernanke, Ben S. 2005. The global savings glut and the U.S. current account deficit. FRB, Apr 14.

Bernanke, Ben S. 2007Jun15. The credit channel of monetary policy in the twenty-first century. Atlanta: Conference on the Credit Channel of Monetary Policy in the Twenty-first Century, FRBA, Jun 15.

Bernanke, Ben S. and Mark Gertler. 1995. Inside the black box: the credit channel of monetary policy. *Journal of Economic Perspectives* 9 (4): 27–48.

Bernanke, Ben and Mark Gertler. 1999. Monetary policy and asset price volatility. Paper Presented at Federal Reserve Bank of Kansas City Conference, Jackson Hole, Wyoming, Aug 26–28. In Federal Reserve Bank of Kansas City, *Economic Review* 84 (4): 17–51.

Bernanke, Ben S., Mark Gertler, and Simon Gilchrist. 2000. The financial accelerator in a quantitative business cycle framework. In J. Taylor and M. Woodford, eds. *Handbook of Macroeconomics*. Amsterdam: North Holland.

Bhagwati, Jagdish N. 1995. US trade policy: the infatuation with free trade areas. In Jagdish N. Bhagwati and Anne O. Krueger, eds. *The Dangerous Drift to Preferential Trade Agreements*. Washington, DC: American Enterprise Institute for Public Policy Research.

Bhagwati, Jagdish N. 1998a. The capital myth: the difference between trade in widgets and dollars. *Foreign Affairs* 77 (3): 7–13.

Bhagwati, Jagdish N. 1998b. Poverty and reforms: friends or foes? *Journal of International Affairs* 52 (1): 33–45.

Bhagwati, Jagdish N. 1999. Free trade: why AFL-CIO, the Sierra Club and Congressman Gephardt should like it. *American Economist* 43 (2): 3–12.

Bhagwati, Jagdish N. 2003. Testimony. Washington, DC, US House of Representatives, Subcommittee on Domestic and International Monetary Policy, Trade and Technology, Apr 1.

Bhagwati, Jagdish N. 2006a. Global warming fund could succeed where Kyoto failed. *Financial Times*, Aug 15.

Bhagwati, Jagdish N. 2006b. Asia must opt for open regionalism on trade. *Financial Times*, Nov 2.

Bhagwati, Jagdish N. and Arvid Panagariya. 1996. The theory of preferential trade agreements: historical evolution and current trends. *American Economic Review* 86 (2): 82–7.

Baghwati, Jagdish N. and T. N. Srinivasan. 2001. *Trade and Poverty in Poor Countries*. New Haven, CT: Yale University, 2001. http://www.econ.yale.edu/~srinivas/trade_poverty.pdf

Bhagwati, Jagdish N. and T. N. Srinivasan. 2002. Trade and poverty in the poor countries. *American Economic Review* 92 (2): 180–3.

BIS. 2001Mar. History of the Basel Committee and its membership. Basel, BIS, Mar.

BIS. 2001Aug. Working paper on risk sensitive approaches for equity exposures in the banking book for IRB banks. Basle, BIS, Aug.

BIS. 2004. VIII. Conclusion: change, uncertainty and policymaking. *BIS 74th Annual Report*. Basel, BIS, Jun.

BIS. 2007May. Semiannual OTC derivatives statistics at end-December 2006. Basel, BIS, May.

BIS. 2007Jun. Highlights of international banking and financial market activity. *BIS Quarterly Review*, June 2007, 15–26.

BIS. 2007Jun24. Foreign exchange markets. *BIS 77th Annual Report*. Basel, BIS, Jun 24.

Bittencourt, Gustavo and Rosario Domingo. 2004. Los determinantes de la IED y el efecto del MERCOSUR. *El Trimetre Económico* 71: 73–128.

Black, Fisher and Myron Scholes. 1973. The pricing of options and corporate liabilities. *Journal of Political Economy* 81 (3): 637–54.

Block, Bill and Kristin Forbes. 2004. Capital flows to emerging markets: the myths and realities. Dallas, Federal Reserve Bank of Dallas, Nov 4.

Blonigen, Bruce A. 2005. The effects of NAFTA on antidumping and countervailing duty activity. *World Bank Economic Review* 19 (3): 407–24.

Bloomberg, Michael and Charles E. Schumer. 2007. Preface to MKC (2007).

BOE. 2007Q1. The Monetary Policy Committee of the Bank of England: ten years on. *Quarterly Bulletin* 2007 Q1, 24–38.

Braddock, Cory L. 2006. Penny wise, pound foolish: why investors would be foolish to pay a penny or a pound for the protections provided by Sarbanes-Oxley. *Brigham Young University Law Review* 2006 (1): 175–210.

Brooks, Rick and Constance Mitchell Ford. 2007. The United States of subprime. *Wall Street Journal*, Oct 11.

Burnside, Craig, Marin Eichenbaum, Isaac Kleshchelski and Sergio Rebelo. 2006. The returns to currency speculation. Cambridge, MA, NBER, Aug.

Caballero, Ricardo J. 2000. International liquidity management problems in modern Latin America: their origin and policy implications. Prepared for the Conference on Fiscal and Financial Reform in Latin America. Palo Alto, Stanford University, Nov 9–11.

Caballero, Ricardo J. and Arvind Krishnamurthy. 2001. Smoothing sudden stops. WP 8427 NBER, Aug.

Caballero, Ricardo J. and Arvind Krishnamurthy. 2004. Exchange rate volatility and the credit channel in emerging markets: a vertical perspective. MIT, draft, May 12.

Caballero, Ricardo J., Emmanuel Farhi and Pierre-Oliver Gourinchas. 2007. An equilibrium model of "global imbalances" and low interest rates. Cambridge, MIT, Aug 9, 2008 in *American Economic Review* 98 (1, March): 358–93.

Cadot, Olivier, Céline Carrère, Jaime de Melo and Alberto Portugal-Pérez. 2005. Market access and welfare under free trade agreements: textiles under NAFTA. *World Bank Economic Review* 19 (3): 379–405.

Cai, Kevin G. 2003. The ASEAN-China free trade agreement and East Asian regional grouping. *Contemporary Southeast Asia* 25 (3): 387–404.

Camdessus, Michel. 1998. Capital account liberalization and the role of the fund. Washington, DC, IMF Seminar on Capital Account Liberalization, Mar 9.

Cameron, Rondo. 1961. *France and the Economic Development of Europe, 1800–1914: Conquests of Peace and Seeds of War*. Princeton: Princeton University Press.

Cameron, Rondo. 1967. *Banking in the Early Stages of Industrialization*. Oxford: Oxford University Press.

Cameron, Rondo. 1972. *Banking and Economic Development*. Oxford: Oxford University Press.

Cameron, Rondo, Richard Sylla, Mira Wilkins and A. A. Fursenko, eds. 1992. *International Banking 1870–1914*. Oxford: Oxford University Press.

Carney, William J. 2006. The costs of being public after Sarbanes-Oxley: the irony of "going private." *Emory Law Journal* 55 (1): 141–60.

Castañeda, Jorge G. 2004. NAFTA at 10: a plus or minus? *Current History* 103 (670): 51–5.

Cavallo, Michele. 2006. Interest rates, carry trades, and exchange rate movements. *FRBSF Economic Letter* 31 (17): 1–3.

CCMR. 2006. Interim report of the committee on capital markets regulation. Nov 30. http://www.capmktsreg.org/index.html

CCMR. 2007a. Committee on Capital Markets Regulation. http://www.capmktsreg.org/index.html

CCMR. 2007b. Update. Mar 13. http://www.capmktsreg.org/index.html

CEBS. 2005. Role, programme and challenges. http://www.c-ebs.org/documents/CEBS.pdf

CEBS. 2006. Quantitative impact study 5. Overview of the results on the EU countries. http://www.c-ebs.org/qis5.htm

CGFS. 2004. Foreign direct investment in the financial sector of emerging market economies. Report submitted by a Working Group established by the Committee on the Global Financial System. Basel, BIS, Mar.

CGFS. 2005Jun. Foreign direct investment in the financial sector – experiences in Asia, central and eastern Europe and Latin America. Basel, BIS, Jun.

Chang, Won and L. Alan Winters. 2002. How regional blocs affect excluded countries: the price effects of MERCOSUR. *American Economic Review* 92 (4): 889–904.

Chen, Shaohua and Martin Ravallion. 2004. How have the world's poorest fared since the early 1980s? *World Bank Research Observer* 19(Fall): 1–41.

Cheng-Chwee, Kuik. 2005. Multilateralism in China's ASEAN policy: its evolution, characteristics and aspiration. *Contemporary Southeast Asia* 27 (1): 102–22.

Chudnovsky, Daniel and Andrés López. 2004. Transnational corporations' strategies and foreign trade partners in MERCOSUR countries in the 1990s. *Cambridge Journal of Economics* 28 (5): 635–52.

Čihák, Martin. 2007. Introduction to applied stress testing. Washington, DC, IMF WP/07/59, Mar.

Clarida, Richard H., Manuela Goretti and Mark P. Taylor. 2005. Are there thresholds of current account adjustment in the G7? NBER, May 9.

Clarke, George R. G., Lixin Colin Xu and Heng-fu Zou. 2006. Finance and income inequality: what do the data tell us? *Southern Economic Journal* 72 (3): 578–96.

Cline, William R. 2005. *The United States as a Debtor Nation*. Washington, DC: PIIE.

Coase, Ronald H. 1937. The nature of the firm. *Economica* 4 (16 Nov): 386–405.

Coase, Ronald H. 1960. The problem of social cost. *Journal of Law and Economics* 3 (1): 1–44.

Coffee, Jr., John C. 2005. A theory of corporate scandals: why the USA and Europe differ. *Oxford Review of Economic Policy* 21 (2): 198–211.

Cole, Margaret. 2007. The UK FSA: nobody does it better? *Fordham Journal of Corporate and Financial Law* 12 (2): 259–83.

Conceição, Pedro and Pedro Ferreira. 2000. The young person's guide to the Theil index: suggesting intuitive interpretations and exploring analytical application. Austin, Texas, LBJ School, UTIP WP No. 14.

Cooper, Richard. 2004. America's current account deficit is not only sustainable, it is perfectly logical. *Financial Times*, Nov 1.

Copeland, Brian R. and M. Scott Taylor. 2004. Trade, growth and the environment. *Journal of Economic Literature* 42 (1): 7–71.

Croke, Hilary, Steven B. Kamin and Sylvain Leduc. 2005. Financial market developments and economic activity during current account adjustments in industrial economies. FRB, Feb.

Cropper, Maureen L. and Wallace E. Oates. 1992. Environmental economics: a survey. *Journal of Economic Literature* 30 (2): 675–740.

Cuevas, Alfredo, Miguel Messmacher and Alejandro Werner. 2005. Foreign direct investment in Mexico since the approval of NAFTA. *World Bank Economic Review* 19 (3): 473–88.

Cumming, Christine M. 2006. Review of recent trends and issues in financial sector globalization. In BIS (2006).

Dasgupta, Partha. 2006. Comments on the Stern Review's Economics of Climate Change. Cambridge, Cambridge University, Dec 12.

Davies, James B., Susanna Sandstrom, Anthony Shorrocks and Edward N. Wolff. 2006. The world distribution of household wealth. Helsinski, UNU-WIDER, Dec 5.

Debreu, Gerard. 1951. The coefficient of resource allocation. *Econometrica* 19 (3): 273–92.

Del Castillo, Santiago Perez. 1993. MERCOSUR: history and aims. *International Labor Review* 132 (5–6): 639–53.

Demirgüç-Kunt, Ash, Enrica Detragiache and Thierry Tressel. 2006. Banking on the principles: compliance with Basel Core Principles and bank soundness. Washington, DC, IMF WP/06/242, Oct.

De Rato, Rodrigo. 2006Apr5. The Managing Director's Report on Implementing the Fund's Medium Term Strategy. Washington, DC, IMF, Apr 5.

De Rato, Rodrigo. 2007Jun18. Keeping the train on the rails: how countries in the Americas and around the world can meet the challenges of globalization. Montreal, Canada, International Economic Forum of the Americas, Jun 18. http://www.imf.org/external/np/speeches/2007/061807.htm

Descamps, Jean-Paul, Jean-Charles Rochet and Benoit Roger. 2002. The three pillars of Basel II: optimizing the mix in a continuous-time model. Basle, BIS, Apr 12.

Deutsche Bundesbank. 2006. Transposing the new Basel capital rules into German law. *Deutsche Bundesbank Monthly Report* 58 (12): 67–88.

Diamond, Douglas W. 1984. Financial intermediation and delegated monitoring. *Review of Economic Studies* 51: 393–414.

Diamond, Douglas. 1994. Corporate capital structure: the control roles of bank and public debt with taxes and costly bankruptcy. *Economic Quarterly* (Federal Reserve Bank of Richmond) 80 (2): 11–37.

Diamond, Douglas W. 1996. Financial intermediation as delegated monitoring: a simple example. *Economic Quarterly* (Federal Reserve Bank of Richmond) 82 (3): 51–66.

Diamond, Douglas W. and Philip H. Dybvig. 1983. Bank runs, deposit insurance and liquidity. *Journal of Political Economy* 91 (3): 401–19.

Diamond, Douglas W. and Raghuram G. Rajan. 2002. Bank bailouts and aggregate liquidity. *American Economic Review* 92 (2): 38–41.

Doidge, Craig, G., Andrew Karolyi and René M. Stulz. 2007. Has New York become less competitive in global markets? Evaluating foreign listing choices over time. Columbia, OH, Dice Center WP 2007–9, Apr.

Dollar, David and Aart Kraay. 2001. Trade, growth and poverty. *Finance and Development* 38 (3).

Dollar, David and Aart Kraay. 2002. Response. *Finance and Development* 39 (1).

Dooley, Michael P., David Folkerts-Landau and Peter Garber. 2003. An essay on the revived Bretton Woods system. WP 9971 NBER, Sep.

Dooley, Michael P., David Folkerts-Landau and Peter Garber. 2004. The revived Bretton Woods system: the effects of periphery intervention and reserve management on interest rates and exchange rates in center countries. WP 10332, NBER Mar.

Dornbusch, Rudiger. 1976. Expectations and exchange rate dynamics. *Journal of Political Economy* 84: 1161–76.

Dow Jones Newswires. 2007Feb10. G7 recommends a move in China's foreign-exchange rate. *Wall Street Journal*, Feb 10.

Duffie, Darrell and Kenneth J. Singleton. 2003. *Credit Risk: Pricing, Measurement and Management.* Princeton: Princeton University Press.

Dugan, John C. 2006a. Testimony. Washington, DC, Subcommittee on Financial Institutions and Consumer Credit, US House of Representatives, Sep 14.

Dugan, John C. 2006b. Testimony. Washington, DC, Committee on Banking, Housing and Urban Affairs, US Senate, Sep 26.

Edison, Hali J. 2007. The Kiwi dollar – Getting carried away? In Hali J. Edison and Dmitry L. Rozhkov, eds. New Zealand. Selected Issues. Washington, DC, IMF Country Report No. 07/151, May.

EEC. 1957. Treaty establishing the European Economic Community. http://europa.eu/scadplus/treaties/eec_en.htm

EIA. 2003. *Greenhouse Gases, Climate Change and Energy*. Washington, DC: EIA.

EIA. 2007. *Annual Energy Outlook*. Washington, DC: EIA. http://www.eia.doe.gov/oiaf/aeo/index.html

Eichengreen, Barry. 1996. *Golden Fetters: The Gold Standard and the Great Depression, 1919–1939*. Oxford: Oxford University Press, New Ed.

Eichengreen, Barry. 2000. The EMS crisis in retrospect. Berkeley, University of California, Nov.

Eichengreen, Barry. 2002. Still fettered after all these years. Cambridge, MA, NBER WP 9276, Oct.

Eichengreen, Barry. 2004. What macroeconomic measures are needed for free trade to flourish in the Western Hemisphere? *Latin American Politics and Society* 46 (2): 1–27.

Eichengreen, Barry. 2006. *Global Imbalances and the Lessons of Bretton Woods (Cairoli Lectures)*. Cambridge, MA: MIT Press.

Eichengreen, Barry and David Leblang. 2006. Democracy and globalization. Basle, BIS WP No. 219, Dec.

Eichengreen, Barry and Michael Mussa. 1998. Capital account liberalization and the IMF. *Finance and Development* 35 (4).

EPA. 2004. *Inventory of US Greenhouse Gas Emissions and Sinks: 1990–2004*. Washington, DC: EPA. http://epa.gov/climatechange/emissions/downloads06/06ES.pdf

Europa. 2007. How is the EU organized? http://europa.eu/abc/panorama/howorganised/index_en.htm

European Union. 2006. Consolidated versions of the treaty on European Union and of the treaty establishing the European Community. Brussels, Official Journal of the European Union, Dec 29.

European Union Parliament and Council. 2006a. Directive 2006/48/EC relating to the taking up and pursuit of the business of credit institutions (recast). Brussels, Jun 30.

European Union Parliament and Council. 2006b. Directive 2006/49/EC on the capital adequacy of investment firms and credit institutions (recast). Brussels, Jun 30.

Feldstein, Martin. 2006. The case for a competitive dollar. Stanford, Economic Summit of the Stanford Institute for Economic Policy Research, Mar 3.

Fetter, Frank Whitson. 1933. Congressional tariff theory. *American Economic Review* 23 (Sep 3): 413–27.

Findlay, R. and K. O'Rourke. 2007. *Power and Plenty: Trade, War and the World Economy in the Second Millennium*. Princeton: Princeton University Press.

Fisch, Jill E. 2004. The new federal regulation on corporate governance. *Harvard Journal of Law and Public Policy* 28 (1): 39–49.

Frankel, Jeffrey. 2005. Mundell-Fleming lecture: contractionary currency crashes in developing countries. *IMF Staff Papers* 52 (2): 149–92.

Frankel, Jeffrey A. and David Romer. 1999. Does trade cause growth? *American Economic Review* 89 (3): 379–99.

FRBO. 2007Aug10. Press release. Washington, DC, FRBO, Aug 10.

FRBO. 2007Aug16. Commercial paper – last released Thursday, August 16, 2007. Washington, DC, Aug 16.

FRBO. 2007Aug17. Press release. Washington, DC, FRBO, Aug 17.

FRBO, FDIC, OCC and OTC. 2007Jul20. Banking agencies reach agreement on Basel II implementation. http://www.fdic.gov/news/news/press/2007/pr07063.html

Friedman, Alan. 1997. But nations appear reluctant: IMF pushing to open East Asian markets. *International Herald Tribune*, Sep 20.

Friedman, Milton and Anna Jacobson Schwartz. 1963. *A Monetary History of the United States, 1867–1960*. Princeton: Princeton University Press, 1963.

FSA. 2007. About the FSA. http://www.fsa.gov.uk/Pages/About/index.shtml

FSF. 2007a. Who we are. http://www.fsforum.org/about/who_we_are.html

FSF. 2007b. Plenary meetings. http://www.fsforum.org/meetings/meeting_9_45.html

FSF. 2007c. Compendium of standards. http://www.fsforum.org/compendium/about.html

FSF. 2007d. What are standards? http://www.fsforum.org/compendium/what_are_standards.html

FSF. 2007e. Why are standards important? http://www.fsforum.org/compendium/why_are_standards_important.html

FT. 2007Feb. We need a clear and predictable price for carbon. *Financial Times*, Feb 2.

FT. 2007Aug10. Credit arbitrage funds. *Financial Times*, Aug 10.

FT. 2007Sep19. U-turn erodes Bank's credibility. *Financial Times*, Feb 19.

Galbraith, James K. 2002. A perfect crime: inequality in the age of globalization. *Daedalus* 131 (1): 11–25.

Galbraith, James K., Ludmila Krytynskaia and Qifei Wang. 2004. The experience of rising inequality in Russia and China during the transition. *European Journal of Comparative Economics* 1 (1): 87–106.

Gapper, John. 2006. New York's days of glory will never return. *Financial Times*, Nov 26.

Gately, Dermot. 2004. OPEC's incentives for faster output growth. *Energy Journal* 25 (2): 75–96.

GATT. 1986. *The Text of the General Agreement on Tariff and Trade.* Geneva: GATT. http://www.wto.org/english/docs_e/legal_e/gatt47_e.pdf

Ge, Weili and Sarah McVay. 2005. The disclosure of material weakness in internal control after the Sarbanes-Oxley Act. *Accounting Horizons* 19 (3): 137–58.

Giannini, Curzio. 2002. Promoting financial stability in emerging market countries: the soft law approach and beyond. *Comparative Economic Studies* 44 (2): 125–67.

Giavazzi, Francesco and Guido Tabellini. 2005. Economic and political liberalizations. *Journal of Monetary Economics* 52 (7): 1297–330.

Giovannini, Alberto and Martha de Melo. 1993. Government revenue from financial repression. *American Economic Review* 83 (4): 953–63.

Goldberg, Linda and Eleanor Wiske Dillon. 2007. Why a dollar depreciation may not close the US trade deficit. *Current Issues in Economics and Finance FRBNY* 13 (5): 1–7.

Goldsmith, Raymond. 1969. *Financial Structure and Development.* New Haven: Yale University Press.

Gourinchas, Pierre-Olivier and Hélène Rey. 2005. From world bankers to world venture capitalist: US external adjustment and the exorbitant privilege. NBER, Aug.

Granger, C. W. J. 1969. Investigating causal relations by econometric models and cross-spectral methods. *Econometrica* 37 (3): 424–38.

Grant, Jeremy and Krishna Guha. 2006. Paulson urges flexible market regulation. *Financial Times*, Nov 20.

Greenberg, Maurice R. 2006. Escape from New York. *National Interest* 86 (Nov/Dec): 29–31.

Greenspan, Alan. 2004Jan3. Risk and uncertainty in monetary policy. Remarks at the Meetings of the American Economic Association. San Diego, AEA, Jan 3.

G7. 1998. Strengthening the architecture of the global financial system – report of the G7 finance ministers to G7 heads of state or government for their meeting in Birmingham May 1998. Birmingham, UK, May 15.

G7. 2006. Statement by G7 finance ministers and central bank governors. Washington, DC, Apr 21.

G7. 2007Feb9. Finance ministers meeting, statement. Essen, Germany, Feb 9/10.

G7. 2007Oct19. Statement of G7 finance ministers and central bank governors. Washington, DC, Oct 19.

G10. 1996. The resolution of sovereign liquidity crises, a report to the ministers and governors under the auspices of the deputies. Basle, BIS.

Gurley, John G. and Edward S. Shaw. 1955. Financial aspects of economic development. *American Economic Review* 45 (4): 515–38.

Gurley, John G. and Edward S. Shaw. 1960. *Money in a Theory of Finance*. Washington, DC: Brookings Institution.

Gust, Christopher and Nathan Sheets. 2007. The adjustment of global external imbalances: does partial exchange rate pass-through to trade prices matter? Washington, DC, FRBO, Feb.

Guzman, Andrew. 2005. The design of international agreements. *European Journal of International Law* 16 (4): 579–612.

Han, Hongyul and Kwang Yong Kim. 2003. FDI environments and policy competitiveness of Asia Pacific economies. *Journal of International and Area Studies* 10 (2): 1–20.

Heckscher, Eli. 1919. The effects of foreign trade on the distribution of income. Reprinted in Howard S. Ellis and Lloyd A. Metzler, eds. *Readings in the Theory of International Trade*. Philadelphia: The Blakiston Co. 1949.

Hellmann, Thomas F., Kevin C. Murdock and Joseph E. Stiglitz. 2000. Liberalization, moral hazard in banking and prudential regulation: are capital requirements enough? *American Economic Review* 90 (1): 147–65.

Hicks, John R. 1939. The foundations of welfare economics. *Economic Journal* 49: 696–712.

Hillgenberg, Hartmut. 1999. A fresh look at soft law. *European Journal of International Law* 10 (3): 499–515.

HM Treasury. 2006. Stern review on the economics of climate change. http://www.hm-treasury.gov.uk/independent_reviews/stern_review_economics_climate_change/stern_review_report.cfm

HM Treasury. 2007a. Postscript of Stern review on the economics of climate change. http://www.hm-treasury.gov.uk/independent_reviews/stern_review_economics_climate_change/sternreview_index.cfm

Ho, Daniel E. 2002. Compliance and international soft law: why do countries implement the Basle accord? *Journal of International Economic Law* 5 (3): 647–88.

Horan, Stephen M., Jeffrey H. Peterson and James Mahar. 2004. Implied volatility of oil futures options surrounding OPEC meetings. *Energy Journal* 25 (3): 103–25.

Hubbard, Glenn R. and John L. Thornton. 2006a. Is the US losing ground? Oct 30. http://www.capmktsreg.org/index.html

Hwee, Yeo Lay. 2006. Japan, ASEAN and the construction of an East Asian community. *Contemporary Southeast Asia* 28 (2): 259–75.

IMF. 1998WEODec. IMF World Economic Outlook, interim assessment. Washington, DC, IMF, Dec 21.

IMF. 2006GFSRSep. The yen carry trade. Global financial stability report: market developments and issues. Washington, DC, IMF, Sep.

IMF Executive Board. 2005. IMF Executive Board reviews the standards and codes initiative. Washington, DC, IMF PIN No. 05/106, Aug 8.

IMF Independent Evaluation Office. 2005. Evaluation report. The IMF's approach to capital account liberalization. Washington, DC, IMF.

IMF Independent Evaluation Office. 2006. Report on the evaluation of the financial sector assessment program. Washington, DC, IMF, Jan 5.

IMF and WB. 2005a. The standards and codes initiative: Is it effective? And how can it be improved. Washington, DC, IMF-World Bank, Jul 1.

IMF and WB. 2005b. *Financial Sector Assessment: A Handbook*. Washington, DC: The International Bank for Reconstruction and Development/The World Bank/The International Monetary Fund.

IMF and WB. 2005c. Financial sector assessment program – review, lessons and issues going forward. Washington, DC, IMF and WB, Feb. 22.

IMF Staff. 2007Apr. The multilateral consultation on global imbalances. *International Monetary Fund Issues Brief*, 07/03 Apr.

IMFWEO. 2007Apr. World Economic Outlook April 2007: spillovers and cycles in the global economy. Washington, DC, IMF, Apr.

Interim Committee of the Board of Governors of the IMF. 1997a. Communiqué. Washington, DC, IMF Press Release 97/44, Sep 21. http://www.imf.org/external/np/sec/pr/1997/pr9744.htm

Interim Committee of the Board of Governors of the IMF. 1997b. Statement of the International Monetary Fund. Washington, DC, Apr 28 http://www.imf.org/external/np/sec/pr/1997/pr9722.htm

Interim Committee of the Board of Governors of the IMF. 1998a. Communiqué. Washington, DC, Apr 16. http://www.imf.org/external/np/cm/1998/041698a.htm

Interim Committee of the Board of Governors of the IMF. 1998b. Washington, DC, IMF Press Release No. 98/47, Oct. http://www.imf.org/external/np/sec/pr/1998/pr9847.htm

Interim Committee of the Board of Governors of the IMF. 1999. Washington, DC, Sep 26. http://www.imf.org/external/np/cm/1999/092699A.HTM

International Monetary Fund. 2004. The IMF's approach to capital account liberalization. Draft issues paper/terms of reference for an evaluation by the Independent Evaluation Office (IEO). Washington, DC, IMF, Jul.

International Monetary Fund. 2006. Standards and codes – implementing the Fund's medium-term strategy and the recommendations of the 2005 review of the initiative. Washington, DC, IMF, Jun 29.

International Monetary Fund. 2007Apr14. IMF's International Monetary and Financial Committee Review Multilateral Consultation. Washington, DC, PR No. 07/72, Apr 14.

International Monetary Fund Staff. 2000. Recovery from the Asian crisis and the role of the IMF. Washington, DC, IMF, Jun.

Ip, Gregg. 2006. Is a US listing worth the effort? *Wall Street Journal*, Nov 28.

Ip, Greg. 2007Aug24. New York fed takes step to bolster credit markets. *Wall Street Journal*, Aug 24.

IPCC. 2001. Human influence on the climate system. WGI: the scientific basis. http://www.grida.no/climate/ipcc_tar/wg1/044.htm

IPCC. 2007Feb2. Media advisory. IPCC adopts major assessment of climate change science. Paris, Feb 2. http://www.ipcc.ch/press/prwg2feb07.htm

IPCC. 2007Feb5. Climate change 2007: the physical science basis. Summary for policymakers. Paris, Feb 5. http://www.ipcc.ch/SPM2feb07.pdf

IPCC. 2007Apr6. Climate change 2007: climate change impact, adaptation and vulnerability. Summary for policymakers. UN, IPCC, Apr 6.

IPCC. 2007May4. Climate change 2007: summary for policymakers, IPCC fourth assessment report, Working Group III. UN, IPCC, May 4.

Irwin, Douglas A. 1998 The Smoot-Hawley Tariff: a quantitative assessment. *Review of Economics and Statistics* 80 (2, May): 326–34.

Johnson, Harry G. 1958. Towards a general theory of the balance of payments. In Harry G. Johnson ed. *International Trade and Economic Growth*. Cambridge, MA: Harvard University Press.

Jones, Jr., Joseph M. 1934. *Tariff Retaliation: Repercussions of the Hawley-Smoot Bill.* Philadelphia: University of Pennsylvania Press.

Joyce, Joseph P. and Todd Sandler. 2007. IMF retrospective and prospective: a public goods viewpoint. Wellesley, MA, Wellesley College, Feb.

Jurn, Iksu and Hong Y. Park. 2002. The trade effects on the non-member countries of the regional integration: the case of the Mercosur. *Multinational Business Review* 10 (2): 23–32.

Kaldor, Nicholas. 1939. Welfare propositions of economics and interpersonal comparisons of utility. *Economic Journal* 49: 549–52.

Kaminsky, Graciela L. and Carmen M. Reinhart. 1999. The twin crises: the causes of banking and balance-of-payments problems. *American Economic Review* 89 (3): 473–500.

Kaplan, Steven E., Pamela B. Roush and Linda Thorne. 2006. Andersen and the market for lemons in audit reports. *Journal of Business Ethics* 70: 363–73.

Kaufmann, Robert K., Stephane Dees, Pavlos Karadeloglou and Marcelo Sánchez. 2004. Does OPEC matter? An econometric analysis of oil prices. *Energy Journal* 25 (4): 67–90.

Kemp, Murray C. 1964. *The Pure Theory of International Trade*. Englewood Cliffs, NJ: Prentice-Hall.

Kemp, Murray C. and Henry Wan, Jr. 1976. An elementary proposition concerning the formation of customs unions. *Journal of International Economics* 6 (1): 95–7.

Keynes, John Maynard. 1936. *The General Theory of Employment, Interest and Money*. London: Macmillan.

Kindleberger, Charles P. and Robert Z. Aliber. 2005. *Manias, Panics and Crashes 5th Edition*. Basingstoke, UK and New York: Palgrave Macmillan.

King, Robert G. and Ross Levine. 1993. Finance and growth: Schumpeter might be right. *Quarterly Journal of Economics* 106 (3, Aug): 717–37.

Kose, M. Ayhan, Eswar S. Prasad, Kenneth Rogoff and Shang-Jin Wei. 2006. Financial globalization: a reappraisal. Washington, DC, IMF WP/06/189.

Kroszner, Randall S. and Raghuram G. Rajan. 1994. Is the Glass-Steagall Act justified? A study of the US experience with universal banking before 1933. *American Economic Review* 84 (4): 810–32.

Kroszner, Randall S. and Raghuram G. Rajan. 1997. Evidence from commercial bank securities activities before the Glass-Steagall Act. *Journal of Monetary Economics* 39 (Aug): 475–516.

Krueger, Anne O. 1983. *Trade and Employment in Developing Countries, 3. Synthesis and Conclusions*. Chicago: University of Chicago Press.

Krueger, Anne O. 1999. Are preferential trading arrangements trade-liberalizing or protectionist? *Journal of Economic Perspectives* 13 (4): 105–24.

Ku, Charlotte and Paul F. Diehl. 2006. Filling in the gaps: extrasystemic mechanisms for addressing imbalances between the international legal operating system and the normative system. *Global Governance* 12: 161–83.

Kuznets, Simon. 1955. Economic growth and income inequality. *American Economic Review* 45 (1): 1–28.

Lal, Deepak. 2000. The new cultural imperialism: the greens and economic development. New Delhi, India, The Inaugural Julian Simon memorial lecture, Liberty Institute, Dec 9.

Lal, Deepak. 2004. *In Praise of Empires*. Basingstoke and New York: Palgrave Macmillan.

Lal, Deepak. 2005a. An imperial denial. *Yale Global*, Jan 6.

Lal, Deepak. 2005b. The greens vs. India and China. *The Globalist*, Jul 8.

Langevoort, Donald C. 2006. Internal controls after Sarbanes-Oxley: revisiting *corporate law's* "duty of care as responsibility for systems." *Journal of Corporation Law* 31 (3): 949–73.

Langhammer, Rolf J. 1999. Regional integration APEC style: lessons from regional integration EU style. *ASEAN Economic Bulletin* 16 (1): 1–17.

Lansing, Paul and Christopher Grgurich. 2004. The Sarbanes-Oxley Act: new securities disclosure requirements in the United States. *International Journal of Management* 21 (3): 292–9.

La Porta, Rafel, Florencio Lopez-de-Silanes, Andrei Shleifer and Robert W. Vishney. 1997. Legal determinants of external finance. *Journal of Finance* 52 (3): 1131–50.

La Porta, Rafael, Florencio Lopez-de-Silnaes and Andrei Shleifer. 1998. Law and finance. *Journal of Political Economy* 106 (6): 1113–55.

Lederman, Daniel and Luis Servén. 2005. Tracking NAFTA's shadow 10 years on: introduction to the symposium. *World Bank Economic Review* 19 (3): 335–44.

Levine, Ross. 1997. Financial development and economic growth: views and agenda. *Journal of Economic Literature* 35 (2): 688–726.

Li, Quan and Rafael Reuveny. 2003. Economic globalization and democracy: an empirical analysis. *British Journal of Political Science* 33: 29–54.

Lin, Heng Hsieu and Frederick H. Wu. 2006. Limitations of Section 404 of the Sarbanes-Oxley Act. *CPA Journal* 76 (3): 48–53.

Lobb, Annelena. 2007Aug12. Lookahead: fixated. *Wall Street Journal*, Aug 12.

Lobo, Gerald J. and Jian Zhou. 2006. Did conservatism in financial reporting increase after the Sarbanes-Oxley Act? Initial evidence. *Accounting Horizons* 20 (1): 57–73.

López-Córdova, J. Ernesto and Christopher Meissner. 2005. The globalization of trade and democracy, 1870–2000. Cambridge, MA, NBER WP 11117, Feb.

Love, Inessa. 2003. Financial development and financial constraints: international evidence from the structural investment model. *Review of Financial Studies* 16 (3): 765–91.

Lucas, Jr., Robert E. 1990. Why doesn't capital flow from rich to poor countries. *American Economic Review* 80 (2): 92–6.

Madsen, Jakob B. 2001. Trade barriers and the collapse of World Trade during the Great Depression. *Southern Economic Journal* 67 (4, Apr): 848–68.

Manning, Mark J. 2003. Finance causes growth: can we be so sure? *Contributions to Macroeconomics* 3 (1): 1–22.

Mansfield, Edward D., Helen V. Milner and B. Peter Rosendorff. 2000. Free to trade: democracies, autocracies and international trade. *American Political Science Review* 94 (2): 305–21.

Mansfield, Edward D., Helen V. Milner and Jon C. Pevehouse. 2005. *Democracy, Veto Players and the Depth of Regional Integration*. Princeton: Princeton University.

Martínez-Zarsoso, Inmaculada and Felicitas Nowak-Lehmann D. 2004. Economic and geographical distance: explaining Mercosur sectoral exports to the EU. *Open Economies Review* 15 (3): 291–314.

McCormack, Richard T. 2005. Looking forward in wartime: some vulnerable points in the global economy. In Peláez and Peláez (2005).

McCormack, Richard T. 2007. Lessons from adjustment of the current account. In Peláez and Peláez (2007).

McKibbin, Warwick J. and Peter J. Wilcoxen. 2006. A credible foundation for long term international cooperation on climate change. Washington, DC, Brookings Discussion Papers in International Economics No. 171.

McKinnon, Ronald I. 1973. *Money and Capital in Economic Development*. Washington, DC: Brookings Institution.

Meade, James E. 1955. *The Theory of Customs Unions*. Amsterdam: North Holland.

MERCOSUR. 2007. Quem somos. http://www.mercosur.int/msweb/portal%20intermediario/pt/index.htm

Merton, Robert C. 1974. On the pricing of corporate debt: the risk structure of interest rates. *Journal of Finance* 29: 449–70.

Milanovic, Branko. 2002. True world income distribution, 1988 and 1933: first calculation based on household surveys alone. *Economic Journal* 112: 51–92.

Miller, Merton H. 1988. The Modigliani-Miller propositions after thirty years. *Journal of Economic Perspectives* 2 (4): 99–120.

Miller, Merton H. and Franco Modigliani. 1961. Dividend policy, growth and the valuation of shares. *Journal of Business* 34: 411–33.

Milner, Helen V. and Benjamin Judkins. 2004. Partisanship, trade policy and globalization: is there a left-right divide on trade policy? *International Studies Quarterly* 48: 95–119.

Milner, Helen V. and Keiko Kubota. 2005. Why the move to free trade? Democracy and trade policy in the developing countries. *International Organization* 59: 157–93.

Mishkin, Frederic S. 1999. Global financial instability: framework, events, issues. *Journal of Economic Perspectives* 13 (4): 3–20.

MKC. 2007. *Sustaining New York's and the US' Global Financial Services Leadership*. New York: McKinsey & Co.

Modigliani, Franco and Merton Miller. 1958. The cost of capital, corporation finance and the theory of investment. *American Economic Review* 48 (2): 261–97.

Mollenkamp, Carrick, Deborah Solomon, Robin Sidel and Valerie Bauerlein. 2007. Gordian Knot: how London created a snarl in global markets. *Wall Street Journal*, Oct 18.

Mussa, Michael, Barry Eichengreen, Enrica Detragiache and Giovanni Dell'Ariccia. 1998. Capital account liberalization: theoretical and practical aspects. Washington, DC, IMF OP No. 172, Sep 30.

Naya, Seiji F. and Michael G. Plummer. 2006. A quantitative survey of the economics of ASEAN-US free trade agreements. *ASEAN Economic Bulletin* 23 (2): 230–52.

Nica, Mihai, Ziad Swaidan and Michael M. Grayson. 2006. The impact of NAFTA on the Mexican-American trade. *International Journal of Commerce & Management* 16 (3/4): 222–33.

Nordhaus, William. 2006. The Stern Review on the economics of climate change. New Haven, Yale University, Nov 17. http://nordhaus.econ.yale.edu/SternReviewD2.pdf

Nourzad, Farrokh. 2002. Financial development and productive efficiency: a panel study of developed and developing countries. *Journal of Economics and Finance* 26 (2): 138–49.

Obstfeld, Maurice. 1994. Risk-taking, global diversification and growth. *American Economic Review* 84 (5): 1310–29.

Obstfeld, Maurice. 1998. The global capital market: benefactor or menace. *Journal of Economic Perspectives* 12 (4): 9–30.

Obstfeld, Maurice. 2001. International macroeconomics: beyond the Mundell-Fleming model. Mundell-Fleming Lecture. *IMF Staff Papers Special Issue* 47: 1–39.

Obstfeld, Maurice and Kenneth S. Rogoff. 1996. *Foundations of International Macroeconomics.* Cambridge: MIT Press.

Obstfeld, Maurice and Kenneth Rogoff. 2005a. The unsustainable US current account position revised. NBER, Cambridge, MA, Jun.

Obstfeld, Maurice and Kenneth Rogoff. 2005b. Global current account imbalances and exchange rate adjustments. Washington, DC: Brookings May 16.

OCC. 2006a. Regulatory impact analysis for risk-based capital standards: revised capital adequacy guidelines. Washington, DC, Office of the Comptroller of the Currency, Sep 11.

OCC. 2006b. Regulatory impact analysis for risk-based capital guidelines; capital adequacy guidelines; capital maintenance: domestic capital modifications. Washington, DC; Office of the Comptroller of the Currency, Dec 12.

OCC. 2006c. Risk-based capital: domestic capital modifications. Notice of proposed rulemaking. *OCC Bulletin 2006–50,* Dec 26.

Ohlin, Bertil. 1933. *Interregional and International Trade.* Cambridge, MA: Harvard University Press.

Ohyama, Michihiro. 1972. Trade and welfare in general equilibrium. *Keio Economic Studies* 9: 37–73.

Olson, Mancur. 1965. *The Logic of Collective Action.* Cambridge: Harvard University Press.

Olson, Mancur. 2000. *Power and Prosperity: Outgrowing Communist and Capitalist Dictatorships.* New York: Basic Books.

O'Neill, Jim. 2007. Insight: dollar story no thriller, but it's compelling. *Financial Times,* May 16.

OPEC. 2005. Annual statistical bulletin 2005. http://www.opec.org/library/Annual%20Statistical%20Bulletin/ASB2005.htm

OPEC. 2007a. About us. http://www.opec.org/aboutus/

OPEC. 2007b. 144th meeting of the OPEC Conference. Vienna, OPEC, Press Release No. 3/2007.

OPEC. 2007c. Crude oil production ceiling allocations. http://www.opec.org/home/quotas/ProductionLevels.pdf

O'Rourke, Kevin H. and Alan M. Taylor. 2005. Democracy and protectionism in the nineteenth century. Dublin, Trinity College, Sep.

Ossinger, Joanna. 2007Aug10. Stocks gyrate after global selloff. *Wall Street Journal,* Aug 10.

Pagano, Marco. 2005. The Modigliani-Miller theorems: a cornerstone of finance. *Banca Nazionale del Lavoro Quarterly Review* 58: 237–47.

Panagariya, Arvind. 2000. Preferential trade liberalization: the traditional theory and new developments. *Journal of Economic Literature* 38 (2): 287–331.

Park, Chang-Gun. 2006. Japan's emerging role in promoting regional integration in East Asia: towards an East Asian Regional Integration Regime. *Journal of International and Area Studies* 13 (1): 53–72.

Paulson, Henry M. 2006. *Remarks on the Competitiveness of US Capital Markets*. New York: Economic Club of New York.

Paulson, Henry M. 2007. Opening remarks. Washington, DC, Treasury's Capital Markets Competitiveness Conference, Georgetown University, Mar 13.

Peláez, Carlos A. 2007. The implementation of Basel II bank capital requirements in Brazil. Philadelphia, University of Pennsylvania Law School, Jan.

Peláez, Carlos Manuel. 1968. The state, the Great Depression and the industrialization of Brazil. New York, Columbia University, PhD diss.

Peláez, Carlos Manuel. 1972. *História da industrializacão brasileira*. Rio de Janeiro: APEC.

Peláez, Carlos M. and Carlos A. Peláez. 2005. *International Financial Architecture: G7, IMF, BIS, Debtors and Creditors*. Basingstoke, UK and New York: Palgrave Macmillan.

Peláez, Carlos M. and Carlos A. Peláez. 2007. *The Global Recession Risk: Dollar Devaluation and the World Economy*. Basingstoke, UK and New York: Palgrave Macmillan.

Perry, Joellen and Greg Ip. 2007Aug11. US rate cut looks more likely. *Wall Street Journal*, Aug 11.

Pigou, Arthur C. 1932. *The Economics of Welfare* 4th Edition. London: Macmillan & Co.

Plaza Accord. 1985. Announcement the Ministers of Finance and Central BankGovernors of France, Germany, Japan, the United Kingdom, and the United States (Plaza Accord). Sep 22.

Plummer, Michael G. and Reid W. Click. 2005. Bond market development and integration in ASEAN. *International Journal of Finance and Economics* 10: 122–42.

Prasad, Eswar S. and Kenneth Rogoff. 2003. The emerging truth of going global. *Financial Times*, Sep 1.

Prasad, Eswar S. and Raghuram G. Rajan. 2005. Controlled capital account liberalization: a proposal. Washington, DC, IMF Policy Discussion Paper 05/7, Oct.

Prasad, Eswar, Kenneth Rogoff, Shank-Jin Wei and M. Ayhan Kose. 2003. Effects of financial globalization on developing countries: some empirical evidence. Washington, DC, IMF, Mar 17.

Rajan, Raghuram G. and Luigi Zingales. 1998. Financial dependence and growth. *American Economic Review* 88 (3): 559–86.

Rajan, Raghuram G. and Luigi Zingales. 2001. Financial systems, industrial structure and growth. *Oxford Review of Economic Policy* 17 (4): 467.

Rajan, Raghuram G. and Luigi Zingales. 2003a. *Saving Capitalism from the Capitalists: Unleashing the Power of Financial Markets to Create Wealth and Spread Opportunity*. New York: Crown Business.

Rajan, Raghuram G. and Luigi Zingales. 2003b. The great reversals: the politics of financial development in the twentieth century. *Journal of Financial Economics* 69: 5–50.

Rajan, Raghuram G. and Luigi Zingales. 2003c. Capitalism for everyone. *The National Interest* 91 (Winter 2003/04): 133–41.

Rajan, Raghuram G. and Luigi Zingales. 2003d. A conversation with Raghuram Rajan and Luigi Zingales. *Crown Business*, Feb. 25.

Ravallion, Martin. 2004. *Competing Concepts of Inequality in the Globalization Debate*. Washington, DC: World Bank.

Reddy, Sanjay and Thomas W. Pogge. 2005. How not to count the poor. New York, Columbia University, Oct 29.

Reinhart, Carmen M. and Kenneth S. Rogoff. 2004. Serial default and the "paradox" of rich-to-poor capital flows. *American Economic Review* 94 (2): 53–8.

Reinhart, Carmen M., Kenneth S. Rogoff and Miguel A. Savastano. 2003. Debt intolerance. *Brookings Papers on Economic Activity* 1: 1–74.

Reuters. 2007Feb10. G7 sees double, feeling force of emerging economies. Feb 10.

Rigobon, Roberto and Dani Rodrik. 2004. *Rule of Law, Democracy, Openness and Income: Estimating the Interrelationships*. Cambridge, MA: MIT.

Rioja, Felix and Neven Valev. 2004. Finance and the sources of growth at various stages of economic development. *Economic Inquiry* 42 (1): 127–40.

Robertson, Raymond. 2005. Has NAFTA increased labor market integration between the US and Mexico? *World Bank Economic Review* 19 (3): 425–48.

Robinson, Joan. 1937. Beggar-my-neighbour remedies for unemployment. In Joan Robinson, ed. *Essays in the Theory of Employment*. London: Macmillan & Co.

Robinson, Joan. 1946. The pure theory of international trade. *The Review of Economic Studies* 14 (2, 1946–7): 98–112.

Rodriguez, Francisco and Dani Rodrik. 2001. Trade policy and economic growth: a skeptic's guide to the cross-national evidence. In Ben Bernanke and Kenneth S. Rogoff, eds. *Macroeconomics Annual 2000*. Cambridge, MA: MIT Press for NBER.

Rodrik, Dani. 1998. *Who Needs Capital-Account Convertibility? Essays in International Finance No. 207*. Princeton: Princeton University.

Rogoff, Kenneth. 2002. Dornbusch's overshooting model after twenty-five years. *IMF Staff Papers* 49 (Special Issue): 1–34.

Rogoff, Kenneth. 2006a. Impact of globalization on monetary policy. Jackson Hole, Wyoming, FRBKC, Symposium on "The New Economic Geography: Effects and Policy Implications," Aug 24–6.

Rogoff, Kenneth. 2006b. Can the IMF avert a global meltdown? Project Syndicate, Sep. http://www.project-syndicate.org/commentary/rogoff19

Rogoff, Kenneth. 2007. No grand plans, but the financial system needs fixing. *Financial Times*, Feb 7.

Romano, Roberta. 2005a. The Sarbanes-Oxley act and the making of quack corporate governance. *Yale Law Journal* 114 (7): 1521–1611.

Romano, Roberta. 2005b. Is regulatory competition a problem or irrelevant for corporate governance? *Oxford Review of Economic Policy* 21 (2): 212–31.

Roubini, Nouriel and Brad Setser. 2004. The US as a net debtor: the sustainability of the US external imbalances. New York, NYU, draft, Nov.

Rubin, Robert E. 1998. Strengthening the architecture of the international financial system, remarks as prepared for delivery. Washington, DC, Brookings Institution, Apr 14, 1998, US Treasury RR-2366, Apr 14, 1998, available at http://www.ustreas.gov/press/releases/archives/199804.html

Sala-i-Martin, Xavier. 2002. The world distribution of income: estimated from individual country distributions. Cambridge, MA, NBER WP 8993.

Sala-i-Martin, Xavier. 2004. Why are the critics so convinced that globalization is bad for the poor? A comment. New York, Columbia University, Oct 19.

Sally, Razeen and Rahul Sen. 2005. Wither trade policies in Southeast Asia? The wider Asian and global context. *ASEAN Economic Bulletin* 22 (1): 92–115.

Samuelson, Paul A. 1948. International trade and the equalization of factor prices. *Economic Journal* 58: 163–84.

Samuelson, Paul A. 1949. International factor price equalization once again. *Economic Journal* 59: 181–97.

Samuelson, Paul A. 1951. A comment on factor price equalization. *Review of Economic Studies* 19: 121–2.

Samuelson, Paul A. 1953. Prices of factors and goods in general equilibrium. *Review of Economic Studies* 21: 1–20.

Sandler, Todd. 2006. Regional public goods and international organizations. *Review of International Organizations* 1 (1): 5–25.

Sandler, Todd and Daniel G. Arce M. 2002. A conceptual framework for understanding global and transnational public goods for health. *Fiscal Studies* 23 (2): 195–222.

Santos, João A. C. 2000. Bank capital regulation in contemporary banking theory: a review of the literature. Basle, BIS, Sep.

Schmukler, Sergio L. 2004. Financial globalization: gain and pain for developing countries. *Economic Review Federal Reserve Bank of Atlanta* 89 (2): 39–66.

Schofer, Evan and Francisco J. Granados. 2006. Environmentalism, globalization and national economies, 1980–2000. *Social Forces* 85 (2): 965–91.

Schumpeter, Joseph A. 1911. *The Theory of Economic Development: An Inquiry into Profits, Capital, Credit, Interest, and the Business Cycle*. Translated by Redvers Opie. Cambridge, MA: Harvard University Press, 1934.

Schumpeter, Joseph. 1940. The influence of protective tariffs on the industrial development of the United States. *Proceedings of the American Academy of Political Science* 19 (May 1): 2–7.

Schumpeter, Joseph. 1942. *Capitalism, Socialism and Democracy*. New York: Harper and Brothers.

SEC. 2003. Final rule: implementation of standards of professional conduct for attorneys. 17 CFR Part 205. January 29. http://www.sec.gov/rules/final/33-8185.htm

SEC. 2006. The investor's advocate: how the SEC protects investors, maintains market integrity and facilitates capital formation. http://www.sec.gov/about/whatwedo.shtml

SEC. 2007. Sarbanes-Oxley rulemaking and reports. http://www.sec.gov/spotlight/sarbanes-oxley.htm

Seligman, Joel. 2004. Cautious evolution or perennial irresolution: stock market self-regulation during the first seventy years of the Securities and Exchange Commission. *The Business Lawyer* 59 (Aug): 1347–87.

Shaw, Edward S. 1973. *Financial Deepening in Economic Development*. New York: Oxford University Press.

Shelton, Dinah. 2006. Normative hierarchy in international law. *American Journal of International Law* 100 (2): 291–323.

Shleifer, Andrei. 2000. *Inefficient Markets*. New York: Oxford University Press.

Smith, Adam. 1776. *The Wealth of Nations*. Chicago: University of Chicago Press, reprinted in 1976.

Smith, James L. 2005. Inscrutable OPEC? Behavioral tests of the cartel hypothesis. *Energy Journal* 26 (1): 51–82.

Stavins, Robert N. 2004. *Environmental Economics*. Cambridge, MA: John F. Kennedy School of Government.

Stevens, Paul. 2005. Oil markets. *Oxford Review of Economic Policy* 21 (1): 19–42.

Stigler, George R. 1971. The theory of economic regulation. *The Bell Journal of Economics and Management Science* 2 (1): 3–21.

Stiglitz, Joseph E. 1988. Why financial structure matters. *Journal of Economic Perspectives* 2 (4): 121–6.

Stiglitz, Joseph E. 1994. The role of the state in financial markets. *Proceedings of the World Bank Annual Conference on Development Economics 1993*. Washington, DC: World Bank.

Stiglitz, Joseph E. 2006. Global public goods and global finance: does global governance ensure that the global public interest is served? In Jean-Philippe Touffut, ed. *Advancing Public Goods*. London: Edward Elgar Publishing.

Stiglitz, Joseph E. and Andrew Weiss. 1981. Credit rationing in markets with imperfect competition. *American Economic Review* 71 (3): 393–410.

Stiglitz, Joseph E. and Bruce Greenwald. 2003. *Towards a New Paradigm in Monetary Economics*. Cambridge: Cambridge University Press.

Stiglitz, Joseph E. and Marilou Uy. 1996. Financial markets, public policy and the East Asian miracle. *World Bank Research Observer* 11 (2): 249–76.

Stolper, Wolfgang F. and Paul A. Samuelson. 1941. Protection and real wages. *Review of Economic Studies* 9: 59–73.

Summers, Lawrence H. 2000. International financial crises: causes, prevention and cures. *American Economic Review* 90 (2): 1–16.

Tang, Donny. 2003. The effect of European integration on trade with the APEC countries: 1981–2000. *Journal of Economics and Finance* 27 (2): 262–78.

Tassell, Tony. 2007. Europe tops US in stock market value. *Financial Times*, Apr 2.

Tett, Gillian, Paul J. Davies and Norma Cohen. 2007Aug12. Structured investment vehicles' role in crisis. *Financial Times*, Aug 12.

Tobin, James. 1978. A proposal for international monetary reform. *Eastern Economic Journal* 4: 3–4. Reprinted as Cowles Foundation Paper 495.

Tornell, Aaron, Frank Westermann and Lorenza Martínez. 2003. Liberalization, growth and financial crises: lessons from Mexico and the developing world. *Brookings Papers on Economic Activity* 2: 1–112.

Trefler, Daniel. 2004. The long and short of the Canada-US free trade agreement. *American Economic Review* 94 (4): 870–95.

USCC. 2006. Capital markets, corporate governance and the future of the US economy. Washington, DC, National Chamber Foundation, Feb. www.uschamber.com/ncf

USCC. 2007a. Commission on the regulation of the US capital markets in the 21st century: report and recommendation. Executive Summary. Washington, DC, National Chamber Foundation, Mar. www.uschamber.com/ncf

USCC. 2007b. Commission on the regulation of the US capital markets in the 21st century: report and recommendation. Washington, DC, National Chamber Foundation, Mar. www.uschamber.com/ncf

US 107th Congress. 2002. Public Law 107–204. Sarbanes-Oxley Act of 2002. http://www.sec.gov/about/laws/soa2002.pdf

USTR. 2006. 2006 special 301 report. http://www.ustr.gov/assets/Document_Library/Reports_Publications/2006/2006_Special_301_Review/asset_upload_file473_9336.pdf

US Treasury. 2006b. Risk-based capital guidelines; capital adequacy guidelines; capital maintenance; domestic capital modifications. Proposed rules. *Federal Register* 71 (247): 77446–518.

US Treasury. 2006c. Risk-based capital standards: advanced capital adequacy framework. Proposed rules. *Federal Register* 71 (247): 77518–19.

US Treasury. 2006d. Proposed agency information collection activities; comment request. Notices. *Federal Register* 71 (247): 77520.

Vanek, Jaroslav. 1965. *General Equilibrium of International Discrimination. The Case of Customs Unions.* Cambridge, MA: Harvard University Press.

Vervaele, John. 2005. Mercosur and regional integration in South America. *International and Comparative Law Quarterly* 54 (2): 387–409.

Viner, Jacob. 1950. *The Customs Union Issue.* New York: Carnegie Endowment for International Peace.

Vlachos, Jonas and Daniel Waldenström. 2005. International financial liberalization and industry growth. *International Journal of Finance and Economics* 10: 263–84.

Volz, William H. and Vahe Tazian. 2006. The role of attorneys under Sarbanes-Oxley: the qualified legal compliance committee as facilitator of corporate integrity. *American Business Law Journal* 43 (3): 439–65.

Vu, Kim T. 2006. Conscripting attorneys to battle corporate fraud without shields or armor? Reconsidering retaliatory discharge in light of Sarbanes-Oxley. *Michigan Law Review* 105 (1): 209–39.

Watkins, Kevin. 2002. Making globalization work for the poor. *Finance and Development* 39 (1).

Wei, Shang-Jin and Yi Wu. 2004. Globalization and inequality without differences in data definition, legal system and other institutions. Washington, DC, IMF and Georgetown University.

Whalen, Christopher. 2003. Revisiting Sarbanes-Oxley. *International Economy* 17 (4): 40–3.

Wilkinson, Max. 2006. Stern's report is based on flawed figures. *Financial Times*, Nov 2.

Williamson, Jr., Richard L. 2003. Hard law, soft law and non-law in multilateral arms control: some compliance hypotheses. *Chicago Journal of International Law* 4 (1): 59–82.

Winters, L. Alan, Neil McCulloch and Andrew McKay. 2004. Trade liberalization and poverty: the evidence so far. *Journal of Economic Literature* 42 (1): 72–115.

Wirl, Franz and Azra Kujundzic. 2004. The impact of OPEC Conference outcomes on world oil prices 1984–2001. *Energy Journal* 25 (1): 45–62.

Wolf, Martin. 2007Feb6. In spite of skeptics, it is worth reducing climate risk. *Financial Times*, Feb 6.

Wong, John and Sarah Chan. 2003. China-ASEAN free trade agreement. *Asian Survey* 43 (3): 507–26.

WTO. 2007. Regional trade agreements. http://www.wto.org/english/tratop_e/region_e/region_e.htm

Yu, Miaojie. 2005. Trade globalization and political liberalization: a gravity approach. Davis, CA, University of California-Davis, Nov.

Zhu, Hong and Ken Small. 2007. Has Sarbanes-Oxley led to a chilling in the US cross-listing market? *CPA Journal* 77 (3): 32–7.

Index

aerosols, 57
antidumping, 13, 25
APEC, 1, 3–4, 15–17, 20–1
applied welfare economics, 48–9, 72, 154, 174, 177–8
ASEAN, 1, 3–4, 17–23, 26
Asian Development Bank, 39
asymmetry of information
    adverse selection, 2, 79, 87, 107–8, 112
    banks, 108, 111
    moral hazard, 2, 79, 107–8, 112

Bank of England, 153, 195–7, 202
Bank of Japan, 195, 197, 199
Banks
    disclosure, 92, 94, 122, 127, 159–60
    foreign, 90
    growth, 78–9
    intermediation, 76, 78
    loss of New York to London, 168
    monitoring, 76, 108, 122
    runs, 95, 106–7
Basel Committee on Banking Supervision, 89, 115–19, 123, 126, 128–31, 133–4, 140, 142–4, 202
Basel II, 2, 106, 114–16, 122, 126–48, 163, 166–8, 179, 195, 201–2, 214
Bhagwati's PTA spaghetti bowl, 3, 7–8, 17
BIS, 118, 130, 144, 202
Board of Governors of the FRS, 147, 150, 191, 195, 197–201

capital account liberalization, 2, 18, 73, 80, 86–101
carbon price, 55, 58, 60–1
carry trade, 202–4
clean air, 48–9, 63
climate change, 52–63
collateralized debt obligation, 198–9, 211
collective action, 16, 46, 52, 54
comitology, 144
Committee on Capital Markets Regulation, 168–79
Committee on the Global Financial System, 87–90
Committee on Payment and Settlement Systems, 115

countervailing duties, 13
creative destruction, 109
credit channel, 180–1
credit default swap, 201
credit/dollar crisis, 201, 211–13
current account, 2, 91–2, 102, 181–94, 202

democracy, 35, 63–72, 125
derivatives, 32, 83–4, 87–9, 132–7, 139, 149, 151, 153, 163, 167–8, 171–2, 198
devaluation, 1, 26, 82, 95–6, 98, 106, 120, 181–2, 185–92, 202, 204–7, 209, 213
directed lending, 81–2, 110–11
discount rate, 49–50, 52, 58, 60–1
displaced workers, 13
Doha Development Round, 17, 34

European Banking Supervisors, 145
European Central Bank, 118, 130, 145, 195–7, 199
European Union, 1, 3–5, 8–10
external financing, 74, 79–80, 95, 180
externalities, 48

financial
    competitiveness of NYC, 168–79
    crises, 2, 19–20, 24, 48, 66, 68, 73–4, 82, 86, 88, 92, 95, 98–108, 112–15, 118–25
    globalization, 86–90
    intermediaries, 74, 76–7, 82
    mercantilism, 82, 100
    repression, 2, 81–3, 92, 96, 108, 110–11
    restraint, 83–5
financial accelerator, 180
financial risk
    counterparty, 132, 139, 190, 199, 201–2, 212
    country, 97, 102, 127
    credit, 88–90, 112, 126–43, 201
    operational, 127, 129, 138–9, 141, 145, 166
Financial Services Authority, 152–5, 174, 176, 178, 202
Financial Stability Forum, 118–19, 202

foreign direct investment
    capital, 12–14, 17, 21–2, 27, 38, 51, 66,
        92, 99, 102, 193
    financial sector, 86–90, 102, 112
fossil fuels, 52–4, 56

G7, 114–15, 119, 121, 179, 181–2,
    191–5, 202
G10, 89, 118–19, 124–6, 179, 194
GATT, 3–5, 28
Glass-Steagall Act, 179, 209, 213
global public goods, 1, 35, 46–8, 63, 72,
    114, 122–3, 125, 144, 193
global warming, 52–3, 56–8, 62–3
governance
    corporate, 99, 117–19, 138, 155
    IFIs, 46, 120, 124–5
    national, 66, 120
    SROs, 148–9, 151, 161–3, 165, 173, 175
Gramm-Leach-Bliley Act, 209
Great Depression, 1–2, 102, 205, 207–9
greenhouse gas, 52–8, 61–2
Greens, 52

hedge funds, 192
house real estate crisis, 2, 181, 194, 200–1,
    209, 212
human capital, 36, 50, 61, 88–9, 97

IEFP, 2
IMF, 41, 65, 70, 91–3, 98, 100–1, 117–25,
    130, 179, 181, 184, 186, 188–9,
    192–5, 209
inflation targeting, 26, 196, 202
international financial architecture, 2,
    93, 194
international trade finance, 102
investment banks, 171, 201, 211
Investment Company Act, 151
IOSCO, 115–17, 130
IPCC, 55–9, 63
IPO, 155, 169–71, 177

Joint Forum, 115, 117

Kuznets curve, 50

leveraged buyouts, 161
liberalization
    economic, 23, 70–1
    finance, 2, 73, 80–6, 111–13, 121, 210
    political, 63, 70–1
    trade, 7–8, 14, 16, 27, 52–6, 65–70,
        111–13

M&A, 19, 27, 87–8, 170
McKinsey & Co, 168–79
market failure, 35, 49, 52, 54, 72, 85, 124,
    154, 167, 211–12
market power, 32, 111
MERCOSUR, 1, 3–4, 24–8
most favored nation, 5, 8, 16–17,
    20, 34

NAFTA, 1, 3–5, 10–15, 20
new institutional economics, 19, 213

OECD, 31–2, 45, 96, 117–18, 130, 187
OPEC, 1, 3, 28–33
ozone, 56

pareto optimality, 6, 49, 73, 84, 211
pass-through
    devaluation, 187–8, 190
    tariffs, 12
pollution, 49, 51, 63
poverty, 1, 18, 35–46
preferential trade agreements
    analysis, 4–8
    customs union, 4–5
    free trade area, 3–5
    rules of origin, 4, 10, 12, 23
private interest view, 2, 108–10, 201,
    211–13
property rights, 44, 112, 124, 175,
    192, 213
public interest view, 49, 63, 124, 201,
    211–13

regulation, 5, 23, 49–51, 55, 58, 86, 92, 94,
    96, 101, 111–12, 114–16, 118–19, 121,
    123–6, 130, 143–6, 146–55, 159–60,
    167–8, 173–8, 182, 192–5, 197, 201–2,
    205, 209, 211–13
Rey Report, 119, 124, 194
risk management, 74–5, 88–90, 112, 119,
    126–8, 140–1, 143, 145–6, 148, 154,
    166, 197, 202
ROSC, 118, 120–3, 195

Sarbanes-Oxley Act, 153, 155–69, 173,
    175–7, 179, 213
SEC, 148–52
SRO, 148–52
standards and codes, 114–25
stock exchanges
    LSE, 155, 169, 172–3
    NYSE, 149, 151–2, 155, 169, 172

stress tests, 120, 122, 140–2
structured investment vehicles, 198–9, 202, 211–12

tariff, 4–8, 12–14, 16–18, 24–8, 37, 44, 67, 69, 207–9
technology, 12, 22, 29, 43, 47–8, 51, 59, 61, 63, 75–6, 79, 82, 85, 88, 90, 152, 171, 196, 209
transaction costs, 19, 33, 49, 74–5, 79, 124, 164, 204

US Chamber of Commerce, 168, 174, 177–9
USTR, 11–12

value at risk, 137

World Bank, 12, 39, 41, 93–4, 114, 117–22, 125, 194–5
World Trade Organization, 3–4, 13–14, 16–17, 20, 22–3, 37, 44, 65, 148